ALLEN L. ☐ P9-DNF-804
EXECUTIVE DIRECTOR

ROSEMONT SCHOOL, INC.
597 N. Dekum St.
Portland, Ore. 97217
(503) 283-2205

Clinical Work with Adolescents

Clinical Work with Adolescents

Judith Marks Mishne

THE FREE PRESS
A Division of Macmillan, Inc.
NEW YORK

Collier Macmillan Publishers
LONDON

The Free Press
A Division of Macmillan, Inc.
866 Third Avenue, New York, N.Y. 10022

Collier Macmillan Canada, Inc.

Printed in the United States of America

printing number

1 2 3 4 5 6 7 8 9 10

Library of Congress Cataloging-in-Publication Data

Mishne, Judith.
  Clinical work with adolescents.

  Includes bibliographies and index.
  1. Adolescent psychopathology. 2. Adolescent psychiatry. I. Title.
RJ503.M57   1986   616.89'022   86-148222
ISBN 0-02-921260-X

To my son Jonathan

I stand between two worlds. I am at home in neither and I suffer in consequence.
                    Thomas Mann, ''Tonio Kröger''

Contents

Acknowledgments

I would like to thank a number of people and institutions for their help. I am grateful to Laura Wolff, my editor at The Free Press, who made valuable suggestions and supported the lengthy preparation of this text. Edith Lewis, editing supervisor, and Kennie Lyman, copy editor, gave particular attention to the technical aspects of preparing the manuscript. Typist Ed Fried proved invaluable in providing moral support and consistent, cheerful, prompt technical assistance.

I have been fortunate in having the opportunity to teach courses devoted to treatment of children and adolescents at the University of Chicago School of Social Work, Columbia University School of Social Work, Smith College School of Social Work, and New York University School of Social Work. Additionally, I have served as consultant at a number of agencies and clinics, and I am indebted to students and trainees in various clinical disciplines for stimulating questions and ideas. They have taught me a great deal about the struggles and pleasures of working with adolescents and parents.

I am grateful to Bellefaire, of the Cleveland Jewish Children's Bureau, for providing my first professional experience in working with adolescents. The late Morris F. Meyer, the director of Bellefaire, was my finest teacher and mentor as well as a very close friend. He conveyed the magic that accrues in effectively reaching a troubled teenager. My professional development was enhanced by my advanced education in Chicago, and I give special thanks to the faculty of the Child Therapy Program of the Chicago Institute for Psychoanalysis for the rich training I received.

PART I

An Overview of Adolescence

Child and Adolescent Therapy: A Historical Perspective

The advent of child psychoanalysis may be dated to 1909, when Sigmund Freud published his report of the psychoanalytic treatment of Little Hans, who was treated for a phobia by his father under Dr. Freud's guidance. Dr. Freud, however, did not focus on adolescence beyond his references to the transformation of puberty in "Three Essays on Sexuality" (1905). Following these publications, it was some time before children or adolescents were treated directly.

In the late 1920s Anna Freud was trying to convert a psychoanalytic interest in childhood as it is recalled by adults into a concern with childhood itself. Under her leadership, the new profession of child analysis was born. In her seminal paper on adolescence (1958), Miss Freud delineated adolescence as a unique and specific period of late childhood, characterized by normative upheaval and turmoil. Miss Freud was assisted in her pioneering explorations of adolescence by Aichhorn, who studied and treated aggressive and delinquent adolescent youth.

Shortly before the publication of Miss Freud's paper, Erikson (1950) made an enormous contribution to our understanding of the experiences of adolescence as the time of life that promotes the sense of personal identity. He articulated his formulation of the major conflict of adolescence, namely, "identity versus identity diffusion." Piaget (1969), in his studies of cognition, delineated the adolescent stage as the time when the capacity for abstract thought, the highest level of intellectual development, is achieved and gives its special quality to the human mind. Blos, in the early 1960s, also made major contributions in investigating and describing the unique stressors and developmental tasks of the teen years.

Keniston (1971) observed that while puberty as a biological state had been recognized, adolescence, as we understand it today, was only discovered in the nineteenth and twentieth centuries. Not only has adolescence been acknowledged, but additionally, contemporary society has begun to support this phase of development by providing educational, economic, institutional, and familial resources for teenagers. This has allowed for the greater possibility of continued psychological growth during the ages 13 through 18. Educational possibilities, recognition and acceptance of the moratorium, and a positive image of postchildhood are now almost universal.

This more realistic appreciation of adolescence relates to social and economic realities. "Increasing industrialization has freed postpubertal youngsters from the requirements of farm and factory labor. The rising standards of economic productivity make the adolescent, especially the uneducated adolescent, a burden on the labor market. Growing affluence enables families and society as a whole to support economically unproductive adolescents in school" (Slaff, 1981, p. 8).

Recently there have been challenges to Anna Freud's view of the normal, expected, necessary turmoil and upheaval of adolescence.* While the debate continues about the length and nature of the adolescent stage, there is agreement on the special needs of this age group. There has been growing recognition, in outpatient and inpatient programs, since the postwar "baby boom" that enormous increases in demand for services for this age group have occurred and that these patients are often difficult to treat. Methods that are effective with children and adults do not suffice with teenagers.

Special separate inpatient and outpatient services for adolescents have been established. The American Society for Adolescent Psychiatry was developed in 1967, "with aims of providing a national forum for adolescent psychiatry, initiating efforts and cooperating with other organizations on behalf of adolescents, and facilitating communication and cooperation among constituent societies" (Slaff, 1981, p. 13). The professional journal *Adolescent Psychiatry* published its first volume in 1971. Issues of particular concern for adolescents, such as college mental health, drug abuse, and delinquency, were recognized as requiring advocacy and improved consultation and treatment resources. Specialization in treatment of adolescents has taken place in other nations, much as it has in the United States. The first international meetings on adolescent psychiatry took place in Jerusalem and in Edinburgh during 1976.

The adolescent psychiatry movement has invited members of allied professions to cooperate in joint clinical work, research, and program development. Genuine sharing, collaboration, and mutual support is crucial in effective work with this population, who frequently require the team approach—the coordinated efforts of psychoanalysts, social workers, psychiatrists, psychologists, nurses, educators, and on occasion, lawyers, child care staff, recreation personnel, and speech, art, music, and drama therapists.

> Adolescents have a propensity for creating problems within the treatment setting because of their reticence about becoming engaged or their inclination to express themselves through action rather than words and feelings.

*See pp. 9–11.

Our responses to the various impasses adolescents typically produce, interestingly enough, have become our most valuable asset in giving us technical guidance to deal with what at first seems to be impossible situations. True, some impasses may, in fact, be difficult: but if we make a frank and non-anxious examination of our feelings, many may prove to be resolvable [Giovacchini, 1985, p. 447].

This text aims to provide a clear and comrehensive presentation of the fundamentals of clinical assessment and treatment of adolescents for use by graduate students and practitioners in the above disciplines. The literature that discusses clinical work with adolescents is dominated by the writing of child psychiatrists and child analysts. It requires that students and practitioners from various professions translate the material for use in their own nonmedical and nonanalytic practices. Proficiency in work with adolescents is a clinical skill only gradually acquired. Nevertheless, early in their training, social work and psychology graduate students, medical residents, nurses, and art, drama, dance, and speech therapists are expected to treat adolescents. Indeed, some settings demand instant expertise in direct work with teenagers and their parents. Enhancement of clinical proficiency, via translation of psychiatric and psychoanalytic principles into more broadly based practice, is the goal of this text.

Specialization in adolescent and/or child therapy can only begin during one's formal professional education. Because of the special dimensions of this field—the unclear communications from adolescents, their particular reticences, resistances, rebelliousness, and propensity for action rather than words and sharing of feelings—work with this population is a specialty, requiring lengthy, ongoing training, experience, and supervision.

Ultimately, to be able to do intensive psychotherapy with adolescents, any aspiring therapist, regardless of discipline, will need some personal treatment. This is necessary in order for the practitioner to develop a therapeutic, objective, emphatic response that embodies the necessary self-awareness and self-observation, and that controls against regression and acting out through, and/or with, adolescent patients. We may or may not have encountered, struggled with, or lived through the identical pain and stresses that our clients experience. But as adolescents, we once all engaged in the same developmental struggles for autonomy, separation, and individuation; we also suffered the same fears of narcissistic injury and failure that our teenage patients are currently experiencing. We once encountered with alarm, anxiety, and excitement our first love, erotic arousal, and sexual and emotional intimacy. Thus, clinical work with adolescents strikes continuous responsive chords in all therapists in a unique, stressful, and universal manner.

Adolescence Defined and Described

In "Three Essays on Sexuality" (S. Freud, 1905), puberty was described as the time of life when the bodily changes occur which give infantile sexual life its final form. During puberty there is subordination of the erotogenic zones to the primacy of the genital zone. Orality and anality have waned, and the child's focus and bodily cathexis are fixed on the phallic genitalia while the mental and emotional life is centered on the loved and forbidden oedipal incestuous objects. New sexual aims and the seeking of new sexual objects outside the family are noted as the main events of puberty.

Anna Freud explained that the newly developed notion of the existence of an infantile sex life lowered the significance of adolescence. "Before the publication of the 'Three Essays,' adolescence had derived major significance from its role as the beginning of sex life in the individual; after the discovery of an infantile sex life, the status of adolescence was reduced to that of a period of final transformation, a transition and bridge between the diffuse infantile and the genitally centered adult sexuality" (A. Freud, 1958, p. 256). In 1922 Jones published a paper that examined the correlation between infancy and adolescence, and noted the recapitulation during adolescence of what had been significant developmental steps during the first five years of life. Jones stated "that adolescence recapitulates infancy, and that the precise way in which a given person will pass through the necessary stages of development in adolescence is to a very great extent determined by the form of his infantile development" (p. 399).

Anna Freud cited Bernfeld as the next prominent observer-researcher examining the adolescent stage of life. Bernfeld described a particular kind of male adolescent phenomenon, the so-called protracted adolescent phase that produces artistic, literary, scientific, and philosophic creation. His conclusions arose out of his clinical work with teenagers in which diaries and poetry were shared. Artistic and creative productions were assumed to be the outcome of inner psychological frustrations and external environmental pressures; neurotic, sensitive youth employed sublimation to deal with conflicts through creativity.

Aichhorn studied the adolescent stage of life through examination of asocial and criminal development in youth who demonstrated faulty superego development and delinquent and rebellious behavior. His seminal, world-renowned text *Wayward Youth* (1935) was a pioneer step in employing psychoanalytic theory in an effort to understand the young offender.

Anna Freud examined the struggles of the ego to master tensions and pressures created by the drives in "The Ego and The Id at Puberty" and "Instinctual Anxiety During Puberty," which became chapters in *The Ego and the Mechanisms of Defense* (1936). She concluded that conflictual process led to character formation and, in some cases, pathological outcomes and the formation of neurotic symptoms. The battle between ego and id during the oedipal stage ends at the beginning of latency and breaks out again at puberty. She stated: "I made the point that, more than any other time of life, adolescence with its typical conflicts provides the analyst with instructive pictures of the interplay and sequence of internal danger, anxiety, defense activity, transitory or permanent symptom formation and mental breakdown" (1958, p. 258).

Following World War II, more publications attempted to define and describe the stage of life known as adolescence. Nevertheless, this increased focus did not improve clinical skill in direct work with adolescent patients. In the 1950s, Miss Freud concluded that adolescence remained, as it had been before, a stepchild in psychoanalytic theory. Problems of engaging and sustaining teenagers in treatment remained formidable, and so material was sought through less than satisfactory avenues, e.g., via the memories and reconstruction of adolescence by adult patients. While facts and events were recalled,

> what we fail to recover, as a rule, is the atmosphere in which the adolescent lives, his anxieties, the height of elation or depth of despair, the quickly rising enthusiasms, the utter hopelessness, the burning—or at other times sterile—intellectual and philosophical preoccupations, the yearning for freedom, the sense of loneliness, the feeling of oppression by the parents, the impotent rages or active hates directed against the adult world, the erotic crushes, whether homosexually or heterosexually directed—the suicidal fantasies, etc. These are elusive mood swings, difficult to reverse which, unlike the affective states of infancy and early childhood, seem disinclined to re-emerge and be relived in connection with the person of the analyst [1958, p. 260].

Repeated treatment obstacles in work with adolescent patients caused Miss Freud to conclude that analytic technique was inadequate to deal with the young patients, all of whom demonstrated rapid shifts of emotional position, revolt, and abrupt and undesired termination of therapy. The obstacles in treatment caused her to conclude that these patients had a lower threshold for frustration, a preference for action rather than verbalization of feelings, and new weaknesses and immaturities of ego structure. She likened this time of life to that of a mourning state, a period of slow and painful recuperation from an unhappy love affair. Because of the narcissistic withdrawal, adolescents have little if any libido energy available with which to explore their past, or relate to the present. The detachment from the parents causes intense and all-absorbing mental suffering.

Repeated clinical observations compelled Miss Freud to conclude that the adolescent upset is inevitable, desired, and "no more than the external indications that inner adjustments are in progress" (p. 264). Balance between id and ego forces must shift to accommodate the accelerated pubescent drive activity. Some degree of adolescent upset is predictable; upset is especially intense when the incestuous oedipal and pre-oedipal fixations to the parents have been exceptionally strong. Delineating between normality and pathology is problematic.

> As described above, adolescence constitutes by definition an interruption of peaceful growth which resembles in appearance a variety of other emotional upsets and structural upheavals. The adolescent manifestations come close to symptom formation of the neurotic, psychotic or dissocial order, and merge almost imperceptibly into borderline states, initial, frustrated or fully fledged forms of almost all the mental illnesses [p. 267].

Miss Freud concluded that normal adolescence is, by its nature, a disruption of peaceful growth, and that any steady equilibrium during the adolescent process is in itself abnormal. The basic disharmony is the norm!

> I take it that it is normal for an adolescent to behave for a considerable length of time in an inconsistent and unpredictable manner; to fight his impulses and to accept them; to ward them off successfully and to be overrun by them; to love his parents and to hate them; to revolt against them and to be dependent on them; to be deeply ashamed to acknowledge his mother before others and, unexpectedly, to desire heart-to-heart talks with her; to thrive on imitation of and identification with others, while searching unceasingly for his own identity; to be more idealistic, artistic, generous, and unselfish than he will ever be again, but also the opposite, self-centered, egoistic, calculating. Such fluctuations between extreme opposites would be deemed highly abnormal at any other time of life [p. 275].

In concert with Miss Freud's formulations, her colleagues continued to view adolescence from an ego psychological perspective, as a moratorium (Erikson, 1950); a normative crisis (Erikson, 1956); and a period of mourning and depression (Laufer, 1966) during which the young person makes a final emotional separation from parents and bids farewell to childhood. As Jones (1922) viewed adolescence as a recapitulation of the early infantile-toddlerhood development, Blos (1962) called it a second edition of childhood. Drawing on the lifelong work and studies of Margaret Mahler, Blos (1968) developed the view of adolescence as a "second individuation" process. However,

> This process should not be thought of as a replica of the first separation-individuation ... Separation-individuation occurs once and only once

during the first 3 years of life: it refers to the infant's gradual recognition and acceptance of the boundaries between his own self and those of the mother" [L. J. Kaplan, 1984, p. 94].

L. J. Kaplan (1984) emphasized the difference between the original separation-individuation of infancy and that during adolescence: "Adolescent individuation . . . involves the reconciliation of genitality with morality" (p. 95). Kaplan cautioned about mistaken notions of adolescence as a recapitulation of the past. Adolescence *revises* the infantile past and the early narcissism is transformed from love of oneself to love of the species. Much as Kohut (1966) discussed transformation of narcissism; Kaplan described the transformations of adolescent narcissism into an "adult capacity for moral dignity, cultural aspiration and ethical ideals" (p. 20).

In contrast to this longstanding traditional view on the inevitability, in fact, the desirability of turbulence during adolescence, a number of researchers recently have suggested that the extreme upset of adolescence is not universal and that the personality upheaval of this phase of life can be reflected primarily in manageable nondebilitating rebellion and depression. Such current research studies have proposed that normal teenagers experience little, if any, of the inner upheaval or acting-out behavior ascribed to them in the classic literature (Douvan and Adelson, 1966). This more recent perspective suggests that rebellion occurs over minor matters and that adolescents continue to share with parents a core of stable values. The findings of Offer (1967), and his initial colleagues (Offer, Sabshin, Marcus 1965), pointed to rebellious behavior solely during early adolescence and then only over minor matters such as dress, household chores, music and curfew. No delinquent acts or great emotional upheaval were evident. Transient feelings of anxiety, depression, guilt, and shame were observed but no debilitating forms of anxiety or depression were noted. These studies reveal that adolescents normatively maintain psychic equilibrium while struggling with developmental tasks, remain able to demonstrate successful social and family adjustment, evidence only mild forms of depression and anxiety, and have only minor disagreements with authority figures. The findings of Rutter et al. (1976) on rural youth ages 14 and 15 substantially agreed with those of Offer, Sabshin, and Marcus. Oldham (1978) suggested a number of factors that perpetuate what he terms the "mythology" surrounding adolescent turmoil. "These factors seem to be professional, cultural, and personal in nature. . . . Our culture persists in its expectations that adolescence can be marked by anything except stability and relatively peaceful growth. Teenagers are frequently typecast as brooding idealists or impulsive delinquents and inherent in both roles is alienation from the adult community" (p. 277). Oldham cautioned against the power of self-fulfilling prophecies and recommended that mental health professionals base their expectations of adolescents, as much as possible, on available data.

More recently Offer, Ostrov, and Howard (1981) described adolescents as confident, self-satisfied, meeting the challenges of maturation with acceptance, ease, and comfortable relationship with parents, sibs, and peers. Mood swings and rebellion are viewed by some as pathological manifestations of severe emotional disturbance. In discrediting the "turmoil" view of adolescence Masterson and colleagues (Masterson and Washburne, 1966; Masterson, 1967b, 1968), and Rinsley, proposed that symptomatic adolescents were not simply traversing a vulnerable and stressful developmental stage, but rather were suffering serious psychopathology and would not "grow out of it." These clinicans emphasized placement in in-patient units and controlling symptomatic behavior in firm and structured milieu settings. While these authors are steadfast in their views, others retain the more classic view of adolescence.

Kaplan (1984) took exception to this revision of the adolescent image and suggested that questionnaires sampling opinions and attitudes cannot constitute valid, in-depth research. Kaplan's definition and description is in keeping with the earlier classic position formulated by A. Freud, Blos, Erikson, Laufer, and others:

> Adolescence represents an inner emotional upheaval, a struggle between the eternal human wish to cling to the past and the equally powerful wish to get on with the future. The purpose of adolescence is not to obliterate the past but to immortalize what is valuable and to say farewell to those items of the past that stand in the way of a full realization of adult sexual and moral potentials. Saying farewell entails considerable grief and longing. In that regard, the adolescent is like a mourner, but a mourner who at first only dimly realizes what she is losing. What the adolescent is losing, and what is so difficult to relinquish, are the passionate attachments to the parents and to those dialogues that had once been the center of infantile existence [p. 19].

There is no suggested compromise or reconciliation between the classic definition and descriptions of adolescence and the newer views formulated by Offer et al. (Offer and Offer, 1975a, 1975b, 1977; Offer and Sabshin, 1963), Rutter et al., Oldham, etc. It should be noted that the newer research has been primarily focused on youth in middle and upper-middle class, white, suburban or rural, intact families in which over 90 percent of the youth are college bound. Given the ever-increasing divorce rates, one must consider the unrepresentative sampling procedures, and lack of study of comparable groups of other socioeconomic, racial, and ethnic groups before generalizing about the adolescent stage of life.

Defining and describing the contemporary adolescent requires some references to current societal changes which have affected familial style and roles, parental employment patterns, and adolescent peer behavioral norms. We are seeing increasing numbers of adolescents reared without consistent parental care. In a high proportion of families divorce almost invariably puts an end to shared parenting. Nagera (1981) voices grave concern about such youth. "I fear that many . . . will be damaged to the point of becoming irretrievable casualties during their own adolescent revolt" (Nagera, 1981, pp. 240–41). The breakdown of the extended family and consistent social ties has resulted from social mobility. The easy availability and use of drugs which cause regression have made it difficult for some adolescents to develop and sustain meaningful emotional involvements with others and to tolerate frustration in the move toward mature adulthood. Adolescents today commonly depend on external factors such as music, peers, and drugs for psychological stimulation. They have little experience in tolerating ambivalence, ambiguity, grief, and mourning.

The above social realities, and increased recognition of the length of time involved in preadult personality consolidation, plus financial dependency and increased academic preparation, have expanded the concept of adolescence and the mastery of age-appropriate tasks beyond the teen and even college years. This expanded perspective of adolescence, including Erikson's concept of "moratorium" (the time for contemplation, role experimentation, or year of work or travel during college) has redefined the adolescent stage of life in contemporary western society.

Early Adolescence

Peter Blos (1962) observed the uneven rate of passage through the adolescent period, noting continuous progressions, regressions, and digressions. "The adolescent may rush through these various phases or he may elaborate on any one of them in endless variations but he cannot altogether sidestep the essential psychic transformations of the various phases" (pp. 52–53). Blos suggested six phases

1. The latency period or introduction
2. Preadolescence
3. Early adolescence
4. Adolescence proper

5. Late adolescence
6. Postadolescence

Presented below are the more commonly defined early, middle, and late periods of adolescence.

Blos (1962) stated that the distinctive character of early adolescence resides in the disengagement from the parents which causes the young person to search, at times frantically, for new attachments and new love objects. Hamburg (1974) observed that this early adolescent stage is a time of great stress even for the model youngster. The efforts at separating from parents coincide with the period of diminished coping skills and high vulnerability. The challenge of dealing with all the biological and psychosocial changes is enormous. Normally, parental values and standards have already been deeply embedded in the young person, but during early adolescence shifts of varying intensity are made toward separation and independence. The search for new attachments is an effort to escape loneliness, isolation, and depressed moods. The more endowed and artistic youngster will attempt to handle the emotional pain through immersion in creative endeavors (e.g., poetry, music, drama, politics, athletics and academics); the impulsive youngster might engage in short-lived delinquent acts. In the more troubled adolescent population, we also see withdrawal into extreme food fads and aesthetic religious affiliations. In the normal search for new interests and attachments, friends are often idealized and the peer group becomes an all-important bridge away from the nest of the nuclear family. Burgeoning sexual feelings are often played out via excessive daydreaming, fantasizing, and masturbation. Romantic relationships and/or the best friend often exemplify the adolescent's search for the missing perfection of the self. Crushes and passionate devotion frequently characterize the friendship ties of the early adolescent. The bisexual or nonsexual stance declines only when the young person makes a genuine entry into adolescence proper, and thereby conforms with gender role, appropriate attire, language, and demeanor.

The early adolescent faces new and dramatic social demands in his or her new role as a teenager, most commonly in the junior high school setting, which was devised to ease the transition from the self-contained classroom and single teacher of elementary school to the rotating classes and multiple-teacher situation of high school (Hamburg, 1974). In reality junior high is rarely a place of gradual transition, but in fact duplicates the conditions and multiple transitions of the high school setting. The academic expectations of junior high involve a sharp and sudden increase of work and achievement pressures. These realities constitute a significant discontinuity with the recent elementary school experience and the friendship circles of the lower grades. There is the need for, and uncertainty about, one's ability to make new friendships.

The biological changes of puberty are considerable, and we now know many specifics of the endocrine changes. Hamburg (1974, p. 106) summarized the current information about puberty as follows: The onset of puberty is determined by the interaction of gonadal hormones and the hypothalamus. The significant change of puberty is the maturation of the cells of the hypothalamus and their escape from the restraining influence of minute quantities of gonadal hormones. We do not know whether such changes alter responsiveness to provocative stimulation or lower frustration thresholds. "Nonetheless, several recent reports suggest a role for sex hormones in relation to personality development in the adolescent and young adult human and draw attention to the promotion of aggressiveness in adolescence by androgen administration" (p. 107). There remains a need for interdisciplinary research on endocrine changes and behavioral changes for a clearer understanding of the interplay of events in the critical period of early adolescence. We have no studies that reliably relate the hormonal changes of puberty to specific measures of anxiety, hostility, or self-esteem. Hamburg concluded by stating that at present the moodiness and hostility of early adolescent males and females is generally observable in interpersonal relationships. It would be helpful, she suggested, if the hormonal contribution to these affective states could be realistically assessed.

All researchers note the dilemmas and stress both for young adolescents who experience slowness or lags in pubescent development and for those whose physical and sexual maturation is rapidly accelerated. For boys, approximately two years after the first appearance of pubic hair, the ancillary hair appears, beginning with down on the upper lip.

> The remainder of the body hair grows slowly and over a lengthy period. During the same period there is an enlargement of the pores and acne is very common, particularly in boys, inasmuch as the characteristic skin changes are due to androgenic activity. The changing of the voice is a somewhat late and gradual process. The change in pitch is due to enlargement of the larynx and lengthening of the vocal chords" [Hamburg, 1974, pp. 109–110].

This voice change commonly begins at about age 14½ or 15, but the final and true pitch is not acquired for several years. At about 11½, initial change in the pubertal male testicles and secretion of male sex hormones is under way. The boys' height spurt begins about a year after the first testicular acceleration, and the peak of the growth spurt is about age 14, though mature height in boys is generally not attained until about 18 years of age. This height change at 12, 13, and 14 is accompanied by noticeable growth in the penis. The first ejaculation will commonly occur at about age 13½.

Girls commonly begin to show pubertal changes about two years earlier than boys. Uterine growth and ovarian follicles begin to develop as early as ages 9 and 10. Breast development is the first external manifestation of beginning sexual maturation, and this may be evident by age 10 or 11, well before the appearance of pubic hair. By age 11, the uterus and vagina show accelerated growth. Once pubic hair is well developed, vaginal secretion begins, and there is growth and remolding of the bony pelvis. About age 13, nipples show pigmentation, and breast development increases toward mature size and shape. Menarche occurs at about age 12½, though full reproductive function may not be attained until a year or two later. Initially, menstrual cycles are often irregular.

These norms or typical ages for pubescent changes are subject to many exceptions and irregularities, as children mature at vastly different rates. The irregularities have many different behavioral consequences for boys and girls. Overall, early maturation has distinct advantages for boys but disadvantages for girls. Hamburg (1974, p. 111) noted that the early-maturing boys are perceived as more "masculine" while the late-maturing boys, who appeared "childish" and slender in their builds, are perceived and treated as less mature and responsible by both adults and peers. The early-maturing boys appear to show more self-confidence and less dependency than do the late-developing males. By contrast, in early adolescence, early-maturing girls are often seen as submissive, self-conscious, and lacking in poise, while late-maturing girls appear to be more outgoing, assured, and confident and are more frequently in positions of leadership.

Bodily changes that produce anything atypical and highly unusual create a sense of discordance, with resultant self-consciousness, shame, and turmoil. The late-maturing boy is perceived as the most severely disadvantaged. "He continues to look like an elementary school boy at a time when it is important for him to be as grown up as possible. He has a developmental lag of about four years as compared to the average girl at the same age and perhaps two years in relation to the age-matched boy" (Hamburg, 1974, p. 112). All researchers document the distress experienced by the boy who is slow to grow and develop. A common outcome is low self-esteem, with compensatory maladaptive patterns of appeasement and overcompliance, or swaggering bravado, anxiety, and provocative, risk-taking, counterphobic, macho, aggressive behavior.

All in all, young adolescents are struggling to come to terms with their body images through an integration of perceptions about them and their own self-perceptions. The psychological outcome is seen as closely related to the course of physical development. The struggle and stigma of the awkward and ungainly child, the obese child, or the sufferer of severe acne is apparent. Similarly, the overendowment or underendowment of breast development in the female creates self-consciousness, often signalled by shyness, withdrawal, and blushing. Looking like one's peers is highly prized, and the very deviant child struggles with this additional burden during a time that typically poses an intense developmental challenge.

The effects of the biological changes of puberty, including a changed body image, are not the only special tasks to master during early adolescence. Increased academic expectations help to make early adolescence a period fraught with fears of inadequacy and failure. Some researchers go so far as to suggest that students who experience a prolonged decline in academic performance in junior high are rarely able to improve at a later point in their academic high school careers. Grades in elementary school are highly related to intelligence; in contrast, in junior high motivation seems to be the important factor. Kagan (1971) stated "the adolescent needs a firmer set of motivational supports that will allow him to work at school requirements while he is trying to fit the catechism of academic competence into the larger structure we call the self" (p. 1006).

Hamburg (1974, p. 114) noted that despite the fact that intelligence per se is not at issue in the school performance during early adolescence, it is important to reexamine the style of cognitive functioning. Inhelder and Piaget (1959) stated that early adolescents have moved beyond formal operational thinking to logic and abstract thinking. However, this and other earlier theories of adolescence actually derived from scrutiny of the older adolescent, which created inappropriate expectations of the younger adolescent. There is more recent research that suggests that most early adolescents have not progressed to abstract thinking and that, in fact, teachers must employ a concrete approach, as the junior high student cannot generalize, use symbols, and process information with objectivity, especially if he or she lacks a positive rapport with the teacher.

Elkind (1967) notes adolescents' egocentrism, preoccupation with their bodily changes, and concern with the responses of others to their appearance as indicative of their concrete thinking. Rebellious and acting-out behaviors are not uncommon in the junior high population, even among formerly cooperative students, who were diligent in elementary school. Experimentation with drugs and alcohol occur most frequently with the younger adolescent population, who struggle to try things, defy adults, and comply with peer groups and social mores. In educational circles, it is generally acknowledged that the junior high school student is the most taxing, as this period of life is characterized by the highest degree of turbulence, unruliness, beligerence, and defiance, all of which greatly interfere with ordered learning and study patterns.

In sum, role changes of early adolescence are numerous. The entry into junior high serves to identify the youngster as no longer a child, but rather, as another participant in the teen culture with a need for a new set of reference persons, values, and behaviors. Not uncommonly, the early adolescent feels compelled to assume a position of exaggerated independence with resultant rebellious attitudes toward adults in general and parents in particular. This is usually combined with a slavish conformity to the peer group, marked by adherence to styles of hair, clothing, musical tastes, and all the various trappings of the youth culture.

Middle Adolescence (Adolescence Proper)

Adolescence proper, or middle adolescence (ages 14–17) is characterized by a more intense emotional life and a turning toward heterosexual love concurrent with increased withdrawal of cathexis from the parents. This process frequently results in impoverishment of the ego; the pain and mourning over the surrender of parent-child ties result in a paucity of ego energy.

> The phase of adolescence proper has two dominant themes: the revival of the oedipal complex and the disengagement from primary love objects. This process constitutes a sequence of object-relinquishment and object-finding, both of which promote the establishment of the adult drive organization. One may describe this phase of adolescence in terms of two broad affective stages; "mourning" and being "in love." The adolescent incurs a real loss in the renunciation of his oedipal parents and he experiences the inner emptiness, grief and sadness which is part of all mourning [Blos, 1962, p. 100].

The articulated adolescent protestation of "leave me alone" may commonly mask dependency and yearning for a meaningful attachment to a significant, consistent, caring adult. What is manifestly asked for is often not what the adolescent actually needs. Emotional dependence can be denied vigorously, thereby confusing parents who mistakenly back off, employ permissive approaches, and surrender needed protective limit setting.

Withdrawal from the parents results in increased cathexis to the self. There is an increase in narcissism and self-preoccupations. Correspondingly, friends and early love objects are narcissistic object choices, based on the ego ideal. "Sexual identity formation becomes the ultimate achievement of adolescent drive differentiation during this phase" (Blos, 1962, p. 89). The teenager is actively seeking and finding new objects outside of the family to replace the earlier passionate ties to oedipal incestuous objects.

The heightened state of narcissism leads to moodiness, self-absorption, and self-aggrandizement. Commonly the estrangement from the family drives the teenager to overvalue peers and new love objects. Object hunger is intense; and in the need to attach to friends, parents are devalued. The narcissistic grandiosity causes the teenager to rebel and demonstrate arrogance and defiance of the parent's authority. Self-esteem requires narcissistic supplies which are now sought through friends and personal achievements. The earlier narcissistic gratifications provided by the parents no longer satisfy, and some adolescents experience mild depersonalization, a new sense of estrangement, and overwhelming yearnings for love. Daydreams and fantasies commonly increase during this time of life; emotional self-absorption can be evident in the use of a diary or journal. "The diary stands between daydream and object world, between make-believe and reality and its content and form change with the times . . . the diary stands foremost in the service of identifactory processes and finally, the diary affords a greater awareness of inner life, a process which in itself, renders the ego more effective in its functions of mastery and synthesis" (Blos, 1962, pp. 94–95).

Identifications and ever-changing attachments are employed as the adolescent struggles in search of meaning and direction. Anna Freud (1963) described the role these identifications play in the love life of the adolescent. Identifications are used to preserve a hold on object relations at the time of the retreat to narcissism. People are used in make-believe friendships and identifications so that the adolescent can exercise his own aggressive and libidinal needs. There is an adaptive experimentation which ultimately strengthens the ego.

There commonly is a heightened sense of awareness; and Blos (1962) cautioned that heightened body-ego feeling should not be minimized. The adolescent's absorption and fascination with his moods, and sensory perceptions promote an intimate sense of self, which evolves into a sense of self-knowledge and boundaries and a growing sense of identity. This self-awareness aids the adolescent in becoming aware of sexual arousal, feelings of anger, and tension. Some authors believe that crushes and tender love precede heterosexual experimentation, though others observe that curiosity or sexual experimentation precedes emotional attachment. The new love object represents prized and precious attributes and characteristics, and threatens newly found independence. There is a longing for and fear of closeness with the idealized newly found object. Blos observes that the emergence of tender feelings marks a turning point for the boy: "the first signs of heterosexuality are manifest and the adolescent elaboration of masculinity is underway" (p.102). The choice of heterosexual love object is commonly determined by its striking similarity or dissimilarity to the parent of the opposite sex.

During middle adolescence, there are two sources of internal danger. One is the weakening of the ego when defenses are inadequate to successfully bind in aggression and depression, and the other is the anxiety aroused by emotional attachment for a sexually desired object. The ego's defenses are marshalled in efforts to avoid a state of panic. Anna Freud (1936) stated that asceticism and intellectualization were the significant defenses of adolescence. Asceticism is ego restrictive, whereas intellectualization allows for more active positive behavior. Blos (1962) considered these defenses typical for European youth; but in his work with American adolescents, he observed cases of behavior and conformity which he viewed as going beyond imitation: "[The] eventual result is an emotional shallowness or sentimentalism due to the overemphasis of the action component in the interplay between self and environment. . . . I call this defense so prevalent in American youth 'uniformism'" (pp. 117–18). Blos posited that this conformity is used as a protection against anxiety and engages several defense mechanisms such as denial, isolation, and identification.

In sum, the middle phase marks an advance in the heterosexual position, as libido is directed away from parental incestuous objects. The stage concludes with "delineation of idiosyncratic conflict and drive constellations" (p. 127), which arouse defensive measures and adaptive efforts. Cognition has become more realistic, objective, and analytical. Interests, skills, and talents have emerged and self-esteem is more stable. Vocational choices are being considered and sorted out realistically, yet unreconciled internal strife still resists transformations. Conflicts are in sharp focus, to be resolved, it is hoped, in the next phase of adolescent maturation.

Late Adolescence

Late adolescence is viewed as a stage of consolidation and stabilization. We anticipate and expect clarity and purposeful actions, predictability, constancy of emotions, stable self-esteem, and more mature functioning. Narcissism has diminished, and there is a greater tolerance for frustrating compromise and delay. Blos (1962) noted:

1. A highly idiosyncratic and stable arrangement of ego functions and interests

2. An extension of the conflict-free sphere of the ego (secondary autonomy)
3. An irreversible sexual position (identity constancy)
4. A relatively constant cathexis of object and self representations
5. The stabilization of mental apparatuses [p. 129]

The developmental task of late adolescence is the consolidation of
personality to facilitate stability in handling work, love relationships,
and one's personal value system. Ritvo (1972) emphasized the older adolescent's need to surrender his narcissistic preoccupations in the move
toward the external world as a source of pleasure and mastery.

Blos reminds us of the oedipal phase with its residues of previous
stages. Resolution of the oedipal crisis requires specific compromise
formations; late adolescence requires that the earlier oedipal residues
be transformed into ego modalities, forming a final, stable, irreversible
sexual identity. Failure in this realm causes what he has described as
sexualization of ego functions, which weakens objectivity, reality testing, and self-criticism, leading to a "resolution of the universal pulls in
one's mental and emotional life. One must be able to distinguish clearly
between self and other, activity and passivity, and pleasure and pain, in
order to achieve a sense of genuine identity" (p. 147).

Anna Freud (1958) noted the following issues as central to adolescence, and their resolution is inclined in the tasks of late adolescence:
(1) impulses: acceptance versus rebellion; (2) love versus hate of parents;
(3) revolt versus dependency; (4) idealism versus narcissism; (5) generos-
ity versus narcissism.

The aforementioned consolidation of personality creates greater
stability and clarity in the emotional and intellectual life of the older adolescent. There is a newly acquired solidity of character. But for the true
artist, this stability can occur only upon the surrender of the introspective hypersensitivity of the younger adolescent. The poetry written
earlier is surrendered; and for many, there is a fading and waning of
creativity and imagination. There is a predictable predisposition to particular kinds of love relationships; drive organization is fixed; and moral
values and ideals are relatively stable. It is generally not until postadolescence that the full moral personality emerges, emphasizing "personal dignity and self-esteem rather than superego dependency and instinctual gratification" (p. 152). Roles and goals have been selected with
a more realistic appraisal of one's strengths and weaknesses.

In late adolescence, the ego ideal, the psychic representation of aspirations and goals, must divest itself of the aim of narcissistic resolution and adjust itself to new and more complex realities. Displacement
is used in the service of finally distinctualizing the ego ideal. Whereas
during latency the ego ideal is concerned with the concrete attainment
and deployment of skills related to industry, competence, etc., in late

adolescence it becomes abstracted and value-ladened. Erikson (1956) referred to the late adolescent superego as ideological rather than parental as in early childhood. The ego ideal, which originates in the stage of primary narcissism and is imbued with an aversion to object-libido involvement, is intimately associated with shifts in libidinal cathexis. The sense of perfection (self-perfection or its externalization) belongs to this narcissistic realm. The growing up to be achieved in adolescence includes closing the gap between ego and ego ideal. In this compression, the cognitive functions of the ego are employed to take a measure both of one's cultural and societal values and of one's own ideals and aspirations, and to modify the latter so that they are more in line with the former. Late adolescents often experience a sense of mourning accompanied by depression in letting go of their wish for perfection. They learn to accept their own limitations and the limit imposed by finite time. Further, they need to give up some deeply held goals and learn to live with uncertainty, ambiguity, and only partially attainable goals.

Solnit (1972) held that the older adolescent searches and longs for support in developing a social conscience. "I believe this represents a universal need which also reflects the unfolding of a biological and psychological force within each adolescent" (p. 98). He quoted Winnicott (1969) who pointed out that adults abdicate their responsibility to adolescents if they ignore them or submit to their points of view or challenges. Solnit posed concern about a lack of visible, institutionalized social alternatives for adolescents to express their independent and rebellious strivings. This thwarts their hope of finding altruistic solutions to their own and to their culture's conflicts. "Altruist aims must be coupled with a rebellion against parental values and finding a 'better than thou' identity" (Solnit, 1972, p. 101).

In an attempt to avoid identity diffusion, the older adolescent may engage in some experiments with negative identity, an identity based upon hostility toward and distance from roles approved by family and society. This experimentation has been described by Settlage (1972) in his account of the development of the individual's integration into the culture in terms of an "in-between space": memories of past experiences between the self and the environment are externalized, worked over in the "mind's eye," and finally internalized and assimilated. When infantile experiences have been sparse or defective, there is an impairment in one's ability to assimilate things cultural and to contribute to one's culture. Settlage (1972) stated:

> An adolescent who has suffered such impairments may fear the loss of self to the culture or tradition (the old danger of fusion or engulfment in the symbiosis) or find himself unable to lend his unique and creative stamp to the culture, to make his mark on it without destroying it. In the case of severe pathology stemming from difficulties in early separation-individua-

tion, there is the risk either of a total alienation from the culture or of a total rejection of it. A creative blending in the in-between, shared space of elements of what is in the self and what is outside the self in the culture is blocked [pp. 77–78].

In late adolescence, there is an increased capacity for abstract thought and organized application of intelligence. While there is no overall resolution of earlier infantile conflicts, we see a more predictable and stable arrangement of derivatives, defenses, and personality style. Patterns have been formed, and less flexibility is discernable. Jones (1922) quoted a letter Sigmund Freud wrote to Ferenczi: "A man should not strive to eliminate his complexes but to get in accord with them: they are legitimately what directs his conduct in the world."

Blos (1962) did not mean to imply that personality development comes to a halt at the conclusion of adolescence. What is firmly and solidly consolidated is the instinctual organization of the individual. New interests, values, and goals are assimilated by the healthy and open young adult. Benedek (1970) emphasized subsequent parenthood as a major new developmental phase. The psychic organization needs to be receptive to alterations after the adolescent stage. However, adulthood does not offer the infinite possibilities of adolescence. Kaplan (1964) stated that those earlier dreams of glory "must be transformed into the life of feasible possibility" (p. 20).

Parenting the Adolescent

Too often parenting literature that stresses adolescent independence and autonomy has been assumed to apply not only to the late adolescent for whom it is appropriate, but to younger teens for whom total freedom is disastrous. At a time of major discontinuity, young adolescents suffer when parental guidance and limit setting is abruptly curtailed; and this often forces the youngster toward uncritical acceptance and attachment to the peer group as a model and major ally. When the peer group is organized around drugs or acting-out behaviors, there is potential for considerable damage and danger.

More recent writers and researchers stress the maintenance of a strong parental coalition against the child's negative choices, wishes, and behaviors. This is easier said than done, as parents are narcissistically vulnerable, due to their own dethronement and to the constant bombardment by the fluctuating ego states and moods of their children.

Parents are bewildered to see a dramatic decline in coping skills, diminished academic performance, and a shift in choice of friends. While adolescents bombard their parents and themselves with concerns about adequacy and attractiveness (which result in mood and affect swings and defiance of parents), the parents, ideally, unite to offer their children a response that embodies empathy and firmness.

Parental sense of humor is not insignificant in the face of the adolescent's sudden indifference, projections, aggression, and withdrawal. Parents can be comforted by knowing that, commonly, the turning of the emotions into their opposites—love into hate, respect into contempt—signifies the hidden but underlying bond between their adolescents and themselves. The adolescent does not expect to be taken literally and reacts with confusion to parents' helplessness and diminished self-esteem.

Cohen and Balikov (1974) suggested that the phenomenon of parental aggression has not been sufficiently valued as a positive and binding force. Schafer (1960) noted the relationship between restrictions and limit-setting roles on the one hand, and nonabandonment on the other. He emphasizes that parental reproaches signify protection and caring. Problems of narcissistic imbalance are frequently followed by maladaptations to hostile impulses with unstable ego-ideal and superego structures. Parental capitulation, distancing, overindulgence, and commands to children to "be happy" to preserve parental narcissism are frequently ingredients in faulty separation-individuation. Parental avoidance of the inevitable struggles and conflicts impedes their and their children's "letting go."

In dealing with the rebellion and withdrawal of the adolescent, parents may be bewildered by confusing advice and/or their own feelings of being overwhelmed. Parents sometimes view their children's problems in terms of the unresolved issues from their own adolescence. For example, parents may try to rebel against their own autocratic upbringing by taking a totally permissive approach with their own children. This, may, and indeed often does, backfire, leading to disastrous and bewildering acting out by their children. Effective parenting must be based on firmer ground than simply offering the child the opposite of one's own youth.

Parental empathy should include a sense of what lurks behind maladaptive behaviors and ugly defensive patterns but must not be misconstrued to convey what Weisberger (1975) called the "understanding fallacy." She cautioned that understanding a child's source of pain and sadness must not mean acceptance of the unacceptable, or "patience beyond endurance." The reality principle must prevail, and parents are mistaken if they attempt to cover up or shield their children from the reality consequences of their behaviors; e.g., by trying to circumvent the rulings of a school or juvenile court. Firmness, empathy, and parental cooperation on the youngster's behalf is the ideal. It is most frequently lacking in households where parents struggle with their own marital, employment, and financial problems.

Bibliography

AICHHORN, A. [1935] (1963). *Wayward Youth*. New York: Viking Press.

_____ (1955). *Delinquency and Child Guidance—Selected Papers*. New York: International Universities Press.

BERNFELD, S. (1938). Types of Adolescence. *Psychoanal. Q.*, 7: whole issue.

BLOS, P. (1962). *On Adolescence*. New York: Free Press.

_____ (1967). The Second Individuation Process of Adolescence. *Psychoanalytic Study of the Child*, 22: 162–86. New York: International Universities Press.

_____ (1968). Character Formation in Adolescence. *Psychoanalytic Study of the Child*, 23: 245–63. New York: International Universities Press.

_____ (1979). *The Adolescent Passage*. New York: International Universities Press.

COHEN, R. and BALIKOV, H. (1974). On the Impact of Adolescence Upon Parents. In *Adolescent Psychiatry, Vol. 3: Developmental and Clinical Studies*, eds. S. Feinstein and P. Giovacchini, pp. 217–36. New York: Basic Books.

DOUVAN, E. and ADELSON, J. (1966). *The Adolescent Experience*. New York: Wiley.

ELKIND, D. (1957). Egocentrism in Adolescence. *Child Development*, No. 4, pp. 1025–34.

ERIKSON, E. H. (1950). *Childhood and Society*. New York: Norton.

_____ (1956). Late Adolescence. In *The Student and Mental Health*, ed. D. H. Funkenstein, p. 76. Cambridge: The Riverside Press.

FREUD, A. [1936] (1946). *The Ego and the Mechanism of Defense*. New York: International Universities Press, chapters 10–11.

_____ (1958). Adolescence. *Psychoanalytic Study of the Child*, 13: 255–78. New York: International Universities Press.

FREUD, S. (1905). Three Essays on the Theory of Sexuality. *Standard Edition*, 7. London: Hogarth Press.

_____ [1905] (1975). The Transformation of Puberty. In *The Psychology of Adolescence—Essential Readings*, ed. A. H. Esman. New York: International Universities Press, pp. 86–102.

_____ (1909). The Analysis of a Phobia in a 5 Year Old Boy. *Collected Papers*, 3. London: Basic Books.

GIOVACCHINI, P. (1985). Introduction: Countertransference Responses to Adolescents. In *Adolescent Psychiatry, Vol. 12: Development and Clinical Studies*, eds. S. Feinstein, M. Sugar, A. Esman, J. Looney, A. Schwartzberg, and A. Sorosky, pp. 447–48. Chicago: University of Chicago Press.

HAMBURG, B. (1974). Early Adolescence: A Specific and Stressful Stage of the Life Cycle. In *Coping and Adaptation*, eds. G. Coelho, D. Hamburg, and J. Adams, pp. 101–24. New York: Basic Books.

INHELDER, B. and PIAGET, J. (1959). *The Growth of Logical Thinking from Childhood to Adolescence*. New York: Basic Books.

JONES, E. (1922). Some Problems of Adolescence. *Brit. J. Psychiatry*, 13: 41–47.

_____ (1955). *The Life and Work of Sigmund Freud*, vol. 2. New York: Basic Books.

KAGAN, J. (1971). A Conception of Early Adolescence. *Daedalus*, Fall 1971, pp. 997–1012.

KAPLAN, L. J. (1984). *Adolescence: The Farewell to Childhood*. New York: Simon & Schuster.

KENISTON, K. (1971). Youth as a Stage of Life. In *Adolescent Psychiatry*, 1: 161–75.

KOHUT, H. (1966), Forms and Transformations of Narcissism. *J. Amer. Psychoanal. Assn.*, 14(2): 243–72.

LAUFER, M. (1966). Object Loss and Mourning During Adolescence. *Psychoanalytic Study of the Child*, 2: 269–93. New York: International Universities Press.

MASTERSON, J. (1967a). *The Psychiatric Dilemma of Adolescence*. Boston: Little Brown.

_____ (1967b). The Symptomatic Adolescent Five Years Later: He Didn't Grow Out of It. *Amer. J. Psychiatry*, 123: 1338–45.

_____ (1968). The Psychiatric Significance of Adolescent Turmoil. *Amer. J. Psychiatry*, 124: 1549–54.

MASTERSON, J. F.; TUCKER, K.; and BERK, G. (1963). Psychopathology in Adolescence IV—Clinical and Dynamic Characteristics. *Amer. J. Psychiatry*, 7: 166–74.

MASTERSON, J. and WASHBURNE, A. (1966). The Symptomatic Adolescent: Psychiatric Illness or Adolescent Turmoil? *Amer. J. Psychiatry*, 122: 1240–48.

NAGERA, H. (1981). *The Developmental Approach to Childhood Psychopathology*. New York: Jason Aronson.

OFFER, D. (1967). Normal Adolescents: Interview Strategy and Selected Results. *Arch. Gen. Psychiatry*, 17:285–90.

OFFER, D. and OFFER, J. (1975a). *From Teenage to Young Manhood: A Psychological Study*. New York: Basic Books.

_____ (1975b). Three Developmental Routes Through Normal Male Adolescence. In *Adolescent Psychiatry, Vol. 4: Developmental and Clinical Studies*, eds. S. Feinstein and P. Giovacchini, pp. 121–41. Chicago: University of Chicago Press.

OFFER, D.; OSTROV, E.; and HOWARD, K. (1981). *The Adolescent: A Psychological Self-Portrait.* New York: Basic Books.

OFFER, D. and SABSHIN, M. (1963). The Psychiatrist and the Normal Adolescent. *Arch. Gen. Psychiatry,* 9:427–32

OFFER, D.; SABSHIN, M.; and MARCUS, D. (1965).Clinical Evaluation of Normal Adolescents. *Amer. J. Psychiatry,* 121:864–72.

OFFER, J. and OFFER, D. (1977). Sexuality and Adolescent Males. In *Adolescent Psychiatry, Vol. 5: Developmental and Clinical Studies,* eds. S. Feinstein and P. Giovacchini, pp. 96–107. New York: Jason Aronson.

OLDHAM, D. (1978). Adolescent Turmoil: A Myth Revisited. In *Adolescent Psychiatry, Vol. 6: Developmental and Clinical Studies,* eds. S. Feinstein and P. Giovacchini, pp. 267–79.

PIAGET, J. (1969). The Intellectual Development of the Adolescent. In *Adolescence: Psychosocial Perspectives,* eds. G. Caplan and S. Levovici, pp. 22–26. New York: Basic Books.

RITVO, S. (1972). Late Adolescence—Developments and Clinical Considerations. *Psychoanalytic Study of the Child,* 27:241–63.

RINSLEY, D. B. (1963). Psychiatric Hospital Treatment with Special Reference to Children. *Arch. Gen. Psychiatry,* 9:489–96.

_____ (1965). Intensive Psychiatric Hospital Treatment of Adolescents: an Object-Relations View. *Psychiatric Q.,* 39:405–29.

_____ (1967). Intensive Residential Treatment of the Adolescent. *Psychiatric Q.,* 41:134–43.

_____ (1981). Borderline Psychopathology: The Concepts of Masterson and Rinsley and Beyard. In *Adolescent Psychiatry, Vol. 9: Developmental and Clinical Studies,* eds. S. Feinstein, J. Looney, A. Schwarzberg, and A. Sorosky, pp. 259–74. Chicago: University of Chicago Press.

RUTTER, M.; GRAHAM, P.; CHADWICK, O.; and YULE, W. (1976). Adolescent Turmoil: Fact or Fiction? *J. Child Psychol. & Psychiatry & Allied Disciplines,* 17:35–56.

SCHAFER, R. (1960). The Loving and Beloved Superego in Freud's Structural Theory. *Psychoanalytic Study of the Child,* 15:163–90.

SETTLAGE, C. (1972). Cultural Values and the Superego in Late Adolescence. *Psychoanalytic Study of the Child,* 27:77–78.

SLAFF, B. (1981). History of Adolescent Psychiatry. In *Adolescent Psychiatry, Vol. 9,* pp. 7–21. *See* Rinsley (1981).

SOLNIT, A. (1972). Youth and the Campus—The Search for Social Concerns. *Psychoanalytic Study of the Child,* 27:98–105.

WEISBERGER, E. (1975). *You and Your Young Child.* New York: Dutton and Co.

WINNICOTT, D. W. (1969). Adolescent Process and the Need for Personal Confrontation. *Pediatrics,* 44:752–56.

PART II

Assessment

An Introduction to Assessment

What constitutes normality in adolescence? What behaviors will abate, and when will the teenager "grow out of it"? Trying to assess what is normal and what is pathological has always been a difficult task, "but for the adolescent age group this seems to have been especially enigmatic" (Mitchell, 1980, p. 200). Olden (1953) noted that adults can empathize more readily with other adults than with children due to differences of ego structure as well as age. Children's egos are in flux, especially during the adolescent years when so many biological, hormonal, physical, emotional, social, and cognitive changes are occuring. These variables cause progressions and regressions, and there is no reliable pattern. Thus, teenagers repeatedly bewilder adults.

There is currently considerable controversy within the profession about the significance of turmoil in adolescent development. This controversy further complicates the assessment process. The traditional view, beginning with the writings of Aristotle and Shakespeare, depicts adolescence as a period of inevitable chaos and disruption. Anthropologists like Mead (1928) have noted tranquility in other cultures; however, traditional psychoanalytic investigation has concluded that in Western civilization adolescent chaotic acting out and rebellion is inevitable, and in fact necessary evidence that the compliant latency phase has ended. A. Freud (1946, 1958) stated that teenagers who remain "good children" are failing to show the signs of inner unrest signifying genuine entry into adolescence. Their excessive defenses are impeding normal maturation and development. Such early psychoanalytic writers as Aichhorn (1935) and Jones (1922) built on Sigmund Freud's ideas concerning biogenetic factors in the development of the personality and stressed the impact of increased sexual and aggressive impulses at puberty, which cause disruption. A. Freud (1946, 1958), Spiegel (1961), and Josselyn (1954) observed what they viewed as normative adolescent upheaval, which looks like neurotic and psychotic disorders or antisocial character pathology but is caused by essentially benign and transient ego failure in adolescence. From a similar perspective Erikson's (1956) concept of normative identity crisis in adolescence is characterized by wide mood swings, social alienation, acting out behavior, rebellion against parents, and frequently temporary academic decline. Blos (1962, 1967) subscribed to the theory of turmoil, which may become a transient, extremely pathologic period, characterized by substance abuse, running away from home, promiscuity, and delinquency. Lindemann (1964) considered a tranquil adolescence an ominous prognostic sign. Unchanged performance and continued adherence to parental values was viewed by these theorists as connoting high risk for development of serious emotional difficulty in adulthood. Those who subscribe to the turmoil and stress account of adolescence attribute the protracted disruption to a lowering of ego strengths combined with an upsurge of sexual and aggressive impulses, which upsets the existent psychic equilibrium.

During the 1950s and 1960s other researchers, using questionnaires and interviews, studied large numbers of adolescents and reached vastly different conclusions. Westley (1958), Grinker (1962), Sibler et al. (1961), and Douvan and Adelson (1966) found little if any of the inner turbulence or rebellious behavior noted by the earlier researchers. In fact, their findings were radically opposed to the traditional accounts. The youth in their samples reported trust of their parents, continuation of common values, good self-esteem based on parental approval, and easy joint participation in rule making in their homes. Masterson concluded from his studies (1967a, 1967b, 1968) that complaints beyond episodic mild anxiety and depression are not found in healthy teenagers. More serious symptoms, such as decreased academic functioning and disturbed familial and social relationships, indicate genuine emotional illness. In follow-up evaluation, those teenagers presenting more serious symptoms evidenced continued symptomatology and moderate to severe disturbance. Masterson believed that there is no basis to presume that affected adolescents will grow out of their difficulties.

Oldham (1978) and others noted that the original psychoanalytic investigations were based on a small sample of patients, which raises questions about normative generalizable theory. Thus, those clinicians who subscribe to the original conceptions may overlook serious nontransitory behavior. Some clinicians may err on the opposite end of the spectrum and overreact to any signs of nonconformity in language, dress, and manner. "It is important for the clinician who evaluates and treats teenagers to critically examine the sources of his or her conceptualization of adolescent turmoil" (p. 277).

It appears that there is no way to reconcile these vastly different perspectives. More research is clearly needed for a fuller comprehension of normality in adolescence. It would appear that the future research samples should be more varied. Generalizations may not be possible, and indeed, we may find a series of norms for different populations. Kernberg (1978) suggested that the "adjustment reaction" label in adolescence is not a diagnostic label, but rather, an alarm signal, pointing to the need to evaluate in depth the personality structure of an adolescent in social conflicts. This evaluation would include the patient's early developmental history and previous level of functioning. Some clinicians predict stability in adulthood based on overall adjustment prior to adolescence; others look for good adjustment after early adolescence as the predictor of stability or pathology after the final stage of consolidated postadolescence.

The perspective to be presented in this text is predicated on as thorough an in-depth assessment of the adolescent patient as possible, including seeking data on the adolescent's early history, familial and peer relationships, social and academic functioning, significant traumas or environmental influences, and mastery of age-appropriate tasks. The diagnostician must attempt to assess drive development, ego and superego development, object relations, self-esteem regulation, and such general characteristics as frustration tolerance, management of affects, e.g. anxiety and depression, sublimation potential, and progressive versus regressive tendencies.

Giovacchini and Borowitz (1974) emphasized object relations and devised an object relations scale. The clinician records the patient's behavior toward him or her, and toward parents and siblings, noting motor behavior and affects (e.g., verbal quality and coherence, anxiety, depression, hate, pleasure, and affection) and patient's attitudes (e.g., cooperativeness, interest or curiosity, submissiveness, dominance, approval or disapproval, optimism, pessimism, and external world or inner preoccupations). A similar detailed examination focuses on the defenses the patient employs, the apparent psychosocial development, and characterological variables, such as self-esteem, identity, and role adequacy. This scale helps therapists substantiate formulations, examine basic concepts, and, it is hoped, leads to conceptual clarification. Adolescence is a period of heightened narcissism, and in the diagnostic phase, assessment of self-esteem or self-regard is particularly important.

Due to the heightened narcissism of all adolescents, the clinician must be clear about the tendency to idealize or deprecate friends, family members, teachers, and other authority figures. It is often difficult to distinguish the norm from a narcissistic personality disorder.

Process and Form of the Diagnostic Evaluation

It is useful to consider specific guidelines at the time of the first contact with an adolescent and his or her parents. Kessler (1966) suggested scrutiny of

1. The difference between the child's chronological age and behavioral age level
2. The frequency and duration of the symptoms
3. The number of symptoms
4. The degree of social disadvantage
5. The intractability of the behavior
6. The adolescent's personality or general adjustment
7. Last, and often overlooked, the degree of the child's inner suffering.

These criteria often aid in determining the child's progression, fixation, or regression in age-appropriate tasks. The objectives in an assessment are to determine how, and in what areas, the child differs from others of the same age; to assess the chronicity of the child's problems; and to appraise areas of strength in the adolescent, and the adolescent's family. This information should then help the clinician formulate some hypothesis about possible contaminating factors, be they past, present, constitutional, or family-induced. One hopes to find out how the family handled the child before the symptoms appeared and how they are currently handling him or her. One attempts to make an assessment of the adolescent's parents along with that of the child to determine subsequent recommendations and what is possible in the future work with the adolescent and/or with the family. One should attempt to determine to what extent parents contribute to the maintenance of the adolescent's problems and, in contrast, to what extent they support healthy aspects of the teenager's personality.

The initial assessment may be tentative, given the above noted enigmas in assessing adolescents. Diagnosis is an ongoing process over the course of therapy, and revisions occur as one gathers new material and information. Kessler (1966) recommended that one's diagnostic formulation include symptomatology, etiology, prognosis, and at least a tentative treatment plan. MacDonald (1965) added for consideration, "the child's conflict, the child's personality and developmental progress, constitutional and organic impairments, major psychological traumas, and, the child's and parents' external world" (p. 601).

At the onset, a therapist hopes to obtain as clear a view as possible of family life, including the familial relationships and structure in the family and extended family: the modes of parenting and discipline, the financial reality and work schedules of parents, the child care arrangements, and the additional support systems or lack thereof (social ties, neighborhood, school, religious affiliation, life style, values, and any other services or systems that have aided and/or involved the family and specifically the adolescent). Because of the importance of the peer group for teenagers, one should ask for both the adolescent's and the parents' descriptions of companions and activities.

Psychological testing need not be routinely done. When it is part of the assessment, the adolescent should be well prepared for the testing process and should be given the reason for it as well as the results. An appraisal of an adolescent's physical condition is essential and may well require a physical and/or neurological exam. Organic pathology must be considered; and attention must be given to chronic physical diseases and disabilities that exact emotional stress, cause learning disabilities or social difficulties, and/or inhibit the subject's ability to work.

It is important to observe how and what the parents and adolescent share with the therapist, not only as to factual data such as the adolescent's developmental history, but emotional attitudes, past and present, which are more telling. Do the parents guiltily describe marital difficulty? Do they project all blame onto the teenager? Is the father aloof and indifferent to the assessment process, merely complying with agency practice or therapist's preference that both parents be seen, or is he actively, empathically concerned about his teenager? What affects are discernable (e.g., apathy, anger, helplessness, or empathy) between parents and adolescent? Is there a cold war, a stony silence in the family or an emotional tone of overreactiveness, seductiveness, and intrusiveness? One is often hard put to determine the realities of conflictual areas in the realm of curfew, companions, dress, accountability, academic expectations, and so forth. At times during the initial contacts, parents and teenager attempt to turn the therapist into a referee or mediator about such matters. Restraint, and withholding premature advice, is the prudent course during the initial contacts when establishment of rapport and early alliance with the adolescent and the parents is essential. Affect and motivation are key prognostic guidelines essential to the ongoing planning of therapy.

In contrast to the current mental health trend toward dispensing with the assessment phase, the view advanced here is that such evaluation is crucial. Some writers note that treatment begins with the first contact, and clinicians in agreement with this will plunge into treatment in the first session. The recent preoccupation with treating large populations has led to ever briefer treatment in the effort to treat more patients in less time. While this goal may be socially valid, it has little to do with the needs of a given patient. Time is rarely saved, and in fact, is usually lost, by the total omission of the assessment process. The distinction between evaluation and treatment is not merely a semantic one. Following the feeling of relief that often accompanies the first visit, adolescents and parents must make a conscious decision to undertake actual ongoing therapy.

The therapist should use his or her discretion regarding treatment recommendations, choice of therapeutic modality, etc.; but it is important that these decisions be based on realistic expectations for the adolescent patient. Thus, when possible, the therapist should avoid lengthy treatment waiting lists or time lags between the assessment phase and commencement of regular therapy sessions. Adolescents commonly are brought for treatment by their parents, schools, police, juvenile courts, and themselves, during crisis; and crisis intervention requires prompt, often immediate attention. The poor frustration tolerance common to adolescents and their propensity for impulsivity and mood swings call for prompt engagement of parents and teenagers.

The engagement-assessment process sets the stage and serves, ideally, as the beginning of an ongoing alliance between the adolescent, the parents, and the clinician. In the initial collection of data, resistance must be respected. Parents and/or adolescent may oppose any sort of inquiry at the teenager's school. An adolescent who abuses drugs and/or alcohol most likely will object to any physical exam or evaluation as part of the assessment process. In all, the evaluation of teenagers rarely proceeds smoothly, in accord with agency- or clinician-determined procedure and time frame. Contact with outside sources of information may well require not only parental permission, but also the adolescent's permission. One cannot effectively engage a teenager in a trusting treatment relationship if one does not inform him or her of the information one possesses or if the information is secured behind the teenager's back.

The initial assessment phase of contact is the logical time to help parents prepare the teenager for his or her initial interview. Ideally, the adolescent is allowed considerable independent input into the decision to seek help. This is obviously not the case, however, when the teenager is a nonvoluntary client, e.g. referred by the juvenile court, school, or some such agency of power. In the absence of such authoritarian referrals, teenagers' fears of stigma or craziness are often such that the adolescent will not initially comply with parental requests that help be sought. Not infrequently the clinician must begin contact with the parents to explore and discover effective means to engage the adolescent. Even when appearing for an appointment, the teenager may vehemently deny all problems, or project all difficulties onto the parents as the persons in need of help. It is unrealistic for a clinician to expect such a defense of denial, and/or projection to be given up quickly or easily. Adolescent clients need to be informed of the confidentiality of their communications, and their right to share or withhold as they wish. It is hoped that they will come to see that they will not be seduced or forced into any disclosure. Commonly the resistive adolescent perceives the clinician as the pawn or tool of the parents, engaged to reshape the teenager into the compliant child he or she believes the parent seeks.

Many parents report their adolescent's opposition, rage, and explosiveness at the prospect of being taken to see a therapist. We can assume that such opposition and tantrums are generalized responses over and beyond the proposed contact with a therapist or mental health clinic. Teenagers generally are not allowed autonomy regarding attendance at school, the necessity of medical and dental appointments or the approval of medical and dental procedures. Often they should not be allowed total freedom of choice regarding therapeutic contact. When severe disability and symptomatology exist, parents need help and support to set and maintain realistic expectations for therapeutic contact. The dilemma of overwhelmed parents who plead that they can't get their adolescent to the sessions is a diagnostic sign that requires further scrutiny of possible parental resistances, ineffectiveness, and ambivalence. It may also be a sign of overriding problems in the home regarding limits and controls. In such situations, the clinician is wise to remain firm and patient, clarifying the situation, rather than allying with the regressive infantile stance of the parents or identifying with parents' covert rejection and helplessness. Firm limits, outreach, and persistance often constitute a form of caring that overwhelmed parents have not been able to provide their teenager. When the referral is nonvoluntary, the clinician is well advised to inform the adolescent about expectations and reality and take a therapeutic stance that will not permit collusion; e.g., if the teenager misses appointments this reality will not be kept in confidence and withheld from parents, school, the juvenile court, probation department or other relevant authority.

Assessment Procedures

Many clinics and therapists have a specific form or policy for collecting evaluative data. They contact parents and the adolescent, and may or may not routinely consult schools and pediatricians. Some initial interviews are in the form of joint family sessions; other treatment centers specify separate sessions for the teenager and his or her parents from the first contact on an ongoing basis. While some clinics, schools, and teenage drop-in centers offer service to adolescents without their parents, others require parental participation or permission if the adolescent is under 16 or 18. These procedures vary depending on agency services, focus, and mandate.

When possible, parental contact is generally useful in determining why help is sought now, the history of the presenting complaint(s), premorbid functioning, and early history; It also provides clarity about the emotional tone and course of events in family life. In addition to child-focused material, the marital situation and parents' personal histories are important to understand. We are familiar with the well-known phenomenon of the repetition compulsion and the frequency with which parents repeat their painful pasts. Parents' own adolescent struggles frequently reverberate during their children's adolescence as they all deal with issues of separation and individuation.

During the assessment phase, the adolescent patient is generally seen immediately so that he or she does not feel manipulated and dissected by parents and a potential therapist. Whenever possible, one wants to promote an age-appropriate sense of responsibility and independence in the adolescent at the onset of therapeutic contact. Exploration and review of the reasons for appointments, acknowledgement of, for example, parental concerns or school's recommendations, and exploring the teenager's perceptions of the reasons for clinic contact, often can be done in the first session. During these initial contacts, the following issues are pertinent in formulating diagnostic conclusions: Are there indications of an emerging set of personal initiatives directed toward peers, teachers, and experiences outside the home and separate from family activities? What is the level of mastery of age-appropriate academic tasks? Is there an ability to make friends, maintain a circle of friends, and share interests and activities with others? Is there a capacity for empathy, good judgment, frustration tolerance, and control of impulses and drives?

Once material is organized and diagnostic impressions are formed, preliminary formulations and treatment plans can be made. Drawing on clinical judgment, practice wisdom and interpretation of observations, one should formulate an integrated description of the adolescent, with clarity about the child's social context and the family's socioeconomic-educational status and life style. This should include a description and preliminary assessment of the parents and a cross sectional view of the child's current functioning (e.g., peer relations, school functioning, relationships with family members, play, work, sexual identity, and self-concept). The diagnostic impressions and formulations should give information about the etiology of the adolescent's major conflicts, anxieties, object relations, modes of dealing with frustration, delay, anger, and guilt.

Often parents and teenager are eager to learn the results of the evaluation, and an informing or follow-up interview can be a crucial point in the early contacts. If adolescent and parent can integrate the findings and commit to the therapy recommendations, it can be a turning point in improving family members' well-being. Often an overly close relationship with the diagnostician can interfere with referral or case transfer. Obviously, a negative experience will also interfere with ongoing work and acceptance of recommendations, which are rarely accepted quickly in any case. Parents, teenager, and clinician need to consider not only the emotional significance of recommendations, but also practical matters, such as fees, travel, time, needs of other children in the family, parents' work schedules, and the like.

Some adolescents are pleased to have a special private person, a therapist to themselves, and others are resentful, angry, and highly resistive to the idea of regularly scheduled ongoing sessions. Drastic recommendations, such as placement or hospitalization, may be met with denial and resistance and flight from the clinic or require considerable time to work through. All in all, the clinician's conclusions and recommendations need to be presented fully, simply, and in clear language, avoiding the jargon of the profession, and time must be allotted for questions. This may be in the form of additional sessions.

Case of Jan: Hampstead Profile Assessment of Adolescent Disturbances

The case of Jan and several others in this text are presented in full to acquaint the reader with the assessment process, the kind of data gathered, the contact with parents, and the diagnostician's observations of the adolescent. The organization of the material or diagnostic evaluation is in accord with the Developmental Process, an application of Anna Freud's Diagnostic Profile (1965) adapted particularly for assessment of an adolescent (Laufer, 1965, 1977). Other case material is presented in vignette form, as the emphasis there is not on assessment but on specific pathologies of adolescence.

The Diagnostic Profile is an instrument used for all diagnostic work at the Hampstead Clinic. Based on a psychoanalytic theory of childhood and adolescent development, the profile serves as a framework for a clinician's thinking and a method of organizing findings. It enables clinicians to assess behavior, symptoms, drive, and ego and superego development in structural, dynamic, economic, genetic, and adaptive terms. Lines of development, mastery of age-appropriate tasks, regression and fixation points, and the interplay of internal and external forces are clarified by use of this instrument. Additionally, assessment of general characteristics like frustration tolerance, sublimation potential, and overall attitude toward anxiety are clarified.

> When diagnosing the mental disturbance of children, the child analyst is confronted with difficulties which are due to the shifting internal scene in a developing individual, and which are not met within adult psychiatry. One of these difficulties concerns the fact that, during development, symptoms, inhibitions and anxieties do not necessarily carry the same significance which they assume at a later date. Although in some cases they may be lasting, and the first signs of permanent pathology, in other cases, they need be no more than transient appearances of stress. . . . Another difficulty for the diagnostician is bound up with the well-known fact that there are no childhood alternatives to the adults' efficiency or failure in sex or work, vital factors which are used in adult psychiatry as indicators of intactness or disturbance. . . . Accordingly, it becomes the diagnostician's task to ascertain where a given child stands on the developmental scale, whether his position is age-adequate, retarded or precocious, and in what respect; and to what extent the observable internal and external circumstances and existent symptoms are interfering with the possibilities of future growth [1962, pp. 149–150].

Referral

Jan A.,* a middle-class black 14-year-old girl, was referred to the clinic by her parents. The parents stated that for the last month Jan had expressed terror about being alone and feared that she was becoming a lesbian. As fearful as she was about being alone, she would closet herself in her room and remain alone and withdrawn for hours, supposedly reading. Jan shared with the therapist the fact that, actually, when closeted in her room, she would read "dirty" books, get excited, and relieve herself by masturbating; she had been experimenting with new modes of masturbation. At the clinic, Jan described her obsessive fantasies and thoughts of an erotic nature about girls, as well as ideas about women having intercourse with dogs. She described being flooded with these images and longed to be normal, happy, and free of these thoughts, like her peers. She continually shared these concerns with her parents in a frantic, frenzied discharge; and apparently their remarks only added fuel to her expanding concerns and did not decrease her staring at and fantasizing about females. She was alarmed by her suggestibility; she feared that whatever she read about or heard might happen to her.

Jan's father, an assistant principal in a high school, expressed grief that he could be effective and helpful with other children but not with Jan; he feared that she would need hospitalization. Both Jan's mother and father currently planned the family schedule to ensure that Jan was not alone. Her mother had taken a leave of absence from her city job, where she was employed on a 3 P.M. to 12 P.M. shift.

Description of the Patient: Appearance, Mood, Affects, Mien

Jan was basically an attractive teenager, but her hair was somewhat disheveled and she looked depressed and agitated. She was very well-developed physically and seemed somewhat self-conscious about it. The most striking thing about this child was her totally undefended outpouring of libidinal material, both at home and at the clinic. She said she worried "every minute," and couldn't stop her thoughts. She would rather stay home than go anywhere. Her primary concern was over her preferences, that she would "convince" herself to become a lesbian; she was terrified by her erotic thoughts and wishes about girls. Her total lack of eye contact initially added to the impression that the therapist was used as an object, or receptacle, into which she could discharge floods of information. She did not relate interpersonally; rather, she "vomited" out her fears, images and accounts of masturbation, speaking nonstop.

Jan did well in school. Her problems had emerged when the school year ended. Peer relationships appeared to be strained. Friends had noted Jan's daydreaming and distracted air, and she feared that they knew something was wrong with her. Jan was attending a city-sponsored activity program over the

---

*The events recounted in the case studies are factual. The names of the participants have been changed to protect their privacy.

summer; she could actively involve herself in the sports program, but generally felt nervous and tense there.

She said she couldn't stand for a man to be around her or looking at her, although she was not "bothered" by her brothers and father. Last fall she had had a crush on a boy, who gave her a present. However, her parents were very strict with her and had curtailed this involvement because they disapproved of boyfriends and presents from boys at her age.

Jan demonstrated a distorted sense of genital differentiation. Her own sexual identity crisis obscured any evidence of a genuine oedipal triadic relationship with her parents. Nevertheless, she did evidence a problematic relationship with each parent. Latency tasks seemed to have been mastered; the advent of adolescence had caused a resurgence of terrifying unconscious incestuous sexual stresses. At this point, Jan believed she had a split self-concept; she spoke of a "lesbian side" and a boy side, as opposed to a more normal "girl side." This seemed to be a defense against a very strong cathexis to her father.

Developmental History

The parents had been married for 15 years. Jan was not a planned child. In fact, her mother was pregnant when she got married. She was 19 when Jan was born; Jan's father was 24 and still in college. The father said that he "spoiled" Jan from birth on. The mother described her pregnancy as "normal," although further questioning brought out the fact that she had severe morning sickness for the first three or four months and then was more comfortable. She did not work during this pregnancy. The delivery was described as normal. The mother did not attempt to nurse Jan. As an infant, Jan did not sleep well. For the first two months, she "mixed up days and nights" and was colicky.

Jan was said to be a good eater and a curious, active baby. Things went more easily by the third month, when the colic subsided and the sleeping schedule stabilized. Jan's mother acknowledged that she was very anxious and distant with her first baby. By four months, Jan was pulling herself up. At six months, she was sitting and starting to crawl. She walked at eleven months and was toilet trained at a year. The mother stated that toilet training only took one month; she started when Jan was eleven months old. Jan used the bottle for a year and never liked or used a pacifier. She never sucked her thumb and was said to have started to coo, babble, and sing in her crib at three months. She was described as speaking plainly at about a year.

When Jan was 1½ years old, she grabbed and ate paper and other peculiar substances, a habit which lasted for a three-month period. Her parents felt that being in an apartment without a backyard made things somewhat difficult with a toddler. Although the eating of paper did not last long, it did appear to signify problems in the mother/child dyad. By the time Jan was about 1½ years old, her father was working full-time at a city job and finishing college on a part-time basis. Her mother had worked full-time only in the last five or six years.

Jan was 2½ when the second child was born. She was described as excited but not jealous. However, she was said to manifest profound jealousy as she got older and currently is very competitive and combative with her brothers. Her parents said she still wanted to get her own way. The father said that now it was a craving for attention rather than sibling rivalry. He also said that maybe he was overindulgent with material things, trying to minimize his daughter's problems which, in fact, worried him terribly. He said that Jan got whatever she wanted (e.g., money, clothes, movies). He felt that they had indulged her materially more than their other children.

Jan did not attend nursery school. Her only unusual illness was whooping cough, which she had in her preschool years. She became anemic at age two and this lasted for a year. No cause was found. Jan was hospitalized for approximately a week at the age of seven or eight, when she was bitten by a dog and had some poisoning and a swollen leg. This occurred when Jan was far away from home visiting her maternal grandparents. No surgery was necessary. Since age three, Jan had spent summers in Alabama with these grandparents. It was most significant that parents attached little importance to this repeated and lengthy separation each year.

Jan entered kindergarten at a parochial school at age five. She did not cry, manifested no separation difficulty, and was eager and excited to start school. She always did well at school, except for one low math grade this last year, which she was able to bring up by the end of the academic year.

Jan was ten years old when her mother started to work on a 3 P.M. to midnight shift. Her parents said Jan had shown no reaction to this at the time. The father apparently did all the homemaker jobs. He would get back from his teaching job before the children returned from school. Jan's mother once switched to the midnight shift in order to be home after school; however, she could not keep it on a permanent basis and went back to her old shift. Her father said that Jan always had been very attached to him, particularly around the age of three. She asked for very little information about sexual differences or how babies are born, and simply was told that "the stork brought them."

Family Background and Possible Significant Environmental Influences

Mr. and Mrs. A. described arguments about the children's discipline. They agreed that he was easier on the children than she was. Mrs. A. rather sarcastically implied, however, that this was the case because he let the children have their own way. She said that the boys would convince him to let them stay out and play until 10:00 P.M., but with her it was 9:00 P.M. and no later, and if their school work was not done on a school night they could not play after 7:30 P.M. She said that they didn't even ask her for a later hour. The father said that he felt it was good for them to be out playing and he felt they should be allowed to stay out later on weekend evenings. He said that he was made to come in early as a child and resented it; he did not want his children to feel the same way.

Father

Jan's father said that, as an assistant principal, he had seen a lot of parents; and he really had some questions about his own wife and what was going on in his own family. He said that perhaps he was not forceful enough; perhaps he should have insisted on his wife's greater involvement with Jan and should have provided Jan with things such as dancing classes. He felt there was an absence of "motherly love." He went on to say that his wife did not talk enough, especially to the children. She was not chatty and did not think of easy casual things to do, like other mothers did, such as taking her daughter shopping. At home, she did not chat and interact with the children in a pleasant way. More often her conversation consisted of orders to the children, such as "do the dishes" and "clean your room." Mr. A. said that he had urged his wife to take Jan shopping and do other pleasant things.

Jan's father said that he came for a large sociable Southern family. He grew up in a house with a yard and had some advantages that his wife did not have. He said that their personalities were very different, in that his wife did not talk or socialize very much, even with her own family. He liked the gaiety of big family meals and visiting back and forth, which Jan's mother seemed less interested in.

The father initially described his marriage as "OK" and later described difficulties. He said that his wife enjoyed bowling, and he lets her go. However, when he went bowling, she seemed to be jealous and concerned. He said that one of the biggest problems was that when his wife got angry, she would not speak, sometimes for as long as a week. He felt that often she would get upset over nothing or over something that she would not share with him. He said that the last week had been a difficult one. In addition to the concerns about Jan, there had been two deaths in the family, one on his wife's side and one on his side. He had offered to help his wife with her relative's funeral, and had been very hurt and upset that she did not offer to help him in regard to his relative's death (for example, by making phone calls to relatives who had come to town for the funeral). It was true that her father had been visiting from out of town; but, in general, she would not reach out by doing any kind of warm, familial thing. He had been telling his wife lately that his relatives wondered if he, in fact, had a wife because she never attended family functions. He said that she seemed to spend too much time playing cards with her friends and was away from the children. He was further concerned that she would arrange their social life so that they would leave the children too frequently. "I get a feeling of emptiness in our household. She just won't talk, although sometimes I think I've gotten used to it."

Mr. A. said that his wife could get very angry at him when he was only joking. He gave an example of his having had a drink or two at a party and having joked about his wife's poor driving ability. She blew up at him and threatened that she would never help him by driving on a long-distance trip. She "seemed to enjoy handling me around my people, trying to humiliate me." He thought his wife was picking excuses to get angry, and he couldn't understand it. He said that this had more or less always been her pattern. She would have spells, get angry, get quiet, and be very remote. Their sexual life was very poor; they had sex no more than once or twice a month and sometimes not at all, and they had had many disagreements about this. He then pondered the thought that Jan's room was next door to theirs and that, although their door was kept closed, perhaps she had heard their arguments and fights. The father said that in the last five to seven years things had gotten worse; it was very bad once his wife started working nights. He often asked her what she expected of him. He said that the household contained no love or affection. What did she think he wanted a wife for? He didn't need a woman to help him manage his money; and he could buy TV dinners or pick up a woman. He wanted more out of marriage. He seemed very upset when he talked about the fact that maybe his wife was happier playing cards and working than being with him. Her excuses when she declined sex were that she was tired or simply didn't feel like it. Mr. A. said that on occasion he even pointed out their sort of problems cited in the Ann Landers column. When he would try to discuss their problems, he sometimes would get so angry that he would leave the house and go out for a drink.

In addition to sex, money was also a problem. Mrs. A. complained about it constantly. In the father's view, she would prefer total control of the money. Mr. A. banked his check and deducted little. He believed that his wife wanted him simply to turn over the paycheck to her so that she could dole out money to him. He did not see her paycheck, had not asked to have control over it, and was concerned at the way she spent money. "She has more clothes than anyone I know. She owns more pants than I do." Mr. A. said that when he attempted to do something to please his wife, such as buying her a dress, she would get suspicious and assume that he was having an affair or something on the side. Because of this attitude, he had stopped buying her presents. He said that he gave her no reason to think he was being unfaithful and felt that she thought he might be wild, like her own acting-up brother. She was not suspicious now because he bought her nothing. He said that once, when he was concerned that perhaps he was not attentive enough to her, he suggested stopping by to watch her in a bowling league; and she accused him of wanting to spy on her. However, now she liked him to accompany her; and they frequently bowled together.

In Mr. A.'s opinion, "the mother shapes the child's life." He felt that there was a lot of conflict in his wife's family; her parents were always at war. Her father drank and chased younger women. He stated that his wife had been greatly affected by seeing her own father chasing young women around. His father-in-law told him that he and his wife battled physically. He and Mrs. A., too, have had quite a few physical battles. They both had tempers, but he felt that hers was excessive. He said that maybe he wasn't easy to live with, but that she subjected him to enormous pressure and tension and, when they fought, she wanted the children, particularly the sons, to defend her. He said that his wife acted very peculiar sometimes, tearing his pajamas, throwing things, and hitting him. Although he got angry, he felt that her screaming and yelling were far worse. He wondered about several families on the block who they were close with and who were currently engaged in separations and divorces. The father said maybe the conflict between him and his wife was alarming to Jan.

Mother

Mrs. A. said that the marriage had been a tense one and might have contributed to Jan's difficulties. There had been much disagreement between the parents over money, bills, and the discipline of the children. The mother said that she paid all of the bills and that her husband often did not tell her when he wrote a check and therefore she could not balance the account and often would get overdrawn. Despite the fact that they argued endlessly about this, her husband would not alter his behavior at all until about two or three months ago. He seemed to be more thoughtful and careful about it lately. She said that they disagreed about how much he should spend on himself. He took fifty dollars out of his paycheck to cover two weeks for him. Mrs. A. felt she did not know what he did with this money. She said sometimes he seemed to spend an inordinate amount of his money on alcohol, mainly for the house. He did go out drinking occasionally perhaps once every two or three months, either alone or with her brother. Very hesitantly she shared the fact that he might go to a bar to drink after they had had an argument.

Mrs. A. said that she and her husband had had many arguments about sex. She never really wanted to have sex and felt that something was wrong with her. Her husband was more outspoken on the subject and talked constantly about the fact that something was wrong or that perhaps she was seeing someone on the side. Her doctor had indicated that perhaps her lack of interest in sex was a side effect of the pill. She had been on the pill for five years and said that she was going to go off it soon. She had told her husband what her doctor had said.

The mother acknowledged that the marriage had been much less happy during the last three years because of the sexual incompatibility. However, she said that she and her husband seemed to be close in regard to shared activities such as bowling, visiting relatives, or attending parties. Mrs. A. was close to tears in talking about the marriage. She seemed under great tension and anxiety during this interview, as she had in the joint one with her husband the week before. She said that she felt teary and upset when she and her husband argued or when she thought about Jan's problem. She felt that her husband was equally worried and concerned about Jan and that neither of them understood their daughter's problem.

In answer to the therapist's question, Jan's mother acknowledged that perhaps her working nights all these years had affected her sexual relationship with her husband, although they used to have sex on the weekends. She talked about her husband not being opposed to her work or even her schedule, because her work had a purpose, specifically, to bring in money so that the family could afford a home. Mrs. A. would cook and have dinner ready so that her husband was not burdened with a lot of household responsibilities when he took care of the children in the afterschool hours. The mother said that in the early years of their marriage they were happy, although things had been very stressful in the last three years.

Their courtship had lasted for almost a year. Mrs. A. was just out of high school, happy and proud and impressed with her boyfriend, who was older and in college. She said that her parents always had liked her husband. Her husband's mother was deceased, and she felt she got along well with her father-in-law. In fact, when her father-in-law remarried, she and her husband and her in-laws had lived together for a three-month period and had had a cordial relationship. She had less cordial contact with her husband's aunts, who apparently felt that no one was good enough for their nephew and disapproved of her. All but one of these aunts were now dead. Her husband would visit this remaining aunt alone, without her. Mrs. A. felt that perhaps things were a little better lately, in that she was cordial and close with the aunt's children.

She felt that extended family issues were not of major importance and that the tension, lack of privacy, and mounting conflict at home adversely affected Jan and her as well. The mother always had an open-door policy; Jan would come and go when her mother was bathing and dressing. In addition, she had been exposed to severe parental fighting and sexual problems, in that their bedrooms were close and privacy was meager. The following environmental factors seemed of great significance: Jan had had her own room for only four years; Jan described memories of kissing and laughing with her brother in his bed, and of engaging in erotic play with a boy cousin at age six or seven (see second interview with Jan).

Interviews with Jan

Without preamble, Jan plunged right in at the beginning of the interview with a flood of worries and preoccupations. She felt that no one understood her or knew what she was talking about. She was upset and preoccupied and felt she was going crazy. She wished she could be normal as before. She was furious with herself for staring at cute girls and was most upset to find herself preoccupied with her mother's legs some weeks ago. She said that when these strange thoughts and feelings first occurred, she could brush them off. By the second week in June, she had developed crying spells and was spending a great deal of time in her room. She would go to her room and pretend that she was someone else, a fantasy figure. She would read dirty books and stuff her bra to look bigger, different, and "be another person." She would talk to herself about how she did not want to become a lesbian and would try to interest herself in ideas about intercourse with a man. She said she had started to masturbate lately. She read a lot about masturbation and used her finger in a masturbatory effort. She said that it hurt her and she was frightened by it, but she continued to do it. She said that she was preoccupied with these issues. Recently, she sent away for a breast exerciser; she didn't know why she had done this as she was well developed physically. She did not know what she was doing or why she was obsessed with these thoughts. Her constant concern was that she was a lesbian, but she also was preoccupied with women having intercourse with dogs. She said that she had a lot of mental images about herself and her dog. She said that her father had told her that some women "go with dogs." She said her father told her that lesbians have penises, but she knew that couldn't be true.

She said that she was uncomfortable when she had her menstrual period and related this to hearing her mother comment that lesbians hate to have menstrual periods. She was 13 years old when her menstrual periods began. Her mother had told her about menstruation, although she had already heard a great deal about it in school. She was concerned that she hadn't started her periods earlier and felt that something would go wrong. She remembered being very happy when she started to menstruate. She said that until recently she had always liked boys. When a boy gave her a box of candy for Valentine's Day, her mother told her she was not old enough to accept presents from boys. She didn't agree, but she accepted the ultimatum. She said it was not an issue anymore, because she hadn't been given any more gifts by boys. She wished she were happy and normal like her friends and were rid of all these worries. She appeared very hysterical and suggestible.

In response to questions the therapists raised about her relationship with her parents, she said at times she felt like screaming because they "bugged" her. She said that they asked her too often, "why, why, why?" She said that she never screamed or argued with her parents for fear of getting hit. But recently, when her mother was nagging her about cleaning her gym shoes, she told her mother to shut up. She said that she did argue with her parents often about money and clothes. She used to argue with them a lot about spending more time with her friends, but they would make her stay home and babysit for her brothers. She often would sneak out of the house to avoid this responsibility. Now she hated being in the house if there was no one there with her. Yet, when they were all at home, she wanted to be by herself in her bedroom with the knowledge that someone was available in the house. She said her father nagged her to do things she didn't want to do. For example, he wanted her to "be happy, see friends, and go places with him." She said her parents generally approved of her schoolwork but had been a little concerned when she got a low mark in math last year. She had improved the mark. She also had received a poor grade in sewing, but they expressed little concern about it.

Jan, wringing her hands and very anxious, went on to say that after she had seen the intake clinic worker she wondered if she had told everything she should. She said that maybe she had omitted the fact that once, when she was in the fifth or sixth grade, she had kissed and hugged a girlfriend on a field trip. She said she was obsessed with the question of whether or not she "felt anything" during that incident. Currently in gymnastics, when she was spotting and holding a girl, she would find herself staring at her hand on the girl's waist. Her friends were asking her what was the matter with her and why she was daydreaming so much. She described her schoolwork as "all right." Actually she had gotten very good marks except for the sewing grade. She was not close with any teachers this last year. She described one short, irritable male teacher, who was her homeroom teacher. From Jan's account, she seemed to have had no major disciplinary problems in school.

In commenting on her relationship with her brothers, she said that it was all right, although they could make her angry. She said they would mess up the kitchen after she cleaned it, and she would become furious, because she was the one responsible for the dishes. She said that she yelled at her brothers a lot. She said now she was less irritable about their activities in the kitchen, since they all took turns with the dishes.

She said she talked to her parents and it helped her only for the moment. She said that her parents were nice, gave her money, and tried to help her, but nothing seemed to be giving her much relief. She talked about an incident at the summer activity program: she heard the word "fag" and thought someone was referring to her. Although her friend reassured her that this taunt was directed at a boy, and not at her, she was upset all day and had a crying spell at home over it. Jan had asked this close friend whether or not she thought she was acting peculiar and strange.

During the school year she had liked, in fact, probably loved, a boy, and she had broken up with him. All this was stated in an overdetermined and dramatic style. She had gone out with him in the seventh grade, but he had liked another girl better. This past year, in the eighth grade, he seemed to have had some feeling for her; but since he hung out with a different crowd, she had not had much daily contact with him in school. She said that she had remained aloof and shy until one day the class went on a field trip to a forest preserve, and she was teased and pushed into kissing him on the bus. Later at the forest preserve, she had seen him show interest in another girl. She described feeling hurt and upset about this.

She said that now she couldn't think about much except her questions and concerns about sex, especially her terror of becoming a lesbian at age 14 and her fear that anything she read about might happen to her, specifically, perversions, such as sexual mating with animals and peeping toms. She said that every time she heard or read something bad, she thought that it might happen to her. The therapist empathized with her concerns, indicated that other children experienced them, too, and told her that she still wanted to see her again. This relieved Jan.

In trying to recount historical material during the second interview, Jan was able to give more than she anticipated when she said she couldn't remember things very clearly. She thought she was about eight or nine years old when her mother started to work. She did not remember much about this, about her feelings, or about anything going on in the family when her brothers were born. She remembered playing outside a lot as a little girl; she had enjoyed playing with the kids in the neighborhood. She talked about playing jumprope and hand-clapping games. She said that her mother told her about the facts of life, although she learned more about this at school. (Jan's mother said that Jan apparently understood the facts fairly clearly, so she did not go into much detail).

Jan said that this spring she started to get upset. She felt that one of the major reasons was the rejection by the first boy she ever liked (see previous interview). She was aware of feeling funny and odd on Memorial Day, when she spent some time with friends of the family and found herself obsessed with looking at one of her mother's friends, who was wearing hot pants. She said that she looked at herself a lot in her room. She liked having her own bedroom for the last four years. Before that, she had shared a bedroom with her brothers. She said they had a big room, and the brothers didn't bother her. She had seen her father undressed once or twice when she was about eight years old. Now, she never saw her father undressed unless she was sitting in her parents' room and her father came out of the shower with his shorts on. She said he did not like her to see him this way. Her mother sometimes undressed in front of her, including taking her bra off. She said that she had always stared at her mother's breasts although recently she had avoided seeing her undressed. Earlier on the day of the interview, she saw her mother in a towel and was obsessed with the thought that her mother had nothing else on.

Jan said that once, when she was about six or seven, she and her brother had kissed and laughed together in his bed. They had pulled the sheet over themselves and giggled until an aunt told them to quiet down. She said she couldn't remember any more about that. She said that at around the same time, she had been playing with her brothers at her grandmother's. She and a boy cousin had pulled their pants down and touched each other's genitals. She remembered beginning to learn about sex in school in the fifth grade. She said that she had thought she could get pregnant and have a baby from touching; she remembered telling her mother about the incident with her cousin for fear that she would have a baby.

She said that her relationship with her father was all right, although sometimes he said things to get on her nerves. She tried to tell him, as well as her mother, her problems and worries. She thought that maybe they really didn't understand how upset and worried she was. She just couldn't get herself to go out and play. She said that she thought about dying, although she did not want to die. She had fantasies about running out in the street and being run over and killed by a car or killing herself with a knife. The images were of the car running her over and bloodying the street and of herself pushing a knife into her stomach, getting blood all over. She said that sometimes she thought it would be better to be a lesbian or die than to feel the way she did now.

Toward the end of the hour, she wondered if the therapist could tell her whether or not treatment could help her. The therapist reviewed with Jan the nature of the diagnostic evaluation that had to precede the planning of the treatment and reiterated that all findings would be shared with her. Jan seemed to be reassured by the thought of ongoing clinic contact.

Diagnostic Impression

The diagnostician felt that Jan showed no change in the three sessions she had at the clinic, one with the intake worker, two with the diagnostician. She did not show any age appropriate watchfulness or caution in establishing some kind of impression and differentiated mode of relating to the two women she saw. She was rambling, flighty, and verbose, and extraordinarily anxious. This caused her to flood and spill in each session. She showed evidence of thought disorder, that is, concrete thinking; for example, she translated her father's observation that some women "go with dogs" to the concrete concept of women having intercourse with dogs. Jan was increasingly decathected to the outer world, absorbed and frightened by her inner preoccupations. Her defenses were not effective and could not bind her severe anxiety and panic. Thus, she was increasingly isolated and withdrawn, regressing to a predominantly narcissistic focus. Reality testing was showing increasing disturbance, as her sense of identity was experienced as unstable and bizarre. Academic functioning showed a striking lack of impairment or regression, thereby connoting the strongest area of her current ego functioning. Jan's basic ego apparatus was intact, with no suggestion of sensory handicap or organicity. However, autonomous ego function showed considerable deficits. Reality perception, cognition, and thinking were distorted. She misheard and misperceived outer events. The lack of synthesis resulted in confusion, a sense of depersonalization, social withdrawal, and preoccupation with sexual ruminations. Drive modulation was poor, as demonstrated by the endless obsessive masturbation and frightening accompanying fantasies. The lack of appropriate repression permitted a surfacing of primary process material. The defense system appeared to be creating secondary interference. Defenses of isolation, projection, and withdrawal exacerbated the sense of estrangement and aloneness.

Jan appeared not to have reached a genuine oedipal stage of development, nor had she achieved separation-individuation that would have enabled her to experience self and object constancy. She was confused about her sense of self, her sexual identity, and her choice of sexual objects, seemingly vascillating between her parents—both of whom seemed to be responded to as maternal objects: the father connoting the more loving, accepting, "good" mother; the mother, the scolding, nongratifying, "bad" mother. The long-standing marital conflicts of the parents had prevented any kind of parental coalition, and Jan feared her father's preference for her over mother. Jan had long been overstimulated sexually—by the early sibling sex play plus being privy to the full extent of her parents' conflicts and sexual problems. Jan had not been able to resolve any portion of the oedipal crisis due to her mother's stern, strict, and cold nature and behavior; the overstimulation from seeing her mother naked or dressing; and the extensive maternal absence at a night work shift. This left Jan at the mercy of her pre-oedipal and oedipal-like incestuous strivings for forbidden objects, i.e., mother, brothers, and father. Her harsh superego introjection of mother's scolding and disapproval put Jan in the position of masochistic surrender; she did not venture into age-appropriate assertiveness, e.g., over the present given her by a boy. Her mother's own sexual withdrawal in her marriage and disapproval of Jan's age-appropriate tentative contacts with boys her age made Jan very guilty about heterosexual strivings. Thus, the lesbian stance was her defense against more egosyntonic sexual stirrings. Jan's mother was casual about the open-door bathroom policy, thereby symbolically teaching Jan that it was all right for them to have this intimacy. This overwhelmed Jan, who nevertheless complied with her mother.

Jan functioned academically; and, fortunately, viewed her fears and anxieties as bizarre and inappropriate. This ego-dystonic reaction to her symptoms reflected still intact portions of an observing ego. The lack of sufficient gratifying early bonding, the repeated summer separations all her life, and the continued lack of maternal warmth created major trauma for Jan in this adolescent, second-edition separation/individuation struggle, whereby she was increasingly homebound, alternatively experiencing overgratification and frustration by her mother and overgratification by her father. Jan was fearful of the strong pulls toward her father or oedipal substitutes—boyfriends her age. In essence Jan unconsciously struggled, but reluctantly complied, with her mother's unconscious message: men are to be rejected and avoided sexually, but the charged interchange between mother and daughter is acceptable. Thus the presenting terror of lesbianism, which in this case signified reengulfment in ungratifying symbiosis with her mother.

Jan's early unsatisfactory history and repeated protracted summer separations since age three created significant arrest and fixation points. In fact, there was no phase dominance, rather points of arrest at every developmental milestone. Latency appeared uneventful; the good child compliance of that period did not disturb the precarious balance between Jan and her mother. As Jan entered adolescence and attempted some age-appropriate heterosexual contacts, her mother drew her back harshly and unempathically. Thus, the developmental tasks of the teen years were being grossly interfered with. In Anna Freud's words, "[T]here is permanent drive regression to previously established fixation points, plus simultaneous ego and superego regression which leads to infantilism, borderline, delinquent or psychotic disturbances" (1965, p. 147).

Treatment Recommendations

Jan presented borderline and psychotic symptoms (see Chapter 3); she functioned more appropriately during the year when there was extensive external structure provided by her school schedule. At the time of the evaluation, she was in a panic, desirous of help, which the diagnostician felt should be offered immediately on a crisis-intervention basis. The most frequently recommended therapeutic intervention for borderline children is individual psychotherapy. Given the nature of her concerns and her struggle to separate and individuate, individual treatment, preferably at least twice a week, was recommended. Family therapy was contraindicated, given the above-noted developmental issues and marital problems, which had already overwhelmed the child. Another therapist could work profitably with her parents offering marital treatment and parent guidance regarding their daughter's age-appropriate need for privacy, peer relationships, and protection from the intimate details of her parents' marital conflicts. It was hoped that the combination of therapeutic interventions would "delineate borders within the domain of borderline" (Pine, 1974, p. 341) and that the extent of ego deviance and details of the lack of phase dominance would become clearer. Greater clarification about the shifting levels of internal disorganization and the nature of the aberration of object relationships would dictate the future details and fuller parameters of therapeutic planning.

The diagnostician recommended that Jan be seen by a female therapist, available on a consistent long-term basis.

> The critical phase-specific preoccupations of early adolescents with their nascent sexuality and their masturbatory conflicts is invested with feelings of shame and the potential for humiliation that make it difficult in the extreme for them to communicate with an adult of the opposite sex. Further, the proximity to consciousness of oedipal wishes and fantasies makes the opposite-sex therapist a potentially dangerous figure for many early adolescent patients. For these reasons I believe that wherever possible, young adolescents are best treated by a therapist of the same sex . . . [Esman, 1985, p. 125].

It was hoped that in the course of the treatment relationship Jan would make a nonthreatening symbiotic attachment and thereby be able to effect a more genuine separation-individuation to facilitate the development of self and object constancy.

Some of Jan's symptoms were very alarming, but in work with children and adolescents, we are repeatedly impressed with the reality that "symptoms, inhibitions, and anxieties do not necessarily carry the same significance which they assume at a later date [and in fact can] be no more than transient appearances of stress, which emerge whenever a particular phase of development makes specially high demands on a child's personality. . . ." (A. Freud, 1962, p. 149–50). In sum, the treatment goal is to attempt to enable this adolescent girl to resume the capacity for progressive development that characterized, despite traumata and less than optimal parenting, her preadolescent years.

Bibliography

AICHHORN, A. [1935] (1963). *Wayward Youth.* New York: Viking Press.

BENEDEK, T. (1970). The Family as a Psychological Field. In *Parenthood: Its Psychology and Psychopathology,* eds. E. J. Anthony and T. Benedek, pp. 109–36. Boston: Little, Brown.

BLOS, P. (1962). *On Adolescence.* Glencoe, Ill.: Free Press.

———— (1968). Character Formation in Adolescence. *Psychoanalytic Study of the Child,* 23:245–63. New York: International Universities Press.

DOUVAN, E. and ADELSON, J. (1966). *The Adolescent Experience.* New York: Wiley.

ERIKSON, E. (1956). Late Adolescence. In *The Student and Mental Health,* ed. D. H. Funkenstein, p. 76. Cambridge: The Riverside Press.

ESMAN, A. H. (1985). A Developmental Approach to the Psychotherapy of Adolescents. *Adolescent Psychiatry, Vol. 12: Developmental and Clinical Studies,* eds. S. Feinstein, M. Sugar, A. Esman, J. Looney, A. Schwartzberg, and A. Sorosky, pp. 119–33. Chicago: University of Chicago Press.

FREUD, A. (1946). *The Ego and the Mechanisms of Defense.* New York: International Universities Press.

———— (1958). *Adolescence. Psychoanalytic Study of the Child,* 13:255–78. New York: International Universities Press.

———— (1962). Assessment of Childhood Disturbance. *Psychoanalytic Study of the Child.* 17:149–58. New York: International Universities Press.

———— (1965). *The Writings of Anna Freud, Vol. 6: Normality and Pathology in Childhood: Assessments of Development.* New York: International Universities Press.

GIOVACCHINI, P. L. and BOROWITZ, G. H. (1974). An Object Relationship Scale. In *Adolescent Psychiatry, Vol. 3: Developmental and Clinical Studies*, eds. S. Feinstein and P. L. Giovacchini, pp. 186–95. New York: Basic Books.

GRINKER, SR., R. (1962). Mentally Health Young Males (homoclites). *Arch. Gen. Psychiatry*, 6:405–53.

JONES, E. (1922). Some Problems of Adolescence. *Brit. J. Psychiatry*. 13:41–47.

JOSSELYN, I. (1954). The Ego in Adolescence. *Amer. J. Orthopsychiatry*, 24: 223–37.

KERNBERG, O. (1978). Diagnosis of Borderline Conditions in Adolescence. In *Adolescent Psychiatry, Vol. 6: Developmental and Clinical Studies*, eds. S. Feinstein and P. Giovacchini, pp. 298–319. Chicago: University of Chicago Press.

KESSLER, J. (1966). *Psychopathology of Childhood*. Englewood Cliffs, N.J.: Prentice-Hall.

LAUFER, M. [1965] (1977). Assessment of Adolescent Disturbances—The Application of Anna Freud's Diagnostic Profile. In *An Anthology of the Psychoanalytic Study of the Child—Psychoanalytic Assessment: The Diagnostic Profile*, eds. R. Eissler, A. Freud, M. Kris, and A. Solnit, pp. 57–81. New Haven: Yale University Press.

LINDEMANN, E. (1964). Adolescent Behavior as a Community Concern. *Amer. J. Psychotherapy*, 18:405–17.

MASTERSON, J. (1967a). *The Psychiatric Dilemma of Adolescence*. Boston: Little Brown.

———. (1967b). The Symptomatic Adolescent Five Years Later: He Didn't Grow Out of It. *Amer. J. Psychiatry*, 123:1388–45.

———. (1968) The Psychiatric Significance of Adolescent Turmoil. *Amer. J. Psychiatry*, 124:1549–54.

MCDONALD, M. (1965). The Psychiatric Evaluation of Children. *J. Child Psychiatry*, 4:569–612.

MEAD, M. (1928). *Coming of Age in Samoa*. New York: Morrow.

MEHLMAN, R. (1980). A Conceptual Model for the Assessment of Developmental Normality. In *Child Development in Normality and Psychopathology*. ed. J. Bemporad, pp. 395–432. New York: Brunner/Mazel.

MITCHELL, J. (1980). Normality in Adolescence. In *Adolescent Psychiatry, Vol. 8: Developmental and Clinical Studies*, eds. S. Feinstein, P. Giovacchini, J. Looney, A. Schwartzberg, and A. Sorosky, pp. 200–13. Chicago: University of Chicago Press.

OFFER, D. (1967). Normal Adolescents: Interview Strategy and Selected Results. *Arch. Gen. Psychiatry*, 17:285–90.

OFFER, D. and SABSHIN, M. (1963). The Psychiatrist and the Normal Adolescent. *Arch. Gen. Psychiatry*, 9:427–32.

OFFER, D.; SABSHIN, M.; and MARCUS, D. (1965). Clinical Evaluation of Normal Adolescents. *Amer. J. Psychiatry*, 121:864–72.

OLDEN, C. (1953). On Adult Empathy with Children. *Psychoanalytic Study of the Child*, 8:111–26. New York: International Universities Press.

PINE, F. (1974). On the Concept "Borderline" in Children, a Clinical Essay. *Psychoanalytic Study of the Child*, 29:341–47. New York: International Universities Press.

RUTTER, H.; GRAHAM, P.; CHADWICK, O.; and YULE, W. (1976). Adolescent Turmoil: Fact or Fiction? *J. Child Psychol. & Psychiatry and Allied Disciplines*, 17:35–56.

SIBLER, E.; COELHO, G.; MURPHY, E.; HAMBUR, D.; PEARLIN, L.; and ROSENBERG, M. (1961). Competent Adolescents Coping with College Decisions. *Arch. Gen. Psychiatry*, 5:517–27.

SPIEGEL, L. (1961). Identity and Adolescence. In *Adolescents: Psychoanalytic Approach to Problems & Therapy*, eds. S. Lorand and H. I. Schawe. New York: Hoeber.

WESTBY, I. (1958). Emotionally Healthy Adolescents and Their Family Backgrounds. In *The Family in Contemporary Society*, ed. I. Goldstein. New York: International Universities Press.

PART III

Adolescent Pathology

1

The Societal Context of Adolescent Development and Pathology

One of the major contributions of Erik Erikson in his seminal text, *Identity: Youth and Crisis* (1968), was the integration of a psychoanalytic developmental perspective and a cultural perspective, whereby adolescent development and value conflicts were viewed against our society's cultural and technological changes, which have affected and altered social, legal, and emotional security and adult role expectations. It is acknowledged widely in psychiatric circles that there has been a progressive change in the personality structure, and hence in the type of psychopathology of Americans during the middle half of this century, along with a progressive reduction of authoritarianism in society. The rigid Victorian moralistic superego has been modified; we now frequently see characterological problems predominating in adults instead of psychoneurotic symptoms in the classical repressive mode. In a workshop discussion at the American Psychoanalytic Association meeting, December 1970, it was readily agreed that there is now much more acting out (in the broad use of the term) of what used to be repressed, and repression is now directed not so much against genitality as against object relationships. This repression is a defense against the trauma of early object loss. The clinical picture produced is of the cool, affectless, narcissistic character, obsessively driven to transient liaisons and to distancing activities and drugs, with impairment of capacity for object constancy and little interest in introspection. "Accompanying this change is the so-called new morality, which rejects sexual restraint and marriage as the primary conditions of heterosexual intimacy and emphasizes present conscious feeling as the basis for authenticity in relationships" (Smarr and Escoll, 1973).

Smarr and Escoll (1973) note that, in addition, American youth have been profoundly affected by the cultural and societal influences of affluence, prolonged education and accompanying prolonged financial dependence on parents, an unpopular and demoralizing war, the threat of nuclear destruction, the pill and other contraception devices, and a prevailing anti-authoritarian political and social spirit, resulting in what the authors call neohumanism. "These three forces, the narcissistic character, the new morality, and neohumanism, have coalesced to form a living style being tried widely in adolescent role playing, emphasizing libertarian rights of existential individuality" (p. 114). This results in widely accepted peer patterns of rejecting parental ideologies, or as Erikson (1968) viewed it, ritualizing life for themselves, and by themselves, against us, i.e., "doing their own thing." Erikson further noted that in revolutionary times the underprivileged and overprivileged frequently reach out to each other, joined in their social marginality against the majority. Thus, both groups of youth can assume an antiestablishment posture, reject the regimented life of work and conformity, prefer immediate pleasure to the notion of future security, and thereby, assume a life style characterized by libidinal, passive-aggressive gratification. The lack of commitment, responsibility, and rejection of the Protestant work ethic and Judeo-Christian values, results in a chasm between parents and youth and a "superego change in middle-class America" (Smarr and Escoll, 1973, p. 116).

For middle class youth, affluence and prolonged education has resulted in a postponement of work. This provides a moratorium on adult choices and responsibilities. Often this time can be wisely used for contemplation, personal development, and the testing of career alternatives. However, obstacles are not uncommon if the adolescent has been overindulged or insufficiently exposed to frustration and delay, and is therefore unable to develop sufficient capacity for sublimation. The resultant impulse-ridden behavior and the low self-esteem, arising out of lack of struggle to master, commonly create feelings of emptiness, boredom, and depression, frequently dealt with by drug usage today. Overindulgence can be the result of familial patterns of parenting, or a reflection of broader cultural trends.

> Under certain circumstances our technical society will encourage adolescents' infantile attitudes and behavior (instant gratification and magic thinking—press a button and it happens!) more than evoking their capacity

for mastery through providing acceptable, attractive channels for the expression of socially constructive and satisfying behavior [Solnit, 1983, pp. 16–17].

The complexity of technology and the need for extensive training for employment in our accelerated society often require that career decisions be made before teenagers can fully explore and ponder future choices and preferences. "In a world that demands more preparation for adult opportunities and rewards, [there is] an increased pressure on adolescents when they need settings that allow time for dreaming, experimenting and exploring their choices as they prepare for adulthood" (p. 17). This pressure is exacerbated by the reality of large-scale youth unemployment affecting the contemporary western world (Levine, 1982). The extent of this problem is a relatively new phenomenon. Any economic recession disproportionately affects working young people, in that, if employed, they are the last hired, the first laid off, and are given the least satisfying positions. Advanced technology has made the youngest workers the most expendable. This population who wishes to work and cannot find employment is vulnerable to boredom, identity diffusion, low self-esteem, guilt, shame, anger, anxiety, and depression. These emotions create a corrosive sense of demoralization and alienation.

Many authors (Bronfenbrenner, 1973; Rosenberg, 1976; Levine, 1979) have raised questions about our societal values and goals, in that our society seems to be obliterating the chance for its young people to believe in themselves by becoming responsible, competent citizens. Economic and social circumstances appear to be spawning individuals who have not tasted mastery or success. Recent figures indicate that the unemployed are not solely from the uneducated lower socioeconomic classes. Now middle-class educated youth are comprising an increasing proportion of that statistic (Coleman, 1974). Some research predicts that unless society involves its youth in gainful work and commitments, chances increase that many normal young people will deteriorate personally, engage in antisocial activities, or be attracted to dissonant asocial life styles and groups in order to feel some sense of belonging and purpose in their day-to-day existence. (Levine, 1978, 1979a, 1979b, 1982). Levine (1982) cautioned that employment (a major problem) is not the sole dilemma for youth who do not feel that they can contribute to their country or community. "Even if full employment is accomplished, . . . we may still have to face the possibility that our current value system will not capture the imagination of many of our young" (p. 36). Caution has been voiced regarding our self-indulgent society, because of the perception in many quarters, that narcissism has now supplanted altruism.

Some authors have suggested that "the social environment today may indeed be imposing unbearable burdens on the more vulnerable members of this generation (Holzman, 1980, p. 314). The baby boom after World War II has created rapid changes in the social order. Diminished quality education, high unemployment, particularly for minority groups, greater exposure to violence via the media, and interruption of attachments by divorce all contribute to young people's feelings of hopelessness. The new freedom in personal relationships has created an atmosphere of superficiality, transience, and impermanence. All in all, "the problems of our time have precipitated mounting sadness and depressive episodes among young people" (Elson and Kramer, 1980, p. 267).

Bibliography

BRONFENBRENNER, U. (1974). The Origins of Alienation. *Scientific American*, 231:53–61.

COLEMAN, J. (1974). *Youth: Transition to Adulthood*. Chicago: University of Chicago Press.

ELSON, M. and KRAMER, J. (1980). Introduction—Vulnerable Youth: Hope, Despair and Renewal. In *Adolescent Psychiatry, Vol. 8: Developmental and Clinical Studies*, eds. S. Feinstein, P. Giovacchini, J. Looney, A. Schwartzberg, and A. Sorosky, pp. 267–69. Chicago: University of Chicago Press.

ERIKSON, E. H. (1968). *Identity: Youth and Crisis*. New York: Norton.

HOLZMAN, P. (1980). Discussion—Vulnerable Youth: Hope, Despair and Renewal. In *Adolescent Psychiatry, Vol. 8, pp. 309–14*. See Elson and Kramer (1980).

LEVINE, S. (1978). Youth and Religious Cults. In *Adolescent Psychiatry, Vol. 6: Developmental and Clinical Studies*, eds. S. Feinstein and P. Giovacchini, pp. 75–89. Chicago: University of Chicago Press.

_____ (1979a). Adolescents, Believing and Belonging. In *Adolescent Psychiatry, Vol. 7: Developmental and Clinical Studies*, eds. S. Feinstein, J. Looney, A. Schwartzberg, and A. Sorosky, pp. 41–53. Chicago: University of Chicago Press.

_____ [1979b](1981). Alienation as an Affect in Adolescence. In *The Adolescent and Mood Disturbance*, eds. H. Golombek and B. D. Garfinkel. New York: International Universities Press.

_____ (1982). The Psychological and Social Effects of Youth Unemployment. In *Adolescent Psychiatry, Vol. 10: Developmental and Clinical Studies*, eds. S. Feinstein, J. Looney, A. Schwartzberg, and A. Sorosky, pp. 24–40. Chicago: University of Chicago Press.

ROSENBERG, M. (1976). The Dissonant Context and the Adolescent Self-Concept. In eds. S. Dragastin and G. Elder. *Adolescence in the Life Cycle*, pp. 97–116. New York: Wiley.

SMARR, E. R. and ESCOLL, P. J. (1973). The Youth Culture, Future Adulthood, and Societal Change. In *Adolescent Psychiatry, Vol. 2: Developmental and Clinical Studies*, eds. S. Feinstein and P. Giovacchini, pp. 113–126. New York: Basic Books.

SOLNIT, A. (1983). Obstacles and Pathways in the Journey from Adolescence to Parenthood. In *Adolescent Psychiatry, Vol. 11: Developmental and Clinical Studies*, eds. M. Sugar, S. Feinstein, J. Looney, A. Schwartzberg, and A. Sorosky, pp. 14–26. Chicago: University of Chicago Press.

2

Schizophrenia

There continues to be considerable controversy about the concept of schizophrenia. There are widely divergent opinions about the criteria for identifying patients as schizophrenic. Despite emphasis on stringent criteria, a wide range of psychopathologies and varied illnesses are listed under the umbrella term "schizophrenia." Clinicians have shifted from overinclusion to exclusion in grouping patients under this diagnosis, yet often including those with extreme forms of affective disorders. There is conflicting opinion about the importance of symptoms versus underlying pathological processes. Controversy is also prominent in theories of etiology and treatment. Through the late 1960s, the psychological frame of reference was the prevailing perspective used to explain the etiology of the illness and to treat the disorder. Since the early 1970s, however, the single most significant trend has been the increased focus on the biological and medical aspects of the disease. In fact, since 1970, the funding of studies focused on the biology of schizophrenia has increased 200 percent. Basic research devoted to biological etiology and to the study of somatic treatments of the disorder far outweighs the study of psychosocial or psychodynamic theories or therapies. In spite of the high prevalence of tardive dyskinesia, the neuroleptic drugs continue to be the major intervention with the schizophrenic population.

Except among patients' rights groups, there has been little protest about this treatment, and the irreversible neurologic damage—like a drug-induced parkinsonism—it causes. Pharmacotherapy has not proven to be a cure for the schizophrenic syndrome.

> In most instances it affects predominately what Eugene Bleuler called the secondary symptoms—that is, delusions, hallucinations, and possibly, thought disorders—but it does not affect the personality structure of schizophrenics. . . . Whatever role the biological matrix may play in some sufferers of the schizophrenic syndrome, currently available drugs are unable to reverse the lack of cognitive development and psychosocial structure which seem to play such a critical role in the syndrome's pathogenesis [Bellak, 1980, pp. 17–18].

Historical Review of the Concept of Schizophrenia

Emil Kraepelin's monograph *Dementia Praecox and Paraphrenia* (1919) offered the first complete account of the symptoms of this disease. His view of treatment and change was a pessimistic one, reinforcing a fatalistic attitude toward mental illness. Arieti (1974) observed that this pioneer investigator presented patients as little more than collections of symptoms, as he raised no questions about the impact of social and familial factors and paid no attention to the structure and content of the patients' thoughts. Eugene Bleuler accepted much of Kraepelin's thinking and, in fact, applied the term *schizophrenia* to the disorder to imply that a schism or splitting of the various psychic functions "was one of the most outstanding characteristics" (Arieti, 1974, p. 13) of the disease. According to Arieti (1974), Bleuler humanized the concept of the disease, by showing that even normal people, when distraught or distracted, show a number of schizophrenic symptoms, such as peculiar associations or incomplete concepts and ideas. Bleuler's key contributions were his study of associations and disturbances of affective life and his attention to autism, withdrawal, and ambivalence. Adolph Meyer was dissatisfied with the emphasis given to heredity and organic factors and chose to reconsider psychological factors, particularly faulty habits of reaction and chronic failure of parental responses.

Sigmund Freud paid only brief attention to the study of psychosis, viewing this severe illness as similar to milder mental disturbances in terms of the presence and attendant repression of unbearable ideas. He posited that a patient's unbearable ideas give way to hallucinatory psychosis: The intolerable idea is rejected by the ego, but the rejection is not successful, and the idea becomes a wish-fulfilling hallucination; thus the unacceptable wishes and thoughts are transferred to others. Freud felt that the essential characteristic of schizophrenia was the change in the patient's relationship with people, and he emphasized the remoteness and withdrawal of emotional attachment; hallucinations and delusions were attempts to reconnect with the world. Arieti (1974) stated that Freud's most significant contribution to the study of schizophrenia was his concept of symbolization. Symptoms, thus, are no longer accepted at a phenomenological level but are viewed as substitutes for something else they symbolize. Freud was pessimistic about treatment and cure because of the enormous difficulties these patients had relating to and emotionally attaching to therapists. Jung departed from Freud and explained the disease from a psychosomatic perspective, reasoning that an emotional disorder produced an abnormal metabolism, which in turn affected the central nervous system, and caused physical damage to the brain. Harry Stack Sullivan is considered the first American psychiatrist who made valuable contributions to our understanding of schizophrenia. Influenced by Freud, he initially emphasized sexual forces and strivings, but later chose to stress the interpersonal relations, the parent/child relationship, and the effects of poor maternal care—tension states, panic, and overwhelming anxiety. Arieti (1974) noted that "an issue which is very important in Sullivan's theory and nevertheless was minimized until recently, is the role of the adolescent period in the engendering of schizophrenia" (p. 27). Blows to one's self-image during adolescence were critical to Sullivan's explanation of the disease. He was always dissatisfied with research that focused primarily on genetic, organic, or intrapsychic forces. He put much emphasis on childhood and adolescent familial environmental factors as well as on regression in the face of assaults on a young person's sense of self esteem. More than prior researchers or his contemporaries, Sullivan was optimistic about the potential for successes in treating the disease through the use of milieu and the interpersonal relationship between patient and clinician.

Contemporary Theories of Causation

Researchers continue to attempt to explain this bewildering, heterogeneous illness. There is vociferous disagreement among those who suggest as its cause: family background, current life stress, and genetic predisposition or vulnerability. Family studies of schizophrenic patients have gone on for many years, particularly in the United States. Faulty family communication, characterized by expressed emotionality, critical comments, hostility, and emotional overinvolvement all are cited as relevant. Such studies have emphasized the importance of disharmonious marriages of the parents and initially focused upon the mother as the major figure contributing to the child's future pathology (Sullivan,

1953, 1964; Hill, 1955; Bateson, Haley, and Weaklands, 1956; Lidz, Fleck, and Cornelison, 1965; Fromm-Reichman, 1984.) Searles (1958) was in the minority in noting positive aspects in the relationship between mother and patient. Lidz (1975) emphasized the patient's negative appraisal of the mother and characterized patients' fathers as insecure in their masculinity, paranoid-like in irrational behavior, and impervious to the feelings of others. Jackson (1956) noted bizarre maladaptive behaviors and patterns of communications in parents of schizophrenics. Lidz and Fleck (1964) highlighted parental inability to nurture and support the integrative development of their offspring.

Twin studies point to the genetic factor as operative in the transmission of the disease. Those examining socioeconomic status point out the consistent finding of a disproportionate number of schizophrenics in the lower socioeconomic classes. This finding is explained by the assumption that the social and economic stress on those in poverty produces illness; additionally, low social class membership among schizophrenic patients is due to their downward mobility, i.e., loss of ability to function as employed, productive, self-supporting individuals. Other studies suggest that immigration and culture change with their attendant stress produce the illness.

> The etiology theory most stubbornly clung to over time states that schizophrenia is a physical disease due to a structural or functional defect in some organ system. The defect does not have to be in the brain. The endocrine glands have also been held responsible for schizophrenia. In the past decade, the search for metabolic poisons in schizophrenia has been spurred on by the study of the psychological or behavioral effects of such substances as mescaline, amphetamines, and lysergic acid diethylamide [Kaplan and Sadock, 1981, p. 307].

Kaplan and Sadock (1981) have enumerated other theories of causality: genetically inborn metabolic error; abnormal levels of blood proteins; aberrant metabolism of bodily products, causing a form of intoxication; and putative central neurotransmitter agents. These authors have concluded that there are many explanations for the cause of schizophrenia but insufficient data to decide which is correct. While genetic factors play a role, they alone do not account for all the etiological variance. ". . . most experts conclude that the schizophrenic phenotypes are the result of environmental factors that elicit or suppress them. Unfortunately, these environmental factors have not been identified" (p. 309).

Characteristics of the Disease

There is agreement on the general manifest symptomatology of schizophrenia, which includes the following features and characteristics: Un-

unsual behavior may appear suddenly or slowly and insidiously, marked by a period of confusion, agitation, and excitement. Decisions and behaviors seem strange, as the individual becomes withdrawn, refusing, for example, to attend school or work, as he or she becomes preoccupied with seemingly unimportant matters. Thinking begins to manifest ideas of reference, that is, things that are said and/or events that occur have a special meaning and are related to by the patient in a special significant fashion. Suspicion may appear and increase as the patient believes that nothing happens by chance but is preordained and directed toward him. Disturbances in relation to reality produce hallucinations, delusions of grandeur, somatic delusions, and a sense of estrangement and depersonalizaton. Disturbances in affects and in emotional or drive control are common, manifest by outbursts of rage, and/or blunted, flat, nonresponsiveness. "Less common are phases of frankly erotic behavior . . ." (Cameron, 1963, p. 607). There are varied levels of disturbance in object relations, manifest in fear of closeness and withdrawal into the self, with loss of interest in people, activities, and the environment. Speech and language show peculiar characteristics. Evasive responses to questions are common, concrete thinking is manifest, and "word salad," (a sequence of words unrelated to one another) appears. Some words are repeated in a stereotyped fashion, called perseveration. Some patients invent personalized condensations and combinations of words, known as neologisms. Some become mute, unable or unwilling to talk. Incoherenece, loose associations, and illogical thinking are frequent. Memory retention, grasp of general information, and calculations may or may not show impairment. Insight and awareness of one's abnormal behavior are absent except in mild or initial states of the illness. *DSM-III* (1980) noted the following types of schizophrenic disorders: Disorganized type, Catatonic type, Paranoid type, Undifferentiated type, and Residual type (pp. 106–108).

Schizophrenia in Adolescence

Middle and late adolescence appear to be critical periods of life, during which the adolescent schizophrenic psychosis makes its appearance. Holzman and Grinker (1977) distinguished between schizophrenia, manifest by a long-standing pattern of apathy, withdrawal and peculiar disorganized thinking, and schizophrenic psychosis, marked by "a severance of reality constraints with many secondary features of psychosis, such as delusions, and hallucinations" (p. 279). In 1970, these researchers studied young adults diagnosed as schizophrenic and noted five prominent features in these patients:

> The first was their striking difficulty in maintaining what we called "organizational coherence," or an inability to keep percepts and ideas from dis-

order, fluidity and disorganization. Even in periods of remission, this quality of organizational instability was noteworthy. The second was the patient's prominent pleasureless demeanor, a quality of affect referred to by Rado (1956) as anhedonia. The third feature was an excessive dependency of these patients on their families, hospital staff and therapists. The fourth was the absence of definitive evidence of general competence; patients achieved less in school, jobs, social life than one would have expected solely on the basis of intellectual levels. A fifth feature was that the precipitating circumstances surrounding the need for hospitalization depressed their self-esteem, highlighting an exquisitely vulnerable sense of self-regard [p. 284].

Striking to these researchers was the relationship among adolescence, schizophrenia and poor competence. In adolescence, schizophrenic patients had manifested high percentages of poor social adjustment, loneliness, and running away, poor school performance, dropping out of school, drug usage, inordinate dependence, and affectionless homes. Findings by other researchers can also be cited: Radnick and Goldstein (1972) noted intrafamilial conflicts, withdrawn behavior by parent(s) and children, social isolation, antisocial behaviors, and excessive dependency on parents. Watt (1972) observed deviant social behavior in early adolescence. Robins (1966) reported infectious illness in early childhood, physical handicaps, eating and sleeping disturbances, and antisocial behavior. Fish and Hagin (1972) emphasized delayed speech development, unclear speech, and social isolation. Holzman and Grinker (1977) concluded that the relationship between adolescence and schizophrenia was "that of a catalyst to a biological reaction. The potential for disorganization is characteristic of the person. The social tasks of adolescence, however, place powerful strains on a vulnerable youth. . . . Responses expose deficits and the strain of the requirement to become competent (and separate and individual) can potentiate disorganization" (pp. 288–89).

Arieti (1974) described the preschizophrenic adolescent as exhibiting a stormy personality and an inability to form a relatively stable self-image or sense of identity. Frequently there is vacillation between aggressive hostility and extreme compliance. Chronic anxiety causes extreme vulnerability. Such youth often live in an atmosphere where catastrophe and doom alternate with grandiose dreams. "They often resort to excessive use of drugs and alcohol. The crisis they go through often weakens them progressively. . . . The school situation, the increasing sexual desires, and the search for a position in a competitive world put his character armour to serious strain" (pp. 113–14). Defenses do not work efficiently or effectively, and there is progressive maladaption and increased failures. The patient becomes increasingly uncommunicative, distant from, and unrelated to his environment.

In considering conceptual life, Arieti (1974) noted that some indi-

viduals make an exaggerated use of concepts, putting things into categories, and thereby omitting individual characteristics. "Some adolescents who later become schizophrenics tend to select the formation of
concepts and categories that have a gloomy emotional load, and these
classes and categories are given an absolute, exceptionless finality"
(p. 116). This affects the image of the self, understanding of others, and
subsequent events and interpersonal transactions. Uncertainty about
one's sexual identification seems quite common in the preschizophrenic adolescent. Sexual life per se is important only as it injures the
self-image. Schizophrenic adolescents and young adults frequently
view themselves as lacking a definite sexual identity, as sexually undesirable or inadequate, as homosexual, or as lacking in sexual self-
control.

When the psychotic break occurs, secondary process thinking dis-
integrates. Primary process thinking becomes prominent. Vague suspi-
cions become rigid and fixed, indefinite feelings become finite, and the
patient experiences events in the form of self-reference, whereby they
feel accused, betrayed and victimized. Old feelings of guilt and self-
blame are directed outward. "No longer does the patient consider himself bad; the others unfairly think he is bad. The danger, which used to
be an internal one, is now transformed by the psychosis into an external
one. In this transformation actually lies the psychodynamic significance of the paranoid psychosis" (p. 124), the most common type of
schizophrenia.

All in all, the world has become a strange and terrifying place. The
patient sees and hears things in a distorted way. People may change dimensions and appear unusually large or small. Hallucinations are often
preceded by the belief that one's thoughts have become audible. Hallucinations can involve every sense, though auditory hallucinations are the
most common. Others involve taste, touch and olfactory sensations.
Fatigue, restlessness, headaches, inability to sleep or communicate
clearly, all are signs of the ongoing psychotic process. Mannerisms such
as tics, grimaces, impulsive gestures, and stereotyped ritualized mo-
tions may be exhibited. Neglect of personal hygiene, generalized social
isolation, and withdrawal into the self is common. Contemporary adolescent schizophrenic patients are less withdrawn and more involved in
antisocial actions.

Schizophrenia must be considered when the adolescent demonstrates any drastic transformation of character, such as sudden scholas-
tic decline, social withdrawal, strangeness in manner, bizarreness of behavior, or unprecedented antisocial acts. The differential diagnosis
between schizophrenia and drug-induced psychosis has become necessary, given adolescents' extensive drug abuse. The use of LSD can provoke a clinical picture similar to schizophrenia, during the immediate

response to the drug. Additionally, this and other drugs can have prolonged adverse effects well after usage has ceased. Arieti (1974) suggested that diagnostic difficulties arise when one suspects that the LSD episode has precipitated a potential schizophrenic psychosis. He believed that the potentiality for schizophrenia would never have reached clinical actualization if specific drugs had not been used.

In commenting on prognosis, Arieti (1974) noted that the nature of the onset of the illness is important—the more acute, the more favorable, in contrast to the slowly unfolding ominous condition that can create massive decompensation and regression. If there has been a specific life stressor, such as loss of a love relationship or employment, or birth of a child, the prognosis is considered better than when the disease appears in the absence of any acute visible precipitant. A premorbid history of adequate age-appropriate functioning and mastery suggests a potentially better outcome than one of an endless succession of failures and maladaption. Affects such as depression and anxiety are viewed as more positive signs than an all-pervasive mood of hopelessness and helplessness and a total acceptance of the illness.

Case of Helen

Helen, a middle class black 13-year-old female, was referred to the adolescent psychiatry clinic by her mother. She has had an extensive history of headaches and stomach pains, and apparently had a standing prescription for phenobarbital. While visiting her father over the recent weekend, she took an overdose of the phenobarbital and was hospitalized for two days. The hospital's medical work-up was negative; no physical basis for abdominal pain, normal EEG, no trace of drug usage, and signs only of the excessive phenobarbital. At the adolescent psychiatry clinic, Helen and her mother both reported Helen's sudden confession to her mother that she was experiencing visual hallucinations. In addition, Helen presented suicidal ideation to the intake therapist. She appeared frightened, confused, and disoriented. On the basis of this material, the assessment was transferred to, and completed at, an in-patient children's hospital, which served latency youngsters and adolescents up to the age of 16.

Helen had been having difficulties for some time but reported that in the recent months things had worsened. She had been suspended from school several times because the school was unable to cope with her confusion, tardiness, disorientation, and wandering about. Additionally, she had endless somatic complaints and made countless visits each day to the school nurse. These frantic visits to the nurse could occur a dozen times in one day. According to the mother, the school requested contact with the parents, but the father refused to come to the school. He blamed the school for Helen's difficulties and said that he was moving to the suburbs, she could live with him and attend a better school. Helen moved back and forth between her parents, fighting with each when she resided with them. Her mother described brief, unsatisfying contact at a neighborhood social agency over the summer.

These school problems and somatic complaints were long-standing, but had escalated lately. Serious school problems surfaced in the second grade, which Helen failed because of low grades and an inability to pay attention. She began having stomach complaints in the second grade, and when she was seven, her appendix was removed. The complaints of stomach pain have been unabating since. Helen's academic achievement in the third grade was described as adequate, but her teachers complained about her somatic complaints, inattention, lateness, and quarrels with peers and teachers. Her mother felt driven to a frenzied state by the incessant calls at her place of work from her daughter and the school with accounts of Helen's complaints about her stomach, headaches, and dizziness.

In the last four months, Helen described fainting. Bickering and quarreling seemed to characterize Helen's relationship with her parents, who both believed she wanted attention, was insatiable, and was never affected by the endless medical workups that found no physical basis for her pain. Helen continued to insist that her pains were real, and that no one listened to her or took good enough care of her.

When Helen was suspended and out of school, her mother felt completely helpless because her daughter slept days and stayed awake all night making incessant phone calls and engaging in nocturnal wandering out of their apartment, unless engrossed in all-night TV programs. In general, Helen was described as moody, irritable, and destructive when she threw temper tantrums. Significantly, tantrums only occurred with the mother, not the father. Helen's mother wondered if her daughter was using drugs, given what she calls her totally irrational unreasonable state of mind. She said her daughter appeared dazed, in a fog, listening to voices. The mother was particulary terrified when Helen wandered out at night. Repeatedly, her mother threw up her hands and forced Helen to go to the father's. "Stay with him, if you won't go to school and he won't help me get you readmitted."

Helen was described as completely denying her role in the conflict at home and with teachers and peers. She went back and forth between her parents' homes, blaming everyone but herself for her problems. In fact, Helen did not refute her mother's account of her actions in her own separate intake sessions with the therapist. She referred to herself as a "mixed up school drop-out" who must make improvements. She showed no overt confusion about her sexual identity, despite a sense of general depersonalization.

Helen and her mother were the only two remaining in their household. Money was tight, and they lived in a lower-middle-income housing project. The mother was employed full-time at the social security office and received no formal alimony or child support. The father occasionally gave some money, though the mother routinely worked overtime to make ends meet. Helen's father taught high school, and had a good salary based on his years of experience and degrees. In fact, he had recently purchased a supposedly lavish home in the suburbs. The father has a B.S. in math; two master's degrees, one in accounting and one in education; and was currently working on his Ph.D. in administration. He had always carried a full-time job and academic program, and his education was a great source of pride for him.

The parents had been separated for eleven years and stated they never sought a divorce because they were Catholic and neither wished to remarry. Their children were described as opposed to a divorce. Three older siblings (a 22-year-old daughter, and two sons, ages 20 and 23) were married and out of the home. Two years before Helen was born, a 5-year-old daughter died of bronchial pneumonia. This child was described as brain-damaged and subject to continuous convulsions. She was described as retarded and following convulsions would regress and have to relearn everything, including toilet training. The mother acknowledged not having gotten over this loss in all these years and stated with emotion and tears that she was continuously amazed at her unending grief.

Helen was the only planned child, born two years after the death of this daughter out of the father's wish to attempt to solidify the marriage. The mother said she reluctantly complied but felt the marriage was too shaky to have a child. Her pregnancy with Helen was fraught with marital problems, the father's physical assaults, and the mother's contracting mumps, which she feared might cause damage to her baby. Delivery was normal, and the mother recalls that Helen was an easy responsive baby who ate and slept well. She was uncertain about other developmental milestones, due to her immersion in her worsening marital problems.

The parents separated when Helen was 2½; since then the mother and Helen have lived in seven different places as the mother tried to improve their housing situation. No overt response to the parents' separation was noted, as the father maintained constant, almost daily contact with his daughter. Helen did manifest fearfulness at being left with sitters once her mother began full-time employment. When Helen was nine, her mother became profoundly depressed when her 19-year-old-younger son eloped. The couple was aided by the father, who drove them to another city to marry. The mother said her husband always undermined her in relation to the children, and none of them finished high school at the appropriate time. The youngest son later gave her pride because he eventually finished high school and at the time of the interview, was in college part-time, had a good job, and had a seemingly solid marriage.

The father, clearly a severely disturbed man, presented a need for total control and, with alarming blandness and not a trace of guilt, stated the following:

> My wife left me because she couldn't stand the fights, but if she had obeyed me, there'd be no trouble. I would not have hit her a lot, knocked her down, blackened her eyes, or whatever. I treated her and the kids the same. Nothing will stand in my way. I need absolute silence to study and would not tolerate the children's noise or her trying to talk to me. I've always had a fierce temper and used my fists, not words. I teach in a tough high school, and I have perfect control of those Black rough seniors. I bring my Judo trophies to class the first day, talk quietly, and let everyone know who is boss.

The father's omnipotent control is evident with his mistress, with whom he has a 5-year-old son.

> She was a typist at work, and when we got involved, I said she must quit work as as not to mix work and private life. She has other kids, needs to work, and

refused to quit; so I fired her, put her and the kids on ADC and support my son with her.

Helen unquestionably has been affected by the extensive conflict she was exposed to between her parents, by her father's omnipotent style, and by her overstressed mother, who has little patience or calm to offer this last, unconsciously unwanted child. Unconscious projective identification seems to be operative, with the mother merging Helen and her deceased daughter. Significantly, both require continuous dosages of phenobarbital, and both are "damaged." Helen appears to be, for the mother, the replacement of the deceased, retarded, brain-damaged sister.

Helen, at the time of the assessment, was an attractive teenager who consistently wore a button which said "Don't bother me. I can't cope." She spilled information about wanting to die, overdosing recently on medicine, and eating safety pins one year ago. She stated that at the time of the interview she couldn't study, concentrate, or sleep. She spoke of endless fantasies about violence, including rape, a suicidal boy who tried to hang himself, jumping off a roof and dying, and shootings. She wished she could go to boarding school and be away from both parents or make them live together again; "but my father has another wife, and I hate their son." Helen rambled on rapidly, often out of context, speaking in a disconnected way about how she could think ahead and predict the future. She also stated she could see people who were dead, like her dead sister and a former neighbor. She described often feeling in another world or in a dream; people sounded like echoes, and were hazy and vague. She said she got strange messages, as when pictures talked to her: "We have a picture of Christ's Last Supper, and he moved his eyes, smiled at me, and got up—like to walk out of the picture. That can't be real. All this makes me sick and dizzy. My eyes blur, my head hurts, and no one believes I'm hurting." In sum, Helen was diagnosed as presenting an acute schizophrenic break at adolescence. Her social withdrawal, depersonalization, hypochondriacal concerns, fantasy life, the impaired ego functions, and hallucinations were classic symptoms of the disease. Her hallucinations and depersonalized state were ego-dystonic; Helen possessed sufficient observing ego to be aware that she "shouldn't" be seeing people who were dead or having conversations with people in a painting. She "knew" that she shouldn't be in a confused dream world.

Helen expressed relief at the idea of being in a children's hospital for a while. She felt she would feel safe in such a place and that people there would know better than her parents how to help her. She felt that after some weeks or months in the hospital—she would want to live with her mother, not her father. "That's because mother and I need each other more than anyone else, and dad is too busy for me."

Bibliography

AMERICAN PSYCHIATRIC ASSOCIATION (1980). *Quick Reference to Diagnostic Criteria. Diagnostic and Statistical Manual of Mental Disorders, Third Edition.* Washington, D.C.: APA.

ARIETI, S. (1974). *Interpretation of Schizophrenia.* 2nd ed. New York: Basic Books.

BATESON, G.; JACKSON, D.; HALEY, J.; and WEAKLAND, J. (1956). Towards a Theory of Schizophrenia. *Behavioral Science,* 1:251.

BELLAK, L., ED. (1980). *Disorders of the Schizophrenic Syndrome.* New York: Basic Books.

CAMERON, N. (1963). *Personality Development and Psychopathology: A Dynamic Approach.* Boston: Houghton Mifflin.

FISH, B. and HAGIN, R. (1972). Visual Motor Disorders in Infants at Risk for Schizophrenia. *Arch. Gen. Psychiatry,* 27:594–98.

FREUD, S. (1924). The Loss of Reality in Neurosis and Psychosis. In *Collected Papers,* 2: 277–82. London: Hogarth.

FROMM-REICHMANN, F. (1948). Notes on the Development of Treatment of Schizophrenia by Psychoanalytic Psychotherapy. *Psychiatry,* 11:263–73.

HARTMANN, H. (1953). Contributions to the Metapsychology of Schizophrenia. *Psychoanalytic Study of the Child,* 8:177–98. New York: International Universities Press.

HILL, L. B. (1955). *Psychotherapeutic Intervention in Schizophrenia.* Chicago: University of Chicago Press.

HOLZMAN, P. and GRINKER, R. (1977). Schizophrenia in Adolescence. In *Adolescent Psychiatry, Vol. 5: Developmental and Clinical Studies,* eds. S. Feinstein and P. Giovacchini, pp. 276–90. New York: Jason Aronson.

KAPLAN, H. I. and SADOCK, B. J. (1981). *Modern Synopsis of Comprehensive Textbook of Psychiatry.* 3rd ed. Baltimore/London: Williams & Wilkins.

KRAEPELIN, E. (1919). *Dementia Praecox and Paraphrenia.* Translated from 8th German ed. Edinburgh: Livingston.

LIDZ, T. and FLECK, S. (1964). Family Studies and a Theory of Schizophrenia. Paper presented at 1964 Annual Meeting of the American Psychiatric Association.

LIDZ, T.; FLECK, S.; and CORNELISON, A. R. (1965). *Schizophrenia and the Family.* New York: International Universities Press.

_____ (1965). The Role of the Father in the Family Environment of the Schizophrenic Patient. *Amer. J. Psychiatry,* 113:121.

RADNICK, E. H. and GOLDSTEIN, M. J. (1972). A Research Strategy for Studying Risks for Schizophrenia During Adolescence and Early Childhood. Paper Presented at Conference on Risk Research, Oct. 1972, Doral Beach, Puerto Rico.

ROBINS, N. (1966). *Deviant Children Grown Up.* Baltimore: Williams & Wilkins.

SEARLES, H. (1958). Positive Feelings in the Relationship between the Schizophrenic and His Mother. *Internat. J. Psychoanal.* 39:569–86.

SULLIVAN, H. S. (1953). *The Interpersonal Theory of Psychiatry.* New York: Norton.

_____ (1964). *The Fusion of Psychiatry and Social Sciences.* New York: Norton.

WATT, N. F. (1972). Longitudinal Changes in the Social Behavior of Children Hospitalized for Schizophrenia as Adults. *J. Nerv. Mental Disease,* 155: 42–54.

3

Borderline Pathology

The borderline syndrome is a confusing and bewildering diagnostic entity, which causes diagnostic dilemmas as well as considerable stress for parents and children and for the professionals attempting to plan and provide services for the adolescent clients who suffer from it. Some background will assist the reader's understanding of this disorder, which always appears first in childhood, never suddenly erupting in adolescence or adulthood.

The theory presented here views this disorder from an ego psychology, object relations perspective which embodies a developmental approach. Specifically offered is a conception of normal and pathological child and adolescent development seen on a continuum, with disorders caused by arrests or fixation in the course of normal chronological development. "Implicit in Margaret Mahler's work is her continuing emphasis on normal development. . . . and the importance of evaluating the adequacy of the symbiotic and separation-individuation phases" (Kaplan, 1980, p. 40). For example, we think of the newborn child, sleeping and eating and unaware of the outside world. The child in the early weeks of life is self-enclosed in what we refer to as the "normal autistic" phase. The denial of the outside human world is due to the extensive proportion of time asleep, the infant's normal stimulus barrier that shuts out household noises, and "the good enough" mother effectively modulating the environment.

> Pleasurable affects, the first manifestations of the differentiating libidinal drive to emerge, are invested in a fused self-object representation, the first intrapsychic libidinal investment. Insofar as that fused structure represents the origin of both self- and other representations, libidinal investment in the self and in objects are originally one process [Kernberg, 1980, p. 25].

Gradually, affects and responses shift; the child is no longer solely responding to inner sensations of hunger, distress, and discomfort. In fact, recent infant research suggests the newborn responds to the mother in the first few days of life, far earlier than suggested in the seminal Spitz studies (Stern, Barrett, and Spiekar, 1983; Stern, 1977; Kennel and Klaus, 1982, 1983). There is a slowly evolving awareness of self and others, namely, gratification from outside in the form of mother. Jacobson (1964) states that the slow differentiation of the self and object representation aids in the differentiation of the self and the external world. Mother is slowly introjected, first in a part-object fashion—the breast, the bottle, the voice, the face, and the comfort and solace provided become linked permanently with her. This is the crucial early bonding and attachment of mother and child. The child who does not make this attachment remains fixed in a self-enclosed world, or regresses back from partial attachment to mother and presents the most profound pathology, that of autism. Mother has not been responded to—or rather has been shut out and responded to negatively. Those who do not find a satisfactory or complete explanation in psychodynamic theories of etiology stress the constitutional and neurological factors that play a part in the creation of autism. Specifically, a defective brain stem or ineffective stimulus barrier—with a resultant bombardment of the infant by stimuli in the environment—may be responsible. Noises are not screened out, and the child is fitful and startles constantly, withdrawing from the mother; and so begins the child's dehumanization and recoiling from the human environment.

Resuming consideration of normal development, we note the next typical step following bonding and attachment, that of symbiosis, most eloquently described by Mahler. She borrowed the term from biology, noting the union of two organisms for their mutual advantage—in this case the child, totally and completely needing the mother, and the mother needing to be needed. The child's fantasy is that mother and child are one, with a common boundary. Over a two-year period, the child begins to separate and individuate, gradually becoming a distinct and complete person in its own right. Before this achievement, the child is engaged in exploration of its small world, rushing back periodically to the safety of mother's lap. Magical thinking and omnipotence permeate the thinking of the toddler. Mother, when gratifying and soothing, is all good; when she frustrates and limits, she is all bad. We note that severe early maldevelopment due to such trauma as parent loss, faulty mothering, or illness in these years causes an arrest or regression, and what Mahler called symbiotic psychosis characterized by the refusal to surrender the magical thinking and omnipotence of toddlerhood. Mother remains a split object, either all good or all bad. Self and other are not distinct and the child feels and acts fused with the mother. This twisted and stunted development is believed to result from massive frustration due to the sudden unavailability of mother. Some very infantile mothers, even without a precipitant, may recoil from their two-year-old who needs limits and protection. They were more comfortable with a tiny baby, whom they could hug and cuddle, and become alarmed at the child's growing self-assertion, exploration, and normal opposition. The other potential contributor to the borderline condition is massive overgratification with no expectations that the child accept limits and boundaries or struggle for mastery, be it in the realm of speech or tolerance for delay. Total indulgence prevents the gradual integration of the reality principle. Again, we see pathology arising out of normal development—the normal stage of symbiosis—when the necessary ingredients of optimal frustration and consistency for normal child development are lacking. The mother may need to hold onto the child because of her own fears of abandonment. She then infantilizes and stifles all normal growth and push for autonomy. Normal development is not fraught with the above stress, and the symbiotic phase comes to an end with a gradual distinction between self and object.

The third major milestone for the young child is that of separation-individuation, and the development of object constancy. Separating and individuating refer to the maturational step of becoming a separate person, with clear self-other boundaries. No longer is there a fantasy of omnipotent control of mother or merger, union, or engulfment by mother. Mother is no longer the split object either all good or all bad. The normally developing child can love irrespective of frustration and can tolerate ambivalence, that is, good and bad feelings toward its parents. The presence and support of the father is crucial to facilitate separation and individuation. Not only does he provide help and support to the mother in the parenting tasks, but he also offers the child the security to surrender the mother safely. Moving away from the primary dyad is possible if there is someone to move toward, thereby creating a triadic mode of relating. This traditional family structure with "good enough" mothering and fathering facilitates the child's entry into a genuine oedipal phase. The parents are permanently introjected by the child, not only the pictorial representation, but the feelings connected to being securely parented. Thus, the normal three-year-old can comfortably attend nursery school with a vivid memory of mother's face, mother's ministrations, and a certainty that mother will be awaiting the child's return and that daddy will soon appear also. This evocative memory soothes the child during absences from the parents. Borderline adolescents have not achieved separation-individuation and self and object constancy and do not have that clear evocative memory. They cannot emotionally recall complete three-dimensional persons, and they continue to split objects into those who are all good and those who are all bad.

This lack of separation-individuation and evocative memory and splitting is well-exemplified by Karen, a borderline adolescent this author worked with for several years in a residential treatment institution. She would vacilate and swing, having to love or hate her social worker, therapist, and unit supervisor. Never could she simultaneously feel neutral, benign, positive, or ambivalent about both; nor could she love or hate both simultaneously. When frantic and frenzied, she would punctuate her screaming outbursts with bulletin notices, or her form of graffiti. She would post the latest written expression of splitting anywhere on campus, proclaiming "J loves me/B hates me" or vice versa. This phenomenon seemed always to correspond with the psychic state of her borderline mother and the mother's repeated agitated and suicidal states, which required numerous hospitalizations. The lack of psychic separation-individuation of mother and daughter was striking and for many years was unaffected by the physical separation inherent in the child's residential placement. Karen continuously acted out her lack of separation-individuation from her mother and demonstrated her lack of object constancy, which was rooted in her mother's lack of consistency and constancy. The symbiotic merger with her symbolic maternal objects during her placement was of a split-object nature and was replayed in her wildly fluctuating all-loving or all-hating stance toward staff and toward herself. This lack of attainment of object constancy, or ability to fuse the good-bad mother, is one of the hallmarks of the borderline state and accounts for the panic, anxiety, and impulsivity of borderline patients, be they children, adolescents, or adults. The distorted object relations often dictate the optimal plan of long-term treatment for the borderline patient.

Historical Review of Research on the Borderline Syndrome

The term *borderline* has come into increasing use in the last thirty years, in describing a severe form of psychopathology. This diagnosis has had a conflicted and confused reputation, and initially was a wastebasket category—applied when we did not know how to label or diagnose. Despite the discomfort of some with diagnosis and labeling, our perspectives suggests that assessment and categorization, properly used, are a kind of empathic shorthand. The intent of such categorization is not pejorative toward clients, but rather, recognizes severe developmental traumata and subsequent ego deficits. In his research on the borderline patient, Knight (1953) noted that the ego labors badly and is a feeble and unreliable ally.

Mental health clinical disciplines have long been puzzled by the etiology and the psychodynamics of the borderline patient, and originally many labels were applied to this bewildering "in-between" pathology. Such labels as "latent" or "ambulatory" psychotic (Zilboorg, 1941) and "pseudo-neurotic" schizophrenic (Hoch and Polatin, 1949), "narcissistic disorder" and "chronic severe personality disorders" were used. The groundwork for examining confusing psychopathology was laid by S. Freud (1914), when he noted the role of the narcissistic defenses of projection and denial in the more severe forms of mental illness. In 1925, W. Reich (1974) placed the impulsive character, the neurotic character, and the psychopath between neurosis and psychosis and observed the ambivalence, hostile pregenital impulses, ego and superego deficits, immature defenses, and primitive narcissistic features of the impulsive personality.

Stern (1938, 1945, 1948) was one of the earliest researchers to delineate the special dynamics, problems, and treatment dilemmas with patients he labeled as borderline. He noted narcissism as the underlying character component of these patients, and, such personality features as:

1. Psychic bleeding, namely intense reactiveness and distress over any and every life occurrence
2. Extreme hypersensitivity and sense of insult and injury at the slightest provocation
3. Rigidity
4. Negative therapeutic reaction with a response of depression or anger to any interpretation that is experienced as an injury to the patient's self-esteem
5. Lack of self-assurance and self-esteem
6. Self-pity and chronic depression manifested by masochistic tendencies and "wound-licking"
7. Pseudo-equanimity despite inner chaos
8. A distorted sense of reality because of excessive projection and denial

Helena Deutsch (1942) described what she called the "as-if" personality; her patients revealed a strikingly uniform tendency to imitate others and take on the characteristics of those around them. Disturbed

interpersonal relationships, characterized by superficiality and clinging, seem to reflect what Deutch noted in the histories, namely a lack of
adequate early mothering with resultant impairment in the processes of
identification, internalization, and normal ego and super-ego formation. In the mid-fifties, Knight (1954) made important observations regarding ego malfunctions and disturbed object relationships. In treating such patients, he advocated modification of the treatment milieu
and the need for limit setting, a more reality oriented approach, and
modification of classic psychoanalytic techniques to promote the treatment relationship and the working through of conflicts.

By the 1950s most clinicians were convinced that these bewildering
patients were not as impaired as schizophrenics, but were more profoundly disturbed than more intact neurotic patients. Parallel with the
examination of adult cases, child therapists were also observing atypical children. In the early 1950s, Margaret Mahler described children
who had a special kind of benign psychosis that made them appear
more neurotic than psychotic. Anna-Marie Weil (1953) noted a similar
sort of child that appeared unemancipated from mother. Ekstein and
Wallerstein (1954) noted children who were similar to the defined adult
borderline patients. These children typically reflected a proneness to be
continuously overwhelmed by intense anxieties and panic reactions.
They were vulnerable to intense ego regression, and even temporary
psychosis, when under severe stress, all the while maintaining reality
testing, despite a tendency towards magical thinking, grandiosity, and
an idiosyncratic, distorted sense of reality.

The vulnerability is caused by basic ego deficits and an inadequate
defense system. Eckstein and Wallerstein (1954) likened ego mechanisms of control to a thermostat. More intact individuals have a reliable,
stable thermostat, and thus have an even temperature or temperament,
whereas the borderline has an unpredictable thermostat, with constant
temperament changes. Reality testing is maintained or quickly recovered after stress-induced regressions have lifted. Ekstein (1966) observed that the children studied at the Menninger Foundation demonstrated markedly shifting levels of ego organization, fluctuating between
primitive and more sophisticated states of ego functioning.

Rosenfeld and Sprince (1963), in their research at Hampstead,
noted the lack of phase dominance; thus a child would simultaneously
evidence marked oral and phallic features. Highlighted in these authors' research was the lack of adequate repression and neutralization.
Chethik and Fast (1970, 1971, 1972), working with children at the University of Michigan Medical School wrote a series of articles attempting
to understand the origin of fixations and arrests. These authors focused
on the infantile period of development in which the child makes the
transition out of narcissism as the developmental source of the child's
pathology.

Contemporary Research on the Borderline Syndrome

The theoretical work of Kernberg (1966, 1967, 1970, 1974, 1975, 1978) and Mahler (1963, 1968a, 1968b, 1972a, 1972b, 1975) provides a major contribution to our understanding of the etiology of the borderline syndrome. Mahler emphasized the essential features of symbiosis and separation-individuation. The hallucinatory or delusional omnipotent fusion of child and mother—the delusion of a common boundary between mother and child—exists from the age of three or four months on. The peak of symbiosis occurs at four to five months, beginning the first subphase of separation-individuation. Stranger anxiety at six to seven months, when the loved one is distinguished from all others, signifies optimal symbiosis. Practicing and rapprochement (crawling or walking away from the mother but scurrying back for emotional refueling) and the simultaneous wish for reunion and fear of reengagement (shadowing and darting away) are highlighted by the important turning point of the twenty-fourth month, when the toddler recognizes that the world is not his or her oyster. Under optimal conditions there is a surrender of secondary narcissism. The final subphase is the consolidation of individuality and the beginning of emotional object constancy, which should solidify by age three. This is the time that the good and gratifying mother, and the bad and frustrating mother are fused into one beloved image and mother is loved, irrespective of gratification or frustration.

This crucial developmental process is perhaps more easily understood if we think of adolescence as the time of separation-individuation, the second time around. The adolescent wishes for independence and autonomy and is in conflict over still-present dependency needs. He or she vacillates between infantile and adult behaviors, wanting the prerogatives of the adult world while at the same time wanting to be cared for: thus the oscillations and reverberations of the adolescent phase. Rebellion and defiance versus dependency—"take care of me"—stances are the common expressions causing the upheaval, as the teenager finally moves into a more genuine emancipated state, culminating in the identity formation of young adulthood.

Often the mother of a borderline child or adolescent is borderline and has failed to separate from her own mother. She fosters the symbiotic union with her child, thus encouraging the continuance of his or her dependency, to maintain her own emotional equilibrium. She is often threatened by and unable to deal with her child's emerging individuality. She depersonalizes the child, cannot see him as he is, but rather, projects upon him the image of her own parents or of a sibling, or she envisions him as a perpetual infant or object and uses him to defend herself against her own feelings of abandonment. The mother clings to the child to prevent separation, discouraging moves towards individuation by withdrawing her support (Masterson and Rinsley, 1975).

Between the ages of 1½ and 3, conflict develops in the child between his own developmental push for individuation and autonomy, and the withdrawal of the mother's emotional supplies that this growth entails. Growth equals loss. Thus, developmental arrest of the borderline occurs either in the narcissistic or early oral phase. The earlier the arrest the more the child will resemble the psychotic; the later it comes, the more he will appear neurotic. However, Mahler and Kaplan (1977) caution against simple equations like symbiosis = schizophrenia, rapprochement vulnerability = borderline, etc. and stress the corrective and pathogenic influences from all the phases which determine later personality organization.

The developmental arrest produces severe defects in ego functioning, persistence of the defenses of ego, object splitting, a failure to achieve object constancy, and thus, the development of a negative self-image. Gunderson and Singer (1975) noted the following features characteristic of most borderline persons:

1. The presence of intense affect
2. A history of impulsive behavior
3. Social adaptiveness
4. Brief psychotic experiences
5. Bizarre, illogical or primitive responses on varied psychological tests
6. Interpersonal relationships that are either transient and superficial or intense, dependent, manipulative, and demanding

Characteristics of this weak ego and superego structure, include: Failure of normal repression, persistence of primitive mechanisms of defense with reliance on projection, introjection, regression, denial, impairment of ego's synthetic function, lack of basic trust, failure of sublimination of raw instinctual impulses, breakthroughs of aggressivity, fluid ego boundaries, deficient differentiation between inner and outer stimuli, poor reality perception, poor frustration tolerance, poor impulse control, and object splitting. There is intense oral dependency and need for affection and approval. There is rage and frustration at the deprivation. The child fears his feelings with destroy self and object. To deal with this fear, he splits. Yet both sides of the split are unrealistic— the all good or all bad mother and the all good or all bad self. An immature primitive superego results in the adolescent's having inconsistent standards, values, controls, and guilt. Ego-syntonic anti-social trends indicate a poor prognosis (Kernberg, 1975).

Kernberg (1966) followed Mahler in his reliance on ego psychology and object relations theory, noting the development of normal and distorted internalized object relationships, and the pathologic chronic characterological organization of the borderline. He emphasized (1978) the basic ego defect and developmental arrest as opposed to the various symptoms, such as anxiety, antisocial behavior,and infantile narcissism, observed in borderline adolescents. As Pine (1974) emphasized "mapping the borders"—high-, middle-, and low-level borderline functioning in children—Kernberg distinguished between the higher or lower levels of organization, depending on the degree of intactness of ego and superego functioning and the quality of object relations. The lower categories included those adolescents presenting infantile personality, substance abuse, and antisocial behavior; the middle range included those adolescents presenting passive-aggressive, narcissistic, and better functioning infantile personalities, and the highest level included better structured hysterical and obessive-compulsive characters. These conclusions of Kernberg's are similar to the conclusions reached by Grinker and Werble (1977) and Grinker (1978), who designated a specific syndrome with a considerable degree of stability and consistency—not a temporary condition that arises out of response to internal or external stress: "The syndrome itself as a process is recognizably stable giving rise to the paradoxical term 'stable instability'" (Grinker, 1978, p. 343).

Borderline Adolescents

Parents' negative attitudes toward the adolescent are introjected unconsciously by the child and become aspects of his own fragmentary self-image. The adolescent feels guilt for leaving or wishing to leave the mother. Guilt erodes his capacity to continue the move toward individuation. James Masterson (1972), in discussing the borderline adolescent, highlights the abandonment depression, which results in frequent acting out behaviors to ward off the depression. The adolescent may initially present mild boredom and difficulty in concentrating in school, then hypochondriacal concerns, followed by excessive physical and sexual activity. More flagrant acting out is expressed via delinquent behaviors, drinking, drug use, sexual promiscuity, slovenly dress, defiance, and running away. Frequently a sexual relationship is used by the youngster to both substitute for and avoid reunion and engulfment by the maternal figure.

Many adolescents diagnosed as borderline have earlier, in latency, presented what appears to be solid and appropriate development, with the borderline features not appearing until adolescence. We now better understand that the earlier "good" adjustment in fact was fragile and the balance maintained was precarious. Under the onslaught of the pressures of adolescence, the initial separation-individuation crisis not mastered in toddlerhood erupts later with drastic reverberations. It appears in florid and dramatic form during pubescence and adolescence. Clinical observation and careful history gathering provide evidence for this syndrome's earlier existence—but in dormant form—until the facing of the second and final separation-individuation crisis necessary as a part of the adolescent process. Hence, the collapse in adolescence and not earlier. Parental divorce, illness, or unavailability frequently precipitates the child's decline, which had been avoided until this constellation of stresses. Adolescence proves to be too much for the teenager crippled by specific ego weaknesses: "(1) predominance of primitive defensive operation of the ego, (2) lack of impulse control, (3) lack of anxiety tolerance, (4) lack of developed sublimatory channels" (Kernberg, 1975, p. 129).

In the evaluation of the borderline child or adolescent, Chethik (1979) reminds us that it is the whole gestalt that determines diagnosis, rather than single symptoms. Chronic and conspicuous problems in ego and superego development often indicate the possibility of this disorder, while neurotic patients will show a minor range of such developmental deviations. Fundamentally, borderlines maintain their capacity to test reality and do not evidence the hallucinatory or delusional problems of psychosis. *DSM-III* criteria for the borderline syndrome include the following: self-damaging impulsivity and unpredictability; intense and unstable interpersonal relationships; inappropriate, intense, and/or out-of-control expressions of anger; identity disturbances manifest by confusion of self-image and gender identity; affective instability; separation anxieties and intolerance of being alone; and chronic feelings of boredom and emptiness.

Differential Diagnostic Questions Regarding Borderline Pathology in Adolescence

Despite Gunderson and Kolb's (1978) claim that borderline patients can be discriminated with great accuracy, in practice diagnostic confusion is common. It is often difficult to distinguish borderline pathology from the typical adolescent turmoil, identity crisis, rapid shifts of role experimentation, depressive states, altered and often impaired parent-child relationships, antisocial acting-out behavior, and heightened narcissism with its transient or more serious hypochondriacal tendencies or excessive preoccupation with physical appearance. While normal adolescence is no longer uniformly viewed as an inevitable period of turbulence, massive regressions characterize much of adolescent psychopathology. "Differentiation between these grave disorders and [normal] regressive shifts . . . sometimes represents a major diagnostic challenge" (Esman, 1980, pp. 287–288).

Because of the heightened narcissism during adolescence, similar confusion and differential diagnostic questions arise in assessing depletion depression (i.e., an inner sense of sad emptiness), disintegration anxiety, and structural deficits (Tolpin, 1978). The current conceptions and controversies about the "narcissistic personality disorder" are particularly pertinent in consideration of the distinctions between entity and borderline pathology during the teenage years. Kohut (1971, 1972) questioned whether we are seeing sexual desires and defenses against them during adolescence or the vicissitudes of the self. "We will find that in certain adolescents the conflict about sex (the resurgence of incestuous sexuality) is paramount, while in others the danger of the dissolution of the self (the reactivation of earlier fragmentation fears) is the main problem" (Kohut, 1972).

Rothstein (1979) posited that Kernberg and Kohut discussed patients differently and in fact may have been discussing different groups of patients. Kohut's group was distinguished by their elaboration of specific narcissistic transferences in the course of treatment and their cohesive narcissistically invested self and object representations. By contrast, Kernberg's lower level group of patients which he labeled as narcissistic personalities, functioned overtly on a borderline level. Rothstein described Kernberg's three levels as, in fact, mildly or floridly borderline, all manifesting distorted object relations and a pathologic, grandiose self.

Kernberg (1978) noted that antisocial behavior in adolescence may be an expression of normal or neurotic adaptation to an antisocial cultural subgroup and thus be relatively nonmalignant. On the other hand, it may reflect severe character pathology and a borderline personality organization, masquerading as an adaptation to an antisocial group. For Kernberg, the diagnosis of borderline in the adolescent patient is based on the presence of severe identity diffusion, primitive defenses (e.g., denial, projection, and splitting), projective identification, and the persistence of reality testing.

Giovacchini (1978) emphasized the borderline adolescent's amorphous personality constructions, rapid personality regression and reintegration, and marginal adjustment to the world. Shapiro (1978) and Shapiro and Zinner (1975) have done family research with borderline adolescent patients. They emphasize shared unconscious assumptions and fantasies that inhibited psychosexual development, with increased tension and symptom formation during adolescence. Anderson (1978) focused on fathering and, borrowing Winnicott's (1953) concept of the "good enough" mother, stressed the absence of a "good enough" father, which deprives the child of the external influences critical to superego formation, with particularly serious consequences in adolescence.

Blos (1967) was the first to view the period of adolescence as a second separation-individuation—a replication of the practicing period, the rapprochement for emotional refueling, and the ultimate push for autonomy, separation-individuation, and self and object constancy. Separation for the borderline adolescent does not evolve as a normal developmental experience, but on the contrary, evokes such intense feelings of abandonment that it is experienced as terrifying. To defend against these feelings, the borderline adolescent overtly or covertly clings to the maternal figure and thus fails to progress through the normal second edition of separation-individuation to autonomy. This clinging can be through fight-or-flight behaviors, such as drug use, running away, delinquent behavior, or defiance. Whatever the form, the effect is to retain parental involvement through worry, anxiety, anger, and commonly futile attempts to limit, discipline, and control the teenager.

Some adolescents fearing individuation and aloneness merge diffusely with cults and other movements, demonstrating their intense need for belonging through engulfment. This is an exaggeration of the more normal adolescent's attachment to the peer group, as described by Buxbaum (1945), where the group is an appropriate transitional bridge away from the family to the outer world.

Many borderline adolescents present an unending pattern of poor impulse control and aggressive outbursts. Fearful of this explosiveness, they withdraw from meaningful social and familial contacts. Some self-medicate via substance abuse and others lose themselves in cults, fantasies, television and the like. What is striking is their lack of sublimation channels, such as interest in academics, politics, painting, poetry, or athletics, available to the more intact teenager.

Some borderline adolescents find "relief" from their depression and anxiety in some form of self-mutilation. This author vividly remembers the constant agitation and impulsivity of a 13-year-old in residential placement, exemplified by her storming off in rages and doing such impulsive things as piercing her ears with an icepick. One never can predict what will occur next, though one can predict agitation, given these children's severe responses to change in the environment (e.g., familial upheaval, and staff changes in institutions).

Specific Therapeutic Methods

The most common therapeutic intervention for borderline clients is individual psychotherapy. Schwartzberg (1978) noted that most authors place special emphasis on the need for intensive, psychoanalytically oriented psychotherapy, which was previously the treatment of choice. Kernberg (1975, 1976a,b, 1977b) has written extensively regarding his view of the need for intensive psychotherapy, an approach he believes is appropriately applied to the adolescent population.

> This approach entails [examination] of the primitive defenses and object relations in the transference of these patients, within a setting of technical neutrality, modified by the establishment of parameters of technique required by acting out, or the severity of certain symptoms . . . and, the need for external structuring during minor or major parts of the treatment [Kernberg, 1978, p. 318].

Like Kernberg (1978), Masterson (1972) stressed the defense of splitting used by the borderline adolescent. He emphasized the need to work through the abandonment depression and the split object relations via the therapeutic alliance and therapeutic transference. He recommended family therapy at more advanced stages of the treatment process. Various combinations of individual and family therapy are recommended, depending on the adolescent's family situation and severity of symptomatology. Shapiro (1978a) and Zinner and Shaprio (1972, 1974, 1975) proposed that a combination of family and individual treatment be considered in all cases where a motivated borderline adolescent seeks help and when the family is available. In general, when an adolescent presents severe impulse problems, acting out, and drug abuse, the family cannot provide sufficient support and structure, and hospitalization or institutional placement becomes necessary. Miller (1980) cited the following indications for hospital care: (1) symptomatic behavior dangerous to the self and others; (2) uncontrolled destructive behavior, such as substance abuse and sexual promiscuity; (3) psychic pain of great intensity or symptomatic attempts at pain resolution that make it impossible for the adolescent to function in an age-appropriate way (assuming the pain cannot be diminished by outpatient interventions); (4) a psychonoxious (familial) environment that makes the patient inaccessible to therapeutic intervention.

Shapiro (1978b) reported observing "family regression that occurs during the adolescence of the borderline patient in which family members respond with retaliation or withdrawal to autonomous or dependent behaviors of the adolescent" (p. 1312). The adolescent dependency needs, and autonomous strivings create conflict because of a regressive shared use of projective identification (Zinner and Shapiro, 1972) "in which the adolescent becomes the bearer of disavowed aspects of the parents" (ibid). Some parents feel devoured by their teenager's dependency needs or wishes and withdraw, out of anxiety about their own wishes to be given to. Conversely, any separation by the teenager is viewed as a "hateful abandonment of the family" (Shapiro, 1978b, p. 1313). Parental contributions and the borderline adolescent's alienation, aggressivity, and inadequately structured self-image, all contribute to family turmoil (Giovacchini, 1973). There is considerable discrepancy among researchers regarding parental pathology. Masterson (1975) found parents of borderline patients to be borderline; Zinner and Shapiro (1972; Shapiro and Zinner, 1975; Shapiro, 1978a) noted significant variability in parental pathology; Singer (1971) using psychological tests found 84 percent of parents to be normal or neurotic. Singer and Wynne (1965) discussed a striking discrepancy between the degree of pathology when family members were interviewed together, versus when interviewed separately, at which time only mild disturbance was noted.

A survey of the literature suggests discrepant attitudes about pharmacotherapy for the hospitalized adolescent. Klein (1975) believed that drug treatment may have special value in the treatment of target symptoms of the "core" borderline adolescent patient, and in his opinion those with particular emotional instability and mood lability frequently respond well to Lithium and phenothiazine drugs. Sarwer-Foner (1977) was opposed to long-term pharmacotherapy, noting that such patients do not in fact use medication, or use it improperly.

> Borderline [patients] often abuse drugs, developing dependency states and physiological addiction to certain categories such as the psychosedative. They are also notorious for not taking medication on an organized basis, but rather, only when it suits them—with the same oscillating patterns that we know so well . . . (medication) can usually only deal with the emerging or emergent aspect of certain descriptive symptoms or acute psychotic(like) states. . . . Its use, however, in adequate doses is often essential in staving off decompensation in an emergency situation or in helping a patient progress in his defenses to at least an acceptable level [Sarwer-Foner, 1977, pp. 359–60].

Group therapy is a frequent intervention for inpatient and outpatient work with borderline adolescents—in tandem with individual and family therapy. Day hospital programs are one of several transitional interventions to assist the adolescent's departure from the hospital and return to the family and community.

We are clearer about the criteria for inpatient and outpatient treatment, but the issues of therapeutic frequency and modality of intervention have not been resolved. Therapy can be supportive, behavioral, or interpretive, all in the context of individual, group, or family approaches. Assessment is necessary to determine:

> (1) the patient's capacity to make a therapeutic relationship; (2) the level of anxiety; (3) the intensity of pain inflicted on self and others; (4) the presence of regressive sympomatology; (5) the conscious motivation for treatment. The failure to make an adequate assessment of which type of ther-

apy and frequency is appropriate can convert a seriously disturbed adolescent into one who is intractably ill" [Miller, 1980, p. 479].

Deficits in self-esteem, self-reliance, autonomy, and object constancy commonly make such adolescents too fragile for group or family interventions. Such individuals frequently cannot share the therapy hour and the therapist's attention. Not infrequently, the parents' personalities act as the primary pathogenic agents, whereby the parents "actually disregard and thereby frustrate important development needs of the child" (A. Freud, 1968, p. 115). In such situations, the parents have failed to provide the "essential ingredients for normal growth: reliable emotional attachment, help with inevitable anxieties, stability, adequate stimulation, basic acceptance of drives, appropriate guidance, and pride and pleasure in achievement" (Tolpin, 1978, p. 169). Many such afflicted adolescents present with empty depression and depletion anxiety (Kohut, 1977), and their disturbances in adolescence are often sexualized as they struggle with faulty self-esteem, a missing sense of direction, and, disturbances of cohesiveness. Because of these characteristics, conventional interpretation or interpersonal communications in group or family sessions are perceived as a criticism and assault. The fragility, narcissistic vulnerability, and paucity of parental empathy suggest the need for one-to-one interventions that embody empathy rather than confrontation.

Individual Psychotherapy: The Optimal Intervention

Because individual treatment is overwhelmingly the major and optimal treatment plan for the Borderline adolescent, this concluding section will focus on the process of individual treatment. First, we must anticipate the vicissitudes of the process and the impediments to change in the adolescent. Kernberg (1977) cautioned that "many borderline patients do not change significantly over years of treatment, despite the efforts of skilled therapists of various orientations" (p. 287). He suggested that negative therapeutic reactions derive from "(1) the patient's unconscious sense of guilt; (2) the need to destroy what is received from the therapist because of unconscious envy of [him or her]; (3) the need to destroy the therapist as a good object because of the patient's unconscious identification with a primitive and sadistic object which requires submission and suffering" (p. 288). Thus, we see the significance of profound pre-oedipal conflict, severe regression, and structural deficits involving early self and object representations. Kernberg (1977), in considering stalemates in treatment, noted "unchanged grandiosity . . . and severe masochistic acting out" (p. 289).

Giovacchini (1974) cited the disturbed adolescent's reticence and tendency to blame the environment for his difficulties, the not uncommon refusal to communicate, narcissistic self-preoccupation, and characterological disorders which threaten the clinician's professional identity. "This adeptness and the accompanying provocative attitude is a manifestation of defensive character traits associated with ego defects" (p. 280).

Clinicians can become resistant to working with the taxing borderline adolescent. Pearson (1968) suggested that the therapist's resistance might have several sources, such as chronic problems with the parents of the adolescent and/or feeling bombarded by the adolescent's fluctuating ego states, primitive expressions—often of rage—and primary process material.

Clinicians' countertransference and counterreactions are inevitable and can prove to be important assessment tools, reflecting, in part, the degree of primitive regression in the teenager and the shifts and changes of tone and emotional attitude in the professional relationship. This information can be profitably used by the therapist. Kernberg (1975) specified dangers to the therapists caused by:

1. The reappearance of anxiety connected with early impulses, especially those of an aggressive nature, which now are directed toward the patient
2. A possible loss of ego boundaries in interactions with specific adolescents
3. The strong temptation to try to control the teenager in consonance with an identification with an object of the therapist's own past
4. Masochistic submission to the adolescent's aggression
5. Disproportionate doubts about one's professional capabilities
6. Nihilistic attitudes about the necessary work with persons and systems on behalf of the adolescent patient

Many clinicians note that the therapist's capacity to experience ongoing concern for the teenager helps in overcoming and neutralizing the aggressive countertransference responses. The key to management of the countertransference of the therapist is restraint (Blanck, 1973).

Despite the general agreement with Kernberg's (1975) comprehensive presentation of borderline personality organization and the vicissitudes of the transference and countertransference phenomena in the treatment of such patients, increasingly clinicians disagree with his major technical recommendation for dealing with the patient's negative transference. He recommended "confrontation with the interpretation of those pathological defense operations which characterize borderline patients as they enter the negative transference" (1975, p. 72). Spotnitz

(1969, 1976) observed that patients suffering from pre-oedipal disorders usually require considerable time for the resolution of resistance. Havens's (1976) reliance on the work of Sullivan emphasized the patients' resistance to interpretations. Kohut (1971) emphasized the narcissistic injury and assault that frequently follow interpretations and cause patients to feel robbed of competence and/or omnipotence, which they may well still need in their defensive repertoire. Epstein (1979) suggested containment, reflection, investigation of the projections, keeping a low profile, and working with transference projections in the here and now.

Giovacchini (1985) emphasized the impossibility of everyone being able to treat all kinds of patients. He observed that in work with borderline adolescents, one must accept the patient's lack of object constancy, destructiveness, and use of a therapist as a "connecting bridge between unconnected parts of the psyche" (p. 459). He cautioned against classic analytic neutrality, which for some patients rekindles their early rejections and abandonments. Thus, a flexible therapeutic style is required, to ensure against trying to make patients do something they do not have the capacity to accomplish.

Technical neutrality and emphatic understanding require the patient and clinician to accept their own aggression and trust that this aggression will not destroy the therapist or the attachment to the therapist. A successful relationship is predicated on the clinician's trust in the ultimate potential of the adolescent. The eventually trusted therapist's cognitive formulations strengthen and broaden the patient's self-modulation and object relations. Warmth and availability are insufficient. Intellectual clarity, consistent concern for the adolescent, limits when needed—all are essential in providing the optimal background for interpretive psychotherapy with borderline adolescents.

Case of Barbara

The Diagnostic Profile assessment of Barbara is presented, followed by a brief account of ongoing treatment. Note the extensive amount of material one can obtain, even when there is no contact with parent(s), school, or other usual informants beyond the adolescent.

Referral

Barbara, a 16-year-old, beautiful mulatto girl, was self-referred and chose a therapist based upon the referral of her boyfriend's mother. She was motivated and most conscientious, initially, about keeping appointments. There were occasional failures due to a broken alarm clock or debilitating depression, but she then took the responsibility of calling, explaining, and rescheduling, complete with much shame and upset. She was seen biweekly free of charge because of her total lack of finances.

The precipitating crisis was the mother's abandonment of Barbara a month and a half earlier; she had left the state with her new male lover and Barbara's younger brother and had not gotten in touch with Barbara since then. Barbara's parents, who had lived in common-law marriage, separated when she was about 10. The current whereabouts of her father were unknown; he was thought to be in the urban area. At the time of her referral, Barbara had no address or phone number for her father and used friends' apartments as temporary crash pads.

The crises of abandonment and lack of housing money were the manifest reasons Barbara sought help. She felt she needed aid and support to get her life together so that she could handle school, part-time work, self-support, and eventual involvement in what appeared to be a potentially promising career in modeling; she also wanted to finish high school and go to college. She originally presented herself as connected with a top modeling agency, but this proved to be a hope and wish rather than a current reality.

Latent issues that led Barbara to seek help were her awareness of both her emotional fragility and her inordinate strengths. She was self-aware, self-observant, and conscious of the distorting impact of the hideous life experiences she had endured as a consequence of her parents' pathology and chaotic life style. She was concerned about her personal, racial, and sexual identity, over and beyond the current crisis agendas, as will be elaborated below.

Initially, Barbara was resistive to the therapist's suggestion of social agency contact or referral to the Bureau of Child Welfare. She did not want to be in a foster home or enter the child welfare system. She was averse to any kind of "reporting on her parents" and thought she could handle things independently. She could not imagine locating her mother, whom she knew to be out of state (somewhere in between Florida and California), or getting her mother to sign any kind of release forms, since "my mother is crazy and unbalanced." Barbara also declined contact at a mental health agency due to her awareness of the impermanence of trainee workers and her inability to tolerate change or loss. She initially presented herself as having money for therapy fees; and by the time the reality of no funds was clear, she and the therapist had connected; and the therapist decided to continue with her on a pro bono basis until such time as she was actually supported or employed and therapy fees could be paid.

After six months of working with the therapist and contact with an informal, unofficial guardian-friend, Barbara finally recognized that existent supports were insufficient, that she was not managing school and work, and that she was entitled to special services and funds for adolescents through the Department of Child Welfare. She struggled with her views of the "crazies, waifs, and junkie teenagers" in group home settings, noting her prejudice about such adolescents and the shame and stigma she would experience residing with such peers. The information the therapist shared with her about two appropriate agency programs somewhat diminished her fears and shame regarding public agency services. She proceeded with these referrals and voluntarily registered herself with and sought placement at a group home.

Description of Patient: Appearance, Mood, Affects, and Mien

Barbara was very tall, very slim, and strikingly beautiful. She had innate style and presence and, despite simple jeans, parkas, and bookbags—the paraphernalia of adolescence—she commanded attention. Her claim that model photographers pressed their cards on her in the street, subway, etc., seemed very plausible. She was very fashion-conscious and could carry herself with aplomb. Her fine taste in the selection of a cap, scarf, or boots gave Barbara a very distinctive and glamorous look.

This young girl's intelligence was as striking as her appearance. She was very articulate, expressive, insightful, and sophisticated in her discussion of any and all issues, ideas, or relationships. In fact, her precociousness hid her little-girl dependency needs. She described enjoyment and prior success with schoolwork; her only academic struggle had been with mathematics. She was self-observant and had ready access to her feelings and affects. Her behavior was incongruous due to her adolescent grandiose stance; she had high expectations of herself and perfectionistic standards and experienced total frenzy and depression when she could not accomplish the impossible. She tended to distort, cover, and deny but was not out of contact with reality or given to lying. She "split," projected, and denied out of shame, mortification and narcissistic injury when she "messed up" or felt she let someone down. When she became increasingly trusting and open in the treatment relationship, she was able to share disagreeable facts, such as being fired from her most recent job due to inaccurate computations on the cash register and total ineptness as a floor salesperson. As the relationship developed, Barbara would call when hysterical or distraught to seek help in sorting things out, get a better perspective, and thereby calm down. Given the distorted mothering she had received, it was not surprising that she lacked self-soothing mechanisms. She responded quickly to the therapeutic contact and saw reality with a less intolerant, harsh, and self-critical view. Slowly she began to learn to partialize and handle things day by day. She had no phone and so called the therapist from the street. If the therapist was busy, she would call again when the therapist was available. She was most responsible about seeking and sustaining the therapeutic contact.

Background and Possible Significant Environmental Influences

Given the crisis agenda that dominated Barbara's initial treatment and the lack of contact with parents, information on her history and background is spotty. All information has been provided by Barbara and is unverified. She stated that her parents were never legally married and resided together, apparently in common-law marriage, until she was ten or eleven years old. The father, Mr. S., was described as a once-affectionate and warm black man who was now an alcoholic and totally unavailable to Barbara and her brother. He supposedly worked as an itinerant chef in cheap restaurants. Mother, white and German, ran off with Mr. S. at age 17, thus estranging herself from her parents in Germany. She worked as a waitress throughout Barbara's childhood. Barbara's early childhood was replete with upheaval, moves, school changes, and chaos. The family moved constantly. As a toddler, Barbara had been in day care, where she was sexually and physically abused. She shared vivid and hideous memories of being beaten and sodomized at age three, while in day care, a situation from which there was no recourse or escape.

When her parents separated the children lived with the mother; at one point the mother, overwhelmed by trying to manage, returned them to the father, but they were terrified by the peer abuse in a rough inner-city school and refused to attend. Thereupon, the mother had them join her in an apartment, which she was sharing with a friend. Barbara soon became aware of the lesbian relationship between her mother and her friend, something initially denied and then admitted by the mother. Conflict between the two women was constant; the lesbian lover was described as jealous and resentful of the mother's attention and attachment to her children. Barbara depicted her relationship with her mother as one in which the roles were reversed, with Barbara mothering her mother and her brother. Barbara had been involved in modeling since age six. She stated that her mother's lesbian lover had pushed her to model to obtain money to support her drug abuse. Barbara described her mother's lover as a "druggie" whom they had to parent. The mother is said to have turned to her daughter for nurturance and help with each and every daily living problem, including sexual difficulties, conflicts with her lover and employer, and financial stresses.

At age 12, Barbara turned for some nurturance for herself to an 18-year-old neighbor, whom she described as weird and isolated but kind. He was a college student. Their relationship became sexual when Barbara was 12½. Barbara was loved, petted, taken to plays and ballets, and exposed to all the finer things by this young man. This helped her to cultivate her air of intellectual sophistication and knowledge about the arts.

She had a range of friends, including gay people in the arts, theatre, and fashion world, rich friends from the wealthy parts of town and poor friends in the Black ghetto areas. She felt confused about who and what she was in terms of personal and sexual identity. She acknowledged confusion about all that she had been exposed to and was involved in. This last year Barbara had chosen to be sexually inactive, despite her involvement with a boyfriend of several years standing. Her boyfriend was aware of her sexual confusion and shifts in gender and object choice, and has a realistic comprehension of Barbara's personal history. He nevertheless remained supportive. While she bemoaned his parental stance, she was also grateful to him for standing by her since her mother walked out. Until Barbara's abandonment and chronic state of crisis these past months, her boyfriend's relative had contemplated formal assumption of guardianship, but she later revised these ideas, feeling it would be too great an undertaking. She maintained an ongoing supportive relationship with Barbara, had her to dinner, accompanied her through all placement planning, and remained available to her on an ongoing basis following placement.

Diagnostic Formulations

Barbara made a pseudo entry into adolescence, characterized by fragility and inordinate vulnerability. Mastery of the developmental tasks of every prior phase and state had been compromised as a result of the chronic lifelong stresses she had endured. Her attainment of separation-individuation, object constancy, and oedipal resolution seems incomplete. Genitality, which served as her most important means of adolescent gratification, had been given up this last year. Regression to the oral phase was manifest in some use of drugs and alcohol when Barbara was depressed. The substance abuse was supported by her peer group. Anorexic eating patterns to maintain model thinness prevailed. At the time of the assessment, she was avoiding a genital oedipal object choice out of fear, confusion, and a need for some kind of sexual moratorium, because of her earlier precocious sexual activity. In a sense, she was exchanging some of the tasks of latency (e.g., industry, work) for those of adolescence, due to the paucity of familial and environmental supports, housing, and funds.

The self was over-cathected for sheer survival. Excessive narcissism was invested in the body. Ego and superego struggled in an attempt to maintain self-regard, mask low self-esteem, and more evenly modulate some feeling of well being. Barbara struggled with dependence-independence, having few people whom she could count on to remain calm, benign, and nonjudgmental. At times, her boyfriend and unofficial guardian got most understandably upset with her. They became unempathic and angry when she failed to fulfill specific commitments, including forgetting or being late for appointments. It appeared that they were somewhat unrealistic in their expectations of her. They had been taken in by her precocious, sophisticated facade, which made her appear and sound like a young adult in her twenties. Barbara had been required to parent her mother; and at the time she entered therapy, she needed parenting and support, which she both wanted and struggled against, because she feared disloyalty to her mother and realistically recognized the limits of people's actual commitments to her. She hungered for a real family and felt rage at what she had never received and could never receive from her family of origin.

Aggression was present in a more modified form than one might expect, given Barbara's history. It would appear that she did receive some affection from her mother and father, as well as the affection and admiration of a number of friends and boyfriends. Thus, aggression was not turned outward onto those in the familial environment or onto the community; instead, when she was upset Barbara would turn her aggression inward onto the self, as shown by recent recurrent agitated depressions. At times, she simply withdrew, did not eat, and tried to sleep to avoid facing problems that she experienced as overwhelming. She shared one episode of wrist-nicking with a razor blade, and one distraught state in which she wished she could "jump" and end all her worries and struggles. The magnitude of her reality problems should not be minimized, especially her lack of money and the limits of what others could provide. On occasion, Barbara felt desperate over how to arrange work, income, finances, school, and housing.

Her basic ego apparatus appeared intact. However, there were defects of perception, memory, and motility. Her ego functions (memory, reality testing, speech, secondary thought processes) also reflected interference. Her drive modulation, her containment and turning inward of aggression, and her sexual moratorium suggested an effort to control herself, to avoid acting out on others. Controls obviously were maintained inconsistently, since she had acted out on herself. There was no drive discharge until anger was turned on herself. Frustration tolerance and self-soothing mechanisms were not consistent. When her defenses broke down, she evidenced regression, frenzy, and brief fragmentation. Her defenses were too precocious and thus brittle and not consistently effective. She lost her prior ability to sublimate. Episode creative sublimation was striking but inconsistent (e.g., on occasion she would write an amazing poem or piece of prose).

The stress of daily living interfered with Barbara's ability to use other sophisticated defenses (e.g., intellectualization and rationalization). She therefore resorted to more primitive defenses such as denial, regression, and withdrawal, with resultant disequilibrium and lability in dealing with anxiety, depression, and aggression.

Barbara could not attend school regularly or handle employment, which compromised her search for an apartment to share or rent. She could not handle affects easily and so experienced guilt, general anxiety, depression, and feelings of shame. Nevertheless, on the positive side, it should be stressed that she was not cynical or without all hope. Her persistence in therapy clearly demonstrated her sense of hope and a growing identification with the therapist. This identification was used in the attempt to control regression and overwhelming depression and to lessen the demands of her harsh superego. Barbara demonstrated conscious guilt, self-criticism, and the capacity for an ego ideal.

Barbara had social relationships; but they were increasingly compromised by her bleak day-to-day existence and lack of sufficient work, study, and structure. Her frustration tolerance, already stretched beyond reasonable levels, was increasingly strained, with diminution of what she could manage. Because of Barbara's growing inability to tolerate frustration, and her heightened anxiety, her therapist became adamant about referral to the Bureau of Child Welfare, relying on the strength of the growing and developing therapeutic relationship and Barbara's begrudging recognition that her approach was not working. The fact that she was coping with anxiety less effectively and had avoided school for a number of weeks—something she had just admitted—reflected the urgent need for intervention. Until recently, Barbara had been preoccupied with grandiose hopes for her future, which interfered with attention to less exhilarating here-and-now tasks and responsibilities. When she achieved, her sense of well-being improved, yet she was understandably very dependent on external approval. Having had so little attention and approval all her life she had insufficient internal approval to allow her to value accomplishments. Her ability for self-observation was uneven and vanished when hurts were too painful to acknowledge, share, and reflect upon.

Barbara suffered more inner conflict than conflict between herself and the object world. She did not cause trouble at school or in the community but rather, withdrew. She experienced internalized conflict between ego and superego, with resultant shame, guilt, and mortification. There was internal conflict between activity and passivity and between masculinity and femininity. There was unresolved ambivalence about her sexual functioning, understandable in light of the sexual abuse she suffered in toddlerhood, her precocious long-term sexual involvement with a college student beginning at age 12½, and her mother's protracted lesbian relationship and shifts from heterosexual to homosexual to heterosexual relationships in the last several years. This regressive picture notwithstanding, given what she had survived, Barbara was impressive. Her ability to engage others and sustain contact with the therapist and her sense of humor and hope were sustaining.

Diagnosis of adolescents in crisis is especially difficult. Nevertheless, Barbara was assessed as borderline with narcissistic, depressive, and hysterical features. While normal adolescents typically evidence a heightened state of narcissism (or adjustment disorder of adolescence), Barbara evidenced earlier disorder and deficit. Barbara's day-to-day situation, history, and personal attributes exacerbated narcissistic pathology. She was preoccupied with a grandiose sense of uniqueness—the child model with aspirations to win fame, fortune, and attention. She could be quite exhibitionistic, having only received attention and admiration for her beauty and brains, not for her child-appropriate needs and normal dependency longings. She had been exploited repeatedly. While she conveyed an air of entitlement, she was not callously exploitative—with a disregard for the personal integrity and rights of others—nor was she lacking in empathy and sensitivity to others.

Treatment

Open-ended group-home care was recommended for Barbara to relieve her of the overwhelming pressures of employment and payment of rent, concurrent with school attendance. Her therapist believed she would calm down when provided with all the financial and educational supports due her from the Bureau of Child Welfare's Special Services for Children. In addition, a group living arrangement would provide needed nurturance and support and would aid in planning and organizing her academic and eventual work programs.

She wanted to continue in therapy with her therapist, which the therapist strongly recommended, because of the strength and significance of the existing relationship and Barbara's understandable fear and avoidance of any more abandonments. (Barbara's fragility and suicidal ideation must also be emphasized.) It was recommended that she continue on a biweekly basis, as she wished, to obtain the support she required.

Barbara gave her therapist permission to confer with Child Welfare and group-home staff. The therapist cautioned on the use of a confrontational style or attempt to puncture this adolescent's grandiosity or sense of specialness and entitlement. She would be able to surrender these characteristics when she felt more secure, and any premature push in this direction would be experienced as a narcissistic assault and injury, with a resultant increase in defenses and narcissistic features. She needed a calm, soothing, and empathic accepting stance by those involved in her care, which would support her voluntary application for services.

Therapist and group-home staff conferred productively, and Barbara entered care in a hospitable milieu. Following voluntary placement, Barbara did experience some relief at being provided the basics of food, clothing, shelter, allowance, and assistance in reentering high school. This enabled her to make and maintain contact with a modeling agency and begin to earn some money and further her long desired career. Model agencies handling many adolescents often assume an unofficial parental stance; and in this case, the therapist was contacted by the model agency. With Barbara's permission, model agency and therapist conferred about her problematic behavior. There were a number of contacts and joint sessions with Barbara, the therapist, and a model agency staff member; and progress began to become more solidified.

While Barbara experienced some shame about her peer group in the residential home, her relationships with staff and children began to improve until a major change in agency administration resulted in staff turnover. This shift in Barbara's living situation coincided with her mother's unannounced and unexpected return—and reconnection with Barbara. These two events disrupted her placement, and Barbara returned to reside with her mother despite her own grave misgivings, her therapist's recommendation, and the advice from the group home's new staff. She demonstrated her minimal frustration tolerances and could not wait for things to settle down and stabilize at the residence. Because of the changes, she no longer could maintain even a pseudoadaption to the environment. As noted earlier, borderline clients have extreme responses to any change in the environment, and the staff turnover coinciding with the abrupt reappearance of her family disrupted Barbara's placement and improved functioning. Her shame and anger interfered with her sustaining contact with her therapist, which led to yet another abrupt disruption, upheaval and loss. Barbara continued to repeat her past, and engage in chaotic impulsive moves and changes of milieu. She was not sufficiently moored in the therapeutic relationship or in her other work and school activities to resist the regressive pull. Thus, she mirrored her mother's pattern of erratic changes and impulsivity, changing her residence much as it had been changed throughout her childhood.

Conclusions

Research findings about treatment of children without the family are "far from optimistic" (Alpert, 1965). The need for genuine guardianship is crucial and, in fact, comes ahead of treatment. Parents or parent substitutes are more important to a child than doctors, and treatment cannot be effective unless proper guardianship is established first (Barnes, 1972, p. 139). We are aware that unvisited children seen by a procession of ever-changing workers are all but doomed to an unsuccessful stay in a residential facility, commonly followed by "revolving door" placements. Despite this knowledge, guardianship is hard to effect for any adolescent abruptly abandoned by parents. The case of Barbara is presented to show the far-ranging therapeutic efforts to offer a borderline adolescent girl crisis interventions, referral, access to services, and outreach, all in a flexible, responsive fashion to attempt to compensate for total lack of available parental figures. The direction of the clinical work was to address the other "23 hours," stabilize Barbara's living situation, respect client self-determination, and work slowly with a 16-year-old abandoned girl, initially resistive to placement and public services. Even when stabilization and placement is effected, results remain precarious, and frequently out of the control of any and all therapeutic efforts. Nevertheless, clinicians must hope, persevere, and try in the face of such young clients' current stress and painful histories.

Bibliography

ACKERMAN, N. (1966). *Treating the Troubled Family*. New York: Basic Books.

ALPERT, A. (1965). Children Without Families. *J. Acad. Child Psychiatry*, 4:163–278.

ANDERSON, R. (1978). Thoughts on Fathering: Its Relationship to the Borderline Condition in Adolescence and to Transitional Phenomena. In *Adolescent Psychiatry, Vol. 7: Developmental and Clinical Studies*, eds. S. Feinstein and P. Giovacchini, pp. 320–38. Chicago: University of Chicago Press.

ANTHONY, J. and McGINNIS, M. (1978). Counseling Very Disturbed Parents. In *Helping Parents Help Their Children*, ed. E. Arnold, pp. 328–41. New York: Brunner/Mazel.

BARNES, M. E. (1972). The Concept of "Parental Force." In *Children Away from Home*, eds. J. K. Whittaker and A. W. Trieschman, pp. 132–39. Chicago and New York: Aldine Atherton.

BERKOVITZ, I. H. and SUGAR, M. (1975). Indications and Contraindications for Adolescent Group Therapy. In *The Adolescent in Group and Family Therapy*, ed. M. Sugar, pp. 3–26. New York: Brunner/Mazel.

BLANCK, G. and BLANCK, R. (1974). *Ego Psychology—Theory and Practice*. New York: Columbia University Press.

BLANCK, R. (1973). Countertransference in Treatment of the Borderline Patient. *Clinical Social Work*, 1(2):110–17.

BLOS, P. (1967). The Second Individuation Process of Adolescence. *Psychoanalytic Study of the Child*, 22:162–86. New York: International Universities Press.

BUXBAUM, E. (1945). Transference and Group Formation in Children and Adolescents. *Psychoanalytic Study of the Child*, 1:351–65. New York: International Universities Press.

CHETHIK, M. and FAST, I. (1970). A Function of Fantasy in the Borderline Child. *Amer. J. Orthopsychiatry*, 40:756–65.

CHETHIK, M. and SPINDLER, E. (1971). Techniques of Treatment and Management with the Borderline Child. In *Healing Through Living*, eds. M. Mayer and A. C. C. Blum, pp. 176–89. Springfield, Ill.: Thomas.

DEUTSCH, H. (1942). Some Forms of Emotional Disturbance and Their Relationship to Schizophrenia. *Psychoanalysis*, 11:301–21.

EKSTEIN, R. (1966). *Children of Time and Space, of Action and Impulse.* New York: Appleton-Century-Crofts.

EKSTEIN, R. and WALLERSTEIN, R. (1954). Observations on the Psychology of Borderline and Psychotic Children. *Psychoanalytic Study of the Child.* 9:344–69. New York: International Universities Press.

EPSTEIN, L. (1979). The Therapist's Contribution to the Therapeutic Situation. In *Countertransference*, eds. L. Epstein and A. H. Feiner. New York: Jason Aronson.

ESMAN, A. (1980). Adolescent Psychopathology and the Rapprochement Process. In *Rapprochement—The Critical Subphase of Separation Individuation*, eds. R. Lax, S. Bach, and J. A. Burland. New York: Jason Aronson.

FAST, I. and CHETHIK, M. (1972). Some Aspects of Object Relations in Borderline Children. *Internat. J. Psychoanal.*, 53:479–84.

FREUD, A. [1968] (1971). Indications and Contraindications for Child Analysis. *The Writings of Anna Freud, Vol. 7: Problems of Psychoanalytic Training, Diagnosis and the Technique of Therapy.* New York: International Universities Press.

FREUD, S. [1914] (1957). On Narcissism: An Introduction. *Standard Edition*, 14: 67–105. London: Hogarth.

GINOTT, H. (1961). *Group Psychotherapy with Children.* New York: McGraw-Hill.

GIOVACCHINI, P. (1973). The Adolescent Process and Character Formation: Clinical Aspects. In *Adolescent Psychiatry, Vol. 2: Developmental and Clinical Studies*, eds. S. Feinstein and P. Giovacchini, pp. 269–84. New York: Basic Books.

_____ (1974). The Difficult Adolescent Patient. In *Adolescent Psychiatry, Vol. 3: Developmental and Clinical Studies*, eds. S. Feinstein and P. Giovacchini, pp. 271–88. New York: Basic Books.

_____ (1978). The Borderline Aspects of Adolescence and the Borderline State. In *Adolescent Psychiatry, Vol. 6: Developmental and Clinical Studies*, eds. S. Feinstein and P. Giovacchini, pp. 320–38. Chicago: University of Chicago Press.

_____ (1985). Countertransference and the Severely Disturbed Adolescent. In *Adolescent Psychiatry, Vol. 12: Developmental and Clinical Studies*, eds. S. Feinstein, M. Sugar, A. Esman, J. Looney, A. Schwartzberg, and A. Sorosky, pp. 449–67. Chicago: University of Chicago Press.

GOLDSTEIN, W. (1981). The Borderline Personality. *Psychiatric Annals*, 11(8).

GRINKER, SR., R. and WERBLE, B. (1977). *The Borderline Patient.* New York: Basic Books.

GRINKER, SR., R. (1978). The Borderline Syndrome. In *Adolescent Psychiatry, Vol. 6*, pp. 339–43. See Giovacchini (1978).

GUNDERSON, J. G., and KOLB, J. E. (1978). Discriminating Features of Borderline Patients. *Amer. J. Psychiatry*, 135(7):792–96.

GUNDERSON, J. and SINGER, M. (1975). Defining Borderline Patients: An Overview. *Amer. J. Psychiatry*, 132,1:1–8.

HAVENS, L. (1976). *Participant Observation*. New York: Jason Aronson.

HEACOCK, D. R. (1966). Modification of the Standard Techniques for Outpatient Group Psychotherapy with Delinquent Boys. *J.A.M.A.*, 58:41–47.

HOCH, P. and POLATIN, P. (1949). Pseudoneurotic Forms of Schizophrenia. *Psychiatric Q.*, 23:248–76.

JACOBSON, E. (1964). *The Self and the Object World*. New York: International Universities Press.

JOSSELYN, I. (1972). Prelude—Adolescent Group Therapy: Why, When and a Caution. In *Adolescents Grow in Groups*, ed. I. H. Berkovitz, pp. 1–5. New York: Brunner/Mazel.

KAPLAN, L. (1980). Rapprochement and Oedipal Organization: Effects on Borderline Phenomena. In *Rapprochement—The Critical Subphase of Separation-Individuation*, eds. R. Lax, J. Bach, and J. A. Burland, pp. 39–63. New York: Jason Aronson.

KEITH, C. H. (1968). The Therapeutic Alliance in Child Psychiatry. *J. Child Psychiatry*, 7:31–53.

KENNEL, J. and KLAUS, M. H. (1983). Early Events: Later Effects on the Infant. In *Frontiers of Infant Psychiatry*, eds. J. Call, E. Galenson, and R. L. Tyson, pp. 7–16. New York: Basic Books.

—— (1982). *Parent-Infant Bonding*. St. Louis: C. V. Mosby.

KERNBERG, O. (1966). Structural Derivatives of Object Relations. *Internat. J. Psychoanal.*, 47:236–53.

—— (1967). Borderline Personality Organization. *J. Amer. Psychoanal. Assn.*, 15:641–85.

—— (1970). A Psychoanalytic Classification of Character Pathology. *J. Amer. Psychoanal. Assn.*, 18:800–22.

—— (1974). Further Contributions to the Treatment of Narcissistic Personalities. *Internat. J. Psychoanal.*, 55:215–40.

—— (1975). *Borderlined Conditions and Pathological Narcissism*. New York: Jason Aronson.

—— (1976a). Transference and Countertransference in the Treatment of Borderline Patients. In *Object Relations Theory and Classical Psychoanalysis*, ed. O. Kernberg, pp. 161–84. New York: Jason Aronson.

—— (1976b). Technical Considerations in the Treatment of Borderline Personality Organization. *J. Amer. Psychoanal. Assn.*, 24:795–829.

—— (1977). Structural Change and Its Impediments. In *Borderline Personality Disorders*, ed. P. Hartacollis, pp. 275–306. New York: International Universities Press.

—— (1978). The Diagnosis of Borderline Conditions in Adolescence. In *Adolescent Psychiatry, Vol. 6*, pp. 298–319. *See* Giovacchini (1978).

—— (1980). Developmental Theory, Structural Organization and Psychoanalytic Technique. In *Rapprochement—The Critical Subphase of Separation-Individuation*, pp. 23–38. New York: Jason Aronson.

KLEIN, D. (1975). Psychopharmacology and the Borderline Patient. In *Borderline States in Psychiatry*, ed. J. Mack, pp. 75–91. New York: Grune and Stratton.

KLEIN, M. (1957). *Envy and Gratitude*. New York: Basic Books.

KNIGHT, R. (1953). Borderline States. *Bulletin of the Menninger Clinic*, No. 17: 1–12.

——— (1954). Management and Psychotherapy of the Borderline Schizophrenic. In *Psychoanalytic Psychiatry and Psychology*, vol. 1, eds. R. P. Knight and C. R. Freedman, pp. 110–22. New York: International Universities Press.

KOHUT, H. (1971). *The Analysis of the Self*. New York: International Universities Press.

——— (1972). Discussion of "On the Adolescent Process as a Transformation of the Self" by Drs. Wolf, Gedo, and Terman. Presented at the Chicago Psychoanalytic Society, 1972.

——— (1977). *The Restoration of the Self*. New York: International Universities Press.

KRAMER, C. H. (1970). Psychoanalytically Oriented Family Therapy: Ten Year Evolution in a Private Child Psychiatric Practice. *Family Institute of Chicago Publication*, 1:1–42.

LAUFER, M. [1965] (1977). Assessment of Adolescent Disturbance: The Application of Anna Freud's Diagnostic Profile. In *An Anthology of the Psychoanalytic Study of the Child—Psychoanalytic Assessment: The Diagnostic Profile*, eds. R. Eissler, A. Freud, M. Kris, and A. Solnit, pp. 57–81. New Haven: Yale University Press.

MAHLER, M. (1952). On Childhood Psychosis and Schizophrenia—Autistic and Symbiotic Infantile Psychosis. *Psychoanalytic Study of the Child*, 8:286–305. New York: International Universities Press.

——— (1963). Autism and Symbiosis: Two Extreme Disturbances of Identity. *Internat. J. Psychoanal. Psychother.*, 39:77–83.

——— (1968a). *On Human Symbiosis and the Vicissitudes of Individuation, vol. 1: Infantile Psychosis*. New York: International Universities Press.

——— (1972a). A Study of the Separation-Individuation Process: and Its Possible Application to Borderline Phenomena in a Psychoanalytic Situation. *Psychoanalytic Study of the Child*, 26:403–24. New York: Quadrangle.

——— (1972b). On the First Three Subphases of the Separation-Individuation Processs. *Internat. J. Psychoanal. Psychother.*, 53:333–38.

MAHLER, M. and McDEVITT, J. B. (1968b). Observations on Adaptation and Defense in Statu Nascendi: Developmental Pressures in the First Two Years of Life. *Psychoanal. Q.*, 37:1–21.

MAHLER, M.; PINE, F.; and BERGMAN, A. (1975). *Psychological Birth of the Human Infant—Symbiosis and Individuation*. New York: Basic Books.

MASTERSON, J. (1972). *Treatment of the Borderline Adolescent: A Developmental Approach.* New York: Wiley.

_____ (1973). The Borderline Adolescent. *Adolescent Psychiatry, Vol. 2,* pp. 240–68. *See* Giovacchini (1973).

MASTERSON, J. and RINSLEY, D. B. (1975). The Borderline Syndrome: The Role of the Mother in the Genesis of Psychic Structure of the Borderline Personality. *Internat. J. Psychoanal.* 56:163–77.

MILLER, D. (1980). Treatment of the Seriously Disturbed Adolescent. In *Adolescent Psychiatry, Vol. 8: Developmental and Clinical Studies,* eds. S. Feinstein, P. Giovacchini, J. Looney, A. Schwartzberg, and A. Sorosky, pp. 469–81. Chicago: University of Chicago Press.

PEARSON, G. (1968). *A Handbook of Child Psychoanalysis—A Guide to the Psychoanalytic Treatment of Children and Adolescents.* New York: Basic Books.

PINE, F. (1974). On the Concept "Borderline" in Children: A Clinical Essay. *Psychoanalytic Study of the Child,* 29:341–47. New Haven: Yale University Press.

REICH, W. (1974). *The Impulsive Character and Other Writings.* New York: New American Library.

ROSENFELD, S., and SPRINCE, M. (1963). An Attempt to Formulate the Meaning of the Concept Borderline. *Psychoanalytic Study of the Child,* 18:603–35. New York: International Universities Press.

ROTHSTEIN, A. (1979). An Exploration of the Diagnostic Term "Narcissistic Personality Disorder." *J. Amer. Psychoanal. Assn.,* 27(4):893–912.

SANDLER, J.; KENNEDY, H. J.; and TYSON, R. L. (1980). *The Technique of Child Psychoanalysis—Discussions with Anna Freud.* Cambridge, Mass: Harvard University Press.

SARWER-FONER, G. J. (1977). An Approach to the Global Treatment of the Borderline Patient: Psychoanalytic, Psychotherapeutic and Psychopharmacological Considerations. In *Borderline Personality Disorders,* ed. P. Hartocollis, pp. 345–64. New York: International Universities Press.

SCHWARTZBERG, A. Z. (1978). Overview of the Borderline Syndrome in Adolescence. In *Adolescent Psychiatry, Vol. 6,* pp. 286–97. *See* Giovacchini (1978).

SHAPIRO, E. (1978a). Research in Family Dynamics: Clinical Implications for the Family of the Borderline Adolescent. In *Adolescent Psychiatry, Vol. 6,* pp. 320–38. *See* Giovacchini (1978).

_____ (1978b). The Psychodynamics and Developmental Psychology of the Borderline Patient: A Review of the Literature. *Amer. J. Psychiatry,* 135(11): 1305–15.

SHAPIRO, E. and ZINNER, J. (1975). Family Organization and Adolescent Development. In *Task and Organization,* ed. E. Miller. New York: Wiley.

SINGER, M. T. (1976). The Borderline Diagnosis and Psychological Test Reviews: Reviews and Research. In *Borderline Personality Disorders,* ed. P. Hartocollis, pp. 193–212. New York: International Universities Press.

SINGER, M. T. and WYNNE, L. C. (1965). Thought Disorder and Family Relation of Schizophrenics IV: Results and Implications. *Arch. Gen. Psychiatry,* 12: 201–12.

SPOTNITZ, H. (1969). *Modern Psychoanalysis of the Schizophrenic Patient.* New York: Grune & Stratton.

———— (1976). *Psychotherapy of Preoepidal Conditions.* New York: Jason Aronson.

STERN, A. (1938). A Psychoanalytic Investigation of Therapy in the Borderline Neurosis. *Psychoanal. Q.,* 7:467–89.

———— (1945). A Psychoanalytic Therapy in the Borderline Neurosis. *Psychoanal. Q.,* 14:190–98.

———— (1948). Transference in the Borderline Neurosis. *Psychoanal. Q.,* 17: 527–28.

STERN, N. (1977). *The First Relationship: Infant and Mother.* Cambridge: Harvard University Press.

STERN, N.; BARRETT, R.; and SPIEKER, S. (1983). Early Transmission of Affects: Some Research Interests. In *Frontiers of Infant Psychiatry,* eds. J. D. Call, E. Galeson, and R. L. Tyson, pp. 74–85. New York: Basic Books.

TOLPIN, M. (1978). Self Objects and Oedipal Objects. *Psychoanalytic Study of the Child,* 35:321–38. New Haven: Yale University Press.

WAYNE, L. C. (1965). Some Indications and Contraindications for Exploratory Family Therapy. In *Intensive Family Therapy: Theoretical and Practical Aspects,* eds. I. Boszormenyi-Nagy and J. L. Framo, pp. 298–322. New York: Harper & Row.

WEIL, A. (1953). Certain Severe Disturbances of Ego Development in Children. *Psychoanalytic Study of the Child,* 8:271–87. New York: International Universities Press.

WINNICOTT, D. (1953). Transitional Objects and Transitional Phenomena: A Study of the First Not-Me Possessive. *Internat. J. Psychoanaly.,* 34:89–97.

ZILBOORG, G. (1941). Ambulatory Schizophrenia. *Psychiatry,* 4:149–55.

ZINNER, J. and SHAPIRO, E. (1972). Projective Identifications as a Mode of Perception and Behavior in Families of Adolescents. *Internat. J. Psychoanal.,* 53:523–29.

———— (1974). The Family Group as a Single Psychic Entity: Implications for Acting Out in Adolescence. *Internat. Rev. Psychoanal.,* 1:179–86.

———— (1975). Splitting in Families of Borderline Adolescents. In *Borderline States in Psychiatry,* ed. J. Mack, pp. 103–22. New York: Grune & Stratton.

4

Personality/Character Disorder

Definition

The diagnosis of personality or character disorders requires evidence of life-long patterns, recognizable by the teenage years.* Thus developing children commonly are viewed instead as presenting behavior disorders. Adolescents in a normal state of disequilibrium often do not present fixed dispositions, patterns, and integrated characteristics. Finch and Green (1979) required three conditions to affix this diagnosis on the young patient: "(1) definitive aberrations of behavior should be present; (2) the youngster's character should be clearly formed into an identifiable pattern; (3) transient situations should not be the primary cause of the aberrations" (p. 236).

Some may view personality disorder as solely an adult phenomena, and an inappropriate "diagnosis for children (and adolescents) whose personalities are still fluid and developing" (pp. 236–37). It is also difi-cult to differentiate certain types of personality disorders from psycho-neurotic disorders. Developmental psychologists distinguish between oedipal and pre-oedipal disorders, and affix this diagnosis on individ-

*The terms Personality Disorder and Character Disorder are used interchangeably.

uals who have not made a genuine entry into the phallic-oedipal phase of development and who present inflexible behavior patterns or personal styles without experiencing subjective pain and discomfort. Cameron (1963) stated that such arrest of the personality occurs early in life and colors the individual's style of coping with the environment. The resultant habitual inflexibility of behavior patterns experienced, in the absence of guilt or anxiety, defends the individual and affects the entire personality. In the more structured and developed normal or neurotic individual, discrete areas of the personality are affected. By contrast, the character-disordered individual's entire personality is affected. The ego functions, affective responses, and object relations are completely skewed. Intrapsychic conflict has been resolved by rigid reaction patterns that often create external conflicts in the environment rather than internal conflicts. The behaviors and rigid patterns permit partial gratification of instinctual wishes, rationalizations of motives, and idealizations of pathological behaviors. Thus, the array of symptoms are ego-syntonic. Missing is the guilt and anguish of the more normal or neurotic individual.

Because such afflicted adolescents do not suffer self-doubts and pain, they are not motivated to seek therapy help to change. Their behavior is disturbing to others but not to themselves. Teachers, parents, and the community often are distraught and worried—in contrast to the bland, unconcerned, stubborn, and unyielding stance of the character-disordered adolescent. The *DSM-III* (1980) classification names the following personality disorders: paranoid, schizoid, schizotypal, histrionic, narcissistic, antisocial, borderline, avoidant, dependent, compulsive, passive-aggressive, and atypical, mixed or other personality disorders. Meeks (1979) noted that "they seem to imply a static and fixed condition with a relatively poor prognosis" (p. 482). Therefore, most therapists working with children and adolescents are reluctant to utilize these diagnoses.

Etiology

There are varied explanations of the etiology of character disorder. Thomas, Chess, and Birch (1968) stressed the importance of temperament as a causative factor in behavior disorders: the mismatch or poor fit of the adolescent's temperament and the environment results in ineffective parental management techniques. Organic or constitutional factors may be critical in the development of personality disorders and antisocial behavior. For example, adolescents with known central nervous system damage demonstrate impulsivity, hyperactivity, and distractibility, which may lead to the development of a behavior or personality disorder. Meeks (1979) emphasized that while organic or constitutional factors may play an important role,

> this should not obscure the fact that they are basically psychological prob-
> lems. Many of these disorders are the direct result of individual and family
> psychological conflict. Moreover, regardless of the inception of the diffi-
> culty, all problems in adjustment to social reality eventually demand reso-
> lution in terms of intrapsychic dynamics. Treatment approaches for any
> established behavior disorder are unlikely to be successful in the absence
> of an understanding of the typical motivations, defensive maneuvers and
> the styles of relating which characterize this group of youngsters [p. 515].

Those who view psychodynamics as the primary causative factor emphasize the experiential etiology and note gross pathology in the environment. This pathology used to be considered a lower-class phenomenon (i.e., only parents who were criminals, alcoholics, and the like produced such teenagers). We now clearly see that the disorder crosses all class lines.

Those emphasizing psychological causative factors note the universal absence of mature and consistent parental love from one or both parents of the character-disordered patient. Parental love is distorted and inconsistent, creating a disturbed environment throughout the patient's childhood. Aggression, often expressed via uncontrolled and unpredictable hostility, is prominent. Frequently, character-disordered adolescents have been witness to, or victims of, unrelenting anger and violence, with resultant feelings of helplessness. Some such adolescents appear to externalize their retaliatory aggression at home, in school, or in society. These adolescents often come from broken homes and evidence pathological narcissism, chronic anxiety, overwhelming tension, and superego lacunae. Adolescent's superego lacunae may mirror those of their parents, in that "parents may find vicarious gratification due to their own poorly integrated superegos which sanction forbidden impulses in the acting out of the child" (Johnson and Szurek, 1952). Parents who are unconsciously permissive or inconsistent in specific spheres of behavior allow their teenagers to act out repeatedly. For example, parents may rationalize their own sadomasochistic impulses by condoning the same in the adolescent, which the adolescent experiences as parental acceptance of the unacceptable impulses.

In addition to superego lacunae and unconscious parental permission, "disturbances in superego development, in which an archaic superego with little tolerance for any impulse gratification overrides the ego and allies itself with the id, may lead to massive destructive acting out as a defense against intolerable feelings of "guilt" (Rexford, 1978, p. 325). Thus, it is a mistake to assume that the adolescent who acts out and presents severe personality or character disorder patterns has no superego. Rather, there is often a faulty, stunted, or primitive superego that relentlessly condemns the adolescent and generates excessive, inappropriate guilt that causes the adolescent to seek punishment repeatedly.

Descriptive Characteristics

The personality development of character-disordered patients is impeded by serious ego and superego distortions. In their description of character-disordered adolescents, Redl and Wineman (1951) cited an inability to cope with boredom, frustration, or aggression, due to poor handling of insecurity, anxiety, and fear; sublimation deafness or a lack of creativity; distorted interpersonal relations; and a poor perception of reality. They described a 13-year-old boy who was caught stealing; he was indignant at his victim for carrying so much money. The poor grasp of reality is further weakened by wishful and magical thinking and omnipotent narcissistic fantasies that ward off low self-esteem, uncertainty about identity, and self-hatred. Adolescents who are immobilized or overwhelmed by conflict over feelings of counteraggression and self-denigration are depressed, sullen, constricted, suspicious, fearful, and subject to intense free-floating anxiety. Redl and Wineman (1951) noted that the most serious problem of adolescents manifesting delinquent behavior is the great hatred resulting from parental rejection and/or mistreatment. Sometimes this hatred is markedly naked and primitive, because the adolescent's aggression was never tempered and neutralized by a strong personal attachment that would have fused aggression and love.

Ekstein and Friedman (1957) suggested that acting out may be an experimental recollection of earlier developmental stages involving the expression, mastery, and use of impulses in problem solving. Grinberg (1968) considered acting out to be closely associated with inadequately mourned object loss and separation. Schwartz (1968) believed that acting out stems from a break in the mother-child relationship at the very height of the ambivalent phase of development (18–30 months) when only the presence of the mother and her tolerance make it possible for the child to express libidinal and aggressive feelings—love and hate of her—while gradually integrating and accepting the unavoidable frustrations and restrictions set by her. Malone and Bandler (1967) described adolescents from disorganized families and unfavorable sociocultural settings who presented impulsive, action-oriented, and generally immature behavior. Most conspicuous was their deficiency in object relations, manifested by a lack of emotional separation from their mothers.

Other authors have emphasized the overt and covert behaviors of fathers of antisocial adolescents. While the parents of antisocial adolescents cannot be placed in any one diagnostic category, "the fathers resemble one another more closely than the mothers and display a strikingly similar attitude towards their sons. They tend to be passive-aggressive men with a high degree of dependency needs and confused sexual identification" (Rexford, 1978, p. 12). The fathers, further, seem to permit, aid, and abet their sons' aggressive activities or to have poor communication due to physical and emotional absences or punitive, obsessive, controlling, and rigid responses to their teenagers. Alcoholism and criminal and psychiatric records abound among the fathers of delinquents.

Frequently, conflicting parental attitudes, behaviors, and actions lead to a failure to establish a parental coalition and thus to a breakdown of generational boundaries where one parent makes a special ally of the adolescent. Traumatic events in early childhood tend to be repeated in acting-out episodes. Greenacre (1978) stated that "the acting out is most forceful and persistent when the child has suffered humiliation in the traumatic episode, being forced from a desired active position to a seemingly devaluated passive one" (p. 219). She stressed the following conditions as contributing to the production of delinquency:

> The conditions of strong stimulation of the very early aggressive and sexual drives of the young child did not permit a separation of the two, and . . . sexuality developed in the service of aggression and narcissism; further, . . . inconsistency of handling was such as to interfere with adequate object constancy to an extent which might strike at the roots of object relationship, promoting ambivalence expressed through action with a minimum of self-awareness. Is it possible that in certain cases of delinquency or criminality in which there is clearly a repetitive patterned form of the offending behavior, there might have been, in addition, a particularly strong fixation at the imitative stage, acting somewhat like an early imprint or engram on the developing child [p. 231].

Treatment Interventions

Because the social, familial, and environmental factors loom so large in the life situation of many personality-disordered adolescents, and because of the very early imprinting of character, treatment of these adolescents remains difficult, frustrating, and taxing. Clinicians, youth authorities, probation officers, teachers, and others face a struggle in work with these disadvantaged and frequently disorganized adolescents, due in part to their superficial mode of relating and apparent lack of genuine feelings. They frequently demonstrate a lack of care for or trust in people as well as the inability to engage in peer friendships or meaningful ties with adults. Their inaccessibility is exasperating and often enraging to those trying to help them. Their lack of emotional response, concern, or anxiety, their patterns of seemingly pointless deceit and evasion, and their negativism, tantrums, and unrelenting delinquency portend enormous obstacles for therapy. In addition, the charisma and reckless verve that accompany the acting out of primitive emotions exacerbate the extremely negative counterreactions and countertransference responses to these adolescents.

Outpatient Psychotherapy

A variety of interventions are currently in use. Thomas, Chess, and Birch (1968) recommended parental guidance for the young adolescent exhibiting a behavior or personality disorder. Their focus was primarily on the adolescent's temperamental style and the parents' management approach rather than the psychological or motivational factors in the parents. More recent interventions of this type are parent effectiveness and behavior modification programs. Meeks (1979) refers to authors Eyberg and Johnson (1974), who noted that although such interventions are beneficial, the parents must be reinforced for desired behaviors within these programs, as the adolescent's behavior does not seem to be a sufficiently strong reinforcer in itself. Other behaviorists report that what works in one setting does not necessarily carry over to other settings (Patterson, 1974). An adolescent might require a dual program at home and school for successful modification of unwanted behavior.

Meeks (1979) noted that outpatient psychotherapy is extremely difficult. However, he did not accept the findings of studies that suggested that it is of no value and noted that "these studies suffer both from the brevity and type of psychotherapy offered and the failure to distinguish diagnostically between impulse-ridden youngsters and those with neurotic behavior disorders" (p. 523). He suggested that positive treatment outcomes do occur with antisocial, acting out children when there is a preponderance of neurotic motivation for the antisocial behavior, relatively low family compliance with the antisocial pattern, and a good fit of therapist and patient.

Treatment techniques with character-disordered children are different from those used with neurotic children. In contrast to the intensive, uncovering, more permissive analytic approach used with the healthier neurotic adolescent, limit-setting and interpretation of reality are necessary with the personality-disordered youth. Jackel (1963) stated that an initial treatment aim is to make ego-syntonic traits and behaviors ego-alien, or ego-dystonic, in the context of building a relationship. Then, one hopes, behaviors will begin to correspond with reality expectations and the previously warded-off anxiety, depression, and discomfort will begin to surface and be better tolerated by the adolescent. With these patients, clinicians should focus on the present, rather than the past, especially early in therapy. Obviously, clinicians must avoid lectures, recriminations, moralizing, and parental attitudes.

Adolescents frequently test therapists, inviting them to break the rules, teasing them and calling them "square," "dull," etc. "The youngster attempts to cajole or intimidate the therapist into collusion in a deception of the adolescent's parents or other authority figures and is rebuffed in the effort firmly but without anger" (Meeks, 1979, p. 524). Therapists must remain benign, secure in their integrity, and committed to an ongoing interest in and attachment to the adolescent, with the goal of understanding the youngster's motivations, true feelings, attitudes, and values. Clarity regarding manifest and latent content is essential, in that an actually guilty adolescent may come across as totally lacking in feelings and empathy for others, valueless, full of bravado, macho, and defiant.

Kohrman et al. (1971) cautioned regarding both the potential for regression due to identification with the patient and anger in the face of the adolescent's resistance to interpretations. Proctor (1959) noted that action-oriented, acting-out adolescents often cause therapists to counterattack via mobilization of the therapists' own infantile superego against patients' id, ego, and superego. This mobilization of the therapist's superego can result in punishment, hostile demands for conformity, or even violent rejection of the patient. As these patients can be maddening, it is crucial to sort out the realistic hatred they engender so that it can be dealt with in treatment. These patients project their own acrimonious self-rebuke (superego) and sadistically attack the therapist verbally or physically for supposed misdeeds or defections. "The patient is then acting as sadistic superego to the therapist while at the same time, the therapist's id is being mobilized by the therapeutic uncovering of the patient's id impulses. This is most trying for the therapist, and it is of little help that the patient is projecting self-criticism and attack by his own superego" (Proctor, 1959, p. 301). Because these adolescents frequently do not want therapy, it begins in a negative phase. Often therapists intellectually grasp these adolescents' fears and resistances, yet emotionally respond as if all behavior could be controlled by the patient if only he or she would try. All of these dilemmas may produce nihilism, hostility, and rejections on the part of therapists. These difficult patients seem intent on forcing therapists to engage with them in a drama, which may not only undermine treatment but may even be threatening to therapists' professional and personal identify (Giovacchini, 1974).

Despite all these vicissitudes, a trusting relationship and therapeutic alliance are required and achievable in the treatment of many character-disordered adolescents. Surviving patients' tests; remaining sensitive to their low self-esteem; staying calm, committed to, and respectful of them; and retaining a sense of humor can carry the clinician forward in the difficult task of engaging such youngsters.

Because of the interpersonal nature of these children's symptomatic behavior, it is rarely possible to work with them in the absence of a fairly intensive alliance with their parents. This may be achieved through collaborative treatment of the parents, regular and periodic contacts with the entire family, or concurrent treatment of the parents and the child in separate sessions. (Most therapists find concurrent treatment technically difficult and potentially disruptive of the therapeutic alliance with both the child and the parents.) The child's "opportunity for an intensely satisfying dyadic relationship which provides . . . ego strengthening, repair of self-esteem, and the internalization of a positive identification figure offers the chance to correct the core disabilities in the behaviorally disordered child" (Meeks, 1979, p. 524).

In addition to individual psychotherapy, group psychotherapy has proved to be of value in work with character-disordered adolescents. Group composition should be balanced: Some youngsters in the group will have relatively strong egos and good frustration tolerance while others will have relatively weak egos and poor frustration tolerance. Younger children are frequently placed in "activity" group therapy, which offers a structured group play situation. One hopes the acquisition of social skills and ego strengthening are accomplished through the children's identification with the leader and interactions with peers. Often adolescents are treated in "rap" groups which offer some educational and/or vocational focus. Outreach work with delinquent adolescents attempts to engage them in socially accepted activities and projects.

Family therapy is another modality frequently employed with character-disordered adolescents; it may be the primary intervention or an adjunct to individual or group psychotherapy. This technique often permits recognition of the important pathological modes of communication, alliances, and roles, within the family. From a therapeutic point of view, the family approach seems to be particularly appropriate when the adolescent's symptomatology is embedded in a state of neurotic family homeostasis. This includes youngsters who are severely scapegoated, those whose parents demonstrate the superego lacunae described by Johnson and Szurek, and some cases where the "antisocial behavior appears to represent a maladroit attempt at separation from a 'binding' or symbiotic family entanglement" (Meeks, 1979, p. 525). There are many situations where family therapy is contraindicated. Offer and Vanderstoep (1975) noted the following circumstances where it is inappropriate: (1) when parents have made a firm decision to divorce; (2) when one or both parents present severe psychotic depression, hardcore psychopathology, or severe masochistic character; and (3) when the adolescent states emphatically that he or she does not want to be in therapy with parents, or only wants group treatment with peers.

Inpatient Psychotherapy

If and when interventions have failed and the adolescent's problems have become too disruptive or dangerous to himself or others, inpatient treatment becomes necessary. There are a number of residential facilities: children's psychiatric units in a hospital, residential treatment institutions, therapeutic boarding schools, and group homes. Treatment approaches and philosophies vary; some settings are closed while others are open, with appropriate adolescents selected to attend public schools off grounds. The range of interventions encompasses milieu therapy, behavior modification and a system of rewards and punishments, and psychodynamically oriented group, individual, and family therapy. Psychoactive medication is frequently used—often excessively—in closed, understaffed facilities. Some facilities offer long-term treatment, while others offer only crisis intervention or short-term placement. Ongoing parental involvement with the placed adolescent— including visits, calls, and passes home, as well as ongoing therapeutic work with the parents—is part of the treatment philosophy and the long-range plans for the adolescent. Such plans may include eventual return home or replacement in a foster home or school.

Currently, placement dilemmas arise out of funding limitations, the cost of care, and staffing problems. Childcare counselors or psychiatric aides vary in their competence, education level, and degree of psychological sophistication. These variables are tempered by the philosophy of the setting and the nature of the supervision and consultation provided to the paraprofessionals employed there. In other countries, where childcare workers have had extensive academic and practical training and are not considered paraprofessionals, they are given greater responsibility, status, salary, and input into the administration and treatment planning of the setting. Given the trauma inherent in separation, it is generally considered prudent to use an inpatient approach only as a last resort, when other interventions have failed and/or the adolescent is in danger or is too disruptive to be handled in the natural home.

The intensity of residential treatment stimulates greater countertransference than does outpatient treatment; and it may arise between staff members, staff and adolescents, and staff and parents. Adequate staff communication and supervision, including sufficient staff meeting time, mitigate against the universal tensions and stresses inherent in such a complex and charged system.

Case of Glen

Glen was a 17½-year-old black male high school dropout who was single and unemployed. He was seen in an outpatient adolescent clinic at the insistence of his parents, who had consulted a probation officer requesting advice and suggestions on how to handle their youngest son. Glen had run away from home the week prior, following an argument with his father over the selection of an expensive pair of boots. The father felt that Glen's choice was impractical and excessively expensive and refused to give him the money for this purchase. Glen refused to accept his father's decision, and the two argued; the father eventually threatened to hit Glen. That night Glen ran away, staying at a friend's house nearby, without his parents' knowledge. He returned home five days later, bland, unconcerned, and indifferent to their worry and fears for his safety.

Glen was the youngest of three siblings. His oldest brother graduated high school and currently worked full-time in a steel company. He had entered college part time and planned to obtain a degree in engineering. His company was currently paying for his courses and would support his college education. The middle brother was a senior in high school. He was a track star and had been awarded a complete athletic scholarship for college in the fall. Both older brothers lived at home, and were described as close to each other, but not to Glen.

Glen's mother was 41 years old, thin, attractive, and intelligent. She appeared sincerely concerned and worried about Glen. The mother was the youngest of five sisters and had always resided in the house she lived in as a child. Her widowed father lived with her and her family until two years before, when at age 78, he died of smoke inhalation caused by smoking in bed. The mother worked as a telephone operator at a motel near her home. She had worked for the past ten years, prior to which she was a full-time homemaker. When Glen was seven she sought employment to contribute to the family finances.

Glen's father was away from the family because his firm transferred him as plant foreman to another city. He accepted the move because he did not want to give up seniority, position, and power. His job gave him great satisfaction. His earnings were high, and he was in charge of 200 people. He came home once a month for three- and four-day weekends. This was the first and only marriage for father and mother. They were relatively unhappy together, not engaging in open hostility, rather "many many cold wars." Recently, the father had been drinking heavily on the weekends at home. He was not aggressive or abusive but slept excessively following his drinking. He interacted minimally with his wife and sons.

Glen was about 5' 8", thin, engaging, and pleasant in manner. He presented himself in a "hip" fashion, wearing several pieces of jewelry, a bandana around his neck, and an earring in one lobe. He and his mother indicated that he was an average student, intent on being part of the crowd. During his sophomore year, his grades declined and he was expelled for poor attendance. His mother felt at a loss as to how to discipline and control him and sent him to reside with his father. He dropped out of school and worked at a job his father got him at his plant. He and his father argued constantly over his failure to save money and his spending it all on clothes and records.

His girl friend announced she was pregnant, and Glen returned home to be with her. He and his girl friend moved in with an uncle; but the uncle, in despair over arguments, asked them to leave. The girl friend and her baby were placed in foster care and Glen returned home to live with his mother and brothers. Reenrolled in high school, he quickly was truant again and soon dropped out. He tried unsuccessfully to find a job, and at home all day, he slept and watched a lot of television.

Glen had frequently run away from home for several days following family altercations, returning of his own volition after four to five day intervals. He had been sexually active since puberty. He denied any history of homosexuality or drug use beyond some experimentation with marijuana and speed. During the course of his diagnostic contact at the clinic, he was arrested for stealing a bike. Glen stated that he took the bike because "I saw it and wanted it." He showed little upset and casually stated he's been stealing clothes and record albums for years and felt no remorse, only regret whenever caught, because he would have a police record. He spoke of another arrest, when he and friends were drinking and smoking pot in a car and were "busted" for being in a stolen car.

Glen was very difficult to engage in diagnostic and treatment sessions. He would oversleep, fail to keep appointments, or arrive very late. He appeared bored and indifferent to making any use of the therapy or the therapist. He had little to offer about worries, goals, or concerns. He spoke childishly of eventually wanting to be a millionaire. He felt forced to come to the clinic by his mother, who had recently spelled out several other ultimatums—that he either find a job, join the army, or get reenrolled in high school. If he did not do one of these things, she said, he would have to move out of the house. He could acknowledge that she was fed up with his sitting around the house all day, doing nothing or getting into one jam after another. Following these limits at home, he and his therapist seemed able to connect on a more sustained basis. Their first goal in treatment was to find a realistic remedial educational program for Glen.

At the conclusion of a protracted diagnostic study, Glen was assessed as presenting a diagnosis of antisocial personality disorder on the basis of truancy, school expulsion, delinquency, thefts, poor academic performance, chronic violation of rules of home and school, initiation of fights and arguments, running away from home overnight, and his lack of remorse over any of the foregoing. In addition, what we knew of the father—his alcoholism and emotional and physical absence—is consistent with the typical family background of antisocial personality-disordered adolescents.

Bibliography

AMERICAN PSYCHIATRIC ASSOCIATION (1980). *Quick Reference to the Diagnostic Criteria from Diagnostic and Statistical Manual of Mental Disorders, Third Edition*, pp. 173–870. Washington, D.C.: APA.

CAMERON, N. (1963). *Personality Development and Psychopathology—a Dynamic Approach.* Boston: Houghton Mifflin.

EKSTEIN, R. and FRIEDMAN, S. W. (1957). The Function of Acting Out, Play Action and Acting Out in the Psychotherapeutic Process. *J. Amer. Psychoanal. Assn.*, 5:582–629.

EYBERG, S. H. and JOHNSON, S. M. (1974). Multiple Assessment of Behavior Modification with Families: Effects of Contingency Constructing and Order of Treated Problems. *J. Consulting & Clin. Psychol.*, 42:594.

FINCH, S. M. and GREEN, J. M. (1979). Personality Disorders. In *Basic Handbook of Child Psychiatry, vol. 2: Disturbances in Development*, ed. J. Nospitz, pp. 235–48. New York: Basic Books.

GIOVACCHINI, P. (1974). The Difficult Adolescent Patient: Countertransference Problems. In *Adolescent Psychiatry, Vol. 3: Developmental and Clinical Studies*, eds. S. Feinstein and P. Giovacchini, pp. 271–88. New York: Basic Books.

GREENACRE, P. (1978). Problems of Acting Out in the Transference Relationship. In *A Developmental Approach to Problems of Acting Out.* Rev. ed., ed. E. N. Roxford. New York: International Universities Press.

JACKEL, M. M. (1963). Clients with Character Disorders. *Social Casework*, 44: 315–22.

JOHNSON, A. N. and SZUREK, S. A. (1952). The Genesis of Antisocial Acting Out in Children and Adolescents. *Psychoanal. Q.*, 21:323–43.

KOHRMAN, R.; FEINBERG, H.; GELMAN, R.; and WEISS, S. (1971). Technique of Child Analysis: Problems of Countertransference. *Internat. J. Psychoanal.*, 52:487–97.

MALONE, C. A. and BANDLER, L. S. (1967). *The Drifters.* Boston: Little, Brown.

MEEKS, J. E. (1979). Behavioral and Antisocial Disorders. In *Basic Handbook of Child Psychiatry vol. 2*, ed. J. Nospitz, pp. 482–530. New York: Basic Books.

PATTERSON, G. R. (1974). Interventions for Boys with Conduct Problems: Multiple Settings, Treatment, and Criteria. *J. Consulting & Clin. Psychol.*, 42:471.

PROCTOR, J. (1957). Countertransference Phenomena in the Treatment of Severe Character Disorders in Children and Adolescents. In *Dynamic Psychopathology in Childhood.*, eds. L. Jessner and E. Pavenstedt, pp. 293–309. New York: Grune & Stratton.

REDL, F. and WINEMAN, D. (1951). *Children Who Hate.* Glencoe, Ill.: Free Press.

REXFORD, E., ED. (1978). *A Developmental Approach to Problems of Acting Out*, rev. ed. New York: International Universities Press.

SCHWARTZ, H. (1968). Contributions to a Symposium on Acting Out. *Internat. J. Psychoanal.*, 49:179–181.

THOMAS A., CHESS, S., and BIRCH, H. G. (1968). *Temperament and Behavior Disorders in Children.* New York: New York University Press.

5

Narcissistic Personality Disorder

Definitions, Descriptions, Etiology

Currently there is considerable controversy about this disorder and the treatment approaches appropriate for it. This is reflected in the variety of labels, perspectives, and theoretical underpinnings applied to it. Patients have been referred to as having: narcissistic character, phallic-narcissistic character, narcissistic character disorder, and narcissistic personality disorder. Employing different frames of reference and models, researchers seem to describe different groups of patients as narcissistic (Rothstein, 1980).

Narcissism is a

> Concentration of psychological interest upon the self. This may range from healthy self-esteem and normal concern about oneself to pathological forms of brooding, and to such severe degrees of self-preoccupation as that of the schizophrenic who stares at his image in the mirror or fantasizes constantly about himself. Under normal circumstances, people's interests are divided between a concern for themselves (narcissism) and for the world of things and people around them (object love). Painful self-consciousness and an increased propensity for shame are the outcomes of conflict over narcissism. On the other hand, pride and pleasure in one's

own body and mind, one's achievements, and in that part of the surroundings which the individual regards as his own, such as his family, his nation, and his possessions, may be regarded as manifestations of a healthy self-esteem. Injury to one's narcissism (e.g., blows to one's self-esteem) tends to evoke severe degrees of anger, often referred to as narcissistic rage" [Moore and Fine, 1968, p. 62].

Sigmund Freud emphasized the ubiquitous nature of narcissism and its "place in the regular course of human sexual development" (1914, p. 73). He also considered narcissism from a developmental perspective as an early normal phase or stage of autoeroticism in the development of object love. From a pathologic perspective, he considered narcissistic fixations and narcissistic object choices as one of the explanations for homosexual attachments (1905 and 1914). In contrast to object love, Dr. Freud (1914) noted several forms of narcissistic love attachments. A person may love "(a) what he himself is (i.e. himself); (b) what he himself was; (c) what he himself would like to be; (d) someone who once was part of himself" (p. 90).

Andreas-Salome (1921) and W. Reich (1949) discussed character formation and the use of narcissistic protective mechanisms to protect the individual from dangers perceived in the environment and from such inner dangers as impulses pushing for expression. Reich's discussion of character disorders showed a continuum from those who are better integrated and attached to people, despite their narcissistic preoccupations with themselves, to those people, such as substance abusers, whom he considered to have regressed to the oral phase. Annie Reich (1953, 1960) discussed the narcissistic injury in men and women: females experience "narcissistic want," a sense of desertion and castration, due to narcissistic injury; and both men and women with narcissistic pathology experience disorders in their identifications, internalizations, and idealizations.

During the last fifteen or more years, we have witnessed increased incidence of narcissistic problems, research, and competing theories of etiology and treatment. The writings of Kernberg and Kohut are central in these reexaminations of definitions and theories of narcissism. Kernberg reserved the diagnosis of narcissistic personality for the group of patients whose "main problem appears to be the disturbance of their self-regard in connection with specific disturbances in their object relations, and whom we might consider almost a pure culture of pathological development of narcissism" (1970, p. 51). The characteristics he enumerates include: a facade of very adequate functioning, good impulse control, and no overtly visible seriously disturbed behavior. The narcissism is apparent in these patients' unusual degree of self-reference, their need for love and admiration, and "a curious apparent contradiction between a very inflated concept of themselves and an in-

ordinate need for tribute from others" (p. 52). Kernberg further described his patient group as possessing shallow emotional lives, a high
degree of boredom, envy, and little empathy for others. He viewed this
population as greedy, parasitic, and lacking appropriate guilt in their exploitative relationships. Behind a surface of charm, such disordered individuals are, in fact, haughty, cold, ruthless, shy, self-conscious, and
extremely self-centered. Grandiosity masks feelings of low self-esteem,
inferiority, and insecurity. Chronic uncertainty, dissatisfaction, and deficiencies in their ability to love impair their personal relationships, despite appropriate superficial social functioning. Kernberg (1974)
stressed "the pathologic nature of their internalized object relations"
(p. 215).

Kernberg (1970) utilized traditional ego psychology and object relations theory and described pathology as arising out of distorted forms of
self-love and object love.

> I propose that a process of refusion of the internalized self and object im-
> ages does occur in the narcissistic personality at a level of development at
> which ego boundaries have already become stable. At this point there is a
> fusion of ideal self, ideal object, and actual self images as a defense against
> an intolerable reality in the interpersonal realm, with a concomitant de-
> valuation and destruction of object images as well as of external objects. In
> their fantasies, these patients identify themselves with their own ideal self
> images in order to deny normal dependency on external objects and on the
> internalized representations of the external objects [p. 55].

Theories of etiology offered by Kernberg include consideration of
constitutional factors, such as a strong aggressive drive, a constitution-
ally determined lack of anxiety tolerance, and severe frustration in the
significant early years of life. "Chronically cold parental figures with
covert but intense aggression are a feature of the background of these
patients" (p. 58). The maternal object is described as callous, indifferent, given to spiteful aggressions or exploitations of the only, beautiful,
talented, or brilliant child. Such children are frequently envied, hated,
and used as a sort of narcissistic extension, which causes the child to
depend on admiration and at the same time, fear dependency, "because
to depend means to hate, envy, and expose themselves to the danger of
being exploited, mistreated and frustrated" (p. 59).

Goldberg (1980) observed that "concern has arisen in 1978 that Kohut's work embodied 'dissent' from traditional analysis" (p. 1) and concurred that, indeed, self psychology is at odds with classical psychoanalysis. While Kohut initially focused on disorders of narcissism, his
revised and expanded theory "gave us the option of considering the self
in both a broad sense and a narrow sense" (p. 3). In examining the varied conceptions of narcissism, Kohut affirmed that it is not the "target"
of the libido, that is, the self versus the object, that defines narcissism,

but rather the "nature" of the libido that determines whether it is narcissistic or otherwise (Teicholz, 1978, p. 835). Thus Kohut (1971) defined narcissism by its idealizing or self-aggrandizing nature, be it attached to the self or to an object. Per Kohut's conception, many patients with narcissistic pathology do not withdraw from the external world, and direct libido inward, onto the self via self-preoccupations, hypochondrias, and the like. Instead, they form attachments of a most desperate intensity due to their need for objects to serve the function of stabilizing a threatened sense of self due to a failure or defect in structural and functional development.

Kohut (1966) was critical of the exaltation of object love over narcissistic love and the tendency to criticize libidinal investment in the self.

> Where such a prejudice exists it is undoubtedly based on a comparison between narcissism and object love and is justified by the assertion that it is the more primitive and the less adaptive of the two forms of libido distribution. I believe, however, that these views do not stem primarily from an objective assessment either of the developmental position or of the adaptive value of narcissism, but that they are due to the improper intrusion of the altruist value system of Western civilization. Whatever the reasons for them, these value judgments exert a narrowing effect on clinical practice [pp. 243–44].

Kohut (1971) was also critical of the use of the traditional medical model for selection of a diagnosis, that is, basing it on a list of symptoms and recurring behaviors. He stated that "the crucial diagnostic criterion is based not on the evaluation of the present symptomatology or even of the life history, but on the nature of the spontaneously developing transference" (p. 23) manifest in the course of the treatment of these patients. Nevertheless, other theoreticians inferred or extracted behavioral descriptions of narcissistic patients from Kohut's writings. Akhtar and Thomson (1982) cited Kohut's accounts of his patients' complaints:

> These patients may complain of disturbances in several areas: sexually, they may report perverse fantasies or lack of interest in sex: socially, they may experience work inhibitions, difficulties in forming and maintaining relationships, or delinquent activities; and personally, they may demonstrate a lack of humor, little empathy for others' needs and feelings, pathological lying, or hypochondriacal preoccupations. These patients also display overt grandiosity in unrealistic schemes, exaggerated self-regard, demands for attention and inappropriate idealization of certain others. Reactive increase in grandiosity because of perceived injury to self-esteem may appear in increased coldness, self-consciousness, stilted speech and even hypomanic-like episodes. Profoundly angry reactions are characteristic of these individuals. . . . Kohut eloquently described this narcissistic rage, the reaction to an injury to self esteem. Its central features are the need for revenge—the inducing of hurt by whatever means—and compulsion in this pursuit, with utter disregard for reasonable limitations [p. 14].

The Kohut patient's central pathology concerns the self and its archaic narcissistic objects. Significant objects are not experienced as separate and independent from the self, yet unlike borderline patients, those Kohut considered narcissistically disordered have attained a cohesive self and have constructed cohesive idealized archaic objects. These patients, unlike borderlines, are not subject to profound or irreversible disintegration. They possess narcissistic vulnerability and resultant depletion depression and disintegration anxiety (Kohut, 1977; Tolpin, 1978). Because of their vulnerability, such patients cannot consistently regulate their self-esteem, or sustain normal levels of anxiety, excitement, and grandiosity. They are subject to embarassment, self-consciousness, or severe shame (Kohut, 1971). Ideals and values are frequently faltering, and ambition and exhibitionism generally drive such patients. Failures large and small can cause mortification, rage, envy, and self-destructive interpersonal relationships.

Kohut's view of the etiology of narcissistic disorders posited two separate lines of development: specifically, he separated narcissistic development from the development of object relations.

> The child's original narcissistic balance, the perfection of his primary narcissism is disturbed by the unavoidable shortcomings of maternal care, but the child attempts to save the original experience of perfection by assigning it on the one hand to a grandiose and exhibitionistic image of the self: the grandiose self, and, on the other hand, to an admired you, the idealized parent image" [1968, p. 86].

Under optimal conditions, there is a taming of the resultant grandiosity and exhibitionism, with subsequent appropriate integration of healthy narcissism into the adult personality. This appropriate narcissism supports the ego ideal, with resultant creativity, stable values, and life enhancing goals.

Pathology ensues if the child suffers far more than the usual unavoidable shortcomings of parental care. Severe early narcissistic traumata cause a fixation of the grandiose self. There is no taming or weaning of the grandiose self. It will not merge with relevant ego content (particularly age-appropriate adequate object relationships) but will remain in its unaltered form as it strives for the gratification and fulfillment of its early more infantile archaic aims. "And if the child experiences traumatic disappointments in the admired adult, then the idealized parent image, too, is retained in its unaltered form, is not transformed into tension-regulating psychic structure, but remains an archaic, transitional object that is required for the maintenance of narcissistic homeostasis" (p. 87). Simply, the idealized parent image continues to be maintained as a self-object. The damaged child defensively continues to idealize the parent to regain or maintain self-esteem by association with the idealized parent image.

By contrast, normally mothers and fathers mirror and respond enthusiastically and with a gleam of pleasure in their eye, until such time as the child no longer depends on maternal empathy, mirroring, and approval. Gradually the parent(s) no longer must be perceived as perfect, all-powerful, and idealized. The real and human, imperfect, but loved parent has become internalized through phase-specific nontraumatic disappointments, and this allows the normally developing child to incorporate the infantile idealizations into their own adolescent and adult ideals, values, and creative activities and emphatic relationships.

Theoretical Controversy

Kohut has been criticized for examining narcissism outside the context of the development of "structuralized derivatives of internalized object relations" (Kernberg, 1973, p. 258); for positing two separate lines of development (Giovacchini, 1976, p. 415); and for disregarding the part played by drives, especially the aggressive drive in the formation of character pathology (Kernberg, 1975; Volkan, 1976). He has also challenged traditional emphasis on the oedipal complex as the central conflict. Ornstein (1974) summarized the argument over early etiologic factors in the development of narcissistic disorders: the question is of "developmental arrest [Kohut's view] versus pathological development" [Kernberg's view]. Possibly one of the main points of disagreement between Kohut and Kernberg is that Kernberg classified narcissistic personality disorder as a subtype of borderline disorder, while Kohut distinguished between the two syndromes, and thereby posited a better prognosis and the analyzability of patients presenting narcissistic pathology.

Kohut and Kernberg—the major theorists examining narcissism—discussed patients very differently, proposed different treatment approaches, and according to Rothstein (1979), may in fact have been discussing essentially different groups of patients. Rothstein's (1980) own definition of narcissistic personality disorder focused on the "character" of the ego: such patients "are defined by their preferred mode of attempting to restore a sense of narcissistic perfection of their self-representation and by the state of integration of narcissism in the egos" (pp. 68–69). The character traits we frequently observe in these patients are their sense of entitlement, and their self-destructiveness in interpersonal relationships. *DSM-III* does list narcissistic personality disorder as a separate entity. The following criteria are noted as characteristic of the patient's long-term functioning: (1) grandiose sense of self-importance or uniqueness; (2) preoccupations with fantasies of unlimited success, power, brilliance, beauty, or ideal love; (3) exhibitionism; (4) cool indifference or marked feelings of rage, inferiority, shame, humiliation or emptiness in response to criticism, indifference of others or defeat; (5) at least two of the following characteristics in interpersonal relationships: (a) entitlement without assuming reciprocal responsibility, (b) exploitiveness, (c) oscillating relationships that shift from overidealization to devaluation, (d) lack of empathy.

Treatment Approaches

The theoretical controversy and differences between traditional psychoanalysts and self psychologists exert substantial influence on the techniques of treatment. Goldberg (1978) stated that the "most significant clinical contribution of Kohut's work has been the delineation, description and elaboration of self-object transferences. . . . Kohut has described several new transference configurations: the mirror transferences and the idealizing transferences. . . . Each of these configurations has regressive as well as progressive or stable manifestations . . . and the [treatment] of a narcissistic personality disorder may consist of movement along one or the other of these developmental axes, or it may involve shifts between the two major forms of narcissistic transference" (pp. 5–6). Goldberg stated that use and understanding of these transference phenomena enable clinicans to avoid "judgmental confrontations in which the psychopathology is reflected to the patients in the form of implicit reproaches for their childish behavior" (p. 6). Kohut's approach in treatment allows the patient to display his grandiosity and to idealize the therapist. Traditional treatment tended to focus on the past for understanding repressed sexual and aggressive wishes. Kohut did not push for resolution of earlier sexual and aggressive content, but rather emphatically listened to the past through the patient's perspective, to discover thwarted developmental needs, in which the self and self-esteem were injured or not confirmed by the parent(s). There is an acceptance of the relative paucity of object love. Treatment goals consist of a "gradual undermining of the grandiosity and exhibitionism of the patient as well as a diminution of his search for unattainable goals" (Goldberg, 1972, p. 5).

Kernberg (1970) described narcissistic patients' needs to deny any dependent relationship, and thus they "persistently devalue the treatment process, deny their own emotional life and confirm the fantasy that the analyst is not a person independent from themselves. . . . All the patient's efforts seem to go into defeating the analyst" (pp. 69–70). Kernberg recommended that the therapist continuously focus on the particular quality of the transference, confront, and "consistently counteract the patient's efforts toward omnipotent control and devaluation" (p. 70).

The handling of countertransference is to share what appears to be the intention of the patient's behavior, that is, the patient's wish to defeat and devalue the therapy and the therapist. "Breaking through" pathological character structure activated in the transference is viewed as demanding and stressful for the therapist, because during treatment

> intense paranoid developments, suspiciousness, hatred and envy, develop. Eventually, after many months and sometimes years of treatment, guilt and depression may appear in the patient; awareness of his aggression towards the analyst may [help the patient] develop guilt over it, and more human concern for the analyst as a person in combination with a heightened tolerance of guilt and depression in general [pp. 71–72].

Kernberg (1974) recommended confronting and interpreting the defensive nature of the patient's grandiosity, and idealizations of self and therapist. "Unfortunately, at times analysts treating these patients accept uncritically some aspects of the patient(s) idealization. To accept the admiration seems to be an abandonment of a neutral position in the same way as does critical over-objectivity" (p. 232). Kohut (1971, 1977) and other self psychologists have taken substantial exception to Kernberg's confrontive approach and his focuses on aggression, specifically early childhood or oral rage, as the key agent in the formation of the narcissistic personality disorder. Kohut (1971, 1977) pointed to the inevitable narcissistic injury and assault that frequently follows confrontation and interpretations, causing patients to feel robbed of competence and/or omnipotence, which they well may still need in their defensive repertoire.

The Adolescent Patient

Tylim (1978) focused on the unusual phenomena of adolescents' withdrawal of cathexis from object representations and the shift of cathexis to self representations. This is caused by instinctual strivings, the rearousal of oedipal incestuous longings, and the availability and nearness of parental objects. Therefore, narcissistic object choice predominates over attachment to object choice (Eisnitz, 1969, 1974). Given these self-preoccupations, the adolescent commonly cannot develop a libidinal self-other object relationship with the therapist. Those with narcissistic personality disorders, and adolescents in general tend to develop narcissistic transferences which appear in varied forms over the course of therapy.

The idealizing and mirror transference phenomena are valuable tools in the treatment of the teenager. "Both types of transference phenomena help the adolescent patient to fill the gap left by the loss of the old omnipotent oedipal object" (Tylim, 1978, p. 283). The therapist becomes a transitional quasi-object, a substitute ego ideal or self-object. "By allowing the patient's idealization, the idealizing transference unfolds freely. The analyst's restraint in interpreting transference phenomena and his actively fostering a realistic therapeutic bond will facilitate the process of idealization" (p. 284). The mirroring back also preserves the adolescent body image from undergoing fragmentations. Laufer (1978) stressed the crucial relationship of the adolescent to his own body: "In my own work, with ill adolescents, I assume that fantasies, feelings and conflicts involve in some way the person's body and the shame or guilt or elation or pleasure he feels in relation to it. . . ." (p. 309).

The narcissistic preoccupations and transference phenomena of the adolescent patient are not necessarily pathologic, but rather, necessary maturational phenomena in the course of normal growth and within the treatment process. Tylim (1978) cautioned regarding the appropriate handling of countertransference responses to adolescent patients' narcissistic transferences. The therapist can directly and indirectly reject the patient's idealizations, periods of admiration, and contempt by lack of understanding of his or her own unresolved narcissism and adolescent conflicts, or, undue stress on conformity and "social adjustment."

In this author's view, contemporary treatment techniques set forth by self psychologists constitute the optimal treatment approach with the adolescent patient, particularly that group suffering from disorders of the self. Teenagers are notoriously difficult to engage and sustain in therapy, and their treatment is commonly interrupted by withdrawal, rebellion, and refusal of future appointments. While Kernberg spoke about counteracting the patient's needs for omnipotent control, adolescents' therapists conversely point to the need to avoid power struggles and negative transference. The heightened narcissistic vulnerability, and underlying shame, envy, and self-consciousness often is marked by grandiosity, a disinclination to ask for help, and a depreciation of the therapist and therapeutic process. The negative transference rarely can be tolerated by the child or adolescent patient. Anna Freud (1958, 1965, 1978) discussed the teenager's inability or unwillingness to maintain a stable therapeutic alliance, tolerate frustration, and engage in introspection.

Aichhorn (1878–1951) was the pioneer in the development of efforts to apply psychoanalytic concepts to the treatment of troubled youth, some of whom today would be labeled narcissistically disordered. Esman (1983) described Aichhorn's original idiosyncratic approach to delinquent youth as "empathic" (p. 3). Aichhorn's fundamental text

Wayward Youth (1935) offered the following thoughts on transference phenomena in work with delinquent youth:

> The necessity for bringing the child into a good relationship to his mentor is of prime importance. The worker cannot leave this to chance; he must deliberately achieve it and he must face the fact that no effective work is possible without it. It is important for him to grasp the psychic situation of the dissocial child in the very first contact he makes with him, because only then can he know what attitude to adopt. There is a further difficulty in that the dissocial child takes pains to hide his real nature; he misrepresents himself and lies. This is to be taken for granted; it should not surprise or upset us. Dissocial children do not come to us of their own free will but are brought to us, very often with the threat, "You'll soon find out what's going to happen to you." . . . To the child we are only another form of punishment, an enemy against whom he must be on guard, not a source of help to him. There is a great difference between this and the psychoanalytic situation, where the patient comes voluntarily for help. To the dissocial child, we are a menace because we represent society, with which he is in conflict. He must protect himself against the terrible danger and be careful what he says in order not to give himself away. It is hard to make some of these delinquent children talk; they remain unresponsive and stubborn. One thing they all have in common: they do not tell the truth. . . . If we take a stern tone with him, he rejects us immediately and we can never get a transference established. . . . the transference must of necessity be (a) very strongly positive if one is to accomplish anything with them [Aichhorn, 1935, quoted in Esman, 1983, pp. 11, 13, 23].

Self psychology has provided us a systemization of Aichhorn's artful practice, characterized by empathy, nonconfrontation, acceptance of the paucity of object love, and a nonjudgmental comprehension of the varied and shifting transference phenomena inherent in the treatment process. Kohut and other self psychologists have focused on a population of patients historically viewed as untreatable, unreachable, and unresponsive. Adolescents have generally been viewed as constituting a sizable portion of the unresponsive and unreachable population. Effective clinical work with adolescents and patients suffering structural deficits and faulty self-esteem requires focus on the patient's ambitions, ideals, values, and humor (Murray, 1964; Kohut, 1966, 1971, 1977; Goldberg, 1972).

Case of Beverly

Beverly was a 15-year-old white Jewish upper-middle-class adolescent who requested therapy for herself, because of her shyness and tension in any and all co-ed social exchanges. Beverly was a very diminutive, attractive, and popular teenager who bemoaned being described as "cute, tiny, and adorable." With great anguish, drama, and adolescent fervor she recounted feelings of humiliation and mortification when friends affectionately joked about, or warmly commented on her tiny hands, feet, etc. She spoke derisively about her dress size, small stature and being shorter than her sister who was three years her junior. Beverly had close friends who included her in all activities. She was an outstanding athlete, excelling in tennis, swimming, and skiing. She actively participated in her school's tennis, swimming, and volleyball teams.

Beverly worked very conscientiously on her school courses and achieved a B + average. School had long been a source of frustration and difficulty due to early learning problems and some suspicion of dyslexia in the primary grades. Her ability to concentrate and persevere was impressive, but she was not satisfied with her achievements. She recognized that some peers and her sister achieved academically with far less time and effort. She was never relaxed about tests and assignments and obsessively ruminated and worried about each paper and report, articulating perfectionist standards for herself.

Just as she felt diminished by her small stature, she felt devalued by the school she attended. She viewed her school as a nonprestigious place and idealized other private schools in her city.

As she devalued herself and her school, she currently devalued her parents. By contrast, Beverly expressed relief and idealization of her therapist as someone who was perfectly attuned to her, sensitive, and all-wise and all-knowing. She "loved" her parents dutifully, but felt they had been and remained insensitive to her feelings, though they generously provided camp, tennis lessons, private school, and the like. In therapy, she shared her personal feelings about family closeness and her desire for personalized attention—such as being given her favorite foods and special presents for birthdays—which went unrecognized by both her parents. Beverly denied any closeness with either parent, and preferred to share her thoughts and her feelings with her therapist and very close friends. Over and beyond the normal adolescent separation-individuation, Beverly indeed had accurately perceived the absence of consistent parental empathy. There had been actual parental impatience with her over the years since the recognition, in first grade, of academic difficulties, which required a change of schools, tutors, and considerable extra help and attention. Beverly's academic achievement was considerable, apparently based on the early educational interventions, Beverly's unusual investment in her studies, and her high intellectual endowment.

It is assumed that relatively minor defects like Beverly's involve a psychological process similar to that which was inferred by Niederland (1965). He stated that "there often ensues from the time of recognition of any defectiveness ('recognition shock') a marked disequilibrium in the relations between mother and child. Some mothers [experience depression] often followed by renewed depression or anxiety states. Others become over-solicitous, seductive or otherwise defective in their mothering functions" (p. 533). Beverly's parents vacillated between irresponsibility, impatience, and irritation and overindulgences. The mother typed all of Beverly's papers and often went to the library to get needed reference books, but could delay and procrastinate in acquiring the needed tutor as Beverly struggled for the first time with a math course. (Geometry, and its theorems and need for abstract thinking, demanded cognitive thinking unlike what was required for arithmetic and algebra.)

Anthony (1976) suggested that one of the major difficulties that results from a deformity or abnormality is the ensuing narcissistic development in both parent and child. Whether disturbances occur first in the mother's and father's narcissistic process depends on their specific vulnerabilities. Anthony stressed the usefulness of the newer self psychology and its understanding of the part-self-object functions. The developmentally appropriate and necessary use of adults as part objects who perform some aspect of the task being mastered was emphasized, as aiding in the dawning intellectual life and cognitive mastery particularly for children with learning disability.

Bach (1975, 1977) examined what he called the "narcissistic state of consciousness" and noted defects in five critical areas: (1) perception of self, including body-self; (2) language and thought organization; (3) intentionality and volition; (4) regulation of mood; and (5) perception of time. He further pointed to subtle learning problems and memory defects. Thus, the learning process inflicts an intolerable narcissistic injury. In the primary grades, Beverly was assessed as having some measure of difficulty and defect in language and thought organization. Her mathematical skills far outweighed her composition and writing skills. Additionally, her exaggerated response to her short stature and disavowal of her extreme attractiveness was striking and suggested an actual defect in the perception of self, the body self.

Bibliography

AICHHORN, A. [1935] (1963). The Transference. In *Wayward Youth*. New York: Viking Press.

AKHTAR, S. and THOMSON, J. A. (1982). Overview: Narcissistic Personality Disorder. *Amer. J. Psychiatry*, 139, 1:12–20.

AMERICAN PSYCHIATRIC ASSOCIATION (1980). *Quick Reference to the Diagnostic Criteria from Diagnostic and Statistical Manual of Mental Disorders, Third Edition*, pp. 177–79. Washington, D.C.: APA.

ANDREAS-SALOME, L. [1921] (1962). The Dual Orientation of Narcissism. *Psychoanal. Q.*, 31:1–30.

ANTHONY, JAMES (1976). The Self and Congenital Defects: Prevention of Emotional Disabilities. Paper read at Association of Child and Adolescent Psychotherapists. Annual Meeting, Oct. 1976, Chicago, Ill.

BACH, S. (1975). Narcissism, Continuity and the Uncanny. *Internat. J. Psychoanal.*, 56:77–86.

_____ (1977). On the Narcissistic State of Consciousness. *Internat. Rev. Psychoanalysis*, 4:281–93.

EISNITZ, A. J. (1969). Narcissistic Object Choice, Self Representation. *Internat. J. Psychoanal.*, 50:15–25.

ESMAN, A. (1983). *The Psychiatric Treatment of Adolescents.* New York: International Universities Press.

FREUD, A. (1958). Adolescence. *Psychoanalytic Study of the Child,* 13:255–78. New York: International Universities Press.

———— (1965). *The Writings of Anna Freud, vol. 6: Normality and Pathology in Childhood: Assessment of Development.* New York: International Universities Press.

———— (1978). The Role of Insight in Psychoanalysis and Psychotherapy— Introduction to the Anna Freud Hampstead Center Symposium held at the Michigan Psychoanalytic Society, Nov. 1978. In *Psychoanalytic Exploration of Technique: Discourse on the Theory of Therapy,* ed. H. P. Blum. New York: International Universities Press.

FREUD, S. (1905). Three Essays on the Theory of Sexuality. *Standard Edition,* 7. London: Hogarth Press.

———— (1914). On Narcissism: An Introduction. *Standard Edition,* 14:69–102. London: Hogarth Press.

GIOVACCHINI, P. (1976). Symbiosis and Intimacy. *Internat. J. Psychoanal. Psychother.,* 5:413–36.

GOLDBERG, A. (1972). On the Incapacity to Love—A Psychotherapeutic Approach to the Problem in Adolescence. *Arch. Gen. Psychiatry,* 26(Jan.):3–7.

————, ED. (1978). *The Psychology of the Self—A Casebook.* Written with the collaboration of H. Kohut. New York: International Universities Press.

————, ED. (1980). *Advances in Self Psychology.* New York: International Universities Press.

KERNBERG, O. (1970). Factors in the Psychoanalytic Treatment of Narcissistic Personalities. *J. Amer. Psychoanal. Assn.,* 18, 1:51–55.

———— (1974). Further Contributions to the Treatment of Narcissistic Personalities. *Internat. J. Psychoanal. Assn.,* 55:215–40.

———— (1975). *Borderline Conditions and Pathological Narcissism.* New York: Jason Aronson.

KOHUT, H. (1966). Forms and Transformations of Narcissism. *J. Amer. Psychoanal. Assn.,* 14(2):243–72.

———— (1968). The Psychoanalytic Treatment of Narcissistic Personality Disorders. *Psychoanalytic Study of the Child,* 23:86–113. New York: International Universities Press.

———— (1971). *The Analysis of the Self.* New York: International Universities Press.

———— (1972). Thoughts on Narcissism and Narcissistic Rage. *Psychoanalytic Study of the Child,* 27: 360–400. New York: Quadrangle.

———— (1977). *The Restoration of the Self.* New York: International Universities Press.

LAUFER, M. (1978). The Nature of Adolescent Pathology and the Psychoanalytic Process. *Psychoanalytic Study of the Child,* 33:307–22. New Haven: Yale University Press.

MOORE, B. E. and FINE, B. O., EDS. (1968). *A Glossary of Psychoanalytic Terms and Concepts.* 2nd ed. Washington, D.C.: American Psychoanalytic Association, vol. 7, pp. 125–243.

MURRAY, J. M. (1964). Narcissism and the Ego Ideal. *J. Amer. Psychoanal. Assn.* 14:482–511.

NIEDERLAND, W. (1965). Narcissistic Ego Impairment in Patients with Early Physical Malformations. *Psychoanalytic Study of the Child,* 20:518–34. New York: International Universities Press.

ORNSTEIN, P. (1974). A Discussion of the Paper by Kernberg on "Further Contributions to the Treatment of Narcissistic Personalities. *Internat. J. Psychoanal.* 35:241–47.

REICH, A. (1953). Narcissistic Object Choice in Women, *J. Amer. Psychoanal. Assn.,* 12:477–511.

_____ (1960). Pathologic Forms of Self-Esteem Regulation. *Psychoanalytic Study of the Child,* 15:215–31. New York: International Universities Press.

REICH, W. [1933–34] (1949). *Character Analysis.* New York: Touchstone.

ROTHSTEIN, A. (1979). An Exploration of the Diagnostic Term "Narcissistic Personality Disorder." *J. Amer. Psychoanal. Assn.,* 27(4):893–912.

_____ (1980). *The Narcissistic Pursuit of Perfection.* New York: International Universities Press.

TEICHOLZ, J. G. (1978). A Selective Review of the Psychoanalytic Literature on Theoretical Conceptualizations of Narcissism. *J. Amer. Psychoanal. Assn.,* 26(4):831–61.

TOLPIN, M. (1978). Self Objects and Oedipal Objects—A Crucial Developmental Distinction. *Psychoanalytic Study of the Child,* 33:167–84. New Haven: Yale University Press.

TYLIM, I. (1978). Narcissistic Transference and Countertransference in Adolescent Treatment. *Psychoanalytic Study of the Child,* 33:279–92. New Haven: Yale University Press.

VOLKAN, V. D. (1976). *Primitive Internalized Object Relations.* New York: International Universities Press.

6

Psychoneurosis

Definition

Technically the term *psychoneurosis* refers to a distinctive, although mild, type of patterned behavioral deviation.

> In the neuroses, only a part of the personality is affected and reality is not changed qualitatively, although its value may be altered quantitatively (i.e., diminished). The neurotic [patient] acts as if reality has the same kind of meaning for him as the rest of the community. In the neuroses, language as such is never disturbed . . . and the unconscious never attains more than symbolic expression [Campbell, 1981, p. 410].

Fenichel (1945) discussed "conflict between drives, that is, the id and the ego" (p. 129). The presence of an emotional disturbance caused by internalized conflict, rather than by environmental stress and deprivation, is the key to a diagnosis of psychoneurosis. Adams (1979) stressed the presence of definite symptoms and the deviation then crystallizing around them: "The symptoms in the neuroses are usually conceived as originating in the child's efforts to cope with fear and anxiety and as continuing to express underlying inner conflict" (p. 194). Childhood and adolescent neuroses are conceived of as clusters of behaviors developed to cope with anxiety. Adolescents generally are aware of anxiety and find numerous ways to conceal the outward manifestations of fear and panic. They may engage in fight-or-flight or nervous compulsive talk or experience distorted psychomotor expression, morbid fears, tics, anxiety attacks, phobic symptoms, depression, and compulsions.

Types of Neuroses

Chronic persistent anxiety neurosis is known as generalized anxiety disorder. Episodic anxiety neurosis is known as panic disorder. The prevailing features are recurring anxiety; panic; and nervousness, fearfulness, and apprehension. Anxiety arises out of a disturbance of the internal psychological equilibrium caused by the ego's striving to control and limit drive expression. When the defenses are successful, the anxiety is contained, and symptoms and neurosis do not develop. Sometimes repression alone can restore the inner psychic balance by keeping all fantasies and affects unconscious. If the repression is not completely effective, additional defenses are marshalled, causing symptom formation, such as conversions, displacement, and regression. The drives achieve partial, though disguised, expression through the symptoms of hysteria (anxiety, hypochondriasis), phobic disorder, or obsessive-compulsive disorder. In treatment, one does not wish to assault the patient's symptoms or defenses rapidly. First, it is important to understand what is being defended against and what consequences are feared from drive expression. Kaplan and Sadock (1981) enumerated varied forms of anxiety including superego anxiety, castration anxiety, separation anxiety, and id or impulse anxiety.

The adolescent suffering from anxiety neurosis often appears skittish, tense, restless, uneasy, indecisive, and irritable. School problems may be present. "As always happens in emotional expression, there is autonomic alerting demonstrated by the following signs and symptoms: diarrhea, dilation of pupils, dizziness, dryness of mouth, fear of imminent death, nausea, palpitations, sweating and trembling" (Adams, 1979, p. 199).

Phobic neuroses or phobic disorders fall into three types—agoraphobia, social phobia, and simple phobia. Phobic responses involve irrational apprehensions and fears of specific situations, activities, or objects. The neurotic patient has a sound observing ego and recognizes the unreasonable nature of the fears (e.g., of bridges, tunnels, elevators, animals, the opposite sex, social situations). Agoraphobia is cited as the most common form, usually appearing in the late teens or early twenties. Social phobias are characteristically associated with adolescence. Simple phobias, especially of animals, are a common if transitory phenomenon during the early oedipal phases of growth and development. Dangers from inner drives and affects are unacceptable, and displacement follows. The sexual conflict originating with early parental objects may be transposed to a seemingly irrelevant object or situation. "It has been demonstrated that, in addition to castration anxiety, other forms of this affect, notably, separation anxiety, are prominent in many phobias" (Kaplan and Sadock, 1981, p. 433). "Phobic anxiety often held, Freud contended, a fear of castration or genital injury at its innermost core" (Adams, 1979, p. 201). The phobic adolescent male may be frozen, rigid, and apprehensive of any and all athletic activities, informal social gatherings, or highly specific impersonal items such as heights, elevators, or bugs.

Obsessive-compulsive neurosis refers to recurrent, persistent ideas and/or repetitive and seemingly purposeful behaviors that are performed in accord with an idiosyncratic set of inner rules or in a stereotyped fashion. The recurrent thoughts or images are often experienced as senseless and repugnant, and effort is made to avoid them. The repetitive acts are performed despite desire to resist them. Recognition of the unacceptable, senseless, and uncontrollable ideas and impulses produces distress and interferes with social and personal functioning. Defenses determine the symptoms and character traits of obsessive-compulsive patients. These patients employ isolation, undoing, and reaction-formation to ward off pre-oedipal and sadistic aggression and ambivalence. The obsessive-compulsive young patient is preoccupied with unconscious conflicts in regard to dirtiness, cleanliness, rebellion versus submission, and activity versus passivity. The consequence is "emergence of earlier modes of functioning of the ego, superego and id" (p. 440). Adams (1979, p. 205) discussed the differentiation between obsessive and compulsive symptoms and youthful schizophrenia. The symptoms can cause handicap and constriction, but as long as the adolescent is aware of the unreasonable nature of obsessive thoughts and compulsive acts, the self-observing ego is operative and there is no actual break with reality.

The neurotic young patient feels that the obsessive thought or the compulsive act must be resisted, as he or she struggles between defiance and anger, and guilt. Adolescents are particularly aware of their lack of ease and spontaneity, and what Adams (1979) calls their search for moral superiority amid faking and "hypocrisy."

Somatoform disorder is the term that has replaced hysteria. It refers to cases of recurrent and multiple somatic complaints for which medical attention is sought but no actual physical illness is found. The disorder often begins during adolescence and can have a chronic and fluctuating course throughout the life cycle. Kaplan and Sadock (1981) and *DSM-III* note the following clinical features: vague but insistent complaints about headaches, stomach aches, nausea, and abdominal pains. Often evident is a high incidence of conversion symptoms, such as loss of voice, double or blurred vision, blindness, fainting, memory loss, seizures, convulsions, trouble walking, paralysis or muscle weakness, and urinary difficulty. This disorder is more common in females than males, and frequent complaints center on menstrual difficulties and sexual indifference or discomfort during intercourse. Pain in back, joints, and extremities, and/or cardiopulmonary symptoms, such as shortness of breath, chest pains, and dizziness, are noted. *DSM-III* notes several types of somatoform disorders: somatization disorder, conversion disorder, psychogenic pain disorder, and hypochondriasis or hypochondriacal neurosis.

DSM-III places psychogenic amnesia, psychogenic fugue, and multiple personality under a final neurotic category—the *dissociative disorders* (hysterical neurosis, dissociative type). These involve a "sudden, temporary alteration in the normally integrated functions of consciousness, identity or motor behavior, so that some part of one or more of these functions is lost" (Kaplan and Sadock, 1981, p. 465). Certain dissociative disorders, like other neurotic disturbances, are rooted in unresolved oedipal and pre-oedipal disorders, dependent longings, and conflicts over drive expression. Amnesia may follow a shock or physical trauma, and fugue state may be exacerbated by heavy alcohol use. The clinical features of amnesia and the fugue state, as enumerated by *DSM-III* (1980), include: disturbance in the ability to recall important personal information; a loss of identity, associated with wandering; and often, assumption of a new identify and life pattern. Multiple personality entails the domination of the patient by one of two or more distinct personalities at any one time, each with a fine range of mental functions, often with different, frequently opposite characteristics. There is often an abrupt and sudden transition from one personality to the next, with a barrier of amnesia between one personality and the other.

Etiology

Neurosis arises out of the child's fantasies and distortions of the parental objects. The environment has not been unpredictable, nor have the parents been pathogenic agents failing to meet their child's developmental needs. The child's anxieties arise from mental distortions, rather than actual stunting crippling parental actions and rebuffs. Adams (1979) considered predisposing or hereditary conditions, such as a child's temperament, intelligence, ordinal position and gender as well as environmental factors, such as parents' modes of communicating and child rearing. Shaw (1966) emphasized the emotional tone and style of a family, including overt and covert communications, excesses of love, and overgratification. External events such as illness, economics, and sociocultural disruptions all play a part in shaping parent-child interchanges and adjustments, particularly during specific vulnerable phases. Family events have a different effect on each child in a family, depending on age, ego development, intelligence, talents, vulnerabilities, and sublimation capabilities. The family's psychological style—aggressivity and emotionality versus inhibition, repression, and strictness—influences the particular forms of childhood neuroses.

Development and Characteristics

Neuroses do not erupt suddenly in adolescence. Common childhood symptoms are sleep disturbances, eating difficulties, inversions, learning problems, compulsive fastidious behavior, perfectionist strivings, depression, aggressivity, inhibitions and irrational fearfulness, which are sufficiently significant to warrant professional help. In childhood the most common neurotic symptoms are anxiety and academic failure. Misery, suffering, and guilt are affect states which accompany the above symptoms. The diagnosis of neurosis in children and adolescents is based upon a clinician's observation of anxiety, the young patient's clear and recognizable capacity for a relationship, and acknowledgment of inner suffering. The early developmental history indicates that separation-individuation has occurred, and the child has attained self and object constancy. This entails a move out of the dyadic bond with mother and an entry into a triadic mode of relating, that is, to both parents. There has been partial or faulty resolution of the oedipal crisis, which is accompanied by castration anxiety, varied degrees of regression, and incomplete or immature superego formation. Nagera (1964) noted that attention to the phase and subphase of the regression aids in our understanding of earlier overt and covert conflicts between the child and significant environmental figures, such as the parents. These earlier conflicts evolve into intrapsychic ones as the young child internalizes parental standards, expectations, and repressed internal drives. Anna Freud (1977) also considered the importance of developmental level, rather than the array of symptoms as significant. "Manifest symptoms may be identical so far as their appearance is concerned, but may differ widely in respect to latent meaning and pathological significance" (p. 35).

Tolpin (1978) cautioned against "cases of mistaken identity," confusion between patients presenting neurosis and those manifesting disorder of structure formation. "It is imperative to distinguish between the central psychopathology of the infantile neurosis, i.e., conflicts between the structures of the personality, and, the central psychopathology which originates in faulty formation of the very structure of the personality itself" (p. 168). Child analyst Marion Tolpin (1978) was one of the first to apply self psychology to the younger patient. She drew on the work of Kohut (1971, 1972, 1977) and enumerated practice principles for clinical work with children and adolescents, distinguishing between those who suffer from classic neurotic pathology and those who suffer from narcissistic personality disorders. This latter group present "structural deficits, faulty self esteem, a missing sense of direction, inadequately formed ideals, fragmentation anxiety or depletion anxiety and depression" (p. 181). The narcissistic disordered patients often manifest a "neuroticlike superstructure" (p. 182). However, despite their similarity to the classic neurotics, they will exhibit different transferences in the treatment process. They will not displace onto the therapists affects originally directed at the parents, as the neurotic patient does; rather, they will exhibit a variety of self-object transferences, using the therapist as a "new edition of the child's prestructural selfobjects" (p. 181). Such patients suffering narcissistic injury cannot benefit from genetic reconstruction and interpretations of conflict "because these interpretations bypass and obscure the central psychopathology; and they inadvertently repeat childhood psychological injuries which lead to artifacts and regressive transferences" (ibid.).

In summary, the young patient who suffers from the classic infantile neurosis suffers from an unresolved oedipus complex; the young patient presenting uneven self-esteem suffers from deficits in the psychic structure in a beginning cohesive self. Thus, in contrast to all other disorders, neurosis represents considerable positive personality growth and is eminently amenable to treatment (A. Freud, 1968, 1971). The neurotic adolescent rarely "acts out," but rather, experiences guilt and anxiety—and considerable inner suffering.

Treatment

The optimal therapeutic intervention for neurotic patients has been classical analysis, but there is much debate about the application of this technique during the adolescent period of life. "The biological influences of drive (id) energy are so forceful and there are so many diverse behavioral possibilities, that the stability of not only psychoanalysis, but any treatment modality of the adolescent is overwhelming to consider and systematize" (Friend, 1972, p. 298).

Commonly adolescence is a period of life which presents labile and regressive potential. "Integrations of psychic and somatic components with sublimation of sexual drive are a developmental task that are never smooth" (p. 302). Mood and affect swings and disturbances of ego attention and concentration are common. Mental and emotional representations and feelings about the parents and self are changing. Moral values shift, and new friends and new ego ideals create superego disequilibrium. The clinician must assess the teenager's capacity to tolerate an uncovering, anxiety-producing mode of therapy in the midst of whatever adolescent upheaval he or she is experiencing. Bernstein and Sax (1978) emphasized intelligence and a psychological sensibility as necessary variables for the successful analysis of an adolescent. "Furthermore, a degree of frustration tolerance, impulse control and intact reality testing are necessary requirements for an analytic process. Children who are overwhelmed by the strength of their instincts should not be analyzed until it is determined that the interpretation of their defenses would not lead to overwhelming panic" (p. 98).

The analytic process requires a capacity for transference and self-other distinctions. These, in turn, are predicated on achievement of some measure of object and self constancy. The adolescent is renegotiating separation and individuation in the pursuit of a final consolidation of object constancy, self constancy and personal identity. Thus, the distinctive adolescent stages and subphases create complex forms of transference. "These developmental considerations enable us to clarify a critical distinction between the transference of neurotic adults and the transference of adolescents. Unlike the former which repeats earlier patterns of interaction, the latter stems mainly from maturational forces and phase-appropriate demands" (Tylim, 1978, p. 279–80). Tylim, citing Jacobson (1964) and Eisnitz (1969, 1974), noted that because of the danger of the immediacy of forbidden incestuous parental objects, the teenager withdraws cathexis from object representations, to cathect the self-representation. Thus, narcissistic object choice overshadows conventional self–other object choice. The transferences commonly formed by adolescents are the idealizing transference and the mirror transference. The therapist becomes a nonincestuous self-object for the teenager, offering reflection and idealization to the patient, with the goal of improving the patient's self-cohesiveness.

Friend (1972) stressed that to be treated successfully, a teenager must have the capacity for an observing ego and a course of development that indicates genital primacy. Severe parental pathology, perceptual and cognitive defects, an excessively rigid defense system, and the lack of a supportive environment all are contraindications for psychoanalysis (Sours, 1978). The importance of the parental stance was underscored by Anna Freud (1968) in her reflection on the impossibility of a successful analysis when the threat (the attacker or seducer) is a real person. In sum, psychoanalysis is indicated when the adolescent's turmoil is a product of his or her inner world, rather than a real conflict between the young patient and his or her community or parental figures.

In addition to the above clinical and diagnostic criteria, practical issues must also be noted. The amount of time (four to five sessions per week), the scarcity of teenagers agreeable to making such a commitment, and the financial expense of such treatment keep all but a very few neurotic adolescents from intensive psychotherapy. Analytically oriented individual psychotherapy, parent guidance, and family therapy are the common interventions offered in public agency practice in mental health clinics and social agencies. If the treatment setting is affiliated with an analytic training institute, where low-fee referrals can be made, psychoanalysis is more easily provided. The goals of therapy, as opposed to those of analysis, more often correspond to the adolescent's and his or her parents' goals for change. Rather than seeking structural change, the patient and family hope for here-and-now symptom reduction (i.e., decrease of anxiety, improvement of social and academic performance) and improved parent-child relationships.

Case of Julian

This case is another example using the Hampstead diagnostic procedure (Laufer, 1965).

Referral

Julian, age 16, was referred to the adolescent outpatient clinic by his mother at what she described as his request. Ms. T. was in the process of seeking help for her younger son and herself and indicated that Julian, her older son, expressed an interest in therapy and having someone of his own to talk to on an ongoing private basis. Julian was described as curious about himself and increasingly given to introspection. He had always been a voracious and precocious reader and had recently immersed himself in the writings of Freud. His previously superior academic record had fallen badly in the last year and a half, and he had become disinterested in academics and athletics, areas in which he previously excelled. He now concentrated only on music and his practicing and independent reading, unrelated to the academic demands at high school. His mother was concerned about his use of marijuana, though she had no clear knowledge about the extent of his usage. The mother emotionally shared her worries about Julian's apparently increasing depression, academic underachievement, shifts in friendships, and increased estrangement from his father. Marital discord had been severe for many years, and after efforts at securing therapy to improve family life, divorce proceedings were initiated 1½ years ago. Julian was most relieved to be offered clinic contact, and telephoned and arranged his own initial appointments.

Julian, the older of two adolescent boys, resided in an urban area, in an old spacious apartment, with his mother and brother. The family was middle class, white, and Jewish. Julian's music and his mother's immersion in art projects and political activism seem to be family preoccupations. Treatment—the mother's attempting to secure it for everyone and her periodic involvement in it—has also been a major family theme. The father is described as the sole family member who has consistently been resistive and uncooperative about entering therapy in an effort to improve family relationships. Julian's physical presentation was in keeping with his mother's account of him and their life style. Like so many adolescents his age, he was most casually attired in jeans, a jean jacket and boots. He seemed to have given little attention to grooming. His hair was quite long and disheveled. He was a lean ascetic looking boy, slight and wiry. He evidenced tension and anxiety initially. As he gradually relaxed, he discussed his concerns about himself thoughtfully, evidencing considerable intelligence, tolerance for self-examination, and psychological mindedness. He was careful and appropriate in what he initially shared, not flooding, spilling, or too quickly attaching. He showed a need to have a relationship before opening up more fully.

First Diagnostic Session with Julian

Julian was ambivalent in presenting his complaints. He described events and history but rationalized and struggled to sort out the significance of his academic decline and marijuana usage. He did not share information about his sexual behavior. He stated that through grade six he had always achieved straight A's. In seventh grade, when he changed schools, his grades were good to fair; and this was very low for him, in his opinion. In the eighth grade his grades were again straight A's. In the ninth grade, he received all C's but said that two courses were honor sections and thus two of the four C's were the equivalent of B's. In the tenth grade, the decline in grades were marked, two D's, one C and a B. Currently, in the eleventh grade, he was receiving D's in English, German, and Chemistry, C in an honors history class, and B in music.

He was scornful of school courses and teachers and felt his education was irrelevant. He was cynical and believed his low grades were ironic, in that currently he felt he was not grinding as he did when he was younger and, in fact, now was a more creative and educated person. He had taken a course in creative writing at the local Arts Center and was to have a play produced at a college nearby. He described voracious reading of Shakespeare, Herman Hesse, Freud, etc,, and much concentration on his music. He played the saxophone and was in a civic orchestra. He started to use marijuana in March. He began using it once every couple of weeks and, over the summer, increased his usage while attending music camp. He spent two weeks with his father and did not smoke then. The remainder of the summer, he used it heavily and now used it heavily and daily, always going to school stoned "cause that's the only way to endure the place." The one exception was Sunday when he never smoked, "because of orchestra practice," and visit time with his father. He did his smoking outside of school, when walking the dog, etc.

Other than the mother's encouragement of Julian's idea to obtain psychotherapy and much discussion about how he is jeopardizing college admission and his future, there had been no handling of his academic decline. His father was described as angry about his grades. His mother had listened to Julian's recent account of his first two sexual experiences and had been at a loss. She seemed to feel it was natural and inevitable that he should currently have sexual involvements. Neither Ms. T. nor Julian indicated any attention from the school regarding his steady academic decline.

His peer relationships were described as recently changed. He reported several boy friends and one girl friend, and being in search of friends like him. He had "dropped all square athletic jocks, fanatic superstars like I used to be." Julian used to be a star baseball player to please his father, who was involved with him in Little League. Now he avoided such activities scrupulously. He also avoided academic grinds and preferred friends who shared his interests in music, art, and literature. His friends wore long hair, used marijuana, and would join him in such activities as attending films, concerts, and plays at the university and going to the museum or the symphony concerts. Many also shared some of his political peace interests. They scrupulously avoided school parties, formal dates, and the athletic events at school. He reported that he and his girlfriend spent much time together, but did not tell of their recent sexual intimacy. His account of peers had an intellectual quality.

He described his major pleasure as his music and the orchestra in which he played. There seemed to be much investment here and a striving for greater proficiency. He bemoaned not being more gifted and naturally talented. Nevertheless, he was not discouraged and practiced religiously. If he missed a day, he described experiencing much anxiety and self-castigation. Reading and creative writing provided a similar focus of investment and concern.

He presented little information about, and mentioned no meaningful relationship with any adults but his parents. The teachers in public school were collectively described as pitiful, ignorant, and stifling of any individuality in the students. Grandparents were not mentioned, though the maternal grandparents were actively involved in his family.

He demonstrated overt hostility and an unconscious high degree of excitement toward his father. His conversation about him centered around his father's unreasonableness, his father's temper, and the impossibility of any discussion with him. Julian spoke of avoiding any and all possible contact, limiting time on Sundays to be as brief as possible, and preferring orchestra practice. He described putting the phone down and walking away from a tirade which could be heard over the phone across the room. He stated fear that if he avoided all contact as he would like to do, child support would be cut off completely. He spoke of rejecting all that his father stood for, including Little League, reactionary politics, and rigid rule of children. His references to mother were very much in contrast and very positive. He spoke of her as his best and closest friend with whom he could and did discuss all thoughts and concerns.

He indicated being very much the man of the family, sharing in concerns and planning for his younger brother, Glen. This was apparently the case throughout his growing up due to his father's consistent absences from the home. Except for Little League and other attempts to please his father, contact with him was meager, while it was always extensive and close with his mother. He described his happiness over the divorce and seemed uncomfortable that the divorce and prior separation of the parents marked the time of his academic deterioration. Julian spoke of resenting his father's wanting to hold on to him and Glen, and insisting on more contact since the divorce than throughout the marriage.

Julian appeared to be in conflict over his identity. His self-concept was of a young intellectual, struggling for clarity and definition of purpose and direction. He planned for college, vaguely, only because it appeared to be the only course open. He had no ideas about work or career. He spoke vaguely about getting a part-time job to earn money for music camp. "But I couldn't get a job and go to work stoned." He was very uncertain and indecisive. For example, at the museum he asked himself: "Why am I here, and do I really enjoy looking at paintings?" He is concerned about being phony and pretentious.

Second Diagnostic Session with Julian

He began by talking about his brother Glen as annoying and puzzling. He went on to complain about Glen at great length and then, rather carefully and thoughtfully, tried to examine what he might do in his brother's behalf since he was the older brother, and they should be closer. Next, he moved on to talk about another problem area for him, his father. He spoke of his relief about the divorce and his rage at the recent court custody hearing. He said his father never was around before, and he resented having to see him regularly for long intervals now. He said that fortunately his orchestra practice on Sundays enabled him to have an excuse to have only half the time tied up with father. He went into great detail about the visitation schedule and made it clear that he would only have meager contact, but for the court order and the threat of his child support being stopped. He indicated having lengthy discussions with his mother about his father, and referred to his fury and contempt for him.

After this flow of talk about others, Julian paused and waited, not able apparently to talk about himself easily. The therapist then made some reference to his mother's comments about his school performance and wondered if he viewed this as a problem. He denied that he did and initially made light of it; only slowly could he speak of it, beginning first with the "rotten system" and his disgust at the way teachers appraised students. Gradually he indicated that the decline in his performance was because his teachers were terrible and work was not relevant. He spoke of enthusiasm about writing, his concern about his possible lack of genuine talent, and how he kept at it. He then spoke of reading a great deal of authors such as Shakespeare and Herman Hesse, and his need to read for hours things he enjoyed; he also spoke of listening to classical music. Julian referred to his intense interest in music and, this year, his playing in a civic orchestra. "I must practice every day, and if I miss I get very angry at myself. I have questions about my talents and, at music camp, felt jealous of others who appeared more naturally gifted." In answer to questions about his interest in treatment now, Julian spoke of thinking it would be an enjoyable and interesting experience for him and helpful in terms of greater self-understanding. He had been reading Freud recently and found the ideas about dreams and the unconscious fascinating. Off hand, he could not think of any dreams but was aware of dreaming.

He then acknowledged that maybe his school work should be looked at, though he did not know how he felt about it and whether he cared except how it would affect college admissions; that seemed to be the thing he wanted to do after graduation. He did not know what he wanted to study there, but wanted to go as he had no better alternative. Julian went on to talk about his total change from a short-haired eager-beaver conformist. He deprecated all of his father's attitude and interests as reactionary, stupid, and empty. The father was pitied and despised for his politics and lack of knowledge of literature and music and all of the things that matter to Julian.

At the end of the session the therapist wondered if Julian had other possible concerns. Julian spoke hesitantly at the end of the interview about using marijuana. He referred to occasionally wondering why he had the need for it and, with some discomfort, admitted to having no control over using it, except on Sunday when he wished to be in good shape for orchestra practice and concerts. The therapist suspected that seeing his father on that day also, had, a more significant impact on his control than Julian was aware of.

Third Diagnostic Session with Julian

Julian began by saying he was glad he had an appointment today, because of the terrible fight he had had with his father on Sunday. They had argued on Sunday about the visitation schedule and yelled and shouted at each other, and the scene had culminated in Julian's throwing his allowance in his father's face, jumping out of the car, and racing into the house. Julian recounted the screaming exchange in much detail and revealed feeling guilty about his behavior, rage, and fear. He asked what to do about it and indicated that with his mother out of town he needed direction.

He next described in detail his refusals to admit his addiction to pot, his scorn of addicted friends, and his recent recognition that perhaps he did not have much control in stopping his use. He spoke of meager attempts to wean himself, which were to him, surprisingly unsuccessful. He wondered what the therapist thought about it. The therapist indicated that it reflected apparent inner problems, which could only be more clearly understood via therapy. Just as Julian denied the possible correlation of his poor grades and the divorce, he was also reluctant to consider any correlation between the divorce and marijuana. He implied that if a therapist told him to stop because usage interferred with treatment, he would simply have to obey and cooperate to help himself in the therapy process.

During the remainder of the interview Julian repeated his lack of respect for his father, and his pleasure about the divorce, which he saw as freeing the family. He spoke in detail about his mother and was fervent in his praise of her, and it was apparent that she was his best and closest friend. He appeared unaware of the affect of intense passion in his description of his relationship with her. There appeared to be no conscious conflict about this closeness.

The intensity about father and mother made his earlier comments about his brother and friends seem pale by comparison.

In conclusion, Julian reported often feeling lost and uncertain about himself, as when he wondered why he was at the museum? and asked "do I really like these pictures?" Julian acknowledged an increasing inability to sort out what he felt and why. This resulted in continuous ambivalence and self-questioning about himself, the nature of "reality," and how he really felt.

Developmental History

Mr. and Mrs. T. had been married for sixteen years. Mrs. T. was 19 at the time of the marriage and Mr. T was 29. There were problems early in the marriage, which worsened as Mrs. T. became more independent. Mr. T. was a travelling salesman, who was always gone all week. Mrs. T., an attractive woman, described trying to raise her sons alone. Mrs. T. had some artistic interest and abilities and actively involved herself in local art classes. In more recent years she had friends and acquaintances in varied liberal political groups as well as the art world. She stated that Mr. T. strongly opposed these friendships because of his supposed reactionary leanings. She described long-standing conflicts about this, and about discipline for the children. In the years immediately before the divorce Mr. T. was described as increasingly depressed, in bed when home on the weekends, and demanding of Mrs. T.'s attention. According to Mrs. T., these problems coincided with his increasing sexual impotence and accusations of her frigidity as well as with increased explosions and complaints about the children, their school work, and long hair, and complaints about Mrs. T. in front of the children.

Money was a chronic area of conflict. For several years Mrs. T. had been working part-time doing free lance market research (interviewing about products), which she did not especially like but continued because of the flexible hours that enabled her to be home with the children after school and at lunch. Money was still a major area of dissension and acting out. Child support payments were late. Mrs. T. acknowledged a prior immature and uninvolved attitude about family finances. She stated that she was not materialistic and never overspent but was inattentive to budgeting and planning. Mrs. T. had only one year of college and no vocational training.

Julian was not a planned baby. He was mistakenly conceived immediately after the honeymoon. At the time of marriage, the mother was a student at college. Once pregnant, she had no plans to work or to continue with school. Her own mother disapproved of the pregnancy, acting as though conception had taken place prior to the marriage. The pregnancy period was described as an unhappy time, because Mrs. T. was alone a great deal due to her husband's business travels. At the time, Mr. and Mrs. T. were living outside the city and Mrs. T. had no car. She was unhappy and mainly slept and read. She described an enormous fight before Julian was born. They were living in an unheated summer house, and Mr. T. was finicky about dinners, despite his always coming home late. Mrs. T. said she exploded, threw a can at him, and announced she would leave. He called her mother who sided with him and was reported as saying, "you rushed this marriage, so stay put. Don't come home. The wedding isn't even paid for." Physically the pregnancy was comfortable, after three initial months of morning sickness. Labor was induced eighteen days past the due date. Other than nervousness about a late baby, and tension over inducement, delivery was normal and easy. Mrs. T. moved to have her baby, staying with her parents a month, due to the overdue delivery.

No nursing was attempted. The mother was nervous because she didn't see Julian for several days, because she had a cold. The circumcision was done in the hospital, and after nine days in the hospital, mother and baby were discharged. Mrs. T. was 20 years old at Julian's birth and said she personified the young tense mother. She did handle and care for Julian and was not as frightened as at the time of her younger son's birth.

Julian was described as a good eater and sleeper. Mother said she had trouble hearing Julian at night, and her husband would awaken her to his cries. Mrs. T. said Julian sucked his thumb and never used a pacifier. He walked at eleven and twelve months and talked at about two years, at which time toilet training was started. The mother was rather vague about the above dates, and could not remember when training was accomplished.

Julian was sent to nursery school at age three½, three months after Glen was born. He shared his room with Glen and gave up his crib for a big bed. He had little contact with the new baby during the first year, as he attended morning nursery school and then he, Glen, and their mother napped in the afternoons. The mother reports that he had little overt reaction to his brother, had no separation problem, and adjusted well to nursery school. The mother said she felt she should spend more time with him than Glen.

Mrs. T. described much involvement with Julian and pleasure in his care, especially when at age four, he began to pick out letters and words. She said she and her husband were in awe at this accomplishment. Julian's father worked long hours, and the children were asleep when he returned from work. Mrs. T. described endless reheating of dinners for him over the years and rage at his apparent lack of awareness of her. "One night I did a crazy thing. I hid under the bed and he came in, didn't realize I was missing and the children seemingly were unattended." Mrs. T. said she resented her husband's unreasonableness, and when he began to travel more and be absent all week, she was relieved. She said she could never share her pleasure in the boys' development, because he acted bored with her accounts, and she assumed he resented her involvement with the children. From birth Julian became very special to her, due to the increased marital discord and the protracted business absences of the father. The father was described as sleeping or watching TV when home. Social life was meager.

Mrs. T. indicated Julian and her art classes were her greatest solace. She had taken art classes since Julian was 4½ and done much art work at home. Julian had a period of night fears at age five, at which time for eight to ten months he would wake up screaming and hysterical and would have difficulty getting back to sleep. He always complained about bad dreams about snakes. Most recently he was described as commenting on his memory of these nightmares and after reading Freud, referred to those fears as "phallic."

When Julian was about 11, the parents' disputes were more overt, and violent verbal scenes were frequent. Hitherto unrebellious, Julian now began to rebel over hair and clothes and refused to discipline himself regarding school work. Mrs. T. stated that Julian was "unrealistic and so idealistic." He was very antiauthority in terms of his views about the administration of the school, among other things and refused to apply himself to anything but the saxaphone. He refused to be prodded to produce and his mother expressed great worry for his future.

Assessment

PHASE DEVELOPMENT

Julian was struggling with a lack of final resolution of the phallic oedipal phase of development. He had achieved separation and individuation, and self and object constancy. His mode of relating was triadic. His romantic passion for his mother was evident in the material he presented and it was substantiated by the developmental history shared by his mother. It would appear that originally at age four and five he identified with his father, conforming and admiring his father's values and commitments to competitive investments in academics and athletics. During adolescence, with the rearousal of oedipal issues, he had not been able to maintain comfortably the prior identification with his father and had regressed to an earlier phase of the oedipal stage. He had demonstrated passage through puberty and into adolescence proper. He demonstrated genitality.

LIBIDO DISTRIBUTION; SELF-CATHEXIS

Libido distribution seemed primarily focused on the self and the mother. Julian was invested in his own evolving identity and search for enduring values, commitments, and intellectual interests. He was very absorbed in personal intellectual and aesthetic pursuits. He was unsure, and self-questioning and his self-esteem was uneven. He presented with the heightened narcissistic preoccupations typical of adolescence. His burning questions and views of himself and others created some measure of grandiosity, as did his deprecation and scorn of his teachers and his school in general, the community, and most significantly, his father.

CATHEXIS OF OBJECTS

He was invested in a small chosen circle of intellectual friends but, indeed, was not free in an age-adequate fashion of intense libidinal cathexis to the original love objects, his parents. He was overly involved in a second edition of the oedipal struggle. The marital discord and divorce appeared to have caused regression. Julian had abruptly detached from his prior identification with his father. He viewed him as the devalued parent and idealized his mother with passion. His recent sexual involvement may have been an effort to get some emotional distance from his mother. Research exploring adolescents' responses to parental divorce has noted that the "divorce left them feeling vulnerable to their own newly strengthened sexual and aggressive impulses. . . ." Also "contributing to the adolescents' anxiety was their divorce-related perception of their parents as sexual persons. This was often a startling discovery for them. Adolescents generally find it comforting to regard their parents as old and sexless. The relative invisibility of sex in the intact family reinforces their capacity to deny that their parents have sexual needs" (Wallderstein and Kelly, 1980, p. 83). Adolescents in divorced families commonly are shaken by having to face their parents' new partners, and Julian was unhappy about the woman his father was involved with, and silent about the man his mother was seeing.

AGGRESSION

Aggression was covertly directed outward toward school authority figures and, more overtly, toward the father. Aggression was also turned on the self in the form of depression and academic decline. Self-medication seemed to be the function of Julian's extensive use of marijuana. He appears to seek some high, defense, and relief from his anger, sadness, and fluctuating self-esteem.

EGO AND SUPEREGO DEVELOPMENT

Julian's ego apparatus seemed to be intact. There were no signs or symptoms of primary defects. There were no signs of basic deficiencies in his ego functions. He was a most intelligent adolescent with a previously superior academic record. Since his parents' divorce, his work had declined considerably. There appeared to be significant secondary interference of defenses with many of his ego functions, possibly additionally complicated by considerable use of marijuana. Defenses evident were regression, intellectualization, rationalization (e.g., of poor school performance), displacement (transfer of some of his hostile feelings from his father onto teachers), and obsessive compulsive ruminations. His defenses appeared mainly directed against the rearoused oedipal longings for his mother and aggression toward his father.

His defense organization was far from effective, resulting in anxiety, regression, breakthroughs of rage at his father, and overly romantic ongoing attachment to his mother. Symptom formation in the form of academic decline, depression, and unstable self-esteem was evident. Defenses employed were age appropriate but not effective in restraining depression, anxiety, and guilt. The ineffective defenses were directed against superego demands and infantile object ties.

Julian has a number of age-adequate achievements. He has a circle of significant friends and age-appropriate intellectual interests. Nevertheless, school work suffers, as he's reengulfed in a hostile oedipal struggle with his father and a highly sexualized relationship with his mother. He appeared guilty and conflicted about his "man of the house position," i.e., the oedipal victory created by his being preferred over his father by his mother. His mother and father had lost their parental coalition that would have helped him resolve and repress the oedipal conflicts and longings.

Points of fixation and regression were noted in Julian's behavior. The oral level was reflected in his oral aggressivity with his father and his possibly dependent use of marijuana. Anal phenomena seemed evident in Julian's failure to complete school assignments—a form of withholding—his disheveled appearance, and obsessive detailed introspection and review of life events. The phallic level was revealed in his oedipal struggles and retreat from his earlier identification with his father. Narcissistic injury and guilty feelings were evident in the deidealization of his father and shifting idealizations and devaluations of himself.

Julian's affects include guilt, anxiety, shame, depression, and cynicism. These moods were due to his rearoused oedipal attachments, his rage and sense of shame about his father, and his guilt and anxiety over winning his mother in the oedipal struggle. Julian had not moved into any close attachments or identifications with new parental substitutes. He identified significantly with his mother, like-minded peers, and intellectual pursuits, in an attempt to cope with guilt and detachment from oedipal objects. His superego development reflected a functioning conscience, a search for an ego ideal, and periodic self-criticism and self-doubt. This was compatible with his above-noted identification with his mother's value system (the arts, liberal politics, the seeking of therapy and self-understanding) and the intellectual and artistic interests of his good friends.

DEVELOPMENT OF THE TOTAL PERSONALITY

Julian's social relationships and attachment to a girl friend were age-adequate efforts to consolidate his masculine identification at a genital level. He struggled with frustration and used marijuana to deal with his heightened anxiety and regression. He was more tolerant of frustration in his artistic and musical activities—his areas of sublimation—than in approaching routine school assignments. His sense of future was rather vague; college was anticipated as the "only logical course to take," but declining grades compromised these aspirations and may well have reflected his apprehension about growing up and being expected to leave home. His sense of achievement centered around music and new intellectual passions, and Julian devalued his prior academic success as mindless "eager-beaver" compliance with his father's demands. Julian had little ability to question positive and negative feelings toward his father because of apparently severe and intense marital and divorce conflicts. Thus, reality events exacerbated problems with his father. In other areas he showed the ability to reflect, observe himself, and acknowledge some measure of difficulty. He requested therapy for himself and was articulate and in touch with varied affects, moods and feelings.

It appeared that Julian reflected gradually increasing depression and regression since his parents' marriage ended in a painful conflictual fashion. This compromised his "final farewell to childhood" and his moving on from the earlier dependent ties to his parents. Julian's conflicts appeared to be internally and externally determined. The parents divorce increased and exacerbated age-appropriate normal internal and internalized conflicts. He was in overt conflict with his father and covert, noncompliant conflict with school authorities, all of which caused guilt and conflict between ego and superego as well as unresolved ambivalence. He was not in conflict about gender identity and had selected activity in his chosen spheres of intellectual pursuit and passivity in areas of lessened current interest, specifically, school and sports. Despite Julian's sublimation potential, poorly managed anxiety and a sense of reactive despair about the dissolution of his family created regressive tendencies. Spontaneous recovery was not expected, and therapy, sought, seemed appropriate and necessary.

Diagnosis

Julian reflected behavior suggestive of considerable reactive regression, which was causing ego damage. We can hypothesize that the parental conflict created additional interference in his final separation-individuation and oedipal resolution, which was semicompromised originally, given his intense attachment to his mother and paucity of contact with his demanding "weekend" father. His regression to early oedipal, and obsessive-compulsive subphases created heightened neurotic conflict at a time of life when he should have been in a position of greater decathexis from parental figures. Instead, he was reengaged in overly intense passionate ties to his mother.

Treatment Recommendations

Treatment appeared advisable, and in fact essential, for Julian at this point in time. He requested help and was aware of his depression and faltering academic functioning. He demonstrated self-awareness, a genuine capacity for insight, and the ability to form a treatment alliance and therapeutic relationship. His mother unquestionably would support his therapy. It was anticipated that once Julian was comfortable with a clinician, he would give permission for some assessment contact with his father. During the assessment interviews, his and his mother's account of the father depicted a man who was resistive and scornful of therapy. Because of Julian's residence with his mother, his father's possible opposition and refusal to pay for treatment would not constitute a barrier, given the sliding fee schedule at the clinic. Analysis could conceivably be recommended as the optimal choice of treatment; however, given the mother's fear of this modality for herself, commuting problems, etc. it was felt that analytically oriented intensive biweekly psychotherapy would be the most realistic intervention.

The initial aims of treatment would be the establishment of a meaningful relationship with Julian to facilitate his being able to tolerate greater distance, gradual decathexis, and neutralization of his passionate bond to his mother. It was hoped that when the mother also connected in her own therapy, she would distance somewhat from her older son as "her best friend, confidant, special son," and move on to greater self-fulfillment in the areas of work and a new romantic relationship, thereby freeing Julian for the age-appropriate final separate-individuation and resolution of renewed oedipal strivings.

Bibliography

ADAMS, P. L. (1979). Psychoneurosis. *Basic Handbook of Child Psychiatry II*, ed. J. Nospitz, pp. 194–235. New York: Basic Books.

AMERICAN PSYCHIATRIC ASSOCIATION (1980). *Quick Reference to the Diagnostic*

Criteria from Diagnostic and Statistical Manual of Mental Disorders, Third Edition. Washington, D.C.: APA.

BERNSTEIN, I. and SAX, A. (1978). Indications and Contraindications for Child Analysis. In *Child Analysis and Therapy*, ed. J. Glenn, pp. 67–108. New York: Jason Aronson.

CAMPBELL, R. J. (1981). *Psychiatric Dictionary*, 5th ed. New York/Oxford: Oxford University Press.

EISNITZ (1969). Narcissistic Object Choice, Self Representation. *Internat. J. Psychoanal.*, 50:15–25.

_____ (1974). On the Metapsychology of Narcissistic Pathology. *J. Amer. Psychoanal. Assn.*, 22:279–91.

FENICHEL, O. (1945). *The Psychoanalytic Theory of Neurosis.* New York: Norton, 1972.

FREUD, A. (1968). Indications and Contraindications for Child Analysis. *Psychoanalytic Study of the Child*, 23:37–46. New York: International Universities Press.

_____ (1971). The Infantile Neurosis—Genetic and Dynamic Considerations. *Psychoanalytic Study of the Child*, 26:79–90. New York: Quadrangle.

_____ (1977). The Symptomatology of Childhood: A Preliminary Attempt at Classification. In *An Anthology of the Psychoanalytic Study of the Child— Psychoanalytic Assessment: The Diagnostic Profile*, eds. R. Eissler, A. Freud, M. Kris, and A. Solnit. New Haven/London: Yale University Press.

FRIEND, M. (1972). Psychoanalysis of Adolescents. In *Handbook of Child Psychoanalysis—Research Theory and Practice*, ed. B. Wolman. New York: Van Nostrand Reinhold Co.

JACOBSON, E. (1964). *The Self and the Object World.* New York: International Universities Press.

KAPLAN, H. I. and SADOCK, B. J. (1981). *Modern Synopsis of Psychiatry III.* 3rd ed. Baltimore/London: Williams & Wilkins.

KOHUT, H. (1971). *The Analysis of the Self.* New York: International Universities Press.

_____ (1972). Thoughts on Narcissism and Narcissistic Rage. *Psychoanalytic Study of the Child*, 27:360–400. New York: Quadrangle.

_____ (1977). *The Restoration of the Self.* New York: International Universities Press.

LAUFER, M. [1965] (1977). Assessment of Adolescent Disturbances—The Application of Anna Freud's Diagnostic Profile. In *An Anthology of the Psychoanalytic Study of the Child—Psychoanalytic Assessment: The Diagnostic Profile*, eds. R. Eissler, A. Freud, M. Kris and A. Solnit. New Haven/London: Yale University Press.

NAGERA, H. (1964). On Arrest in Development, Fixation and Regression. *Psychoanalytic Study of the Child*, 19:222–39. New York: International Universities Press.

SHAW, C. (1966). *The Psychiatric Disorders of Childhood.* New York: Appleton-Century-Crofts.

Sours, J. (1978). The Application of Child Analytic Principles to Forms of Child Psychotherapy. In *Child Analysis and Therapy*, ed. J. Glenn, pp. 615–46. New York: Jason Aronson.

Tolpin, M. (1978). Self Objects and Oedipal Objects—A Crucial Developmental Distinction. *Psychoanalytic Study of the Child*, 33:167–84. New Haven: Yale University Press.

Tylim, I. (1978). Narcissistic Transference and Countertransference in Adolescent Treatment. *Psychoanalytic Study of the Child*, 33:279–92. New Haven: Yale University Press.

Wallerstein, J. and Kelly, J. (1980). *Surviving the Breakup—How Children and Parents Cope with Divorce*. New York: Basic Books.

7

Delinquency

Few pathologies have been so extensively researched as adolescent delinquency. Opinions still conflict regarding etiology and appropriate meaningful treatment. It is important to realize that "*delinquency* is not a psychological or medical term, but a legal one, and that it refers to behaviors rather than to the person who is behaving" (Esman, 1975, p. 229). Esman (1955) reminded us of the wide range of diagnostic categories for assessed youth who manifest antisocial behavior. No consideration of antisocial youth is possible without mention of the pioneering work of August Aichhorn. Aichhorn did not psychoanalyze his delinquent patients, because they lacked the needed psychic structure for an uncovering, anxiety-inducing treatment. However, he did initiate psychoanalytic interest in the field of delinquency and utilized a psychoanalytic developmental perspective in his attempts to understand the symptomatic behavior of the children he worked with. He viewed delinquency as an outcome of early childhood deprivation, which caused a psychic imbalance, unconscious conflicts, and disharmony in the interactions of ego and superego. The symptomatic behavior was thus viewed as a defense, an attempt to help the delinquent master external reality. Aichhorn's conceptualizations drew upon traditional psychoanalytic concepts, namely, unresolved oedipal issues, conflict over incestuous wishes, failure to identity with the same-sex parent as a role model, and sibling rivalry. Aichhorn (1935) wisely noted the lethal combination of deprivation and overindulgence and described cases of delinquency caused by an "excess of love," disproportionately found in well-to-do homes, which caused "great sorrow and despair." Material overindulgence, and maternal overgratification due to paternal absence was (and remains) common in such situations. In addition to intrapsychic conflict, Aichhorn emphasized the impact of social disorganization as stimulating delinquency. He developed nonpunitive therapeutic programs for the children in his care.

Winnicott (1973), like Aichhorn, linked antisocial behavior with deprivation. "When a deprivation occurs in terms of a breakup of the home, especially an estrangement between the parents, a very severe thing happens in the child's mental organization. Suddenly his aggressive ideas and impulses become unsafe" (Winnicott, 1973, p. 367). He suggested that the antisocial acts are unconscious expressions of a hope to be able to engage "someone who will listen back to the moment of deprivation, or to the phase in which deprivation became consolidated into an inescapable reality. The hope is that the boy or girl will be able to re-experience in relation to the person who is acting as psychotherapist, the intense suffering that followed immediately the reaction to deprivation" (p. 370). Suffering was described as "acute confusion, disintegration of the personality, falling forever" (p. 370). This view is comparable to Aichhorn's emphasis on deficiencies of the ego ideal, due to a weak or nonexistent parental identification, thus narcissistic trauma, and attempts to control the other and the world, and to search for the mother over whom he or she has rights (Winnicott, 1956).

To understand delinquency, violence and aggression have been extensively studied, and competing theories have been offered. Biologically oriented clinicians view man as a born aggressor, who must be trained and tamed. Others reject this conception of inborn aggression and view it instead as "learned behavior, and the component we can ascribe to biology is the capacity to respond in an aggressive or violent fashion" (Kalogerakis, 1974, p 323). We have been taught that love conquers hate, in that by displacement, neutralization, sublimation, or fusing the aggressive drive with libido (Hartmann, Kris, and Lowenstein, 1949), aggression is tamed. Kalogerakis (1974) took issue with the concept of aggression as innate and thus normal and not to be curbed or contained.

Currently considerable research is underway to attempt to establish what areas of the brain control aggressive and violent behavior.

> To date, the most clearly implicated area is the limbic system of the brain, particularly the amygdala. Genetic issues have received much attention—since reported chromosomal abnormalities have been found in mentally

retarded male patents in England who had been institutionalized as dangerous, violent or criminal. Hormonal factors . . . have thus far not been conclusively linked to human aggression. The percentage of violent individuals whose destructive impulses arise from biological sources is unknown but is probably quite small. The histories of individuals with organic impairment are often filled with a multiplicity of psychosocial forces that have contributed to an anti-social, aggressive life style; sorting out the respective influences is difficult but essential for a differential diagnosis [p. 327].

Lewis, Shano, and Balla (1979) studied a group of nonincarcerated delinquent children and found more serious medical histories than in a matched group of their nondelinquent peers. The delinquent group evidenced more accidents, illnesses, and head injuries than the nondeliquent group. This outcome of child abuse, with trauma to the central nervous system, and resultant brain damage, combined with social deprivation and parental psychopathology, creates the volatile delinquent, who can inflict, or experience, a violent death.

In considering a psychosocial explanation of violence, it is critical to distinguish between aggressive impulses and weakened defenses that cannot inhibit their expression. The classic environmental statement assumes aggressive acts arise out of frustration. Later researchers incorporated the idea that cultural beliefs and norms of behavior determine whether or not aggression will be exhibited in response to frustration. Others cite imitation as a critical variable shaping expressions of aggression (Bandura and Walters, 1959, 1963). Being attacked will stimulate aggressive retaliation, and case histories of violent offenders are replete with violent and aggressive attacks on them throughout their childhoods. Similarly, most child-abusing parents were abused in their childhoods. We therefore speculate that imitation and identification with the aggressor cause aggressivity. Social forces are cited as spawning violence, and a number of studies (Yablonsky, 1963; Wolfgang and Ferracuti, 1967) mention subcultures of violence. Impaired ego functioning and an inadequate defense system leave the individual unable to exert appropriate controls over rage and aggressive impulses.

In recent years, with the reduction in large-scale formal gang organizations, we see and hear a lot about isolated random individual acts of violence by panic-stricken, traumatized adolescents. Marohn (1974) noted that such outbursts look like transient psychotic bouts, but he viewed them as "traumatic states characterized by an inability to control overwhelming impulses, leading to a state of helpless vulnerability." Certain youths, often borderline adolescents, evidence severe ego deficits—poor judgment, poor reality testing, impaired impulse control—and they are therefore repeatedly overwhelmed. For the same reason, violent outbursts can occur in individuals suffering from psychosis, mental retardation, or an organic or neurologic disease.

A. Freud (1967) defined trauma, as a shattering, devastating event or series of events which causes internal disruption by putting ego functioning and ego mediation out of action. Greenacre (1967) noted childrens' fragmentation under the impact of traumatic stimulation, which is reflected in behavior that is disorganized, frenzied, hyperactive, aimless, replete with tantrums, rage attacks, and diffuse irretractability. The early psychoanalytic ego psychologists such as Bowlby (1951) and Spitz (1965) pointed to the critical and vulnerable first two years of life. The mothering provided then is basic in installing the capacity to love and later provides the child protection against expression of rage and aggression. We see explosiveness accompanying the emotional isolation of remote schizoid individuals. Substance abuse, notably of alcohol and amphetamines, diminish self controls, and affect the abuser's judgment and sense of reality, and are frequently unquestionable causes of violence.

Sociocultural factors must be included in examination of acts of violence. "The decrease in the overall national death rate, accompanied by the increase in the death rate among youths, suggests the existence of signficiant socio-cultural determinants within their acts of violence. . . . [There is] a significant difference between white and nonwhite youth" (Nichtern, 1982, p. 141). Nichtern (1982) observed that between 1971 and 1975, the Vietnam War period, aggression became a "way of life for an entire generation. . . . It was the first major war that was fought within our homes as a television war. . . . Such exposure to violence on a repeatedly daily basis during the early stages of development cannot be dismissed as an innocent process but may have served as a preconditioning system to a developmental state characterized by its own aggression" (Nichtern, 1982, pp. 141–142).

For some delinquents their deaths are intimately intertwined with their own psychopathy (Marohn et al., 1982). For others, violence and aggression "should be recognized—as the result of the blending of sociocultural forces with the essence of adolescence. . . . If we are to look at adolescents' behavior as the focal point of violence, we do them and ourselves an injustice. For they are us. They are our prototype. They mirror all that we are, and all that we created in our society and culture" (Nichtern, 1982, p. 143). The Vietnam War, the nuclear threat, the easy availability of weapons, the high unemployment rate, and the presence of uncared for street people, all impair any self-sustaining psychological environment for adolescents, already vulnerable due to personal and familial vissicitudes. Additional major variables noted were social changes within the family, mobility and dislocation of ties, working mothers, and child care assumed by multiple surrogates, the increased divorce rate, and out of wedlock births; all have contributed greatly to the mounting social instability of the family and thereby the increased incidence of violence and acting out among adolescents. As would be anticipated, the most extreme forms of violence are seen in adolescents who suffered an early loss of object relatedness. "[Their] aggressive and violent acts appear to be irrational and have elements of depersonalization and dehumanization along with complete loss of control over impulses. Often the thought processes are unrelated to acts of aggression" (p. 143).

In attempting to examine the causative factors that adequately explain delinquency and aggressivity, we are stuck with no consistent set of variables. Kalogerakis (1974) is adamant in stating that there is no one particular family pattern or child-rearing practice that fosters delinquency.

> Many combinations can produce the same result. Many violent individuals have emerged from fatherless situations, but equally as many are from so-called intact homes. Some are only children, while others have several siblings and may occasionally represent the only member of the sibship to have fallen into violent ways. Ordinal position is generally not significant. To find any pattern one must examine the personalities of the parents, the roles of individual family members and the specific messages transmitted to the future aggressor [Kalogerakis, 1974, p. 33].

He observed from his work with aggressive and delinquent adolescents that there is always another violent member in the family. While it is usually a parent, it can be an older sib or significant relative. Anxiety levels are generally high in such homes and the common finding is the existence of violent feelings.

A number of the earliest studies of antisocial acting out focused on the weak or defective superegos in the delinquent youth. Johnson and her associates working with pairs of children and parents, discovered unconscious messages and sanctions through which parents promote antisocial behavior. In order to gratify their own repressed impulses, they give their children "covert" subtle permission to act out. Nonverbal cues and skewed messages all coalesce to produce what Johnson called lacunae in the superegos of the delinquent children, who appeared normal, appropriate, and law-abiding in specific areas of day-to-day living. We find the following phenomena, in varying combination and degrees, in the backgrounds of aggressive and delinquent youth:

1. Parental rejection
2. Family discord—intense conflict between parents
3. Punitive discipline
4. Inconsistency concerning discipline
5. Parental permissiveness of aggression
6. Maternal lack of self-esteem
7. Frequent parental threats
8. Lack of parental control
9. Parental deviance [Kalogerakis, 1974, pp. 332–33]

Violence among the parent figures of aggressive adolescents, willful deprivation, arbitrariness or lack of fairness in applying discipline "correlates very high with aggressive responses and, in the absence of outright brutality, is the most important single factor in creating destructive rivalry and hostility to authority" (p. 333). Kalogerakis (1974) points out that when a child's normal expression of anger is interfered with, aggression and violence are the inevitable outcome. By the time of adolescence, vulnerability, low self-esteem, and powerlessness can combine to produce a violence-prone person and the right provocation can lead to a significant explosion.

Self-destructive impulses, a wish to kill and be killed, can be interwoven. Menninger (1935) stated that suicide is a "death in which are combined in one person, the murderer and the murdered." Just as suicide can be an example of murder, murder can be a form of suicide, when the victim represents the murderer in the latter's unconscious. Freud (1901) and Menninger (1935) also considered fatal accidents as atypical forms of suicide. Litman (1967) suggested that more emphasis on helplessness, dependency, and libidinal issues was appropriate in considering suicide. Other authors have linked adolescent suicidal behaviors to disturbance in oedipal development, causing deficits in sexual identity and superego formation. (Shrut, 1968; Margolin and Teicher, 1968) More recent research views the role of hostility toward the child as equally important in adolescent suicide as the teenager's turning aggression upon the self (Rosenbaum and Richman, 1970; Eisen, 1976).

Marohn et al. (1982) pointed to desperate struggles against rage and despair on the part of violent juvenile delinquents. The young people studied evidenced "deficiencies in cognitive controls, leading to difficulties in responding to affective stimuli in a reflective norm. Impulsivity, poor interpersonal relationships and depressed affect were found. None demonstrated signs of psychosis" (Marohn, et al., 1982, pp. 165–66). Narcissistic imbalance (Marohn, 1977) and grandiosity characterize adolescent delinquents. Often, deidealization of archaic parental images is accompanied by disruptive behaviors, narcissistic rage, and irrational violence as the adolescent attempts to overcome feelings of self-fragmentation and emptiness. "What appears to be violent behavior is in reality a massive discharge phenomenon, the result of an ego overwhelmed by internal stimulation" (p. 209).

Adolescent Gangs

Any consideration of adolescent delinquency must include discussion of gangs and their social and psychological dynamics. Copeland (1974) suggested that gangs are appropriately examined in the context of societal interaction but also as a phenomenon of adolescent psychology. A gang is a company of persons acting together for some purpose, usually of a criminal or antisocial sort. This gathering can have positive and negative influences, in that groups and role models for identification are part and parcel of the adolescent search for identity. Too frequently gangs will distort "ego skills necessary for adaptation to the mainstream of society. Negligible education, absence of social skills and minimum preparation for a life work are common problems on egress from the gang (p. 341). When gangs stake out their territory, a neighborhood is composed of members as well as prisoners, forcing cooperation, tacit submission, compliance, and at times, even nonvoluntary enlistment, of other youth. Street corners, abandoned buildings, and bowling alleys are common sites selected by urban gangs for their headquarters. Playgrounds and surrounding blocks often constitute the turf of a given gang. Gangs usually have a rigid social structure of bosses, leaders, and followers. The system emphasizes power and recruitment and control of members. Defection, rebellion, cowardice, or betrayal to the police or another gang are generally viewed as serious crimes or dangerous infractions, dealt with by "court systems" in the gang structure. Girls may gravitate to and hang onto boys' gangs, though more recently, they form their own parallel groups. In both groups, antisocial acts, coercive measures, and motor activity "rather than cognitive function is the style of this social interaction" (p. 344). Nicknames that are descriptive of physical traits of roles in the gang are common (Thrasher and Short, 1962).

Liquor, drugs, and weapons are common armentarium in gangs. "It has been observed by some youth workers that the greater a gang's tendency to use drugs, the decreasingly violent it becomes" (p. 345). Hand guns and knives are common weapons used against rival gangs and for acts of violence, assault, and robbery to generate monies for the coffers of the gang. Intended and unintended violent acts are common, within and without the gang structure. Gangs commonly fill their neighborhoods with a sense of helplessness, and commonly, fear for the younger children who will be forcibly recruited. Often an urban black or hispanic ghetto may identify with the gang's rebellion against the majority white society.

> Racial integration of gangs is almost unknown, although an occasional white may be found associated with a black gang. Racism per se does not appear to be a conscious vital theme for black gangs, and conflict with white gangs seems to be more a function of the ethnic clash noted in transitional communities than a reflection of well-formed anti-white philosophy. This is consistent with evidence that these teenage gangs are relatively naive ideologically [Copeland, 1974, p. 347].

Specific findings have been offered to attempt to describe the youthful members of violent gangs. Reid (1971) observed that the families of such adolescents are "often devitalized and fatherless, and rarely generative of feelngs of security or esteem. Parents of gang members were frequently gang participants in their own adolescence, and mothers of members, incapable of diverting their sons, often appear to deny the significance and magnitude of the sons' violence.

Gang members frequently go to jail for major crimes, following repeated attempts at outpatient treatment, parole, diversion programs, and placement in adolescent correctional facilities. Such youth generally have had protracted academic problems, no success in athletics, and chronic familial conflict. Conflict with teachers, police, and parole officers is commonplace. The lack of positive meaningful contact with adults strengthens the gang's insular nature, and its primitive, impulsive, and self-destructive behavior patterns. Rarely can gangs be broken up by outside forces. The 1950s and 60s were characterized by outreach interventive approaches. Youth workers attempted to gain the gang's trust and acceptance, in order to then rechannel members into more constructive pursuits. In recent years, groups like the Black Panthers attempted to assume a position of leadership vis-à-vis violent adolescent gangs to emphasize black unity, ethnic pride, the destructiveness of drug use, and the folly of blacks fighting blacks.

Media reports indicate that large-scale black violent gang warfare has diminished. We currently hear somewhat more about Hispanic and Chinese gangs. In the 1970s, the violent gang was viewed as an aberrant form of adolescent development. From a sociological perspective Cloward and Ohlin (1960) pointed out that violence is characteristic of urban minority youths' adolescent development and is an integral portion of the youth subculture. Additionally, gangs and violence have been viewed as genuinely adaptive behavior in the frightening ghetto. The presence of, and general acceptance of, violence, depicted on televison and film routinely in the larger culture and ghetto subculture has played a significant part in continuation of the aggressivity of the gang.

Older adolescent and adult manifestations of youth gangs can be seen in a social affiliations in urban areas, and in prisons. Some members never "outgrow" or leave the gang, move away, or settle down and marry. Older members can continue gang affiliations while serving jail terms, during which time they struggle for continued outside connections and for control of prisons, with similarly incarcerated followers. Others on the outside "graduate" into positions of power in organized crime syndicates that focus on the numbers racket, drug traffic, prostitution, and the like.

All adolescents struggle with self-fragmentation, self-definition, idealization of others, deidealization of parents, fear of merger, intimacy and abandonment. Delinquents struggle with these issues and with varying pathologies: depression, impulsivity, psychosis, and borderline states. Frequently they defy parents, admire antisocial values, and experience serious difficulties with self-esteem, ambition, object relations, and control of rage in the face of frustration. Clinicians and researchers were, and are, optimistic, nevertheless. Winnicott viewed antisocial behavior as a sign of hope; likewise Marohn stated that the "juvenile imposter's presentation may be blatant grandiosity or naive idealization but it is the delinquent's best prognostic sign" (p. 210). The delinquent's refusal to simply give up leaves room for clinical intervention and improvement.

Case of Philip

Philip, age 16, was referred to the mental health clinic by his mother, on the advice of her own therapist. She had been in treatment for close to a year, since her husband's death, because she felt depressed, overwhelmed, and confused. The mother was a very attractive youthful Puerto Rican who did not look enough to have a 16-year-old son, and three younger children, ages 13, 12, and 9. The mother listed many complaints and concerns about Philip, who she thought had gotten worse than ever since his dad's death. She recognized the impact of the loss of his father and her young lover's recent part-time residence in the home as possibly contributing to Philip's increased rebelliousness. However, he had, historically, been erratic in school attendance, defiant, and involved with peers who caused trouble in the community. Currently she was very worried about his activities and actual safety and could not in any way reason with, or control, him.

Philip was a tall, healthy, well-built boy, sloppy in his attire, with shirt half out of his pants, scuffed boots, and longish hair. His eyes had a somewhat glazed look. He would unzip his motorcycle jacket, but would not remove it, always poised for flight, and never appearing relaxed or completely involved in his sessions. In a matter-of-fact style, he acknowledged not going to school very often, preferring to hang out with his friends. He avoided school because he thought it was boring, and

> I just don't want to go. When I cut class I go across the street. There's a park there. I meet a bunch of the guys and we drink some and play basketball. The school sends a note home when the cuts mount up. Mom used to get mad at me, but now she doesn't. I guess she's given up trying. So we don't scream and fight about it anymore.

In the course of four diagnostic sessions, Philip was open and revealing about the full extent of his delinquent activities. He matter-of-factly described how he and his friends would grab other kids who angered them and slap them around, not really hurting them but scaring them. Philip and his buddies drank, smoked and hung out doing "the same old stuff," talking a lot about cars and what they did with them.

> You see, Gary has got a master key to Fords, Pontiacs, and Chryslers. So we just get into a car and go driving. We don't have to struggle to hot wire them because of the key. We go all over town looking for excitement. Sometimes we go to this place called Beer Can Beach and do fish tails, doughnuts, and race. Do you

know what a doughnut is? It's running the car in circles, and a fish tail is getting it to stand almost on end. We get three guys in front and four in the back, and one guy stands outside and watches. Sometimes we race a lot—speed, chase after cars—and sometimes we go to states nearby to get more cars. We get one for almost each guy. It takes the police about a week before they look for them in this city. It's smarter this way. We've gotten two Cadillacs and a Buick and a Ford that way. I got into an accident yesterday. I was doing a doughnut and I was going too fast. I just missed an oncoming car and I slammed into a parked car. It's a good thing I'd been practicing doughnuts at the beach, or it would have been a lot worse.

Session after session Philip spilled to his therapist, nonstop, describing how he continually sought excitement. Much of the excitement came from the cat-and-mouse game with the police, trying to outwit the police, realizing when the police seemed to be getting onto them—which curtailed car thefts for intervals of a couple of days or weeks. During these quieter periods Philip would hang out at home and sleep a lot. His mother was worn out from yelling at him and said little to him. He said her yelling was at its worst after his father died.

After Dad died, she didn't take care of my brothers and sister. She didn't discipline them, so I did—even if I had to hit them around. I would have to tell them when to come in and other things. She'd do nothing but be angry at how I'd taken charge. We would fight all the time.

Philip's father apparently was a heavy drinker and had an accident at work and ended up in a wheelchair. He was around the house a lot. He handn't been home much before his accident, generally frequenting local bars. After he recuperated some, he started to wheel himself in his wheelchair to the corner bar, or he would get a friend to take him out of the apartment. Philip's mother, in an effort to control these trips to the bar, moved the family upstairs with grandparents hoping that her husband couldn't get downstairs and out so easily. Philip related that nothing seemed to interfere with his dad's determination to get to a bar.

After a while, he would just slide down the stairs and get down to the bar somehow, getting a friend to come over and carry him down the block. He was often sick, with breathing problems from cigarettes, I guess. The day he died he had been to the bar. He started having trouble breathing and started to turn blue. He really looked bad so I told my mom and she got an ambulance to take him to the hospital. He died there that very day.

Philip denied that his dad's death had been a shock, because he'd been prepared for it for a while because of the breathing difficulty. However, later, he found the finality hard to accept and believe.

I kept expecting him to come back, like from a vacation. All of us felt that way. My mom and I would talk about him all night. Nobody hardly slept for weeks. Finally, my brothers and sister started to sleep and then my mother. I was the last. In all of our minds, it was always as though he could come home.

Subsequently, Philip often spoke of his father and repeated the above events, demonstrating rage and disappointment in his dad and some guilt in feeling that way now that he was dead. He related recurrent battles and conflicts with his mother as well as schemes to curtail stealing cars; he and his friends wanted to work on and soup up cars, and if they kept a stolen car for a protracted period, they might get caught. To date, they stole, used, raced, and then abandoned all the autos they confiscated. The decision to stop stealing autos was based on the following plan:

> We're going to pool our money together and buy a car we can share and fix up. We have this money from when we went out of state and stole a lot of furniture. We'll go back to that same store for more furniture—if we need more money for our car. But we want to lie low—at least in relation to car stealing. Two of my friends got caught and will probably do time. They have lots of curfew violations—since they're on probation and ignore all the rules.

Philip slowly began to recognize that he and all his friends could easily land in jail for a long time. He was amazed that he was discussing this issue with his therapist—since he and his friends refuse to think about, or talk about, the possible consequences of their criminal activities.

During his therapist's brief vacation, he was arrested for stealing a car after the following sequence of events: After a fight with his mother, she threw him out of the house telling him not to come back. He joined his buddies and they took off for nine days in a stolen car. They brought attention to themselves when they ran through a red light and then were chased by the cops.

> We tried to outrun them. I guess I like being chased. It's a game—trying to outsmart the police to see who is better. You have to think fast and know all the streets and where you're going. It's a thrill. Things are so boring most of the time. I like the chase—and getting away. I've been shot at several times. That's why my mother yells at me. She thinks I'm crazy and will get shot, hurt, or killed. In the chase Benny raced and turned corners on two wheels, and because it was icy we slid into a fence. We jumped out then and tried to run. The other guys got away. They had good running shoes, sneakers, and my boots were ragged and I was slowed down. A cop tackled me, and they took me to jail. My mother came down and got me out. She wasn't mad. I guess she missed me after nine days.

Philip's therapist listened to him ponder in a disbelieving way the idea that he could get shot and killed. He described imagining a bullet going into his back while being chased by a cop. He half heard the therapist voice her concerns, the futility of lectures, and possibly talking things out if he could not control his actions. Discussion with the appointed probation officer revealed shared concerns on the part of the court and therapist. As the rules of probation were spelled out, e.g., 6:00 P.M. curfew, both conceded the apparent impossibility of Philip's complying or cooperating. Philip's mother had shared his extensive soft drug history at the hearing. Parent and concerned professionals concurred on his depression, thrill-seeking to avoid the depression, and his apparent repetition of his deceased father's self-destructiveness. Philip quickly informed his therapist that he hadn't conformed to the stipulations of probation—being home by 6:00 P.M. and reenrolling in school, or finding regular employment—for half a moment. In fact, he had taken off from home for two days following being put on formal probation. Philip sneered at his mother's and her brother's attempt to boss him around. He related getting so angry at his mother that he felt like hitting her and knocking her down: "The reason I don't is because I respect her—even love her, I guess. Anyone else . . . and I'd slug them silly."

Philip's dangerous and self-injurious behavior demonstrated his inability to utilize outpatient therapy, even when it was buttressed by the structure and efforts of control and consequences inherent in the juvenile court probation system. Almost with relief, he accepted the collaborative planning and arrangements made by his probation officer, mother, and therapist, for psychiatric hospitalization financed and supported by the local juvenile court. After threats to run away, he cooperated with his admission to an adolescent long-term inpatient unit. This safe containment afforded him, his family, and the involved professionals a respite in which to see whether he could utilize treatment and internalize the existant external controls, so that he would be able to return home, attend school, and maintain distance from his delinquent former peers. Treatment was to focus on his depression, which was currently being warded off by his maniclike, dangerous delinquent behavior. Should this adolescent need protracted care and limits, beyond what is available at home and school, following hospitalization, he would be placed in a group home or residential treatment facility (see Chapter 22).

Bibliography

AICHHORN, A. [1935] (1955). *Wayward Youth.* New York: Meridian.

_____ (1964). *Delinquency and Child Guidance—Selected Papers.* New York: International Universities Press.

BANDURA, A. and WALTERS, R. H. (1959). *Adolescent Aggression.* New York. Ronald.

_____ (1963). *Social Learning and Personality Development.* New York: Holt, Rinehart and Winston.

BOWLBY, J. (1951). Maternal Care and Mental Health. Monograph Series No. 2. Geneva: World Health Organization.

CLOWARD, R. and OHLIN, L. (1960). *Delinquency and Opportunity.* New York: Free Press.

COPELAND, A. (1974). Violent Black Gangs: Psycho and Sociodynamics. In *Adolescent Psychiatry, Vol. 3: Developmental and Clinical Studies,* eds. S. Feinstein and P. Giovacchini, pp. 340–52.

EISEN, P. (1972). The Infantile Roots of Adolescent Violence. *Amer. J. Psychoanal.,* 36(3):211–18.

ESMAN, A., ED. (1975). *The Psychology of Adolescence—Essential Readings.* New York: International Universities Press.

_____ (1975). Diagnostic Categories of "Delinquency." *J. Amer. Probation & Patrol Assn.*

FREUD, A. (1967). Comments on Trauma. In *Psychic Trauma*, ed. S. S. Furst, pp. 235–45. New York: Basic Books.

FREUD, S. (1901). The Psychopathology of Everyday Life. *Standard Edition*, 6:1–279. London: Hogarth, 1960.

GREENACRE, P. (1967). The Influence of Infantile Trauma on Genetic Patterns. In *Psychic Trauma*, ed. S. S. Furst, pp. 108–153. New York: Basic Books.

HARTMANN, H.; KRIS, E.; and LOWENSTEIN, R. H. (1949). Notes on the Theory of Aggression. *Psychoanalytic Study of th Child*, 3, 4. New York: International University Press.

JOHNSON, A. (1949). *Searchlights on Delinquency*, ed. K. R. Eisler. New York: International Universities Press.

KALOGERAKIS, M. (1974). The Sources of Individual Violence. In *Adolescent Psychiatry, Vol. 3*, pp. 323–39. See Copeland (1974).

LEWIS, D. O.; SHANO, K. S.; and BALLA, D. (1979). Perinatal Difficulties, Head and Face Trauma and Child Abuse in the Medical Histories of Serious Youthful Offenders. *Amer. J. Psychiatry*, 135:419–23.

MARGOLIN, N. L. and TEICHER, J. D. (1963). Thirteen Adolescent Male Suicide Attempts: Dynamic Consideration. *J. Amer. Acad. Child Psychiatry*, 7:296–315.

MAROHN, R. (1974). Trauma and the Delinquent. In *Adolescent Psychiatry, Vol. 3*, pp. 354–61. See Copeland (1974).

_____ (1977). The "Juvenile Imposter": Some Thoughts on Narcissism and the Delinquent. In *Adolescent Psychiatry, Vol. 5: Developmental and Clinical Studies*, eds. S. Feinstein and P. Giovacchini, pp. 186–212. New York: Jason Aronson.

MAROHN, R.; LOCKE, E.; ROSENTHAL, R.; and CURTIS, G. (1982). Juvenile Delinquents and Violent Deaths. In *Adolescent Psychiatry, Vol. 10: Developmental and Clinical Studies*, eds. S. Feinstein, J. Looney, A. Schwartzberg, and A. Sorosky, pp. 147–70.

MENNINGER, C. (1935). Purposive Accidents as an Expression of Self-Destructive Tendencies. *Internat. J. Psychoanal.*, 17:6–16.

NICHTERN, S. (1982). The Sociocultural and Psychodynamic Aspects of the Acting Out and Violent Adolescent. In *Adolescent Psychiatry, Vol. 10*, pp. 140–46. See Marohn et al. (1982).

REID, L. (1971). Youth worker, Department of Public Welfare, City of Philadelphia, personal communication.

ROSENBAUM, M. and RICHMAN, J. (1970). Suicide: The Role of Hostility and Death Wishes from the Family and Significant Others. *Amer. J. Psychiatry*, 126:1652–55.

SHRUT, A. (1968). Some Typical Patterns in the Behavior and Background of Adolescent Girls Who Attempt Suicide. *Amer. J. Psychiatry*, 125(1):69–74.

SPITZ, R. (1965). *The First Year of Life: A Psychoanalytic Study of Normal and Deviant Development of Object Relations*. New York: International Universities Press.

THRASHER, F. and SHORT, J. (1962). *The Gang.* Chicago: University of Chicago Press.

WINNICOTT, D. W. (1973). Delinquency as a Sign of Hope. In *Adolescent Psychiatry, Vol. 2: Developmental and Clinical Studies,* eds. S. Feinstein and P. Giovacchini, pp. 364–71. New York: Basic Books.

_____ (1956). The Antisocial Tendency. In Collected Papers. New York: Basic Books, 1958.

WOLFGANG, M. E. and FERRACUTI, R. (1967). *The Subculture of Violence.* London: Louistack.

YABLONSKY, L. (1963). *The Violent Gang.* New York: Macmillan.

8

Academic and Vocational Underachievement

Work has always had a great deal to do with how people identify themselves and are identified by others. Study and academic achievement are the "work" activity of children and adolescents and, similarly, afford status, mastery, or a sense of failure. Both work and study are major components of self-esteem and a determinant of the esteem of others. Psychoanalysis has had a long and fruitful association with education. "It has been said that through most of the history of psychoanalysis, there have been bridges which lead from one area of psychoanalysis to the area of education" (Ekstein and Motto, 1972, p. 72).

Educators, psychologists, and psychoanalysts have engaged in infant and child study to observe how, from earliest infancy, the human child engages in active efforts to master its environment and to place and identify persons and objects in its environment. The watching child learns how and what to perceive through a complex process of seeing, touching, hearing, grasping, throwing, and imitating and identifying with parental love objects. Increasingly complex interactions, transactions, and cognitive development propel the child to learn, at first, out of love for the parents. With greater separation and individuation, the child progresses onward to learn in a more autonomous style and out of an evolving love of learning. Similarly, adult work appears to be the outcome of a lengthy process of individual development, which starts in early childhood and passes through many stages, phases, progressions, and regressions.

Academic learning and adult work relate to events, experiences, and relationships encountered during critical, vulnerable, and formative periods of development. Work, like the ability to learn and love, is influenced by many unconscious motives. Responses that later appear as the adult's patterns of work do not, like learning patterns, appear in infancy, but at the time of childhood, when the youngster is first confronted with formal schooling. The psychodynamic psychoanalytic literature on learning is extensive; but in contrast, meager attention has been paid to the problems and psychopathology of work. Nevertheless, Johada (1966) noted the importance of "an almost casual remark which Freud made in a footnote in 'Civilization and Its Discontents'" (p. 623). Freud (1930) said that "work is man's strongest tie to reality" (p. 80). Thus, "the absence of work should leave him less solidly in touch with reality. This is indeed the case, as several studies of unemployment have demonstrated (Johada, 1966, p. 626).

Satisfaction gleaned from work and study is in proportion to the extent that the various forms of reality testing lead to pleasurable experiences on an eventual adult level. Freud observed that work offers the possibility of "displacing a large amount of libidinal components, whether narcissistic, aggressive or even erotic, onto professional work and onto the human relations connected with it" (Freud, 1930, p. 80). Needless to say, public education, work, and working conditions today do not uniformly offer such potential for pleasures; this reality was recognized by Freud who stated that the "great majority of people only work under the stress of necessity" (p. 80). Chosen professional activity that provides special satisfaction is rare. Psychologists studying work have divided work and leisure into two intersecting facets of social life around which we organize our daily waking experience. Neulinger (1974) defined leisure as the act of being "engaged in an activity performed for its own sake, to do something which gives one pleasure and satisfaction, which involves one to the very core of one's being" (p. xi).

Presented below is an overview of adolescent psychopathology manifested by academic and vocational underachievement or failure. The reader will be offered a perspective that examines the inner world of the adolescent and the outer reality as exemplified by family systems, school systems, and the world of work. We will see how social and cultural forces interact with personal endowment, deficits, and familial experiences in the development of problems with learning or work.

Overview

It has become increasingly widely recognized that academic achievement and work are not at all innate human activities. Children must learn to become students, and adolescents and young adults must learn to become workers. The process of becoming a student and a worker today takes place in an ever-more-complex social setting, and individuals vary in their abilities to master the essential developmental steps and life demands.

For some, achievements proceed smoothly; for others, pressure, progressions, regressions, and strain are continuous; and performance is achieved at varying degrees of emotional cost. For a minority, mastery of academics or work proves to be an impossible task. Why is this latter group unable to learn or work? Some young people appear unable or unwilling to work despite adequate mental and physical aptitudes. Others are handicapped physically, intellectually, and/or emotionally.

The relatively new professions of educational and vocational rehabilitation have recognized that it is not enough to provide a disabled adolescent a caring teacher, a fine academic setting, or vocational training. Clearly, successful study and gainful employment are end points in a long-range developmental process, building certain requisite experiences in early and middle childhood.

Developmental Impairments

Psychological Impairment

Many troubled youths reveal a developmental impairment, rooted in early childhood experiences, which becomes plainly visible during adolescence, when the demands for forward development occur in the midst of concurrent regressive pulls. Despite what might have been excellent superficial earlier adaption, prior difficulties surface in a variety of emotional and behavioral manifestations, frequently in the form of academic decline and inability to work or obtain employment.

Such developmental impairments, which cross social, racial, and class lines, can frequently be explained as resulting from empathic failures on the part of parents. Burch (1985) described a particular type of adolescent, who manifests precocious identity components, while his infantile grandiosity remains in unmodified form. Adolescents such as this cannot tolerate even minimal frustration, and they maintain the illusion that they must be the perfect child. The resultant poor self-esteem regulation, withdrawal, and high degree of manipulative and demanding behavior often crystalize into poor academic achievement and poor to nonexistent work performance. So much is expected that nothing is good enough but all A's and/or a stupendous career; thus, little is attempted. Because of inherent vulnerability, such youths attempt to preserve narcissistic equilibrium by avoiding such central developmental tasks of adolescence as academic achievement and eventual vocational choice.

The adolescents described by Burch exhibit the kinds of narcissistic disturbances described by Kohut (1968, 1972, 1977), Kernberg (1975), and Goldberg (1980). Such youths do not present with normal adolescent narcissism and heightened self-reference. Rather, their difficulties are caused by a subtle but substantial developmental arrest. Borderline adolescents present a more severe developmental arrest. Their failure to separate and individuate and achieve object and self constancy frequently results in more varied forms of performance failure in the work and school arenas. If learning and employment connote autonomy and greater independence, borderline youths hold back from achievement, fearful of such forms of separation and individuation, terrified of being abandoned or reengulfed by the maternal object.

Minimal Brain Dysfunction and Learning Disabilities

From the early 1920s and the advent of the child guidance movement until approximately the late 1950s, children and adolescents presenting "behavioral and/or learning problems were considered to be suffering from psychogenic disorders. This view was especially common around the time of the Second World War, when the influence of classical psychoanalysis was at the height" (Gardner, 1980, p. 269). More recent work attributes some psychiatric disturbances to neurophysiological disorders, i.e., dyslexia, hyperactivity, and minimal brain dysfunction. Gardner (1980) noted that an increasing number of children are being diagnosed as "organic," and that, in fact, the pendulum has shifted excessively: "If the disease has not become pandemic, the diagnosis certainly has" (p. 269). Differential diagnosis is problematic given the confusions about criteria. Impulsivity, distractability, and hyperactivity are considered symptoms of this syndrome; but of course, they may also be caused by ego deficits and anxiety. It is generally agreed that minimal brain dysfunction (MBD) involves developmental lag and impairment, visual and auditory processing problems, and motor coordination (e.g., hand-eye) problems.

Neurological development proceeds at varying rates, but within

certain norms, unless genetic factors, central nervous system disturbances, or other malfunctions interfere. "Any entity that deleteriously
affects nerve cells, central nervous system connective tissues, cerebral
blood and spinal fluid, and brain skull size may impair neurological development" (Gardner, 1980, p. 270). Specific disease processes can
cause developmental lags. Briefly, the following have been found to have
serious secondary effects: seizures, traumas, head injuries, injections,
prematurity, post-natal infection, maternal substance abuse, radiation,
dehydration, pre- and post-natal nutritional deficiency, lead poisoning,
and cardiovascular disease. Neurologists look for what is called soft
neurological signs, alerted by parental concerns about delayed reflexes
or lateness in reaching developmental milestones, like standing, talking,
walking, comprehension, or bladder and bowel control. Other warning
signs are discernable difficulties in fine and gross motor coordination,
motor impersistence, or the "inability to sustain certain voluntary motor acts initiated on verbal commands" (Garfield, Benton, and Mac-
Queen, 1966). "Motor overflow" is another sign of minimal brain dysfunction, and occurs "in association with and in addition to the specific
act that the child has been requested to perform" (Gardner, 1980,
p. 289). Visual processing, i.e., "the ways in which the brain receives,
scans, identifies, integrates, classifies and utilizes visual information"
(p. 296) is critical for learning and work performance, and impairment
in one or more of these functions is found in children and adolescents
with MBD. Poor visual memory, visual distractibility, and impaired
body image are other characteristics of this dysfunction. Auditory processing can be similarly deficient; this disease affects discrimination of
different sounds, sound source, and differentiation between signficant
and insignficant auditory stimuli. Affected is "understanding the hearing of sounds, reproduction of pitch, rhythm and melody and combining speech sounds into words" (Chalfant and Scheffelin, n.d.).

Specific learning disabilities like MBD cause academic difficulties
for afflicted children, adolescents, and young adults. Criteria are confusing, but the term generally refers to

> learning problems in which the defining characteristic is the failure to
> learn, in spite of average or better intelligence, and in the absence of such
> primary contributing factors as emotional disorders, sensory impairment
> and gross neurological dysfunction. The interference with learning ap-
> pears to originate within the child and is not the result of poor teaching or
> cultural differences [Jansky, 1980, p. 305].

The student has difficulty with some or all of the following school subjects: arithmetic, spelling, reading, writing, composition, and foreign
language.

There is some consensus as to the kinds of nonacademic performance deficits that accompany failure in the primary subjects. There is less agreement, however, as to the way these associated problems interact with the printed language and arithmetic difficulties. Nor has it been determined whether learning disabilities constitute a single syndrome of deficits or several rather distinct clusters of deficits [p. 306].

Children with learning disabilities frequently have a family history of relatives who had trouble with learning or mastery of some aspect of language. Not uncommonly, these children have a low birth weight and then seem to progress fairly adequately. Careful inquiry often reveals subtle forms of delay, often in some aspect of language development such as comprehension, difficulty in following directions, short attention span, and varying degrees of developmental and emotional immaturity. Unpredictable motility, fearfulness, trouble separating from the parent, protracted thumb and finger sucking, poor frustration tolerance, lack of curiosity, and poor fine motor coordination are common traits of such children.

When these cognitive deficits and resultant difficulties are detected early, tutoring, psychotherapy, and parent guidance can be very effective. Despite deficits, compensatory approaches can be taught to facilitate learning, and attendance in regular classrooms can be maintained. Such children require and respond well to calm, organization, and structure. They can handle carefully selected academic work that allows opportunity for practice so that gains are firmly established. Learning in small and manageable doses, supportive psychotherapy for child and parents, tutoring, and close collaboration with teachers can ensure a successful outcome.

Accurate assessment of the basic organic interference assists the clinician in "appreciating the patient's core experience of defectiveness and powerlessness, and aids in transmission of empathy and understanding to the patient and to the avoidance of common countertransference problems and therapeutic impasse" (Crabtree, 1981, p. 317). Psychotherapy sessions—like tutoring and educational sessions—need to be tailored to meet the individual's needs. These patients require brief structured and well-focused sessions, characterized by repetition and particular concreteness in communication. Following group or residential care, many require extra focus and structure to sustain ongoing abstinence from alcohol and drug abuse and impulsive acting out. Special education is often necessary to compensate for deficiencies in basic social and vocational skills.

Cohen (1985) stated that 10 to 15 percent of the school population is learning disabled. The disabilities which interfere with reception, e.g., perception, integration in sensory processing and synthesis, remembering, and expression are "bodily rooted events that adversely affect the operation of one or more aspects of autonomous ego functioning" (p. 177). These children are particularly vulnerable to significant emotional stress: in fact, "there are virtually no learning-disabled children or adolescents who do not evidence significant psychological conflicts and concerns" (p. 177). In later adolescence and young adulthood, there are distinct problems in work and learning more advanced and complex academic material.

Cohen (1985) observed that the learning disability creates problems due to cognitive disability and to the psychological correlates of being learning disabled. These include more than a sense of frustration, failure, poor self-image, and low self-esteem. Frequently such long-standing problems interfere with working independently and being able to compete without due anxiety. Fears of being an impostor, or damaged, can interfere with sound decisions about intellectual and career aspirations. The learning disabled youth's total personality may be affected by "(1) an unusually high propensity to experience distress and anxiety, (2) a low-level chronic depression" (p. 180). Resultant feelings are those of helplessness and humiliation and a belief that accomplishments fall short of expectations. In fact, recent research is beginning to show that there may be a link between learning disabilities and biologically based depressive illness (Brumback and Staton, 1983). The learning disabled adolescent's self-representation appears uniquely different from the nondisabled adolescent's. The sense of being dumb, damaged, weak, and vulnerable appears to crystallize during latency and, without therapeutic intervention, remains throughout life. "It was surprising to discover, however, that, even in optimal situations [with empathy and support from parents and teachers], the learning disabled adolescent was still plagued by psychological concerns" (p. 185).

Anxiety and depression exacerbate difficulties in mastery and cognitive learning, despite pockets of superior talent. In recent years, authors have noted that many dyslexics have precocious and superior talents in a number of nonverbal skills, such as art, architecture, engineering and athletics (Geschwind, 1983; Porac & Coren, 1981). This uneven picture may contribute to a lack of cohesive sense of self or a lack of integration of self-representation. Such negative or fragmented self-representations interfere with a stable sense of identity, the "adolescent passage," and the setting of realistic expectations. The learning disability creates a steady and insidious cumulative trauma, similar to other physical handicaps, with resultant uneven self-esteem, frequent grandiosity alternating with a sense of helplessness, and frequent rigid defensive and coping strategies. "Such a continuously deliberate, purposive and tense self-direction involves a special kind of self-consciousness" (Shapiro, 1981). Rigidity, maintained to avoid impulsivity and loss of control, interferes with educational, professional and psychological maturation. Long-term intervention and support can assist such youth in selecting and attaining career aspirations which draw on their strengths and can help them avoid fields in which their deficits would interfere.

Sociocultural Deprivation

Deficits and impairment inevitably result from sociocultural deprivation. Lief and Zarin-Ackerman (1980) noted synonyms for the term deprivation: "disadvantaged, high risk, culturally poor, disorganized and crisis oriented." While these terms have historically been linked with economically impoverished families, more recently, we have recognized that such descriptions in fact often fit families that are middle class or even affluent. Marans and Laurie (1967) suggested that sociocultural deprivation arises out of deviant child-rearing skills commonly found in the "culture of poverty." These authors noted that these families rely on magical thinking and on a disavowal of facts, circumstances, and reality. Deprivation and lack of nurturance of the parents in their own childhoods leave them unable to provide an average, expectable, good enough environment (Hartmann, 1958). Thus, their children lack adequate tactile, visual, auditory, and affectionate stimuli in the first years of life. Erratic, inconsistent stimuli "in lower-class disorganized families tend to be delivered in an arbitrary manner—sometimes too often, sometimes not often enough" (Lief and Zarin-Ackerman, 1980, p. 367) and generally in response to the parent's whim or need, rather than the child's. Many authors speak of resultant parentified children, with precocious survival skills; stunted emotional and cognitive development; and minimal trust, self-respect, or confidence.

Common presenting problems of children and adolescents raised in such circumstances are aggressivity, tantrums, depression, hyperactivity, delinquency and violence, and profound academic difficulty. School problems are reflected in underachievement or academic failure due to truancy and absenteeism, behavior problems, and learning disabilities. Alternative school placement is frequently required; and many such youths are placed in special education remedial programs, day treatment programs, and/or group residential facilities, such as group homes, residential treatment facilities, and hospitals where school programs are available. With adolescents manifesting such a wide range of problems, "including physical, financial, social, cultural, and educational factors in various combinations, . . . cases [are] extremely complicated" (Lief and Zarin-Ackerman, 1980, p. 368). They require varied and combined interventions, involving concrete services, access and referral, environmental manipulation, and supportive counseling. Many programs for such youths and families entail day treatment, day care, educational classes in parenting, and group and/or individual treatment for parents. Helping families trust helpers, make use of public services, overcome apathy, and find housing, health services, and work are common goals. Parents are helped to find alternative ways of disciplining their children. Efforts in such cases are geared to the "main or contributing deprivation, i.e., [parents'] inadequate understanding of the developing needs of the infant and growing child and/or inability to respond appropriately to those needs" (p. 390). By repeating their childhoods with their children, these parents intergenerationally transmit psychological, physical, and cultural impairments that result in school failure, school dropout, delinquency, addictions, and crime. Gainful employment remain all but beyond such populations.

Case of Jill

Jill, age 15, was referred for treatment by her parents. Her father initiated the contact, because his daughter was now living with him after her mother had given up attempting to contain her in her home. The father described being at his wits' end and totally overwhelmed by the problems Jill presented. Jill did not attend school and came and went as she pleased. Her father, like her mother before, had no control over her actions, whereabouts, or activities. The parents both reported that Jill refused to attend school or be enrolled in any therapeutic alternative school program. She was academically far behind her class at this point. She stole from both her parents, told endless lies about her activities and whereabouts, and became hysterical and violent, tearing the house apart when forced to look at the truth. Other truant children were brought into the parents' homes when they were away at work. No parental efforts at limits and discipline had worked, and no change occurred during a year when Jill kept sporadic contact with a clinician at an outpatient adolescent clinic. Neither parent had confidence in any juvenile residential facility or psychiatric hospital setting, seeing each as a nonsolution, a holding action, and a place from which, they predicted, Jill would simply run away.

Jill stopped going to school late in the sixth grade, at which time she was described as resistive to authority, fighting rules at school and at home. Her mother did not learn of her school truancy for a complete year, as the overcrowded public school was remiss and inconsistent in sending any communication to the parents, and Jill was ingenious at intercepting the mail. Jill would leave the house each morning, supposedly for school, and return home after her mother had left for work. She would go back to bed, watch television, or bring friends into the house in her parents' absence. Ultimately, Jill's mother was informed of the situation by Jill's younger sister, Karen, who had become nervous and agitated due to continuous fights with Jill and her knowledge of her sister's activities. Jill had tried to embroil her sister in her activities, involving her with truant friends and encouraging her, at age nine, to smoke pot.

Prior to the sixth grade, Jill demonstrated substantial learning disabilities, despite her obvious intelligence and articulate manner. Dyslexia was eventually recognized, and she was enrolled in a special program in her school, where she received individualized tutoring and support. She responded well to this program and obtained excellent grades. When she entered middle school no such support existed, and Jill fell in academic achievement and began to associate with a rougher, nonachieving peer population. The parents never kept a close watch on their children because of their own stresses and their ultimate separation at the time that Jill would have entered the seventh grade. The lack of any parental coalition in this family was most striking. The parents, both white, middle-class intellectuals, proclaimed a radical life-style: they never married, but lived together in a common-law relationship for thirteen years. Their last years together were characterized by the father's excessive drinking, protracted absences, and adulterous relationships. It was not until a year or more after they separated that the mother learned from mutual friends that her "husband" had fathered several other children and had, in a sense, a second family with his mistress. Jill knew of this second family and often hung out in their home when she truanted. The mother held her former "husband" and his mistress responsible for concealing Jill's activities, thereby preventing her from taking some meaningful steps before Jill was older and totally out of control.

When Jill appeared for her first therapy contact, she conformed to her parents' description. She looked considerably older than 15—a most attractive, articulate, well-groomed adolescent, who presented an affect of "cool" sophistication and street savvy. She described wishing and needing to be on her own, in her own apartment, free to see her friends and come and go as she pleased. Her precocious self-presentation appeared to be a well-established facade, masking considerable depression and low self-esteem, particularly when she later acknowledged her lack of any and all basic reading, writing, and arithmetic skills. These deficits prevented her from being able to hold down jobs she had secured as a waitress or countermaid at hamburger or pizza fast food stores. She could not compute bills or handle the cash register. So, her current day-to-day life consisted of "hanging around," visiting with friends, and picking up whatever odd jobs she could find (cleaning, walking dogs for people, and baby-sitting). Money earned was spent on partying, bars, and disco dancing until 4:00 A.M. Her only age-appropriate activity appeared to be consistent contact at a teen drop-in center, where she involved herself in such activities as classes in jewelry making and drama (though she could not easily read a script, she compensated with excellent memorization skills).

Jill never moved into an ongoing treatment relationship because of the following events: The father's drinking precluded his following any supportive advice from the therapist; and in a typical drunken stupor one evening, he exploded and tried to lock Jill in their apartment, after wild threats to throw her out of his home. She ran away, departing out the window, stealing money and credit cards, with which she charged close to $2,000 worth of clothing for her friends. Her whereabouts remained unknown for close to a year. She would occasionally call her parents and converse briefly, refusing to see them or tell them where she was. Similarly, she would leave messages on the therapist's answering machine with no return phone number and, thus, no possibility for arranging a resumption of contact.

The therapist continued to be available to the parents, providing specific advice, referral, and support. They were advised to report Jill's running away to the police and appropriate juvenile authorities. Initially they—the father particularly—were averse to this action, loathing this form of limit setting, "calling in the pigs," and giving Jill a record. The therapist shared her exploration of resources and procedures at juvenile court with the parents. Specifically, if they filed a P.I.N.S. petition (Persons in Need of Supervision), if and when Jill was found, the parents and their daughter could have some leeway, e.g., to request a treatment facility as opposed to a mandatory juvenile court placement in the rather brutal available correctional facilities.

The therapist believed that Jill might become involved in illegal activity. Furthermore, the parents were advised that if Jill was not reported, they, as her parents, could be tried and judged as neglectful. These legal realities moved the parents to undertake the appropriate steps. Initially the father could not envision such action as protective, caring or a needed limit that could conceivably benefit Jill. He could only articulate some minimal guilt over his explosiveness, which he viewed as precipitant to her running away that fateful night of her departure.

After a year, Jill was arrested in a drug raid. She had been residing with a peer group that operated a business selling soft drugs. When she was brought into juvenile court, she, her parents, and the authorities worked out an emergency placement in a crisis unit of one of the better child welfare agencies in the city. While in this setting, Jill responded to a caring note from the therapist, and they had a short-lived correspondence. Based on the assessment of the crisis unit and the therapist's diagnostic material, Jill was placed in a private long-term residential treatment facility. The father's financial resources provided for this placement. Jill's parents remained in contact with Jill and cooperated with the staff of the residential facility.

Bibliography

BERKOVITZ, I. B. (1985). The Adolescent, Schools and Schooling. In *Adolescent Psychiatry, Vol. 12: Developmental and Clinical Studies*, eds. S. Feinstein, M. Sugar, A. Esman, J. Looney, A. Schwartzberg, and A. Sorosky, pp. 162–176. Chicago/London: University of Chicago Press.

BRUMBACK, R. A. and STATON, R. D. (1983). Learning Disabilities and Childhood Depression. *Amer. J. Orthopsychiatry*, 53(2):262–63.

BURCH, C. A. (1985). Identity and Foreclosure in Early Adolescence: A Problem of Narcissistic Equilibrium. In *Adolescent Psychiatry, Vol. 12*, pp. 145–61. *See* Berkovitz (1985).

CHALFANT, J. and SCHEFFELIN, M. (n.d.). Central Processing Dysfunction in Children: A Review of Research. *National Institute of Neurological Diseases and Stroke, Monograph No. 9.* Washington, D.C.: U.S. Government Printing Office.

COHEN, J. (1985). Learning Disabilities and Adolescence: Developmental Considerations. In *Adolescent Psychiatry, Vol. 12:* pp. 177–96. *See* Berkovitz (1985).

CRABTREE, L. H., JR. (1981). Minimal Brain Dysfunction in Adolescents and Young Adults—Diagnostic and Therapeutic Perspectives. In *Adolescent Psychiatry, Vol. 9: Developmental and Clinical Studies*, eds. S. Feinstein, J. Looney, A. Schwartzberg, and A. Sorosky. Chicago: University of Chicago Press.

EKSTEIN, R. and MOTTO, R. L. (1972). Psychoanalysis and Education: An Historical Account. In *In Search of Love and Competence*, ed. R. Ekstein. Los Angeles: Reiss-Davis Study Center. Distributed by Brunner/Mazel, New York.

FREUD, S. (1930). Civilization and Its Discontents. *Standard Edition*, 21:59–145. London: Hogarth.

GARDNER, R. (1980). Minimal Brain Dysfunction. In *Child Development in Normality and Psychopathology*, ed. J. Bemporad, M.D., pp. 269–304. New York: Brunner/Mazel.

GARFIELD, J.; BENTON, A.; and MacQUEEN, J. (1966). Motor Impersistence in Brain-Damaged and Cultural-Familial Defectives. *J. Nerv. Mental Diseases*, 142:434–40.

GESCHWIND, N. (1930). Biological Associations of Left-Handedness. *Annals of Dyslexia*, 33:29–40.

GOLDBERG, A. (1980). *Advances in Self Psychology.* New York: International Universities Press.

HARTMANN, H. (1958). *Ego Psychology and the Problem of Adoption.* New York: International Universities Press.

JANSKY, J. J., PH.D. (1980). Specific Learning Disabilities: A Clinical View. In *Child Development in Normality and Psychopathology*, ed. J. Bemporad, M.D., pp. 305–36. New York: Brunner/Mazel.

JOHADA, M. (1966). Notes on Work: In *Psychoanalysis: A General Psychology*, eds. R. Lowenstein, M. Newman, J. Scher, and A. Solnit, p. 622–33. New York: International Universities Press.

KERNBERG, O. (1975). *Borderline Conditions and Pathological Narcissism.* New York: Jason Aronson.

KOHUT, H. (1968). The Psychoanalytic Treatment of Narcissistic Personality Disorder: Outline of a Systemic Approach. *Psychoanalytic Study of the Child*, 23:86–113. New York: International Universities Press.

_____ (1972). Thoughts on Narcissism and Narcissistic Rage. *Psychoanalytic Study of the Child*, 27:360–400. New York: Quadrangle.

_____ (1977). *The Restoration of the Self*. New York: International Universities Press.

LIEF, N. R. and ZARIN-ACKERMAN, J. (1980). Sociocultural Deprivation and Its Effect on the Development of the Child. In *Child Developments in Normality and Pathology*, ed. J. Bemporad, M.D., pp. 362–92. New York: Brunner/ Mazel.

MARANS, A. E. and LAURIE, R. (1967). Hypothesis Regarding the Effect of Child Rearing Patterns on the Disadvantaged Child. In *The Disadvantaged Child*, vol. 1, ed. J. Halmuth, pp. 17–41. New York: Brunner/Mazel.

NEULINGER, J. (1974). *The Psychology of Leisure: Research Approaches to the Study of Leisure*. Springfield, Ill.: Charles C. Thomas.

OZAWA, M. (1982). Work and Social Policy. In *Work, Workers and Work Organizations: A View From Social Work*, ed. S. Aradas and P. Kurzman, pp. 32–59. Englewood Cliffs, N.J.: Prentice-Hall.

PORAC, C. and COREN, S. (1981). *Lateral Preferences and Human Behavior*. New York: Springer.

SAWHILL, I. (1976). Women with Low Incomes. In *Women in the Workplace: The Implications of Occupational Segregation*, eds. M. Blaxall and B. Reagan. Chicago: University of Chicago Press.

SHAPIRO, D. (1981). *Autonomy and Rigid Character*. New York: Basic Books.

9

Chronic Illness

Any long-term illness or physical disability poses enormous problems for the child or adolescent, the family, and the responsible community's educational and health services. Illness that begins in childhood creates more stress than one starting later in life because of the vulnerability of the undeveloped young person. Illness can cause life-long crippling distortions in physical, social, educational, and emotional development. Chronic illness of long duration is generally characterized by slowly progressing symptoms or chronic fixed disability. Some conditions cause deterioration and eventually are fatal, while others, such as diabetes, hemophilia, cardiac conditions, asthma, and renal failure need not be fatal, but produce serious ailments and "pose severe physiological and psychological complications which strain the child's and family's adaptive skills" (Levy and Nir, 1980, p. 338).

Below is a list of the more common chronic conditions of childhood. Division of illnesses according to system involved:

Nervous system and sense organs: Seizure disorder, spina bifida, cerebral palsy, deafness, blindness
Respiratory systems: Asthma
Cardiovascular system: Congenital deformation, rheumatic heart disease

Gastrointestinal system: Malabsorption syndromes, gastric and duodenal ulcers, ulcerative colitis, megacolon, colostomy

Genitourinary system: Nephritis, chronic urinary tract infection, genital ambiguity, kidney transplants

Hematological system: Hemophilia, leukemias, hemoglobinpathies

Immunological system: Allergies

Collagen disease: Rheumatoid arthritis, lupus

Endocrine system: Diabetes, thyroid disorders, obesity, adrenogenital syndrome

Dermatological system: Albinism, neurodermititis, psoriasis, eczema

Skeletal-muscular system: Scoliosis

Genetic disorders: Trisomies, cleft lip, cleft palate, Tay-Sacks disease

Other conditions: Amputation, searing due to burns, optic fibrosis, cancer, sequilae of accidents [Levy and Nir, 1980, p. 339]

The psychosomatic perspective focuses attention on the emotional components of physical diseases. Grinker (1953) emphasized an "integrated process of transactions among many systems—somatic, phychic, social and cultural" (p. 188). Physical problems create stigma for the patient as well as a frightening ongoing experience due to the expectation of pain and a shortened life span. Overall, it is generalized that the earlier the illness, injury, or deficit appears, the greater are the emotional, social, and educational risks—and the more tenuous the early parent-child bonding. Maternal anxiety, depression, and preoccupation often occur and interfere. The early literature focused on a child's premorbid emotional state and his or her reaction to acute illness, pain, hospitalization, and separation; only gradually have the longer-range effects—compromised development and diminished quality of life—been recognized. Children and adolescents afflicted with such serious illnesses commonly respond with grief, worry, suppressed anger, feelings of inadequacy, and emotional immaturity and behavior deviancy.

The effects on the family are enormous. The child's chronic illness and ensuing psychological problems deplete energy and are very costly both in terms of emotions and of actual dollars and cents. Parental guilt, particularly over genetic illness, can be enormous. Normal siblings feel and are neglected because of the enormity of the chronically ill child's demands. Commonly, parents are overprotective and excessively permissive with the ill child, who often functions as a despot ruling the home. On occasion, avoidance and withdrawal are denial responses of the child's illness and reality needs. Barely repressed rage and resentment by parents is frequently handled with rejection and isolation of the sick child. There is a high divorce rate and social isolation among parents of chronically ill youths because of the enormity of the emotional pressures. Worry, financial concerns, and minimal understanding of the illness all greatly affect family life. The endless therapy appointments with physicians, psychotherapists, and educational and physical rehab personnel, and the overwhelming amount of physical care, special foods, and special equipment needed, affect every minute of day-to-day life.

Obviously, school life is profoundly affected by a child's chronic illness. Low academic performance, a high degree of absenteeism, social isolation, and problematic pupil-teacher relationships are common.

In many situations, the children are depressed, apathetic, feeling dehumanized by varied medical procedures, out of control, dependent, fearful, and unable to tolerate any academic expectation or task or relationship with their teachers. Children who develop more adequately in the face of chronic illness appear to mirror parental attitudes and coping skills. "It has been found that crisis intervention approaches are useful when both parents are seen during the crisis stage of their child's illness . . . [later] some form of psychological support as well as education must be provided for [parents] nurses, teachers, etc." (Levy and Nir, 1980, p. 358).

Teachers of chronically ill children, like their parents, face emotional hazards and stress. They may be overprotective and set unrealistically low expectations for performance; this stance may alternate with anger and a disappearance of empathy and concern, and harsh handling can ensue. Some teachers have been drawn to this work because of their own illnesses or handicaps, which may or may not have been appropriately worked through. In the best cases, these teachers can provide inspiration and serve as a role model for chronically ill youth.

Case of Walter

At age 13 Walter was referred for evaluation and treatment in an in-patient children's hospital. The precipitant was his involvement in an incident of stealing in a department store, following which he was put on probation. Walter had a history of significant learning difficulties and explosive acting out in school. Reports from school portrayed a boy who at times appeared flagrantly out of contact with reality, threatening peers, behaving wildly and self-destructively, and functioning academically on a fourth grade level. On other occasions, when there appeared to be no provocative stimuli in the environment, he behaved adequately and reasonably. Walter was described as withdrawn and immature at home. He had few friends, watched too much television, and gorged himself on food. He cried often about the death of his natural father and a brother.

Walter, a Black Baptist, was the third of five children. His oldest brother, age 19, lived away from home; the next brother, who would have been 16, was deceased; his 12-year-old sister lived in a foster home; and his 7-year-old brother was at home. Walter's mother, age 36, worked on a cleaning crew servicing office buildings. In the last year she remarried, but the stepfather appeared to be a peripheral family member, and there was little evidence of a relationship between him and Walter. The mother-son relationship appeared to be primarily a symbiotic attachment, characterized by projective identification, hostility, and rejection. His mother stated that Walter was like her and his troubled sister.

The developmental history reflected chronic severe and mild illness. Walter was born prematurely (seven months gestation) when his sister was only eight months old. The mother said the pregnancy was uneventful, but that Walter was born "with his face the wrong way and feet first" so a breech procedure was necessary. Birth weight was 2 pounds 12 ounces, and an incubation of approximately two months was necessary. There were feeding problems from the beginning. Walter was very sickly from birth onward, and then he had pneumonia twice at 13 months of age, followed by measles and anemia. He was hospitalized at 13 and 15 months, for anemia, infected adenoids, and a bout of pneumonia. Walter's mother described him as having been a weakling from birth, and said that a heart condition was discovered during the numerous hospitalizations. In his first year of life he looked like a newborn and continuously vomited up his milk. At 14 to 16 months he developed bronchitis, and he required several more hospitalizations before the age of three. As an infant and toddler he rocked continuously in his crib— and now he rocked his right leg when asleep.

All developmental achievements were significantly delayed. Walter did not begin to walk until 19 months of age, and though he tried to talk at two years of age, actual words were barely discernable until age three. Speech was essentially unintelligible when he entered kindergarten at age five, and he could be only fairly well understood at age six. His mother was vague about when toilet training was attempted and achieved, and was understandably preoccupied with relating the myriad of health problems. She reported that Walter had always had nosebleeds and breathing problems. The breathing difficulties were due to his heart condition, and all of these problems had worsened as a result of his enormous weight gain, which began at the age of two. For some years Walter had suffered considerable arthritic pain, mainly in his ankles and wrists. His sleep was disturbed by the pain; aspirin was used continuously day and night.

When Walter was four years of age a fire started in the home and killed the second oldest son. The mother was at work at the time and the father was supposed to have been caring for the children. He was out drinking and the oldest child was in charge. In the attempt to rescue the four children, one was not gotten out and died. Everyone suspected Walter of starting the fire, since he had started to play with matches around that time. He was the only child who could not talk about the tragedy—and a half year later he was often discovered in front of the picture of his deceased brother saying, "I'm sorry. I didn't mean to."

In the following year, when Walter was five, his father died of an aneurism. Walter's mother reported emotionally going to pieces. Walter was considerable agitated, and frequently stayed home or ran away from kindergarten. He had never developed the ability to make friends and was always picked upon. He reacted passively until adolescence, when he became explosive. Truancy and repeated fire-setting had been ongoing symptoms. More recently, the fire-setting was replaced by stealing.

During the assessment, Walter presented initially as a fairly well related child. He showed appropriate anxiety about the pending hospitalization, coupled with hope that he would be helped to change. Initially he described school problems and conflicts with peers. His discussion of his dead father and brother was accompanied by free and open weeping. Anxiety about being separated from his mother was not noted.

However, subsequent sessions once he was hospitalized included endless recountings of scary incidents in the neighborhood, such as fires, roofs falling in, boys jumping from windows, and people getting hit by cars. He often seemed to deteriorate physically during the therapy sessions. His eyes would glaze over and his thoughts would become quite loose, and the accounts took on a frightening, frenzied, obsessive quality. He did respond to the therapist's assurance that he now was protected from the scary events, and could reintegrate in the treatment hour. However, often in his dorm he demonstrated confused thinking, blurring past and present, and also some delusional paranoid thinking that staff and peers were planning to hurt him. He reported episodes of hallucinations and depersonalization and accounts of conversations with his deceased relatives.

Understandably, Walter depicted a very uncertain external world where danger could strike unexpectedly at any time. He became angry and agitated, threatening others when he felt unprotected, picked upon, or left out. Venting anger at staff and children frightened him and he then turned the rage onto himself, gorging on food, pounding his hands on the floor, picking off scabs until he bled, and banging his head against the wall. He stimulated nosebleeds and seemed to take pleasure in dripping blood all over himself.

The intervention recommended for this borderline adolescent was long-term in-patient care. He seemed, when stressed, to have recurrent psychotic episodes, which he recognized as "crazy, wild episodes." His sense of reality was distorted, but he was not out of touch with reality. Walter had endured numerous severe traumas; the losses of brother and father were the most significant. It was probable that his playing with matches (a classic borderline symptom) did indeed cause the fire in which his brother died. This child was blamed for this accident—despite the reality that it occurred as an outcome of the father's negligence.

The compromised and delayed development that Walter demonstrated was, however, distorted prior to the above traumatic events. His chronic illness since birth, and the life-long existence of a heart condition, obesity, and arthritis, kept him bonded to his mother with no opportunity for separation and individuation. Mother and son shared a constellation of fears about his very survival, and the heart condition, breathing difficulty, and nosebleeds kept them permanently bonded in a symbiotic tie that embodied engulfment, abandonment, overprotection, and rejection, as the mother struggled to parent and resented the endless emergencies, special needs, and strain of taking care of Walter.

Bibliography

GRINKER, R. (1953). *Psychosomatic Research*. New York: Norton.

HAGGERTY, R.; ROGHAMANN, K.; and PLESS, I. (1975). *Child Health in the Community*. New York: Wiley.

LEVY, A., M.D. and NIR, Y., M.D. (1980). Chronic Illness in Children. In *Child Development in Normality and Pathology*, ed. J. R. Bemporad, pp. 337–61. New York: Brunner/Mazel.

SEELTZ, H.; SCHLESINGER, E.; MOSHER, W.; and FELDMAN, J. (1972). *Long-Term Childhood Illness*. Pittsburgh: University of Pittsburgh Press.

10

Anorexia Nervosa and Bulimia

Overview

Anorexia nervosa has been known to medicine for almost three centuries, but its incidence is now increasing dramatically, reaching, in the 1980s, almost epidemic proportion in the United States. In 1918, Freud commented upon a neurotic response in pubertal and adolescent girls "that expresses aversion to sexuality by means of anorexia" (p. 106). Biochemical, endocrinological, sociological, psychological, and psychoanalytic research have examined this disorder and offered varying theories of etiology and treatment prescriptions. Extreme emaciation is the most obvious sign of anorexia nervosa. Casper (1982) observed that this syndrome occupies a unique position among the psychiatric disorders because the patient herself has a stake in propagating the illness. Thinness is "her own accomplishment, borne through prolonged deprivation, hunger, sacrifice, and against her parents' protests. For many months, sometimes years, all other activities, pleasures, and even moral values have become subjugated to the one goal" (p. 433). Casper observed that the patient values the process of being thin as a way of life. Self-starvation becomes "a misguided striving for individuality" that gives patients a sense of purpose and uniqueness and denies the actual emaciation "in the erroneous belief that they have attained a state of exquisite, enviable slenderness" (p. 433).

Wilson, Hogan, and Mintz (1983), members of the Psychosomatic Study Group of the Psychoanalytic Association of New York, previously led by Dr. Melitta Sperling, have presented a new hypothesis. They stated that "as a diagnostic term anorexia nervosa is a medical misnomer and should be replaced by 'fat phobia' or 'phobic fear of fat' which are true psychodynamic descriptions of this syndrome" (p. xi). While acknowledging the heterogeneity of anorexic patients, the variations in drive endowment, constitutional factors, and gender and familial compositions that affect each child's maturation, they "believe it is the domineering and controlling personality of the mother (and/or the father) that profoundly warps and inhibits the normal development of the anorexic-prone child" (p. 2).

Casper (1982) believed that the syndrome could not be completely explained on a psychological basis; and she suggested an interplay of constitutional, biological, and psychological forces. But Wilson, Hogan, and Mintz (1983) stated that all the symptoms of anorexia nervosa are emotionally caused, and thus they classified the disorder as a psychosomatic illness. "That the psyche can stop menstruation is to us patently psychosomatic" (p. 2). These authors also differed with Bruch's contention (1982) that "the patient's persistent malnutrition creates psychological problems that are biologically, not psychodynamically determined" (p. 1535).

Just as there are conflicting etiologic theories, there are also opposing treatment approaches. Bruch (1961, 1962, 1965, 1970, 1973, 1974, 1978a) recommended psychotherapy, rejected psychoanalysis, and insisted on early weight gain and hospitalization. Minuchin, Rosman, and Baker (1978) and Palazzoli (1978) recommended family systems therapy. Bettelheim and Cohler (1975) recommended residential treatment in what they described as an object-relations therapy approach. Other clinicians and researchers have recommended psychoanalysis; and this group is opposed to any and all behavior modification, coercion to eat, and hospitalization or placement, except for true emergencies. (Mushatt, 1975, 1980, 1982; Sperling, 1978; Mintz, 1983; and Wilson, 1983).

Clinical Picture

Whatever the different explanations regarding cause and treatment, there is agreement regarding the recognizable clinical picture presented by patients diagnosed as anorexic and bulimic. Anorexia is defined as the adamant conscious refusal to eat, to the point of self-starvation; in extreme cases, it can be so severe as to cause death. The obsessive pursuit of thinness is the overriding theme of life, and no amount of familial concern and warnings by family and physician can dissuade the patient from food refusal. The anorexic pattern is most common in adolescent girls, although it has also been observed in women of all ages and, increasingly, in adolescent boys. Malnutrition and emaciation are blandly denied, and earlier childhood obesity and shame over fatness are cited as reasons for initiating and perpetuating the diet. Food is picked at and eaten minimally and often surreptitiously; or conversely, the noneating pattern may be displayed with provocativeness. Commonly, jogging and other forms of exercise are employed to burn up calories. "Characteristically, there is hyperactive, energetic-appearing behavior that is in marked contrast to the patient's sick appearance and that serves to deny this helpless state" (Mintz, 1983, p. 85). These patients do not feel hungry, or they deny hunger and a longing for favorite foods.

> The incongruity of the starved, emaciated skeleton who complains of a fear of eating and getting fat is difficult to reconcile unless one recognizes that the starvation covers up a strong unconscious impulse to gorge. It is this impulse that the patient unconsciously recognizes and fears. In some patients, the clinical syndrome involves alternating bouts of starving and gorging. Typically, sustained periods of starvation with weight loss and emaciation alternate with momentary bouts of bulimia in which tremendous amounts of foods are ingested and then vomited up, with no net weight gain" [p. 86].

Overeating can replace anorexic self-starvation. While anorexics deny the impulse to eat, bulimic patients gorge themselves, eating nonstop, and then use laxatives and/or vomit, as they are terrified of weight gain. Both bulimic and anorexic patients commonly describe a similar family history of earlier heaviness or obesity; parental preoccupation with food and diet; and frequently, parents with chronic weight problems. Gorging and vomiting are commonly secret activities, recognized as out-of-control patterns that cause self-loathing and disgust. The enormous amount of food that is gobbled up is often junk food or whatever is available. Like the alcoholic, driven out at night to purchase liquor, bulimics will recount with shame a late night foray to purchase any and everything available—sandwiches, pizza, ice cream, cakes—all of which are then devoured at once. Bulimic patients tend to be more impulse-ridden than their overcontrolled anorexic counterparts; and this may take the form of sexual promiscuity, delinquency, lying, and deception.

Psychodynamic and Familial Factors

"It should be clear that if the impulse to eat and gorge is unconsciously defended against by the need to starve, then the underlying conflicts are the same whether the patient is starving or gorging, too thin or too heavy. The conflicts are merely responded to with different sets of defenses" (Wilson, Hogan, and Mintz, 1983, p. 88). The two-sides-of-the-same-coin relationship between bulimics and anorexics cannot be overemphasized; thus psychoanalytically oriented clinicians reject treatment approaches that emphasize normal body weight and ignore psychological functioning. Sours (1974); Volkan (1976); Sperling (1978); Wilson, Hogan and Mintz (1983); and Mintz (1983) have cited a series of repetitively seen familial and behavioral patterns, object relations, and ego deficits that result in both groups of patients being described as insecure, dependent, and immature, with marked attachments to parents, which may be concealed by overt pseudo-independence and hostility. (Mintz, 1983). Mintz noted corresponding parental uniformity:

> They are rigid, controlling, demanding, infantilizing and very attached to their children. One or both parents are very much involved in the child's life, to the point of intrusiveness and interference with the child's maturation and independence. At the same time, the parents are concerned about the well-being of the child and attempt to cooperate with the child's recovery. A great deal of control is exercised by the parents over the life of the child. Most of the time, the child passively accedes to this domination. [p. 88].

Overt defiance and adolescent rebellion are repressed and defended against by the food refusal, which staves off parental attack. Similarly, anorexic patients withdraw from and avoid real-life problems and cope with conflict by focusing on food and dieting. The dieting and food refusal commonly is supported by specific ego deficits, most importantly, distortion in body image. Patients can be emaciated but see themselves as heavy. Those with less severe ego deficits and distortions can recognize and acknowledge their excessive thinness. Casper (1982) for one, suggested biological and constitutional factors to explain the distorted body boundaries. "For example, the perceptual disturbance in the experience and integration of the body image, such as body-size overestimation and the failure to 'feel' emaciated and bony may be biologically rooted. Without this distortion, it would be virtually impossible for emaciated patients to assert that they feel just right" (p. 432). Bruch (1977) observed that patients express bewilderment about their inability to see themselves realistically, almost as if their body were not their own or as if the body were separate from the self. "Lasting recovery involves the development of an active and positive acceptance of one's own body and concern for its health" (p. 295). The disturbed body image commonly accompanies distorted body awareness, expressed in the absence of hunger, fatigue, sexual feelings, or sensitivity to pain, and deficits in identifying emotional states (p. 296). Depression and anxiety can be unnoticed or masked. Because of these perceptual disor-

ders—delusions and body distortions—Bruch suggested a core schizophrenia. Goodsitt (1977) suggested instead the diagnosis of borderline
psychosis for those patients presenting a picture of primary anorectics
(p. 305). He did not believe in the existence of an actual perceptual disorder, but rather in a disturbance of the self that includes the body.
Drawing on Kohut's (1971) examination of "self-pathology," Goodsitt
posited an unattainable, noncohesive sense of self, which interferes
with the patient's processing external stimuli, be it food or information.
"It is a well-integrated self that allows one to feel in control and not just
an empty receptable subject to foreign preoccupation. The anorectic's
experience of bodily helplessness indexes a lack of integrity of the sense
of self" (pp. 306–7). Cohler (1977) suggested the borderline syndrome in
his explanation of the etiology of the anorexia syndrome: "The anorectic patient becomes disturbed as a result of a life in which, almost from
birth, body signals have been distorted and denied. Not having been
able to achieve differentiation and individuation from her mother, the
anorexic patient develops the feeling that she is only one aspect of her
mother's personality (p. 378).

Food refusal often follows adolescents' sense of being powerless
and of having no permission to make decisions in their earlier years.
Anorexics can "force" other family members to eat, doing what adolescent anorexics feel has been done to them, and thereby identifying with
what they feel was the overcontrolling mother (Bruch, 1978).

Food refusal often is not the sole passion of anorexic adolescent
girls. Perfectionist striving for superior academic records is also frequently observed. "The markedly driven patient who studies constantly
and voices dissatisfaction with anything but perfect grades often dis-
tresses the parents who recognize the drivenness and hopelessly attempt to persuade the patient to work less and enjoy herself more"
(Mintz, 1983, p. 91). The adolescent ignores the parents' concerns about
excessive study and sleeples nights, just as she ignored their concerns
about weight loss in her quest for control and perfection.

Prior to adolescence, the usual history of anorexic and bulimic patients is markedly similar, in that these children routinely are described
as nontroublesome, good, cooperative, healthy and responsive. Parents
commonly cannot remember battles of the spoon and forced-feeding episodes, or disciplinary actions or marital conflicts that forced the child
into a submissive position. "Normal phases of separation-individuation,
especially negativism, aggression and exploration suffer the most interference" (Mintz, 1983, p. 93). The careful accurate history generally reflects separation anxieties and clinging to the mother, alongside tranquil preadolescent phases and stages. Good academic performance and
obedience did not diminish with the advent of pubescence and adolescence. Because of the parental demands for obedience and conformity,

normal adolescent rebellion is too frightening to consider; thus self-starvation and illness is employed as a form of safe self-assertion that will incite parental worry rather than anger. The patient's guilt over the normal aggressivity and increased sexuality of adolescence "requires" self-punishment in the form of deprivation, illness, and regression to the earlier infantile bond to the mother. Eating, chewing, and biting are activities too aggressive to be tolerated. In some anorexics, eating is associated with terrifying sexual fantasies. "Both starving and gorging patients have unconscious pregnancy fantasies, fears of oral and genital damage and a preoccupation with a flat abdomen" (Mintz, 1983, pp. 94–95). Psychoanalytic theory suggests that bulimic gorging-vomiting patients, unconsciously are "attempting to relieve, as well as undo, the rape; to eject the semen; the baby; the passive yearning for perpetual infancy without responsibility and the symbiotic attachment to the mother" (p. 95). Just as the adolescent clings to the parent(s), the parents cling also, atempting to control, intrude, and dominate the child's every activity, especially when and if anorexia diminishes and is replaced by acting out and aggression, even though these behaviors are normal and age appropriate.

The overwhelming ties between child and parents are often played out in the selection of peer relationships. Strong symbiotic ties are formed to domineering and demanding friends—if friends are possible at all, in the face of overconsuming parent-child bonds. Fears of dependency, separation, and sexual feelings cause many adolescent girls to deny or cancel, by weight loss, any pubescent bodily changes. Self-starvation will diminish breast development and the body's filling out in feminine proportion and will halt or disturb menses.

It is agreed that anorexic and bulimic patients commonly present immaturity, excessive dependency, frequent protestations of perfection, grandiosity, and omnipotence. These narcissistic disturbances and the patients' uneven sense of self-esteem (Goodsitt, 1977) correspond to the distorted object relations, namely, the pre-oedipal problems of separation and individuation and unresolved oedipal conflicts. "The anorexic female's unresolved pre-oedipal fixation to the mother contributes to psychosexual problems, including severe oedipal conflicts, [and] depending on the degree of regression, the pregenital characteristics of narcissism, ambivalence, some degree of bisexuality and a low frustration tolerance will be more or less evident" (Sperling, 1978, p. 171).

Hogan (1983) examined the pregenital characteristics that distinguish between the anroexic and bulimic patient. "The abstaining anorexic seems to present a more obsessional character structure with obsessional defenses. The gorger-vomiter is more likely to present an over-ideational hysterical character structure, with hysterical acting out and other hysterical defenses" (p. 147). Hogan also observed that the bulimic patient's more overt and covert patterns of provocative acting out apparently reflect a less strict superego than the abstaining anorexics. "Some patients with neurotic character structures and appropriate pregenital problems may discover and use [bulimia and vomiting] to replace neurotic or psychosomatic symptoms and to reinforce their defenses against unwanted oedipal pressures" (p. 148).

Overall, the heterogenity of anorexic and bulimic patients, and the approaches to them, must be emphasized. Food refusal and gorging and vomiting are neurotic symptoms manifested by a wide range of patients, who present various psychopathologies, including psychosis, borderline states, character or personality disorders, and neurosis. Clinicians and researchers who subscribe to emotional causation offer psychodynamic modes of treatment. Others who emphasize biological and organic etiological factors employ a range of interventions, such as appetite-stimulating drugs, behavior modification, and operant techniques.

Treatment

Successful treatment of anorexic and bulimic patients requires appropriate management of food to reinstitute normal nutrition for physical well-being and the resolution of the underlying psychological and family problems. "Weight gain alone is an unreliable sign of rehabilitation. Relapses are frequent and the histories of those with fatal outcome illustrate the fallacy of considering reinstitution of weight alone a cure" (Bruch, 1971). Blinder, Freeman, and Stinkard (1970) reported on a case of a young woman who gained adequate body weight but committed suicide following her discharge from the hospital. Technical and philosophic dilemmas are inherent in treating this disorder, and in evaluating patient's progress. "A psychoanalyst is undoubtedly going to have a different criteria for satisfactory adjustment than a pediatrician" (Halmi and Larson, 1977, p. 349).

While claims of success have been made for a number of approaches, including implantation of the pituitary gland, insulin injection, electro-convulsive shock therapy, drugs, behavior modification, family therapy, and psychoanalysis, Bruch (1977) noted the lack of information about long-range outcomes. She also raised questions about all the above modes of intervention. She observed that patients subjected to any forcible approach—drugs, shock, restraints, and the withholding of desirable activities and granting of privileges as a reward for weight gain—experience such hospital programs and behavior modification as brutal coercion. Family treatment can interfere with familial disengagement and the needed separation and individuation. Psychoanalytic interpretation "contains elements that represent for the patient the painful repetition of old patterns, namely, of being told by someone else what to see and think, with the implication of being incapable of knowing his own mind. The life long profound sense of ineffectiveness is thus confirmed and reinforced" (p. 300). Thus she recommended psychoanalytically oriented ego supportive psychotherapy, an effort to repair conceptual deficits and distortions, recognize affects, and feelings of powerlessness, helplessness, and isolation. The active participation of the patient is sought in the treatment process, to try to stimulate more self-direction, self-acceptance, and self-respect. Opponents of hospitalization Palazzoli (1978), Sperling (1978), Wilson, Hogan and Mintz (1983), and Hogan (1983) have noted the coercive measures routinely applied in hospitals, the patient's manipulations that successfully split staff, the patient's regression, and other negative aspects of hospitalization. Thus, many researchers reserve this extreme intervention for only the most acute cases—those which present severely regressed behavior, profound emaciation causing illnesses, convulsions from electrolytic imbalance, cardiac arrhythmias, or severe depression and suicidal impulses (Mintz, 1983c).

Anorexia Nervosa: Case of Martha

Martha identified her self-starvation as beginning at age 12, when she attended a dance camp and was harshly warned about getting fat and thereby being unfit as a dancer. While her interests in dance were not long-standing, she remained fanatically obsessed with her weight and ate little, if anything. On the rare occasions when she gave in to familial urging and pressure, she would vomit up the relatively normal portion of dinner she had consumed. In college, she would both deny being thin enough and complain about her emaciated breastless appearance and her erratic or nonexistent menstrual periods. She diminished her most extraordinary attractiveness by maintaining a bony, undernourished figure.

She was immaculate, perfectionist, and demanding of herself in a myriad of ways; but she was continually dissatisfied, especially when she compared herself to her siblings. Her three brothers all excelled in the adolescent achievements of academics, athletics, and peer status. The brothers were accepted at prestigious colleges, and then at equally outstanding graduate schools in medicine, law, and architecture.

Martha's family of origin was upper class, white, and Jewish, a Southern family of means and social status. Her father, an outstanding journalist in his community, did some university teaching. He was described as an involved parent, devoted to his children's accomplishments and development, while simultaneously being a "free thinker" and believer in "open" marriage. The parents had long-standing marital discord and the mother repeatedly contemplated separation and divorce. She could neither tolerate her husband's free lifestyle nor leave him and therefore suffered a protracted depression, finding her gratification in her children. She was a most attractive woman, but her self-esteem was low due, in part, to her decision not to continue managing an art gallery and her resulting lack of a profession and career when her children were grown and out of the home. She had an erratic work history and episodic attendance at graduate school once her children were older.

Martha's mother articulated guilt and anger at her husband for "causing" Martha's problems. She claimed that during her daughter's first years of life she was not always emotionally available to this newest baby because of her rage and depression at discovering her husband's first adulterous relationship. This caused what the mother believed was erratic, often harsh and angry care of Martha during the first year or two of her life and excessive sharing with her daughter of the strains and stresses in the marriage when Martha entered adolescence. The father was described as disavowing this explanation of the etiology of his daughter's difficulties and endorsed a strictly medical explanation. He advocated weight gain to appropriate body weight to restore regular menarche and displayed little interest or attention of his relationship with his daughter or to Martha's feelings about herself. Just as he denied the significance of these dynamic considerations, he also denied the significance of this adolescent's retreat from romantic attachments, so in contrast to her brothers' relationships with their steady girl friends.

Martha reported improved weight control following a course of individual therapy that combined a behaviorist and psychodynamic perspective. While she might be instructed to bring food to a therapy session and "eat" with her therapist, they also discussed her familial relationships—with particular focus on her overdependency on and protectiveness of her mother, competitiveness with her brothers, and estrangement from her father. She took gradual pleasure at her own acceptance to a journalism program at an Ivy League university. The therapy furthered Martha's genuine separation and individuation from her mother. She was helped to be less embroiled in her parents' ongoing marital difficulties and therefore freer to form a relationship with her father, without the earlier feelings that such a connection would be disloyal to her mother.

Bulimia: Case of Debby

Debby formally sought therapy during and after college for what she called long-standing "eating disorders." She had struggled with weight control since early adolescence when she experienced rapid weight gain as she entered puberty. Before that time, she had been very slender, so slim that during latency her parents continuously urged her to eat more at each meal. Food preparation and overeating characterized a good portion of family life. Following the postpubescent sudden weight gain, Debby felt ungainly and unattractive and for years was preoccupied with crash diets, starvation periods, and secret private eating binges, followed by vomiting. As an intelligent and well-read older adolescent, she rightly assessed herself as shifting continuously from anorexic to bulimic patterns and behaviors. Mortification was demonstrated in her accounts of binging at night, when she consumed incredible amounts of junk food, dashing out for more pizzas, french fries, cakes, sundaes, and sodas until she made herself bloated and nauseated.

In college, Debby found short-lived relief. She was seen both in individual and group short-term therapy. The approach was described as behavioral and educational. The individual therapist and group leader both lectured and advised about proper nutrition and regular eating habits; and the patients were instructed to keep journals, recording weight, food intake, and episodes of binging or starving, with some attempt to correlate mood and environmental and interpersonal factors with out-of-control eating and vomiting periods. Debby felt some support from peers in the group and from her individual therapist, herself a prior eating-disorder patient. However, Debby felt she learned little that she did not already know about herself and, additionally, was uncomfortable with the amount of personal information about her own life and problems that the therapist shared in their sessions.

In the second course of treatment, Debby was seen in individual psychoanalytically oriented psychotherapy. While she did report binging and self-starvation episodes, she became more in touch with her sense of shame, low self-esteem, and mortification at being out of control. She was able to examine her quest for perfection, her strivings for the perfect body, and her dislike of her body due to her preoccupations with the slightest imperfection. Since she was an aspiring dancer, the weight issue was endemic to her environment and was reinforced by her peers, who all struggled to remain extra-thin and compared and contrasted diets, appetite suppressants, and other techniques. However, in therapy, Debby moved from the surface level to underlying personal issues related to her familial relationships; she was a twin and was the "older" perfect child who was always controlled, well-behaved, and often protective of her more erratic twin sister.

Debby grew up on the West Coast, in an upper-middle-class, liberal, educated family. Her parents, both lawyers, were caring and giving, but often unresponsive and unempathic, due to marital strains and her father's recurrent bouts of depression. Debby's mother had gone back to work a few months after the twins were born, leaving them in the care of a consistent and loyal housekeeper who worked for the family a dozen years. This absence of the mother was something both mother and daughter later considered as a less than optimal arrangement, which affected both sisters as well as the mother, who felt a continuous sense of guilt about her inconsistent early mothering and her emphasis on her career instead of her young children.

Debby examined issues of strains in attachment and separation and individuation from her parents and her twin. The insight she gained enabled her to experience more ego growth, increased frustration tolerance, a capacity to self-soothe without ingestion of food, and better drive modulation. She was able to surrender wild diet schemes and eating binges and could maintain an appropriate weight more comfortably. These accomplishments were accompanied by more age-appropriate grooming, grocery shopping, food preparation, and economic self-sufficiency. She began attending practice and dance classes regularly, in contrast to her past erratic patterns. All in all, Debby grew to be able to take better care of herself. Mood and affect correspondingly became less labile, and self-esteem improved.

Bibliography

BETTELHEIM, B. (1975). The Love That Is Enough: Countertransference and the Ego Processes of Staff Members in a Therapeutic Milieu. In *Tactics and Techniques in Psychoanalytic Therapy, Vol. 2*, eds. P. L. Giovacchini, A. Flarsheim, and L. B. Boyer, pp. 251–78. New York: Jason Aronson.

BLINDER, B. J.; FREEMAN, D. M. A.; and STINKARD, A. J. (1970). Behavior Therapy of Anorexia Nervosa: Effectiveness of Activity as a Reinforcer of Weight Gain. *Amer. J. Psychiatry*, 126:77–82.

BRUCH, H. (1961). Transformation of Oral Impulses in Eating Disorders: A Conceptual Approach. *Psychiatric Q.*, 35:458–81.

_____ (1962). Perceptual and Conceptual Disturbances in Anorexia Nervosa. *Psychosomatic Med.*, 24:187–94.

_____ (1965). Anorexia Nervosa and Its Differential Diagnosis. *J. Nerv. Mental Disease*, 141:555–66.

_____ (1970). Psychotherapy in Primary Anorexia Nervosa. *J. Nerv. Mental Disease*, 150:51–67.

_____ (1971). Death in Anorexia Nervosa. *Psychosomatic Med.*, 33:135–44.

_____ [1973] (1975). Anorexia Nervosa. In *American Handbook of Psychiatry*, vol. 4, 2nd ed., ed. M. F. Reiser, p. 79. New York: Basic Books.

_____ (1974). Perils of Behavior Modification in the Treatment of Anorexia Nervosa. *J.A.M.A.*, 230:1409–22.

_____ (1977). Anorexia Nervosa. In *Adolescent Psychiatry, Vol. 5: Developmental and Clinical Studies*, eds. S. Feinstein and P. Giovacchini, pp. 293–301. New York: Jason Aronson.

_____ (1978). *The Golden Cage: The Enigma of Anorexia Nervosa*. Cambridge, Mass.: Harvard University Press.

_____ (1982). Anorexia Nervosa: Therapy and Theory. *Amer. J. Psychiatry*, 139:1535.

CASPER, R. (1982). Treatment Principals in Anorexia Nervosa. In *Adolescent Psychiatry, Vol. 10: Developmental and Clinical Studies*, eds. S. Feinstein, J. Looney, A. Schwartzberg, and A. Sorosky, pp. 431–54. Chicago: University of Chicago Press.

COHLER, B. J. (1975). The Residential Treatment of Anorexia Nervosa. In *Tactics and Techniques in Psychoanalytic Therapy, Vol. 2*, pp. 385–412. See Bettelheim (1975).

_____ (1977). The Significance of the Therapist's Feelings in the Treatment of Anorexia Nervosa. In *Adolescent Psychiatry, Vol. 5*, pp. 352–84. See Bruch (1977).

FREUD, S. [1918] (1955). From the History of an Infantile Neurosis. *Standard Edition*, 17:7–122. London: Hogarth.

GOODSITT, A. (1977). Narcissistic Disturbances in Anorexia Nervosa. In *Adolescent Psychiatry, Vol. 5,* pp. 304–12. *See* Bruch (1977).

HALMI, K. and LARSON, L. (1977). Behavior Therapy in Anorexia Nervosa. In *Adolescent Psychiatry, Vol. 5,* pp. 323–51. *See* Bruch (1977).

HOGAN, C. (1983). Object Relations. In *Fear of Being Fat—The Treatment of Anorexia Nervosa and Bulimia,* eds. C. P. Wilson, C. Hogan, and I. L. Mintz, pp. 129–49. New York: Jason Aronson.

KOHUT, H. (1971). *The Analysis of the Self.* New York: International Universities Press.

MINTZ, I. L. (1983). Psychoanalytic Description: The Clinical Picture of Anorexia Nevosa and Bulimia, pp. 83–113; Psychoanalytic Therapy of Severe Anorexia: The Case of Jeanette, pp. 217–44; Anorexia Nervosa and Bulimia in Males, pp. 263–303; An Analytic Approach to Self Starvation and Amenorrhea, pp. 335–44. *See* Wilson, Hogan, and Mintz, eds. (1983).

MINUCHIN, S.; ROSMAN, B. L.; and BAKER, L. (1978). *Psychosomatic Families: Anorexia Nervosa in Context.* Cambridge, Mass.: Harvard University Press.

MUSHATT, C. (1975). Mind-Body Environment: Towards Understanding the Impact of Loss on Psyche and Soma. *Psychoanal. Q.,* 44:81–106.

_____ (1980). Melitta Sperling Memorial Lecture, presented at the Psychoanalytic Association of New York, Feb. 25.

_____ (1982). Anorexia Nervosa: A Psychoanalytic Commentary. *Inter. J. Psychoanal. Psychother.,* 9:257–65.

PALAZZOLI, S. M. (1978). *Self-Starvation: From Individual to Family Therapy in the Treatment of Anorexia Nervosa.* New York: Jason Aronson.

SOURS, J. (1974). Anorexia Nervosa Syndrome. *Intern. J. Psychoanal.,* 55:567–76.

SPERLING, O. (1978). The Concept of Psychosomatic Disease. In *Psychosomatic Disorders in Childhood,* ed. O. Sperling, pp. 3–10. New York: Jason Aronson.

VOLKAN, V. D. (1976). *Primitive Internalized Object Relations: A Clinical Study of Schizophrenic, Borderline, and Narcissistic Patients.* New York: International Universities Press.

WILSON, C. P.; HOGAN, C.; and MINTZ, I. L., EDS. (1983). *The Fear of Being Fat—The Treatment of Anorexia Nervosa and Bulimia.* New York: Jason Aronson.

11

Depression and Affective Disorders

I. Depression

"There are no better accounts of adolescent depression that those given by gifted and introspective young people themselves" (Anthony, 1970, p. 841). Such accounts of "deadly despair, and total emptiness, the unspeakable melancholy, the crushing, bleak and desolate joylessness" (pp. 841–42) reflect helplessness, a sense of oppression and agony. Anthony noted that such feelings are frequently described and thus appear to be part of the normal depression of adolescence. By contrast, the clinical depression of adolescence usually evolves out of developmental phases of earlier childhood rather than those of adolescence itself. Differentiating between normative depression and clinical depression is difficult, but generally the presence or absence of significant mood disturbance in earlier childhood is of diagnostic and prognostic importance. Until the relatively recent longitudinal studies by a number of researchers such as Masterson (1967), Offer (1967), and Rutter et al (1976), it was believed that psychopathology, notably depression, could be attributed to normal developmental turmoil and age-appropriate ego regression. Laufer (1966) wrote about object loss, mourning, and depression during the adolescent years, as the young person bids a final farewell to childhood and the close dependent ties to parents. But Carlson (1981) stated that while we recognize that adolescence "is not without its age-appropriate miseries we now realize that the natural history of psychiatrically ill teenagers is to become psychiatrically ill adults (p. 411).

We view the normative state as a painful transient interlude, reactive in nature, whereas the clinical expression has less connection to the period of adolescence per se and is seen as a pervasive sadness, related to earlier upheavals during childhood.

Anthony (1970) reported that

> in a general review of [clinical] adolescent depressions, one is confronted, as in adult cases, with certain repetitive findings; narcissistic types of object relations, conflicts of ambivalence, lowering of self-esteem, regression to oral and anal fixation points, ego helplessness, aggression turned against self, masochistic character structure, precipitation by object loss or narcissistic injury, and conflicts over shame and guilt [p. 845].

Other researchers, such as Sperling (1959) and Toolan (1962), cite early history manifestations of depressive equivalents, such as eating and sleeping disturbances, colic, crying, head banging, negativism, temper tantrums, truancy, running away from home, accident proneness, and antisocial behavior. In adolescence the equivalents generally noted are boredom, restlessness, manic behavior, and seeking of stimuli and excitement. Additionally, depressed adolescents commonly exhibit adolescent anxieties, learning inhibitions, anorexia, bulimia, addiction, and sexual identity confusions. Specific upheaval or traumatic events like illness, accidents, and parent loss, can alter the course of development.

> Children raised in a home shrouded in a pall of oppressive tyranny, hostility, despair, unreasonable parental expectations . . . run a high risk of becoming depressed. When such children reach adolescence, the sexual and aggressive drives may overwhelm them so that separation evokes helplessness, futility and despair [Burman, 1980, p. 371].

In 1943, Edith Jacobson, one of the foremost researchers on depression, spoke of a narcissistic breakdown causing loss in self-esteem, feelings of helplessness, inferiority, weakness or the evolution of a sense of moral worthlessness and sinfulness. She distinguished between pre-oedipal and oedipal depression. The pre-oedipal type is based on a strong symbiotic tie with the omnipotent mother, causing discrepancies between ego and ego ideal with narcissistic imbalance and shifts in self-esteem, creating frequent feelings of shame, weakness, and mortification. Orality and propensity for addictions and narcissistic relationships are typically based on the overwhelming tie to an inconsistent mother who generally has been both overindulgent and critical. The oedipal level depression results in more mature guilt and moral masochism. The hostility directed toward the parents during the oedipal struggle is deflected back onto the self as parental idealizations break down and guilt over angry feelings emerges. Hopelessness and sadness can, in extreme cases, lead to suicidal ideation. Adolescents from such pain-riddled childhoods can overreact when romantic teenage relationships are broken off. Thus, depression during the adolescent years is a continuum, with a range of presenting symptomology and ages of onset.

While there is some controversy over the notion of "masked depression," we do find it as the underlying feeling—even if not initially reported—of the adolescent patient who presents varied forms of delinquency and acting out. Berkovitz (1981) cited late adolescence as a critical period for dealing with depression and feelings of powerlessness and hopelessness. These feelings, if overpowering, can lead to action "violent or controlled, intentional or accidental, random or a mixture of these" (p. 477).

If earlier emancipation, separation and individuation have not resulted in competent autonomy, the young person is overwhelmed with a sense of failure and "time running out." The culmination of long-standing inability to express aggression adequately interferes with the development of autonomous identity with not infrequent erruptive results, and the extreme impulses of homocide and suicide may alternate. Drugs may be used as a self-medication to blur these highly charged feelings, but the drug use, secondarily, will lessen the control of impulse due to diminished ego function. Berkowitz's only optimistic observation of these dire proceedings is that violent actions or accidents "seemed to function almost as traumatic events around which external as well as internal changes become organized, especially the formation of a new, more responsible, less narcissistically oriented superego and a new relationship to family and society" (p. 479).

It is necessary to attempt to clarify whether one is talking about a depressive mood, which occurs as a response to a variety of stressors and disappears when they do, or about depression as a serious and lasting affect and, therefore, an illness. "In depressive illness one has the depressive syndrome which is out of proportion to environmental stressors and is not relieved with environmental manipulation. Furthermore, there is ample evidence from the adult psychiatry literature that the entity of depressive illness has psychological, biochemical, pharmacological and genetic cohesion" (Carlson, 1981, p. 412). Thus we attempt to distinguish between misery and anguish and depression proper.

Some authors (Woodruff, Goodwin, and Guze, 1974) differentiate between depressed adolescents without pre-existing psychiatric disorders, who are diagnosed as having a primary affective disorder, and those with previous emotional disorders, who "have a secondary affective disorder" (p. 412).

II. Affective Disorders

Primary affective disorder can manifest itself early in childhood or adolescence. Until recently bipolar affective disorder, or manic-depressive illness, was considered uncommon in young people especially early adolescents. Carlson and Strober (1978) indicated that this assumption was based largely on misdiagnosis. One of the legitimate diagnostic dilemmas in recognizing the bipolar affective disorder or manic-depressive illness in teenagers is that one is often seeing the first episode, or only one side of a process which will in the future become bipolar. A patient can present an unipolar depressive picture with dysphoric mood, loss of interest, hopelessness, impaired concentration, irritability, slowed thoughts, initial insomnia, anorexia, weight change, auditory hallucinations, feelings of worthlessness, agitation, excessive worry, loss of energy, psychomotor retardation, somatic complaints, and suicidal thoughts or acts (Carlson and Strober, 1978).

Feinstein (1982) offered a behavioral profile of manic-depressive children and adolescents and noted the presence of most or all of the following characteristics:

1. Early evidence of affective instability. As early as one year of age parents recognize a pattern of affective extremes.
2. Dysphoric reactions to early stages of separation-individuation. The child has little ability to dampen down or achieve a low-keyed state. Separations usually lead to exaggerated reactions to loss frequently manifested as temper tantrums or periodic hyperactivity.
3. Dilation of the ego with persistence of grandiose and idealizing self-structures owing to failure of normal transformation of narcissism. This may manifest itself as an outgoing, dramatic quality with a theatrical flair. Many histories reveal early interest in [performances and competitions] and an early willingness to [be on stage].
4. Infantile circadian patterns tend to persist with reactions governed by inner, affective impulses rather than shifting to the environmental patterns of the family. Bizarre eating and sleep patterns and impulsivity may continue in spite of all efforts to enforce normal daily rhythms.
5. There is very frequently a family history of affective disorder. In addition to the presence of bipolar and unipolar patterns, equivalent states such as alcoholism or compulsive gambling may be elicited [pp. 258–59].

A secondary affective disorder is reflected in similar depressive symptoms as noted above, but it occurs with no prior *affective* psychiatric history. To further confuse the clinician we see "depressive equivalents," e.g.: truancy, disobedience, excessive drug use, delinquent behavior, hyperactivity, and aggressiveness, in adolescents with primary *and* secondary depression (Feinstein, 1982). Carlson (1981) noted that though

> symptom frequencies are similar, youngsters with secondary affective disorder are not surprisingly a more disturbed lot. They are frequently aggressive, irritable, delinquent, hyperactive, and more frequently hopeless and suicidal. Many of these characteristics, often designated as depressive equivalents, probably reflect these aggressive teenagers' other psychiatric disorders [p. 418].

Statistics suggest more familial illness in the histories of adolescents with secondary affective disorder. Although systematic follow-up studies have not been carried out, clinical observations reveal the following in cases of secondary affective disorder. First

> the depression remits, either of its own accord or with antidepressant medication, and the original psychiatric problems remain unchanged. Second, these youngsters present more complicated treatment problems, are more often suicidal, and more often have chaotic family situations which result from and then perpetuate the inherent psychopathology [pp. 419–20].

Bipolar illness and schizophrenia are frequently confused and misdiagnosed in adolescents because of their puzzling and atypical presentation. There is considerable conflict and uncertainty about the contributions of genetic predisposition, the role of family stress, as well as possible underlying neurophysiological mechanisms. These uncertainties pose major questions about treatment, including the choice between psychotherapy or lithium. Ginsberg (1979) noted that, at present, we assume that there are biochemical, psychological, genetic, physiological, and hormonal aspects that are relevant to mania. Current *DSM-III* (1980) criteria for bipolar disorder include distinct periods of elevated, expansive or irritable moods, manifested by increase in activity, pressured speech, flight of ideas, grandiosity, distractibility, and reckless activities. Manic patients may be euphoric, carefree, and open in exhibition of affects without concern for reality or the feelings of others.

By contrast, clinicians more commonly see adolescents in the depressive phase of the illness. The teenager may have lost interest in all activities and all sense of pleasure and may complain of poor appetite; feeling slowed down; and being unable to sleep, study, or concentrate. The loss of energy, feeling worthless, and being preoccupied with thoughts of death are all common characteristics. Some researchers note the similarity to patients who are borderline; and Akiskal (1981) described cyclothymic disorders where interpersonal problems were paramount, demonstrated by romantic losses and shifts in relationships, substance abuse, and episodic promiscuity. Generally noted are episodes typical of borderline patients, such as impulsivity and unwarranted extreme anger, mood shifts, fear of being alone, and accounts of boredom and feelings of emptiness.

In sum, specific clinical features are common when the manic-depressive illness emerges during puberty and adolescence. Feinstein (1982) cited:

1. Severe adolescent rebellion manifested by negativism, overconfidence and insistence of a feeling of well-being
2. Exaggerated self-esteem with grandiose conceptions of physical, mental and moral powers and over-commitment to adolescent tasks
3. Heightened motor activity manifested by restlessness, hyperactivity and in some examples, by the compulsive overactivity of anorexia nervosa . . .
4. Exaggeration of libidinal impulses [which] may surface as a sudden change from an inhibited child to an aggressive, sexually acting-out adolescent . . .
5. Gradual emergence of a cyclic, bipolar pattern of affect disorder but often manifesting itself as marked instability with short periods of depression and mania rather than the longer periods typical of adult manic-depression. Suicidal ideation is frequently noted [Feinstein, 1982, p. 263–64]

A less severe picture of adolescent depression is that of psychoneurotic intrapsychic depression. These teenagers display a high level of ambivalence toward their parents, "more so with one than another, dating back to early childhood; the child has experienced a traumatic loss by way of divorce, separation due to death or abandonment, the birth of a sibling or despair associated with parental incompatibility" (Burman, 1980, p. 372). Because of the recognized need to separate and function more autonomously, the more intact but depressed teenagers generally feel hopeless, overwhelmed, and despairing. These feelings may alternate with short-lived temper outbursts, drug abuse, and delinquency; but these symptoms are generally brief, transient, and reactive. This type of depression is viewed to be in the service of the ego running its course, allowing a respite so that more sophisticated defenses can be mobilized to enable the adolescent to move from one developmental phase to the next, to bear the stress of the recurrent bouts of disequilibrium until integration, consolidation, and personal stability are regained. The brittle hypercritical superego in the highly developed neurotic adolescent contributes to the aforementioned depression when the teenager falls short of expectations and accomplishments deemed worthwhile. This loss of self-esteem is generally transient, and when the super-ego matures and regains resiliance and flexibility, there is more self-tolerance for mistakes or shortcomings.

It is critical to monitor and carefully assess depression in adolescents to distinguish among neurotic depressions, the more severe bipolar affective disorders, and either of the above superimposed on a personality riddled with significant ego deficits, as we see in the borderline adolescent. Suicide occurs more frequently among adolescents than adults. (This will be elaborated in the following chapter.) Nevertheless, Kestenbaum (1982) encouraged us:

> On a positive note, I would like to add that young patients with an affective disorder are often among the brightest, most sensitive and creative individuals we encounter. They are often endowed with special gifts and should be encouraged to develop them, whether in the sphere of music, art, literature or human relationships. They are most capable of tenderness and empathy when they do not feel threatened themselves. By helping such children negotiate the difficult adolescent years (because they do need protection from the intensity of their drives as well as from the events of the external world), we are protecting them from future psychotic breakdown or at least ameliorating such breakdowns as well as enhancing the quality of everyday life. Thus the rewards of "at-risk" research [and clinical treatment] speak for themselves [p. 253].

Case of Kathleen

Kathleen entered therapy at age 15, feeling down and hopeless, desirous of help, and agreeing with her teacher's concerns about her academic struggle and the problems she had concentrating and handling her work. She was a white, upper-middle-class adolescent, who had experienced great stress for many years, dating back to her parents' marital discord, and exceptionally stormy divorce when she was ten. She and her brother had not been able to maintain ongoing relationships with both parents. Kathleen allied with her mother and, in fact, did not see her father for years until her entrance into therapy. Her brother had contact with the father and was estranged from his mother and Kathleen.

Kathleen said that at age ten, she initially felt great relief that the parents' fights had ended. Later, she felt self-conscious and very sad that they no longer had this "great and perfect" family.

At the onset of treatment, Kathleen described her sadness and despair at the current distance and perpetual conflict between her and her mother and new stepfather. This conflict took the form of cold estrangement and overly controlled silences, which alternated with her mother's total dependency on Kathleen. She would insist that Kathleen travel with her to the suburbs and protect her from ever spending so much as an evening alone, when her husband was out of town on business. In Kathleen's words: "I've been her mother for so long, her moral support. Look at these notes I left her daily, written when I was, ten, eleven, and twelve. I can't belief I wrote this stuff constantly. Isn't it terrible for any little girl to feel so worried and responsible?" These are the notes of childhood that Kathleen shared:

Dear Mom,
I want you to make sure that you're going to be all right. I just want to say that when you walk in the door of the lawyer's office, put some pride in you. Don't let Dad overcome you. Stand straight like a soldier. Think to yourself that you're the right one. Just wanted to give you some tips.

Love,
Kathleen

Dear Mom,
I hope you have a good day. I'm going to miss you. I will be in gym practicing for tonight and I think you will like the show. Now remember, don't be sad. Think of happy things like flowers, butterflies, springtime and Mother's Day. Love you so much.

Love,
Kathleen

Dear Mom,
I don't want you to feel badly. I know this is a very sad time for you, but keep your spirits up. The world is not at an end yet—you've got to think happy. I love you very much. You're the best mother there ever was and that's the truth. You're very special to me. Don't be sad. I love you. Roses are red, violets are blue, sugar is sweet and so are you. Keep your spirits up.

Love,
Kathleen

Kathleen suffered from the adolescent depression described by Anthony (1970). She demonstrated joylessness; shame and guilt; ambivalence; lowered self-esteem; regressions to oral fixations; ego helplessness; and aggression turned against the self, precipitated by object loss and narcissistic injury following her parents' divorce. Her mother's moodiness and rage at her ex-husband and son frightened Kathleen, so that she did not dare defy her mother. The mother's lack of empathy toward both her children and narcissistic preoccupations with endless material acquisitions in her new marriage were striking. The revenge themes and endless litigations with her former husband preoccupied this fearful and helpless woman and resulted in incessant demands upon her daughter for loyalty, unquestioning compliance, and companionship. She remained markedly insensitive to Kathleen's academic concerns and age-appropriate peer and social interests.

Kathleen's treatment provided her support, a place to ventilate, and assistance in sorting out her own social and academic concerns. Her social interchange with peers and her grades improved, with consequent improvement in her self-esteem and sense of acceptance in school. She was accepted at the art institute of her choice but then became ambivalent and anxious about the prospect of living away from home. She dreaded the thought of college and having to manage day-to-day functioning apart from her mother. She engaged in depressed and isolated self-destructive behaviors following high school graduation. She would walk her dog for hours in the park, withdraw to her room, covertly drink excessively; and over the summer, when mother and stepfather were out of town, she nicked her wrists. On another occasion, she took a heavy dosage of hoarded medications prescribed by the psychoanalyst who assisted her therapist with case management. However, extensive therapeutic work over the summer enabled Kathleen to follow through with plans to enter college in the fall, despite her anxiety, depression, and fear of functioning autonomously.

Bibliography

AKISKAL, H. S. (1981). Subaffective Disorders: Dysthymics Elyclothymic and Biopolar II Disorders in the "Borderline" Realm. *Psychiatric Clin. N. Amer.*, 4(1)25–46.

ANTHONY, E. J. (1970). Two Contrasting Types of Adolescent Depression and Their Treatment. *J. Amer. Psychoanal. Assn.*, 18:841–59.

BERKOVITZ, I. (1981). Feelings of Powerlessness and the Role of Violent Actions in Adolescents. In *Adolescent Psychiatry, Vol. 9: Developmental and Clinical Studies*, eds. S. Feinstein, J. Looney, A. Schwartzberg, and A. Sorosky, pp. 477–92. Chicago: University of Chicago Press.

BURMAN, S. (1980). The Response of Parents to Adolescent Depression. In *Adolescent Psychiatry, Vol. 8: Developmental and Clinical Studies*, eds. S. Feinstein, P. Giovacchini, J. Looney, A. Schwartzberg, and A. Sorosky, pp. 367–78. Chicago: University of Chicago Press.

CARLSON, G. A. (1981). The Phenomenology of Adolescent Depression. In *Adolescent Psychiatry, Vol. 9*, pp. 411–21. See Berkowitz (1981).

CARLSON, G. A. and STROBER, M. (1978). Manic-Depressive Illness in Early Adolescence: A Study of Clinical and Diagnostic Characteristics in Six Cases. *J. Amer. Acad. Child Psychiatry*, 17:138–53.

DSM-III (1980). *Diagnostic and Statistical Manual of Mental Disorders, Third Edition*. Washington, D.C.: American Psychiatric Association.

FEINSTEIN, S. C. (1982). Manic-Depressive Disorder in Children and Adolescents. In *Adolescent Psychiatry, Vol. 10: Developmental and Clinical Studies*, eds. S. Feinstein, J. Looney, A. Schwartzberg, and A. Sorosky, pp. 256–72. Chicago: University of Chicago Press.

GINSBERG, G. L. (1979). Psychoanalytic Aspects of Mania. In *Manic Illness*, ed. B. Shopsin. New York: Rauer.

JACOBSON, E. (1943). Depression: The Oedipus Complex in the Development of Depressive Mechanisms. *Psychoanal. Q.*, 12:541–60.

_____ (1954). The Self and the Object World: Vicissitudes of the Infantile Cathexis and Their Influence on Ideational and Affective Development. *Psychoanalytic Study of the Child*, 9:75–127. New York: International Universities Press.

KESTENBAUM, C. (1982). Children and Adolescents At Risk for Manic-Depression Illness—Introduction and Overview, pp. 245–55. See Feinstein (1982).

LAUFER, M. (1966). Object Loss and Mourning During Adolescence. *Psychoana-*

lytic Study of the Child, 21:269–93. New York: International Universities Press.

MASTERSON, J. F. (1967). *The Psychiatric Dilemma of Adolescence.* Boston: Little Brown.

OFFER, D. (1967). Normal Adolescents. *Arch. Gen. Psychiatry*, 17:285–90.

RUTTER, M.; GRAHAM, P.; CHADWICK, O. F. D.; and YULE, W. (1976). Adolescent Turmoil: Fact or Fiction. *J. Child Psychol. & Psychiatry*, 17:35–36.

SPERLING, M. (1959). Equivalents of Depression in Children. *Jewish Hillside Hospital*, 8:138–48.

TOOLAN, J. (1962). Depression in Children and Adolescents. *Amer. J. Psychiatry*, 118:719–24.

WOODRUFF, R. A., JR.; GOODWIN, D. W.; and GUZE, S. B. (1974). *Psychiatric Diagnosis.* New York: Oxford University Press.

12

Adolescent Suicide

Each year, approximately four hundred thousand teenagers attempt suicide and five to ten thousand are successful. Exact numbers are unknown, because many suicides are recorded as accidental deaths, and only a psychological postmortem could reveal whether the accident was actually a deliberate attempt at self-destruction. What is known is that the rate of suicides by teenagers has risen more than threefold in the past twenty-five years and that this increase is genuine and not the result of better reporting of the problem (Brody, 1984). How can we explain this horrifying phenomena? Are familial, societal, and cultural changes responsible for the increase? We can ponder whether suicide is contagious and whether or not publicity of one or two such deaths stimulates other unhappy adolescents to follow suit. We are currently witnessing an increase in suicides in an unlikely population, youth from affluent suburbs, children with above average abilities and opportunities. Questions are raised about the role drugs and alcohol play.

One of the basic theories related to suicide was first formulated by Freud (1917, 1921, 1924), who viewed the suicidal person as ambivalently loving and hating an object that is lost or appears lost and unavailable. The cherished and lost object is introjected and this possession or incorporation represents an attempt to preserve it and simultaneously destroy the hated object. Guilt over recognition of destructive impulses toward the lost love object is followed by a turning onto the self the aggressive hostile feelings, all of which then leads to suicidal behavior as the way of acting out these feelings and lessening the guilt.

Gould (1965) noted that this conceptualization was formulated essentially for adults and does not account for all suicides. Durkheim in 1950, Jackson in 1957, Ziboorg in 1936, Wahl in 1957, and Hendin in 1964 combined sociological and psychodynamic factors in their analyses of suicide. Hendin (1969) examined the phenomenon from a psychosocial perspective, emphasizing psychodynamic, ethnic, and cultural factors and their impact on child-rearing practices and marital relationships. More recent research has emphasized contemporary societal trends that exacerbate the complexity of the adolescent developmental period. The widespread breakdown of the nuclear family including the prevalence of divorce, diminishes "shared parenting and provides little reality against which to resolve oedipal conflicts" (Miller, 1981, p. 327). The weakening of the extended family and social ties, the greater mobility of families (intact and separated ones), and the easy availability of drugs have all hurt adolescents' abilities to sustain meaningful relationships. Increased numbers of youth experience inner emptiness; depend excessively on external stimuli in the form of drugs, alcohol, peers, music; and maintain a stance of devaluing living. Suicide becomes a common technique of conflict resolution (Miller, 1980). Gould (1965) made the critical point that "we are not dealing with a discrete clinical entity, but rather with a symptomatic act which may have multiple causes in varying combinations. Like most symptoms, the suicide attempt is overdetermined and represents an effort to resolve several conflicts or tension states" (pp. 229–30).

Children have a very incomplete and distorted sense of time, and of death. Young children, with their limited capacities for abstract thought, do not believe that death is final and absolute, but rather see it as a reversible phenomenon. "As difficult as it is for many adults to conceptualize their own death, it is quite literally beyond the grasp of the child" (p. 230). Cultural attitudes and mores discourage speaking about death directly, so euphemisms like going to heaven, going to sleep, and passing on, contribute to the sense of the unreality of death. Some researchers suggest that the reappearance of actors who have "died" on television or in films stimulates the child's belief in the reversibility of death. Many troubled adolescent youth maintain an early childhood attitude toward death and so, while attempting suicide, do not really believe that it could or would actually happen. "They seek the experience of death without dying, or they may wish to frighten others. Paradoxically, a failed suicide attempt by a person may reinforce the individual's sense of omnipotence. A conviction about the ease of the act and the probability of survival is reinforced" (Miller, 1981, p. 329).

At-risk adolescents are those who have suffered parent loss, particularly if the parent has suicided. Borderline and psychotic youth certainly are vulnerable due to ego impairments, such as distorted sense of reality, impulsivity, and poor frustration tolerance. Young people with no sure sense of self, or any sense of an internalization of structure and self-discipline, are frightened and at the mercy of impulses. On the other end of the continuum are young people who have been overstructured and overprogrammed. Some children snap under the strain of intense ambition in upwardly mobile families. They feel obliged to earn top academic marks and succeed in every activity and cannot tolerate not fulfilling their perfectionist goals (Brody, 1984). The withdrawn, highly isolated adolescent who lacks significant friendships and emotional investment in others is also at risk due to the depth of his or her despair and feelings of emptiness. Some of these adolescents have been unrecognized as depressed for years. They would be considered appropriately diagnosed as schizoid or overtly schizophrenic.

The loner college student who commits suicide is generally described as isolated and hopeless, and less likely to send out communication signals for help (Peck and Schrut, 1971). The loner is more commonly male rather than female, white rather than nonwhite, very aware of feelings of sexual inadequacy with doubt about ever being able to relate romantically to a woman. Common clinical diagnoses are borderline state, schizoid personality, and depressive character. Identifying and engaging these loner at-risk youths is a major accomplishment (Peck, 1981). Substance abusing, wildly acting-out adolescents, with histories of car accidents are another group of at-risk teenagers. Youths who are excessively suggestible and subject to extreme forms of altruism and self-sacrifice frequently acquire an ascetic stance; they are easily influenced by social and peer pressures and can destroy themselves through public self-immolation. Miller (1981) described the aftermath of reports of monks burning themselves to death in Saigon; this produced imitators in Prague and elsewhere in the West. "The suicide is symbolically designed to save the world or to convey to the world an awareness of its deficiencies" (p. 334).

Some youths with no sense of self, seeking closeness, join cults and are subject to directives and orders from charismatic leaders, even to the point of group self-destruction, as exemplifed by the mass suicides in Jonestown, Guyana. Accident-prone youth can accidentally suicide, even in a closed psychiatric hospital, where self-destructive behavior becomes part of the contagious patient mores.

Self mutilation is often highly eroticized and is apparently designed to project helplessness and rage onto the environment and at the same time, to have the environment return negative attention. Typical behavior includes suicide threats; cutting wrists, arms, abdomen or thighs; and put-

ting hands through glass. Although such behavior is rarely directly suicidal it may lead to accidental suicide" [p. 336].

The organization and interactions of the family of the at-risk suicidal adolescent have been major areas of study and research. These
studies point out that suicidal youth experience greater family disorganization than nonsuicidal youth and that continued suicidal behavior
may be associated with an inability ever to achieve adequate, reasonable, and neutralized family relationships. The family disorganization
can emanate out of poverty, unemployment, parent loss, health problems, marital conflict, and/or negative attitudes that chronically characterize parent-child relationships.

Some adolescents attempt suicide in response to actual or threatened parent loss by divorce, separation, death, or abandonment. A
greater percentage of suicidal patients had suffered parent losses before
age 12 as compared with psychiatrically disturbed, nonsuicidal patients
(Stanley and Barter, 1970). A greater percentage of suicidal adolescents
had experienced parental divorce, separation, and/or remarriage during
the onset of adolescence (Jacobs, 1971).

Family conflict characterized by overt anger, rejection, and communication problems is commonly present in families of suicidal adolescents (Sabbath, 1971; Teicher, 1970). Quarreling and lack of parent
support, strife, and distrust are frequently in the lives of despairing
youth (Cantor, 1976). Hendin (1969) in his study of young blacks (ages
19–35) noted a relationship between suicide, violence, and rage. Other
studies point to the intensely ambivalent nature of the parent-child relationship, especially the mother-child relationship (Friedman et al.,
1972; Hendin, 1969; Resnik and Dizmang, 1971). Rejection of the adolescent characterized the histories of many suicidal adolescents. Rejection
can be manifested by parental indifference and denial in response to
the problems their children present. Sabbath (1969) went so far as to
suggest the concept of the "expendable child," which results in an adolescent's sense of total abandonment, followed in some cases by an attempt to comply with overt and covert parental messages to "get out."
Rosenbaum and Richman (1970) interviewed family groups of nonsuicidal and suicidal individuals of all ages and found that the suicidal person was an object of aggression, who could only accommodate and save
the family by removing himself. Another form of rejection has been
noted in the reconstituted family, and in every case, the stepparent was
seen by the adolescent as unwanted (Jacobs, 1971; Teicher, 1970). The
aggression toward the unwanted new parent gets turned against the
self. Family conflict and family disorganization, with resultant multiple
caretakers, is perceived through the eyes of the adolescent as another
form of rejection (Dizmong et al, 1974).

Parental characteristics have been studied to attempt to identify what qualities typify parents of suicidal adolescents. The psychological and physical health of the parents obviously contributes to the etiology of adolescent suicide. Fathers have frequently been insignificant or absent, especially during early years of male adolescents who attempt suicide (Friedman et al., 1972). Maternal deprivation and role reversal, with the child having to parent the parent, are also frequent (Teicher, 1970). Parental alcoholism (Marks and Haller, 1977; Senseman, 1969), demanding or domineering behavior, interracial marriage and insistence on success, (Peck and Schrut, 1971) are other parental characteristics. Not uncommonly this parental group remains remarkably bland and does not react with what would be normal anger, worry, fear, or confusion (Yusin, Sinay, and Nihiras, 1972). Often they show only silence and withdrawal and/or indifference to their children. They are unlikely to contact a psychiatric facility about the suicidal crisis (Petzel and Riddle, 1981, p. 350).

Parents who have legal problems, immature or abnormal personalities, and/or severe marital stress produce the most vulnerable adolescents. Parents' severe physical illnesses, e.g., diabetes, cancer, high blood pressure, or cardiac problems, often force adolescents into a parental role, caring for parent(s), sibs, the household, and even the family business. This compromises adolescence, and repression of normal aggressivity results commonly in the anger being turned back onto the self. Familial disciplinary techniques are profoundly affected by parents' emotional and/or physical illnesses.

Adolescents with suicidal patterns generally perceive their parents' discipline as unfair and as a form of rejection (Jacobs, 1971; Teicher, 1970). Such discipline usually takes the form of parental nagging, withholding of privileges, withdrawal, and inappropriately bland responses to crisis. On the other hand, some frantic adolescents document harsh physical punishment (Duncan, 1977). "In general, reports suggest that parents of suicidal adolescents underreact to misbehavior, or at least fail actively and explicitly to communicate their reactions, concern and disapproval, resorting instead to ignoring, withholding and withdrawal" (Petzel and Riddle, 1980, p. 353).

School adjustment is important to ascertain because "school is the second major social system in which adolescents are involved" (p. 353). While not all suicidal adolescents have trouble in school, difficulty with academic performance has been the most frequently reported school factor associated with adolescent suicide. There may or may not also be problems in school attendance, school behavior, and peer relationships. Significantly, unsatisfactory scholarship has not been a major reason for school avoidance for suicidal adolescents. Other problems, such as illness, pregnancy, prior suicide attempts and behavioral problems, ex-

pulsion, or suspension keep teenagers away or stimulate them to attempt to make frequent school changes (Teicher, 1970). Commonly reported about suicidal adolescents are their frequent clashes with peers
and teachers and their general lack of friends and social life. Suicidal
adolescent girls are reported as less likely to have behaved well in school
than suicidal boys or than other emotionally disturbed girls (Marks and
Haller, 1974); they are more likely to have adjustment problems, low
grades, and patterns of disciplinary difficulty and truancy.

A range of problems associated with sexuality are cited in this at-
risk group. Fears and concerns about homosexuality, pregnancy, or
promiscuity are frequently reported. Paternal sexual assault is often
mentioned. Roberts and Hooper (1969) wrote of a sexualized life style of
suicidal adolescents, which includes promiscuity; homosexuality; and
multiple, premature, or precipitous marriages. A relationship, even a
marriage, is frantically sought, as the adolescent seeks remedy for a lack
of familial closeness or for a sense of emptiness. The teenager may seek
a partner to help ward off feelings of fear and abandonment during the
second separation and individuation from the mother. A more highly
developed adolescent, struggling with reawakened oedipal concerns,
may urgently need a partner to diminish the sexual attractiveness and
significance of the parent of the opposite sex. Loss of the partner stimulates suicide gestures. Love conflicts are the most common reason for
the adolescent's suicide attempts (Otto, 1972).

There appears to be a high correlation between suicidal behavior
and a negative outlook, or sense of hopelessness and helplessness. Jacobs (1971) enumerated a series of events that usually must occur to
stimulate a teenager to overcome moral and social constraints against
suicide. Specifically cited is the adolescent's feeling faced with an intolerable and unsolvable problem that is not an isolated incident, but is in
the context of a long-standing sense of failure and comes with the expectation of more failed efforts. This sense of life's being an insolvable
dilemma arises out of increasing social isolation. All dilemmas and
problems are projected onto others. The sense of hopelessness and helplessness becomes overwhelming.

Some studies (e.g., Levinson and Neuringer, 1977) have postulated
that the suicidal adolescent may feel helpless, not because he feels overwhelmed by actual phenomena, but because he cannot cope with his
environment due to possible cognitive deficiencies. Petzel and Riddle
(1981) noted that the contribution of cognitive functioning to adolescent
suicidal behavior has been a neglected area of study. They reported
studies that found suicidal adolescents lacking in problem-solving capacities and available responses to stress. These adolescents often have
distorted attitudes about death and a negative, constricted outlook. Cognitive functioning is impaired by substance abuse, and all studies indi-

cate that "adolescents addicted to drugs are at higher risk for suicide attempts than those who are nonaddicted, but addicted adolescents do not constitute a large proportion of youthful suicide attempters" (p. 387).

No distinct connection between media content and suicidal behavior has been demonstrated. There appears to be an increased risk of suicide among young males during wartime. Lack of employment opportunities or meager economic conditions increase adolescent suicidal behavior. Increased geographic mobility is associated with a greater frequency of at-risk adolescents. Physical illness can be a noteworthy factor for suicidal behavior. Periods of social disorganization, migration, and immigration contribute to higher incidence of suicide attempts. Except for a high proportion of Puerto Rican Catholic adolescents attempting suicide, Jews and Catholics, as a whole, have a much lower suicide rate than Protestants. More girls than boys attempt suicide, but more male adolescents actually succeed. This may be due to boys' greater preference for the lethal methods of fire arms and hanging, whereas girls employ more passive, less effective means such as ingesting pills.

Gould (1965) described types of suicide motivations:

1. The wish to gain support and strength through joining the powerful lost loved object
2. Death as a retaliation for abandonment or threat of abandonment
3. Manipulation and blackmail to obtain love and attention and to punish the other
4. Atonement for one's sins by dying
5. Self murder, as a displacement for what cannot be directed outward
6. Distintegration of the personality, i.e., hearing of voices commanding death
7. A last cry for help, in the hope that someone will save the adolescent [pp. 240–41]

It is crucial to note that little is known about the successful suicidal adolescent. Little follow up has been done to gain information about the deceased youths or about their families. What is known has been gleaned from studies about adolescents attempting and threatening suicide. "It is not valid to generalize results from one group to another . . . [However] there are indications that those adolescents who complete suicide are even more isolated, less visible and more disturbed than those attempting suicide" (Petzel and Riddle, 1981, p. 386).

Attempters are young people particularly vulnerable to loss or possible loss. They overreact to even minor stress and are ineffectual in controlling rage, depression, and anxiety; they frequently engage in a flurry of activity to avoid boredom and a sense of emptiness. Sadness, tenseness, perfectionistic standards, irritability, impulsivity, and susceptibility to suspiciousness are commonly found. Female adolescents commonly display overwhelming despondency, flat affect (though sometimes accompanied by dispassionate tears), few or no friends, and poor judgment. Commonly noted is a history of unreliable friends, family, and interpersonal support, which has become worse just prior to the suicide attempt (Teicher, 1970 and Jacobs, 1971). The suicide gesture or attempt is the extreme, desperate attempt to relieve what for the adolescent is an intolerable situation.

Case of Juan

Juan was a 14-year-old Puerto Rican boy, referred for treatment by his mother at the suggestion of a social worker who was a friend of the family. He had had several psychiatric hospitalizations because of two serious suicide attempts. At the time of the referral for outpatient treatment, Juan had run away at midnight from the hospital and was hiding out at the home of an adult friend, maintaining phone contact with his mother, and refusing to come home, unless she promised he could stay at home and not be returned to the hospital.

The hospital reports described Juan as angry and defensive, not working in therapy, and showing no gains in insight or self-control. He evidenced no motivation for treatment, but the reports recommended that he be continued in a long-term closed and secure setting. The unit director at a state hospital felt helpless in the face of recent policy conflicts between the hospital and the fire department. He described the fire department's prohibition of locked windows, which had resulted in several adolescent patients' running away at night, when staff coverage was lighter than during the day. Because of prevailing conditions at the hospital, he recommended outpatient work be attempted, if Juan's mother could control his activities and school attendance. Given her history of difficulty in handling Juan, the prognosis at onset appeared guarded.

Juan's behavior problems dated back to the fourth grade, when he was frequently truant from school. He was identified as becoming depressed at the onset of puberty, two years before his first hospitalization. The depression markedly intensified one year before the assessment, when he made his first suicide attempt by taking three-fourths of a bottle of antibiotics, following a fight with his girl friend. Initially, he was referred to, and seen in, a special outpatient child depression clinic. The staff there felt he responded positively to the medication (Imipramine in dosages up to 225 mg. a day) and noted a decrease in depression and irritability. However, Juan was discharged from the clinic after five months because of poor compliance and failure to keep appointments.

Juan's mother and her common-law husband described Juan as being very changeable in mood. One day he was sweet and gentle; the next day he had a devilish look on his face and seemed to be looking for trouble. They said he was erratic in his exchanges with them and with his younger brother.

He could get into violent fights with his brother, destroying his toys and punching him very hard. The parents were fearful that he would really hurt his brother.

Juan's second suicide attempt followed an argument with his mother over his late hours. He had arrived home very late and fought when his mother attempted to admonish and reason with him. In the course of the argument, he threw a fire extinguisher against the wall of the kitchen. When the argument subsided and his parents went to bed, Juan wrote several suicide notes to his family and close friends, went into the bathroom and took twenty or thirty 325 mg. Tylenol tablets. He reported going to bed hoping to "wake up dead," clearly a disavowal that he could destroy himself. He awoke early the next morning and phoned a nurse at the depression clinic which had treated him the year before. She phoned an ambulance, which took him to the hospital emergency room where he was treated with Syrup of Ipecac and Mucomyst. His hopsital emergency room care was uncomplicated, but he required constant supervision as he was assessed by the psychiatric consultant as a suicide risk. Therefore, with parental consent, he was then transferred to a psychiatric inpatient setting.

Juan showed preoccupation with suicidal ideation, and a fascination with death, violence, and violent crimes. He spoke of identifying with the character played by Charles Bronson in the movie *Deathwish*. At the time of admission to the inpatient psychiatric hospital, Juan was dressed in black and was wearing two live rifle bullets. He described his mood as "sad." His affect appeared constricted, and he was guarded and made little eye contact during the interview. There was paucity of speech, and he was hesitant and spoke in a soft voice at a normal rate. There was no evidence of psychomotor agitation or retardation, bizarre thoughts, delusions or hallucinations; memory appeared intact. Suicidal ideation was admitted. Judgment and insight were poor, and Juan did not believe he needed hospitalization or any treatment. He was admitted as an involuntary patient.

Juan came from a working-class Puerto Rican family. He was the oldest of his mother's two sons fathered by different men. His brother was three years younger and was described as more communicative and less moody and erratic than Juan. The mother was a most attractive, small, harassed women, clearly bewildered, frightened, and overwhelmed by her son. She acknowledged delegating too much to Juan when he was younger—and having a nonparental, siblinglike or marital relationship with him in the immediate past, considering him the man of the household. The mother had sole financial responsibility for herself and her boys and had frequently been overwhelmed by struggling to maintain employment and provide her children adequate care and supervision. She had relied on her mother, sister, and relatives in Puerto Rico to care for them. There had been separations and a variety of residences for the boys and the mother in the past.

At the time of the interview, the mother's lover of several years was residing with the family, awaiting his divorce; and he and the mother planned to marry. This man appeared to be a strong, secure, stable, and caring father figure. He was deeply resented by Juan, who felt his authority in the home had been usurped. Juan defied him and his mother and stayed out late, associated with rough, acting-out children, and was frequently truant from school. Presumably he was not involved with drugs or actual crime, though the parents feared this in the future, given his current peer affiliations, history of petty shoplifting, and contacts with street gangs. At the time of his outpatient therapy, following his elopement from the hospital, he was obsessively preoccupied with a brigade of youths committed to subway safety. He wore army camouflage fatigues, boots, and a beret, and carried a nightstick. With elaborate grandiosity, he proclaimed that he was a brigadier general, in his organization.

During the course of hospitalization, Juan's behavior ranged from pleasant and cooperative to hostile and sarcastic. He did not appear depressed, sad, or given to tears. These affects were noted at home. He demonstrated good ability to relate to adults and peers and exhibited humor and warmth toward the other adolescents. Continued preoccupations with violence and violent crimes dominated his interests; and he clipped endless articles about crimes of violence against women or crimes involving dismemberment and mutilation committed by teenagers against their parents. All of these he stated should be controlled by the police and adolescent gangs "warring for peace and order." When angry, he would make verbal threats of violence to peers and hospital staff, but he did not act out aggressively, as he did at home and on the streets of his neighborhood.

After some opposition, he was tested on two separate occasions. Intellectual functioning was in the low average (87) range on the verbal scale, very superior range (133) in performance, with an average full scale at 110. The enormous discrepancy between the verbal and performance tasks seemed to be due to his unusual manual and visual-motor skills and his failure to acquire age-appropriate academic skills and knowledge. His general knowledge and reading and arithmetic skills were particularly poor. This action-oriented rather than verbal means of problem solving stimulated impulsivity, since it was coupled with an inability to think through and anticipate the consequences of his actions. No signs of psychotic thinking were evident. Reality testing was unimpaired. Grandiosity was noted; Juan could not tolerate having his depression viewed as rooted in his sense of rejection and deprivation. His mother was this adolescent's lifeline, and his attempts to separate and accept his stepfather caused his current decompensation.

During the course of Juan's hospitalization, he remained angry and defensive and did not work in therapy. Thus he showed no gains in insight or motivation for continued therapy. Long-term hospitalization was recommended because his need for a closed, protected setting; and at the conclusion of the family's limited insurance coverage, he was transferred to a well-staffed long-term adolescent unit in a state hospital. He was opposed to continued care and threatened legal action to get himself discharged. He presented himself as a victim of other people's ideas. In the second hospital, he showed no evidence of psychosis and no delusions; he presented a full range of affects and related directly with a good amount of eye contact. Nevertheless, his history of suicidal, impulsive behavior and his noncompliance with inpatient and outpatient therapy and reasonable parental limits suggested his continued need for a safe, closed, structured setting.

In the hospitals, and later as an outpatient, he described a repeated experience of seeing a lady dressed in a white veil standing in his room as he was about to fall asleep. He described her as "my admirer" or "she is ready to marry me." He said he believed that the apparition was really there and was not a hallucination. He claimed not to be afraid of it as he believed it to be his guardian angel. Also he claimed to experience hearing his name called sometimes by a relative or a friend, but when he went to the door, no one was there.

This hallucinationlike experience appeared to be linked to his mother—his guardian angel—and his mother's Hispanic absorption in witchcraft, spells, curses, devils, and the like. Juan, emotionally unseparated from her, shared her spiritual system and her concerns and preoccupations with feeling haunted. With great fear, the mother described how she placed charms over doorways and elsewhere, and shared her fears—with what she claimed was complete openness for the first time. She feared the curse from her lover's legal wife. She linked her son's crying and sleep disturbances with her own similar symptoms. The mother described how Juan got obsessed with devils (drawing devil faces) and ideas of death as possibly related to her fear of the devil and his wish to "rescue" her. He often dressed in black and claimed he had to stalk the cemetery and confront the Devil.

Outpatient treatment could not be sustained because Juan's old behavior problems erupted and escalated after his first week at home. He kept late hours, despite parental rules and requests; was truant from school; and fought in the playground, resulting in school suspensions and nocturnal wandering. Juan quickly became erratic or very tardy in attending therapy sessions. He seemed afraid and also relieved at sharing thoughts, images, and fantasies in sessions, in the context of a growing degree of rapport and attachment to the therapist. After one month at home, Juan had regressed to sleeping on the floor, crying, and throwing temper tantrums. He articulated grandiose toddlerlike fantasies of superhuman techniques of survival, e.g., how he could live even if he tied his hands and ankles, weighted himself with stones, and lept off one of the many high bridges into the Hudson River.

His "stepfather" and mother became convinced of the necessity for rehospitalization. The stepfather was quick and responsive, whereas the mother seemed more confused, apprehensive, and fearful of her son's hatred of her if she signed him in, even though she acknowledged that she could not protect or limit him at home. Juan's rehospitalization proceeded smoothly. His mother described with amazement her son's actual relief at his parents' decision to accept his therapist's recommendation that he required a closed and protected setting.

Bibliography

BRODY, J. (1984). Personal Health—Detecting the Signs and Preventing Teenage Suicide. *New York Times*, 7 March 1984.

CANTOR, P. C. (1976). Personality Characteristics Found Among Youthful Female Suicide Attempts. *J. Abnormal Psychol.*, 85:324–29.

DISMONG, L. A.; WATSON, J.; MAY, P. A.; and BOPP, J. (1974). Adolescent Suicide at an Indian Reservation. *Amer. J. Orthopsychiatry*, 44:43–47.

DUNCAN, J. W. (1977). The Immediate Management of Suicide Attempts in Children and Adolescents: Psychological Aspects. *J. Family Practice*, 4:77–90.

DURKHEIM, E. (1950). *Le Suicide.* Glencoe, Ill.: Free Press.

FREUD, S. [1917] (1957). Mourning and Melancholia. *Standard Edition*, 14:243–60. London: Hogarth Press.

_____ [1921] (1961). Ego and Id. *Standard Edition*, 19:12–66. London: Hogarth Press.

_____ [1924] (1961). Economic Problems of Masochism. *Standard Edition*, 19:159–70. London: Hogarth Press.

FRIEDMAN, M.; GLASSER, M.; LAUFER, E.; and WAHL, M. (1972). Attempted Suicide and Self-Mutilation in Adolescence; Some Observations from a Psychoanalytic Research Project. *Internat. J. Psychoanal.*, 53:179–83.

GOULD, R. E. (1965). Suicide Problems in Children and Adolescents. *Amer. J. Psychother.*, 19:228–46.

HENDIN, H. (1964). *Suicide and Scandinavia.* New York: Grune and Stratton.

_____ (1969). Black Suicide. *Arch. Gen. Psychiatry*, 21:407–22.

JACKSON, D. (1957). Theories of Suicide. In *Clues to Suicide*, eds. E. Shneidman and V. Farberdev, pp. 11–21. New York: McGraw-Hill.

JACOBS, J. (1971). *Adolescent Suicide.* New York: Wiley-Interscience.

LEVENSON, M. and NEURINGER, C. (1971). Problem-solving Behavior in Suicidal Adolescents. *J. Consulting & Clin. Psychol.*, 34:490–11.

MARKS, D. A. and HALLER, D. L. (1979). Now I Lay Me Down for Keeps: A Study of Adolescent Suicide Attempts. *J. Clin. Psychol.*, 33:390–400.

MILLER, D. (1981). Adolescent Suicide: Etiology, and Treatment. In *Adolescent Psychiatry, Vol. 9: Developmental and Clinical Studies*, eds. S. Feinstein, J. Looney, A. Schwartzberg, and A. Sorosky, pp. 327–42. Chicago: University of Chicago Press.

_____ (1980). The Treatment of Severely Disturbed Adolescents. In *Adolescent Psychiatry, Vol. 8: Developmental and Clinical Studies*, eds. S. Feinstein, P. Giovacchini, J. Looney, A. Schwartzberg, and A. Sorosky, pp. 469–81. Chicago: University of Chicago Press.

OTTO, U. (1972). Suicidal Acts by Children and Adolescents—A Follow-Up Study. *Acta Psychiatrica Scandinavia* (Supplement).

PECK, M. (1981). The Loner: An Exploration of a Suicidal Subtype in Adolescence. In *Adolescent Psychiatry*, vol. 9, pp. 461–66. See Miller (1981).

PECK, M. L. and SCHRUT, A. (1971). Suicidal Behavior Among College Students. *HSMHA Health Reports*, 86:149–56.

PETZEL, S. and RIDDLE, M. (1981). Adolescent Suicide: Psychosocial and Cognitive Asspects. In *Adolescent Psychiatry*, vol. 9, pp. 343–98. See Miller (1981).

RESNIK, H. L. P. and DIZMANG, L. H. (1971). Observations on Suicidal Behavior in American Indians. *Amer. J. Psychiatry*, 127:58–63.

ROBERTS, J. and HOOPER, D. (1969). The Natural History of Attempted Suicide in Bristol. *Brit. J. Medical Psychology*, 42: 303–12.

ROSENBAUM, M. and RICHMAN, J. (1970). Suicide: The Role of Hostility and Death Wishes for the Family and Significant Others. *Amer. J. Psychiatry*, 126:1652–55.

SABBATH, J. C. (1971). The Role of the Parent in Adolescent Suicidal Behavior. *Acta Paidopsychiatria*, 38:211–20.

_____ (1969). The Suicidal Adolescent—The Expendable Child. *J. Amer. Acad. Child Psychiatry*, 8:272–85.

SENSEMAN, L. A. (1969). Attempted Suicide in Adolescents: A Suicide Prevention Center in Rhode Island Is in Urgent Need. *Rhode Island Medical Journal*, 52:449–51.

STANLEY, E. J. and BARTER, J. F. (1970). Adolescent Suicidal Behavior. *Amer. J. Orthopsychiatry*, 40:87–95.

TEICHER, J. D. (1970). Children and Adolescents Who Attempt Suicide. *Pediatric Clinics N. Amer.*, 17:687–96.

WAHL, C. (1957). Suicide as a Magical Act. In *Clues to Suicide*, eds. E. Shneidman and V. Farberder, p. 11–12. New York: McGraw-Hill.

YUSIN, A.; SINAY, R.; and NIHIRA, K. (1972). Adolescents in Crisis; Evaluation of a Questionnaire. *Amer. J. Psychiatry*, 129–574:77.

ZILBOORG, G. (1936). Differential Diagnostic Types of Suicide—Archives. *Neuro Psychiatry*, 35:270–91.

13

Reactive/Adjustment Disorders

Definition

This category of pathological responses is reserved for disorders that arise out of a reaction to an event or a situation in the external environment.* The response is viewed as an attempt to cope with stress, "not as a result of internalized conflict" (Kessler, 1979, p. 173). Many kinds of traumatic events or crises can stimulate and perpetuate a reactive disorder. Kessler (1979) noted the following: excessive or inadequate stimulation; illness, accident, and/or hospitalization; loss of a parent; and school pressures. The suddenness or chronicity of a situation affects the extent of influence on a young patient. "In making the diagnosis of reactive disorder, the dynamic state of the child and the nature of his reaction should be emphasized rather than the kind and degree of stress" (p. 173). Nagera (1966) emphasized that the child lacks the ego capacity to cope with specific developmental demands and therefore reacts to

*Reactive and Adjustment are used synonymously, the former more commonly in reference to children, and the latter in reference to adolescents.

developmental interferences with abnormal symptoms, defenses, and behavior. This sequence may or may not lead to permanent conflicts and deviations. Neubauer (1972) raised questions about the reversibility of symptoms, which in fact differentiates transient reactive disorders from fixed neurotic and character problems.

Etiology

Kessler (1979) emphasized the concept of vulnerability, based on endowment, intelligence, ego perception, age, and critical stage or phase of development, when the event occurs. Individual differences and age affect whether children and adolescents will be more or less successful in dealing with stress. Coping and adaptation depend on the competence and strength of adaptive ego functions. Thus, the traumatic neurosis occurs in response to an event in the environment, in contrast to classical neurosis, which arises out of internalized, long-standing structural conflict. A sudden, intense, and traumatic injury overwhelms the ego and the capacity to sustain organization and integration of normal functioning.

The *DSM-III* (1980) classification of mental disorders characterizes the adjustment disorder of adulthood as a maladaptive reaction to psychosocial stressors and emphasizes that the disorder is not an exacerbation of one of the other mental disorders. "The basis of the disorder lies in the concept of trauma as psychic overload, with a subsequent partial or complete feeling of helplessness, accompanied by regression and inhibitions" (Kaplan and Sadock, 1981, p. 579).

While reactive disorder is a response to environmental stress, symptoms do not always appear immediately, nor do they subside when the stress ceases. The severity of the stress is not always predictive of the extent of regression and temporary impairment. The clinician must be aware of cultural expectations and values, basic personality organization, and familial supports or lack thereof. *DSM-III* (1980) "Quick Reference" does rate psychosocial stressors as typically causing minimal, mild, moderate, severe, extreme, and catastrophic stress. Children or adolescents might experience minimal stress from a family vacation, mild stress, from beginning a new academic year, moderate stress from the birth of a sib, a family move, or chronic parental fighting. Severe stress is caused by the death of a peer, parental divorce, hospitalization (physical illness and surgery), and harsh parental discipline; extreme stress is caused by a death in the immediate family and physical or sexual abuse; catastrophic stress is created by multiple family deaths, and exposure to a devastating natural or abnormal disaster.

Characteristics

Reactive disorders and adjustment disorders are universal. Anna Freud stated that, in fact, we can speculate "that the absolute absence of such stress would find our 'fortunate' young adult vulnerable and poorly equipped to cope with the realities of his life" (Eissler et al., eds., 1977, p. 177). We recognize a reactive disorder following a trauma or stress, when atypical behavior ensues. Emergency defensive responses have been mobilized. Unattended, adolescents suffering from a reactive disorder frequently bind in anxiety and/or depression in some form of fixed psychopathology. The relief of the stress will not lead to reversibility as quickly and readily as it usually does with a younger child. The degree of disturbance depends on the nature of the shock, its suddenness, and the duration of the strain.

Depression, anxiety, mixed emotional features, disturbances of behavior, and regression are common reactive responses. Additionally, withdrawal, work inhibition, or academic decline may ensue. Adolescents can present exacerbated versions of typical teenage apathy, moodiness, irritability, and/or hyperactivity.

Treatment

Treatment interventions should be based on prompt but careful assessment of the adolescent's basic endowment, strengths and vulnerabilities, level of psychological development, past history, and response to the current events. The realities of familial and extrafamilial structure and support are significant. A wide range of therapeutic interventions can be considered, including crisis intervention; individual, family, and group treatment; and medication. Often a combination of approaches is desirable. Treatment offered promptly at the time the reactive disorder appears can provide immediate relief as well as preventive benefits. Not uncommonly, children and adolescents who experience reactive disorders and are not treated "later succumb to adult life stress-producing situations in a similar fashion. Earlier life failure at coping with stressors may be a culmination of repeated, disproportionately intense life responses and vulnerability" (Mishne, 1984, p. 258).

It is important to emphasize the increased growth and strength that can accrue from the effective mastery of a reactive disorder. All developmental interferences are not necessarily perceived as automatically causing permanent damage to the evolving, developing adolescent. "Eventually the stress abates and/or the ego adapts and begins once more to seek an even keel. In the phase of reorganization, there may be a full integration of the experience into the personality with subsequent recovery of adequate function, or even resilience and confidence in the ability to cope with stress" (Kessler, 1979, p. 176). The goal of any treatment intervention is to aid and promote such mastery, to support the adolescent's regaining old coping skills, and, to promote the development of newly acquired strengths and adaptive capacities.

Case of Roberta

Roberta, age 14, was referred for an evaluation at the children's clinic, upon the request of her father's attorney and the court, to assess whether her father should pay outstanding psychotherapy bills to Roberta's prior therapist. According to the parents' divorce decree, Roberta's father was responsible for extraordinary medical bills, but his prior consent was to be requested. The mother had taken her daughter for treatment without seeking her former husband's approval. The judge had dismissed the mother's petition for payment of the bills, because she was in violation of the original divorce decree. However, the father said he would pay the past bill and any future bills if his daughter was in need of treatment.

The mother saw Roberta's problem as resulting from the recent divorce and as beginning when the parents began discussing their marital breakup. The father dated his daughter's problems as evident some years earlier, as he guiltily acknowledged that his extramarital affair and severance of a marriage of twenty-three years must have some impact on his four children. According to the mother, Roberta suffered constant and frequent crying jags and an inability to sleep at night. She wandered the house at all hours and often entered her mother's room at 2:00 and 3:00 A.M. in tears. In the manner of a much younger child, she took a stuffed animal to bed with her in a futile attempt to comfort and soothe herself. She had recently become quite withdrawn, rarely leaving the house. She attempted to curtail and limit her mother's social activities and would not retire until her mother returned from an evening out. She most recently refused to see her father and his new wife. She cut off all contact following his remarriage. She had demanded visits with him alone; and when he refused to exclude his wife, she announced that he no longer existed as a father. Roberta was supported by her mother in her requests for exclusive visits with her father. Roberta's two brothers, also at home and in high school, followed suit and refused to spend time with their father, his second wife, and her teenage son. Roberta's oldest brother, attending college, did visit with his father and seemingly better accepted the remarriage.

Roberta's problems seemed to be contained at home and within her family. She was a superior student, and exhibited no unusual behavior outside the home. She had good study habits, concentrated effectively on her school work, and was conscientious in all her tasks. She got along with peers, and socialized appropriately during the course of a school day. She appeared excessive in her nonrebellion, compliance, and overly affectionate manner with her mother, whom she constantly hugged and kissed.

Roberta was a Jewish, slim, attractive, frail-appearing little girl. She was well dressed and well groomed—shy and kittenish in her manner. She spoke softly and cautiously, acknowledging a need for help, "but, I don't want it." She believed her problems would diminish with time. She complained about sibling conflicts with her brothers and denied any difficulties in regard to her father because "I've erased him. I consider him as though dead."

The clinician was impressed with this adolescent's disillusionment with her father, whom she now viewed as a "lying, cheating adulterer, who no longer exists for her." The recent symptoms appear to be due to the trauma of the divorce. Roberta was a much wanted baby, who progressed in an easy, normal fashion. Her developmental milestones were all appropriate. Her mother recalls a delightful, cuddly baby, toddler, and young child, who seemed happy, curious, and relaxed. Overall, the picture presented was that of solid, healthy development, and a normal beginning adolescence, which then collapsed following the parents' separation. The mother had not resolved the marital breakup for herself, and the three children still at home appeared to mirror her rage and disbelief that the father had another life outside their family, and remarried so quickly after separation.

Roberta demonstrated considerable regression in her clinging and renewed dependence on her mother. Defenses of repression, displacement, and withdrawal to handle her rage and renewed oedipal wishes for her father were now causing secondary interference and arrest. This teenager was profoundly affected by her father's betrayal and departure and the changes in her mother, who is no longer the calm, contented, and nurturing parent of the past. Roberta appeared to have attained a phallic oedipal level of development and seemingly had a successful normal latency period. She no longer demonstrated age-appropriate progression, but rather arrest and regression in the face of her experiencing her father as divorcing and betraying her, setting her aside in favor of his new wife. How much of this was due to her overidentification with her mother and how much was due to the original unresolved oedipal conflicts is not clear. Diagnostically, she was assessed as a neurotic child, evidencing reactive symptomatology as a result of the divorce. It was speculated that she would have continued normal development had the family break-up not occurred.

Treatment recommended involved therapy for Roberta and her mother, as well as for the father, who recently expressed grief at the "loss" of three of his children. There were no guarantees regarding treatment outcome or whether the children would accept their father at some future point. Perhaps if the parents had sought help sooner, in the early stages of their separation, the children would have been better prepared for the divorce. The mother was viewed as a key person in all treatment planning; she might well not be able to tolerate Roberta's possible future "forgiveness" of her father and, thus, needed help for herself to allow her children freedom to function more independently in relation to their father. It was hoped that her need for their alliance and allegiance would diminish with time and effective therapeutic interventions.

Bibliography

AMERICAN PSYCHIATRIC ASSOCIATION (1980). *Quick Reference to the Diagnostic Criteria from Diagnostic and Statistical Manual of Mental Disorders, Third Edition*, pp. 167–69. Washington, D.C., APA.

EISSLER, R.; FREUD, A.; KRIS, M.; and SOLNIT, A., EDS. (1977). *An Anthology of the Psychoanalytic Study of the Child—Psychoanalytic Assessment: The Diagnostic Profile*. New Haven: Yale University Press.

KAPLAN, H. and SADOCK, B. (1981). *Modern Synopsis of Psychiatry III*. 3rd ed. Baltimore/London: Williams & Wilkins.

KESSLER, E. (1979). Reactive Disorders. In *Basic Handbook of Child Psychiatry, vol. 2: Disturbances in Development*. ed. J. Noshpitz, pp. 173–84. New York: Basic Books.

MISHNE, J. (1984). Adjustment Disorders. In *Adult Psychopathology—A Social Work Perspective*, ed. F. J. Turner, pp. 249–59. New York: Free Press.

NAGERA, H. (1966). *Early Childhood Disturbances, The Infantile Neurosis, and the Adulthood Disturbances*. New York: International Universities Press.

NEUBAUER, P. (1972). Normal Development in Children. In *Manual of Child Psychopathology*, ed. B. Wolman. New York: McGraw-Hill.

14

Cults, Communes, and Religious Movements

" 'Cults of unreason' have been particularly attractive in periods of uncertainty" (Evans, 1974). However, never before have these movements been so popular and open, and never has there been such a search for a new awareness and lifestyle.

> In the past decade the emergence of a surprisingly large number of fringe religious groups or exotic cults using modern, psychologically oriented recruitment practices, which some people believe is a form of thought control, have enlisted a large number of middle-class educated youth. Between the ages of seventeen and thirty, these youth are attracted by promises of making the world a better place, finding God, or living in an ideal society" [Feinstein, 1980, p. 113].

Thought reform, with a psychological momentum of its own, arises out of the combination of intense character traits and a grandiose ideology that presents absolutist convictions about man and the world. Lipton (1963) noted that cults manifest specific characteristics—namely, milieu control of communications, leading to disruption of the balance between the self and the outside world; mystical manipulation with a sense of higher purpose; demands for purity, with a simplistic division of everything into good and bad; a preoccupation with confessional procedures to achieve personal purification and surrender of the self to the group; an aura of sacredness that prohibits members from questioning basic assumptions; frequently the development of an idiosyncratic private language that constricts individuals; doctrinal restrictions imposed on individuals' views; and the creation of a hierarchy to dispense rewards or punishments to those deserving either.

Cults follow a dominant leader, generally a living person who makes claims to be divine, God incarnate, the messiah, or God's emissary. The leader further claims to be omnipotent and infallible. Thus members must offer total and literal acceptance of the claims of the leader, his doctrines and dogma. S. Levine (1980) noted that cults need not be religious; some are political or even therapeutic. He cautioned that not all should be viewed as evil or dangerous; in fact, some forms of cults have existed in North America for at least one hundred years, offering solutions or salvation during times of stress.

S. Levine (1978) and Levine and Salter (1976) studied and worked with groups representing many religions, including Hare Krishna, Unification Church, Divine Light Mission, Children of God, Jesus People, Scientology, and Process and Foundation Churches. These groups attract young people who are susceptable to ideologies, rigid belief systems, and mass movements. These tend to be alienated, demoralized youth who lack commitments and a strong sense of self and appear receptive to easy answers. Levine found that the ages of the members ranged from 17 through 35; the median age was 21.5; and there was a preponderance of girls in the younger age groups. Those 106 interviewed tended to be educated and middle class. In fact the majority had had some college education, and it was there that they became attracted to one of the religions. Those from more well-to-do families seemed most attracted to the Eastern religions such as Hare Krishna. Eighty percent were single, and the married followers were predominantly Scientologists. The Eastern religions attracted a majority of Roman Catholic and Jewish followers. Seventy percent came from relatively large intact families where parents' marital relationships were rated fair to good. Almost all parents were strongly opposed to their children's conversions. Drug and alcohol use had existed to varying degrees prior to conversions.

The interviewers were impressed with the intelligence and perceptiveness of some of the members, primarily those whose leaders were charismatic and articulate. Members appeared to be followers rather than leaders. Most claimed to have joined religious groups because of feelings of loneliness, sadness, and estrangement or because they felt they were drifting; some joined because of a disastrous personal or familial crisis; a few were seeking to fill the void in their life; and a small number were seeking to help society or humanity. Reasons cited for staying in the religious group were not primarily spiritual or religious—rather, the majority reported feeling secure and more self-confident and able to improve interpersonal relationships.

Keniston (1968) was one of the first to describe alienated American youth, who manifested disillusionment with traditional politics, opposition to the Vietnam war, and impatience with the slow gains of the civil rights movement. His studies showed that distrust was a primary variable in the alienation syndrome. The American culture was perceived as untrustworthy, corrupt, mechanical, and dull; intimate relationships were viewed as always ending in disappointment; and life, as dark, isolated, and meaningless, lacking purpose or ideals. Pessimism abounded in this alienated group. Rejecting traditional American values of success, self-control, and achievement, they sought meaning in their lives and openness to new experiences.

Their lifestyle embodied intellectual passion and a single-minded dedication to their artistic, athletic, or philosophical interests. They frequently remained cynical, detached observers or wanderers, involved in religious and mystical experiences. Keniston's research group described themselves as socially undesirable, angry, confused, hostile, neurotic, and impulsive. Failure was a cardinal virtue for them, and not "making it" or dropping out were respected patterns in their lifestyle. Their unhappiness was attributed to their families, colleges, American culture—in short, the prevailing human condition of their time of life. As a group, Keniston noted their lack of optimisim, tranquility, or calm and instead, their intense convictions, vehemence, scorn, and passion in their search for some meaning in life. The adolescence of these alienated college students was characterized by extreme turmoil, including intense asceticism, tentative delinquency, rebellion, speed in cars and motorcycles, drinking, and unsatisfying sexual relationships.

Keniston's group came from families close to the norm of the American family; and therefore he predicted an increase in the phenomenon of alienation, created in large measure by our society, with its increased technology, bureaucraticization, and dehumanizing features, which estrange a distinct segment of talented and perceptive youth. In 1966, he stated that he suspected that most reflective Americans were alienated from their society and culture. His predictions seem borne out in the searching and affiliative ties of considerable numbers of youth and anticipate the findings of S. Levine and others. "[In fact] never have these movements been so popular and open; never has there been such a concerted search for a new consciousness and lifestyle" (S. Levine, 1978) because of feelings of alienation, from peers, families, and society (Bourquignon, 1974; Castaneda, 1968, 1971, Roszak, 1969).

Religious affiliation provides a strong belief system, a coherent system of values, and "second, and perhaps more important . . . the rapid development of a sense of belonging of communality, of being an integral part of a group which shares the members' feelings and aspirations. These two experiences, believing and belonging, serve to produce a significant increase in the individual's self-esteem" (S. Levine, 1980, p. 125). Levine further reported that the similarities among the groups far outweigh their differences; they all share the charismatic intense emotional appeal that inspires devotion and inspiration in their followers. Amid rituals, rules, rigid hierarchies, the "quasiintellectual theological tone," the high-powered fund-raising procedures or tithes, each group promises personal salvation. S. Levine (1980) observed various degrees of flirtation with violence, bizarre procedures, dishonest proselytizing techniques, and irregular uses of funds. None of this, however, is as important as the members believing, belonging, and expressing an improved sense of self-esteem. All the varied groups provide simple answers which diminish anxieties and "existential dilemmas," making life for the followers more secure and comprehensible.

Parents' response to their children's initial interest and entry into a cult is, typically, amusement and confidence that this is a transient interest, followed by agitation, and anger. Some parents try to understand, and to learn about the religion that attracts their child; but these attempts at patience, empathy, and interest are generally short-lived and are followed by anger, punishments, or bargains in an attempt to reestablish familial contact and maintain such age-appropriate tasks as homework. Sometimes things quickly escalate; and help is sought from clerics, relatives, and clinicians to no avail. Prospective followers are described as resigned to their parents' lack of understanding and presumed decadent, self-destructive lifestyles. While the follower feels euphoric about his or her emerging affiliations, families are regarded as blind, misguided, and pitiable. The young person is described as unambivalent, secure, and joyful at finding "real answers to life's dilemmas"; they are egocentric, often tolerant of parents fears, or derisive, angry, and impatient, without any genuine sensitivity or emotional empathy. "The converted young person develops a closed-mindedness to conflicting ideas and arguments, often seeing them as ridiculous or even sinister. A garrison mentality develops, which is engendered and encouraged by the [religious] group. He is now well-nigh unreachable" (S. Levine, 1980, p. 127).

Most cults turn their members away from the world, including their parents and their parents' beliefs and ways of life. Nevertheless, while cautioning against total praise, some researchers (S. Levine, 1980, and Noyes, 1966) stress the positive aspects of some of these groups. Levine noted that frequently a member was in physical and emotional disarray prior to joining his or her cult or religious group and, shortly thereafter, "looked, felt and acted better. Some had voluntarily seen mental health professionals during their earlier period of personal deterioration to no avail" (p. 127).

Most researchers report that help is rarely sought prior to conversion and entry into cults or religious groups. Parents deny or dismiss the phenomena and/or attempt to reason, discuss, cajole, or, later, make demands and ultimatums. These parental behaviors commonly further seduce and propel the prospective member toward the excitement and mystery of a forbidden cult. If a mental health clinician is available during the critical time he or she must take actions to which therapists are generally adverse, such as, outreach, home visits, lengthy and irregular sessions, and extended family network treatment to draw in potentially helpful relatives who can be valuable when the potential convert is still semiopen and vulnerable. Later the young person will be closed and inaccessible. Feinstein (1980) reported that parents are viewed as demonic, and the cult convert is lost in rituals, meditation, chanting, and the like. All therapeutic interventions require an evaluation to determine whether we are dealing with a relatively stable adolescent or one decompensating due to psychosis. According to S. Levine (1980), however, psychosis and required hospitalization are uncommon.

Once the adolescent has become a committed religious or cult member, families frequently contact professional mental health workers. Commonly, little can be done beyond securing information and providing support for the parents, who are generally in a state of shock and grief, mourning their child and questioning where they went wrong. Parents often become obsessed, cannot rest, and "become countercult proselytizers, every bit as rabid and intolerant as those they fear and detest" (S. Levine, 1980, p. 129). They may benefit from contact with other similarly afflicted parents, and learn about other people's experience with cults. Usually, the cult member wil not see any clinician, viewed as they are by the religious group as dangerous tools of the parents. S. Levine (1980) noted the common reaction of the cult member to any professional clinical worker: open hostility, a condescending manner, bemused tolerance, smugness and arrogance, screening out via prayer and rituals to avoid any and all verbal exchange and contact, proselytizing, and only occasionally guarded openness. Sometimes the "patient member" is "chaperoned" by an older member of the cult when he or she sees the clinician. S. Levine and others reported that there are few inroads possible at this particular juncture. It is not until the convert is plagued with self-doubt and an identity crisis that he or she can be convinced to leave the cult. If the cult member recognizes the dishonest acts, exploitations, and hypocracies of the religious group, it will stimulate questions about his or her commitment. If this is shared within the cult, S. Levine (1980) pointed out, the cult will apply pressures of

shame, offers of love and support, and threats, which can effectively intimidate and stifle any more autonomous thinking. If such questions are
shared with outside friends and relatives and if the member can be gotten away from the cult for a period of time, he or she may never wish to
return.

S. Levine (1980) opposed calling this process of support deprogramming, and instead viewed it as sensitive listening and interviewing,
through which the convert is helped to face and share his or her fears
and anxieties. At such a juncture, it is crucial that the clinician and relatives spend long hours with the convert to help him or her through the
cathartic process and into actual psychotherapy, which can commence
only when the individual finally wrenches himself away and returns to
his family or a semblance of his former life (p. 131). Most researchers report that teenagers are in a fragile and vulnerable emotional state after
escaping from or leaving the cult. S. Levine (1980) reported culture
shock and the dire need for rehabilitation, insecurities about the future
and resumption of a normal life, and overriding shame and guilt. Guilt
over having initially abandoned the family and, now again, having left
friends and peers who remain in the cult causes low self-esteem,
doubts, and self-recriminations. Frequently, leaving a cult is a drastic
step for the family and the cult member, and such a youth can resemble
"a state seen following a psychotic alteration of consciousness" (Feinstein, 1980, p. 118). Episodes of drifting into fantasy and panic are frequent. "A period as long as eighteen months may be necessary to recreate a sense of cohesiveness and personal competence" (p. 119) to deal
with altered states of consciousness, identity diffusion, and ideas of reference. Singer (1979) reported the monumental failures most professionals have in aiding cult departures because of their lack of knowledge of cult mores and their propensity to view all cult contact and
membership as a sign of pathology. Excultists are commonly overwhelmed with very real fear, be it spiritual and religious fear or terror of
physical retaliation by the cult. Excultists often exhibit depression, regret, and ruminative behavior. They commonly describe flashbacks,
fears and confusion, and hearing the liturgy, songs, and sermons of the
cult.

"Deprogramming," defined by S. Levine (1980), entails coercion,
subterfuge to kidnap or lure the cultist away, detention—perhaps in
locked facilities—and hyperstimulation—constant input, confrontation,
and browbeating to wear the individual down and substitute a better belief system. Levine emphasized the major ethical, legal, and psychological concerns deprogramming arouses, and cited numerous failed depro-
grammings, which resulted in total estrangement from families and
return to the cult or religious group, or the actual appearance of being

brainwashed and subsequent emotional decompensation. He cautioned that deprogrammers

> fail to impress me with their sensitivity, intelligence and efficacy. This is an unpleasant, dangerous, and avowedly illegal procedure. If means to an end excuses the process, we should at least have confidence in the ends— unfortunately, this is not always the case. But anyone who has worked extensively with cultists and their families can easily see how parents are driven to this alternative. It is very difficult for a mother and father to see their child after years of upbringing, shared joys and pains, love and aspirations, enter a way of life which they consider to be sinister or dangerous. It is a frustrating and poignant situation [p. 133].

Who enters cults and fringe religions? Studies point out that while such individuals were not overtly psychotic, a "significant number could be described before their conversion as anxious, depressed, as borderline, or, as having personality disorders" (S. Levine, 1978, p. 79). Most reported being unhappy and alienated before conversion. Many were what Grinker, Grinker Jr., and Timberlake (1971) called homeolites, that is, follower-type personalties. Ungerleider and Willisch (1979) concluded that dependent, immature young people received what they sought, namely, external controls, interpersonal constancy, and group approval. Fringe religions and cults consistently attract young, white, well-educated middle-class youth from stable backgrounds, who generally have unremarkable earlier drug, emotional, or sexual histories. These groups of youth exhibit dissatisfaction with their situations and demonstrate slow resolution of the adolescent identity crisis. In all, they are not viewed as a particularly pathologic group and, in fact, "do come out [leave the cult] on their own, or with general encouragement" (S. Levine, 1980, p. 134). Families are encouraged to maintain channels of communication; but generally, a situation of complete estrangement develops; and clinicians are advised to attempt to mediate between the cult member and family and friends, educate both, confer with community institutions and groups regarding specific approaches to the situation and most importantly, to provide psychotherapy to families and cult members where possible.

Rural communes, like religious cults, have become refuges for middle-class youth (E. Levine, 1980). These communes are very different from urban religious groups in that they do "not subscribe to or share a doctrine that infused or dominated their daily activities and way of life" (p. 139). E. Levine (1980) reported that these noncreedal rural communities numbered approximately three thousand between 1960 and 1970 and were made up of youths with some college education and frequently previous "attractive occupations and well-paid jobs." Some inhabitants were divorced or separated young women with children, and some were floaters with no direction to their lives. Communes have not been extensively researched, but what findings do exist suggest groups of people in search of an ideal lifestyle and "equalization" of all important social relationships in a setting where they could achieve the individuality they saw as impossible to achieve in urban settings. As they encountered difficulty arriving at unanimous major decisions, they began to perceive how unrealistic their goals were. Dominant personalities and arbitrary decisions emerged (Berger, Hackett, and Miller, 1974, and Rothchild and Wolf, 1976) as did informal power structures. The hopes for utopian social equality eroded over disputes about assignment of chores and resultant conflicting interests and preferences. Resistance to routine but important tasks and the pursuit of personal preferences caused many commune collections to dissolve in a matter of months or, at most, after only a very few years. Communes were frequently chosen as escapes from personal, social, and familial difficulties, or anomic existences.

Child care proved actually to be of little interest to commune members, despite verbal commitments to children's needs and proper parenting, which members felt they had missed to varying degrees in their childhoods. Children received very little parenting, guidance, or supervision by parents who generally remained remote and unconcerned on any and all matters related to their offspring. Thus children adopted parental values and hedonistic behaviors, "impulse gratification, self-centered pursuits, and living in, and for the present" (E. Levine, 1980, p. 144) in anomic cultures. Parental apathy and aimlessness resulted in parental indulgence, indifference, benign neglect, and inconsistency. Children were viewed as smaller equals, not needing any authority or structure, permitted adult prerogatives like smoking marijuana and being allowed and encouraged to indulge in early adolescent sexual experimentation. School attendance in nearby towns was irregular, due to parental inability to rise regularly and feed and bus children to school. Children were not provided adequate facilities and qualified teachers or supervisors. They were everyone's and, consequently, no one's responsibility, out of parental philosophies about freedom, adult interference, and direction.

Parental preoccupations with self-exploration, discussions, and aimless day-to-day pursuits resulted in grossly deficient socialization of their young. Thus, the children showed impaired ego and superego development, poor impulse control, and no respect for parental authority. "In their later years, therefore, we can hypothesize that such youngsters will very likely be even more impulse ridden and unconcerned about others, with faint interest in and commitment to the future. Their lives appear to be the ideal breeding grounds for severe characterological deficits (p. 145).

E. Levine (1980) differed with those who suggest that communes offer young people new and more meaningful beliefs and ways of life than are available in the mainstream of society. On the basis of his research, he suggested that those who opted for the all-but-unlimited freedom of rural communes little understood the limits and meaning of freedom and responsibility and that much of their lives was given to indulging themselves in gratifying infantile needs. Indeed their directionless and anomic existence was partly responsible for the inability of communes to endure. "From today's perspectives, rural communes seem to be an archaic subcultural offshoot" (p. 148). In considering why such a number of youth have turned against their religions and their families to cults and communes, E. Levine (1980) concluded that nuclear family parents have few and feeble standards to instill and that among "the upper and middle classes, overemphasis on narcissism, impulse gratification, and disregard for the future arises out of assimilation, excessive residential mobility, affluence, and industrialization, leading to erosion of family cohesiveness and decline in parental authority (Levine and Shaiova, 1971, 1974, 1977).

Material affluence permits many parents to engage in overinvolvement and overindulgence. Aichhorn (1935) described a type of delinquency he attributed to an "excess of love," disproportionality found in well-to-do homes and a source of "great sorrow and despair." These parents refrain from the use of authority and limits and, instead, provide excessive attention to their children's wishes, thereby failing to assist the child to adopt and use values, limits, and standards central to development of sound egos and superegos. Such youth with unresolved dependency needs are overly susceptible to the influence of peers, self-gratification, and hedonistic living. As narcissistic character disordered individuals, they are victims of an anomic society. Thus they seek the rigid structure of cults for needed direction (E. Levine, 1980). While cults have approximately fifty thousand members, some suggest that the tragedy in Guyana may dissuade future youth from joining such groups (Fromm, 1941).

We must recognize that these affiliations have come in the wake of the disintegration of traditional social institutions. A religious renaissance usually correlates with "political conditions such as war with urban migration or with any kind of event that is dislocating to the nuclear family" (Zaretsky, 1980, p. 28). Esman (1972) pointed out that as these institutions decay and as schools, leaders, and parents are devalued, adolescents grasp hungrily at new idealized parent-surrogates. Johnson (1975) and others noted the faulty separation and individuation of cult and commune members: "they must continually recreate those families to survive; but at the same time, like all adolescents, they must reject their families of origin" (p. 533). These individual youth seek intimacy and belonging and affiliate out of feeling unconnected. Their adolescent search for identity is a crucial task which commonly constitutes the core of all treatment.

Case of Gina

Gina, a married older adolescent, sought therapy for her oldest child when the daughter was six years old. Because of the stress associated with her child's academic and social failure and her own marital turbulence, Gina could focus only minimally on sharing her early background. Gina and her husband were an intelligent, attractive, young Jewish couple who presented themselves in a "hip" counter-culture fashion, characteristic of the drug rehabilitation community of which they were semileaders. They also represented tough, lower-middle-class, New York Jewish background that they had rebelled against since early adolescence. Gina entered treatment in connection with her child's treatment. Her husband refused to participate in any kind of ongoing therapy, occasionally agreeing to erratic sessions in response to milieu planning for his child.

Gina was a slim, attractive, blond woman always attired in clothes reminiscent of the late 1960s flower children. She was the younger of two sisters brought up in a working-class community. She described her parents as constantly fighting in a home fraught with financial anxieties because of father's passivity and lack of success in any and every venture or job. Gina's mother was described as the dominating member of the family, who verbally and emotionally abused her husband and children. Despite the mother's forceful personality, no actual limits or discipline existed for the children. Gina felt no warm positive identification with any aspect of family life and described closeness only with her much older sister, who fled the family home for work in a far-away state following her high school graduation. Gina experienced this as a real abandoment. She also expressed anger and resentment over her family's view of female children as not deserving of college or advanced education or training. She went to work following high school graduation and made a hasty marriage to escape her parents' home. Her husband, an only child, had been in severe academic and behavioral difficulty since age 10, and at 15 or 16 dropped out of high school. He joined the Air Force, was unable to tolerate the discipline and got out of the service by lying and saying that he was a homosexual. He drifted, and when they married, he and Gina lived at a marginal level, immediately becoming heavily involved in drug use. Gina said that her first unplanned pregnancy terrified her and contributed to her escape into drugs; during this time she used amphetamines and snorted heroin. Heroin continued to be used by this overwhelmed young couple, who proceeded to have unplanned children in rapid succession. The parents related many shocking stories of their drug abuse, violent quarrels, shooting up their babies with drugs, and Gina's prostitution for money for more drugs. Following endless unsuccessful efforts to detox, work, and function normally, the couple placed their children with Gina's mother and entered a therapeutic community.

At the time they applied for psychotherapy for their child, Gina and her husband were involved at a high administrative level in a sizable drug rehabilitation program. They worked endless hours and acknowledged their "addiction" to their program and their need for structure and activity. This interfered with the time and energy needed for them to function as parents. The relative calm in the marriage was short-lived, and drug use on the father's part resurfaced. In response to his adulterous liaisons, drug use, and physical attacks on Gina, she announced a need to flee far away to avoid being tempted by her husband's pleas for reconciliation. Gina chose to conclude all drug abuse work and all connection with her husband and their lifestyle abruptly. Without funds and any other marketable skills, she moved herself and her children to the West Coast, clear that she required some kind of group organization that would provide her support and structure.

Gina kept in contact with her therapist by phone and by mail and reported the following. Feeling that she had exhausted all expectations for familial support (because during her prior residence in a therapeutic community her mother had cared for her children), she did not turn to her parents at this crisis point. Fleeing her husband, she felt she had no recourse but to seek a group that would provide security and sanctuary in this disastrous period of alienation. Clearly Gina conformed to S. Levine's (1980) observation that a new member of a cult is often in physical and emotional disarray prior to joining the group. Gina first affiliated with a rural Yogi commune. She became concerned about her children in so unstructured a milieu. Recognizing her own overindulgence and apathy and her inability to get them to school, stop their use of marijuana, and other negative behavior, she sought more direction, rules, and doctrine in the Unification Church. Her final correspondence with her prior therapist was a registration of relief at acquiring a sense of belonging, greater security, and more self-confidence, all of which would bolster her against any illusions of a safe return to her husband. She had always recognized her dependency, first on her sister, then on her husband and drugs, and then on a drug rehabilitation program. She noted her continued need for a leader and rules to live by, external controls, and group approval and so expressed relief at her commitment to cult membership.

Bibliography

AICHHORN, A. [1935] 1963. *Wayward Youth.* New York: Viking.

BERGER, B.; HACKETT, B.; and MILLER, R. (1974). Child Rearing Practices in the Communal Family. In *Intimacy, Family and Society*, eds. J. Skolnick and A. Skolnick. Boston: Little Brown.

BOURGUIGNON, E. (1974). *Religion, Altered States of Consciousness and Social Change.* Columbus, Ohio: Ohio State University Press.

CASTAÑEDA, C. (1968). *The Teachings of Don Juan: A Yaqui Way of Knowledge.* New York: Ballantine.

ESMAN, A. (1972). Adolescence and the Consolidation of Values. In *Moral Values and the Superego Concept in Psychoanalysis*, ed. S. C. Post. New York: International Universities Press.

EVANS, C. (1974). *Cults of Unreason.* London: FS&G.

FEINSTEIN, S. (1980). The Cult Phenomena: Transition, Repression and Regression. In *Adolescent Psychiatry, Vol. 8: Developmental and Clinical Studies,* eds. S. Feinstein, P. Giovacchini, J. Looney, A. Schwartzberg, and A. Sorosky, pp. 113–22. Chicago: University of Chicago Press.

FROMM, E. (1941). *Escape from Freedom.* New York: Rinehart.

GRINKER, SR., R.; GRINKER, JR., R.; and TIMBERLAKE, J. (1971). Mentally Healthy Young Males: Homeolites. In *Adolescent Psychiatry, Vol. 1: Developmental and Clinical Studies,* eds. S. Feinstein, P. Giovacchini, and A. Miller, pp. 176–255. New York: Basic Books.

JOHNSON, A. B. (1975). Drifting on the God Circuit. In *The Psychology of Adolescence,* ed. A. Esman, pp. 524–34. New York: International Universities Press.

KENISTON, K. (1968). *Young Radicals.* New York: Harcourt, Brace and World.

LEVINE, E. (1980). Rural Communes and Religious Cults—Refuges for Middle-Class Youth. In *Adolescent Psychiatry, Vol. 8,* pp. 138–63. See Feinstein (1980).

LEVINE, E. and SHAIOVA, C. (1971). Equality and Rationality in Child Socialization: A Conflict of Interest. *Israel Annals of Psychiatry and Related Disciplines,* 9(2) 107–16.

———— (1974). Biology, Personality and Culture: A Theoretical Comment on Etiology of Character Disorders in Industrial Society. *Israel Annals of Psychiatry and Related Disciplines,* 12(1):10–28.

———— (1977). Anomie: Its Influence on Impulse Ridden Youth and Their Self-Destructive Behavior. In *Adolescent Psychiatry, Vol. 5: Developmental and Clinical Studies,* eds. S. C. Feinstein and P. Giovacchini, pp. 73–81. New York: Jason Aronson.

LEVINE, S. (1980). The Role of Psychiatry in the Phenomena of Cults. In *Adolescent Psychiatry, Vol. 8,* pp. 123–37. See Feinstein (1980).

LEIVNE, S. and SALTER, N. (1976). Youth and Contemporary Religious Movements: Psychosocial Findings. *Canadian J. Psychiatry,* 21:411–20.

LIFTON, R. J. (1963). *Thought Reform and the Psychology of Totalism.* New York: Norton.

NOYES, J. H. (1966). *Strange Cults and Utopias of Nineteenth Century America.* New York: Dover.

ROSZAK, T. (1969). *The Making of a Counter Culture.* New York: Doubleday.

ROTHCHILD, J. and WOLF, S. (1976). *The Children of the Counter-Culture.* New York: Doubleday.

SINGER, M. T. (1979). Therapy with Ex-Cult Members. *National Association of Private Psychiatric Hospitals J.,* 9(4) 15–18.

UNGERLEIDER, J. T. and WILLISCH, D. K. (1979). Cultism, Thought Control and Deprogramming: Observations on a Phenomenon. *Psychiatric Opinion* (January):10–15.

ZARETSKY, I. (1980). Youth and Religious Movements. In *Adolescent Psychiatry, Vol. 8,* pp. 281–87. See Feinstein (1980).

15

Substance Abuse

I. Drug Abuse

Therapists concerned with adolescent patients who use drugs can find relatively few extensive dynamic studies of substance abusers. Rado's (1933) early work dealt with adult drug addicts; and he stressed, not the toxic agent, but the impulse to use it which makes an addict of a given individual. In one of the first studies of drug-abusing male adolescents, Hartman (1969), like Rado, stressed defects in ego and development, which were manifested by a poor frustration tolerance, poor tolerance for depression and a constant need to change a low mood into a high one. Early object relationships and present ties were assessed as unsatisfying. Hence, the adolescent's attempts to overcome these lacks and resulting estrangement through psuedocloseness and fusion with other peers who are drug takers.

In addition to specific familial patterns and resultant pathologies in drug taking adolescents, cultural and sociological factors unquestionably play a role in adolescent drug experimentation and substance abuse. H. Deutsch (1967) pointed to more permissive parenting, fewer parental restrictions, and less setting of standards as encouraging drug use. Advertising and cultural endorsement of satisfying one's impulses contribute in some measure to drug use. The peer pressure to act out in groups, the ridicule of "square kids" was, and is, a major impetus for drug use. It is important to note the great variations among drug-taking adolescents. Hartman (1969) reported the findings from a study group of the American Association for Child Psychoanalysis:

1. Some used drugs only a short time as a rebellious acting out against a parent or against their analyst.
2. Some were neurotic or depressed before taking drugs. These were involved in and felt compelled to take drugs for a long time, but were able to sustain [psychological] therapy.
3. In some patients their capacity to function in life was very much restricted and aggravated through their involvement with drugs, and for them, drugs became imperative and treatment ineffective [p. 385].

Classical psychoanalysis frequently could not be employed or continued with this latter group of teenagers. In the sample studied, the clinicians noted more pathology among the mothers than the fathers of the adolescent drug users, in that the mothers showed more uncontrolled aggression than the better controlled fathers. Seductive behaviors by mothers and inconsistency and distance in fathers were noted.

A high proportion of the teenagers appeared orally fixated or regressed in libidinal development. Aggression was either overrepressed, or wildly out of control. The superego was markedly regressed under the influence of drugs, and ego functioning became similarly impaired and deteriorated in nearly all cases. The majority of the group were markedly depressed before using the drugs and most felt less depressed when on drugs. Object relations became much more superficial and social contacts were mainly with other peers similarly involved in substance abuse. Relationships were best described as infantile, with a prevalence of merger and fusion fantasies. Sexual relationships were autoerotic and narcissistic; masturbatory activities prevailed over any resemblance of a meaningful attachment to a specific partner.

In the group reported by Hartman (1969), almost half started drug use during treatment, thereby acting out in the transference and attempting to avoid conflicts realized in the therapy. The need to escape early memories and trauma in childhood was apparent. Consciously, these teenagers reported wanting peer acceptance and relief from depression. Unconsciously, the need seemed to be to replace a lost object—often the parent—as the adolescent struggled to separate and individuate. Divorce and parent loss, death or severe illness of a parent or themselves were prominent factors in the histories of these young patients. Nearly one hundred percent of the small group began drug abuse with marijuana and moved on to use amphetamines, methadrine, hashish, barbiturates, and heroin. Hartman found Rado's study of adults applicable to drug-taking adolescents. Rado (1933) stressed: (1) their basic depressive character and early wounded narcissism; (2) their intolerance for frustration and pain; (3) poor object relationships; (4) the artificial technique to maintain self-regard and the change from a realistic to a pharmacothymic regime which creates severely disturbed ego functions and conflict with reality.

It is important to consider the specific drugs used and the varied patterns exhibited. Wieder and Kaplan (1969) noted substance abuse that is transient, occasional, recurrent, or chronic and that some adolescents take drugs or alcohol in secret, while others dramatically flaunt their addiction. These authors believed that a "chronic need for specific pharmacological effects or 'craving' derives from developmental and structural deficits and distortions" (p. 400). Thus, the traumata in early ego development create fixation and encourage regression, most often in cases of borderline and psychotic personality structure. In these cases substance abuse is a form of corrective self-medication.

Drugs are seen as representing "good" and "bad" objects. In the argot of the addict, his supplier is often called "mother" and his supplies "mood food" (Wieder and Kaplan, 1969, p. 401); heroin becomes "mother heroin." The earliest prototypes of druglike experiences probably are of milk, breast, and mother.

Research indicates that optimal child development requires sufficient satisfaction, gratification, *and* frustration. Spitz (1965) stressed the need for infants and toddlers to be exposed to optimal amounts of imposed frustration, "for ultimately, the capacity to tolerate frustration is at the origin of the reality principles" (Spitz, 1965, p. 172); and the child needs practice in containing aggression to ensure pleasure and mastery. The fusion of the aggressive and libidinal drive and the discharge of them onto a single partner, the mother, is a prerequisite for normal object relations and mastery and competence in daily living. Parenting that provides too much or too little relief has damaging effects on ego and superego development and decreases tolerance for pain and disappointment, often forerunner conditions for substance abuse, given the anxiety, depression, and fluctuating self-esteem common to the normal adolescent process. Drugs often hold a seductive promise of effortless relief and pleasure without any active mastery, struggle, or attempt at coping.

> The individuals who either start drugs in early adolescence or who perpetuate conflict resolution with them have already manifested greater regressive disorganization in the course of the adolescent process because of structural deficits originating in early childhood. Intoxication at first offers them a temporary resolution, palliating through chemical alteration of psychic energy equilibria. With chronic use, the ego becomes more compliant to id demands, more passive when confronted by anxiety, and in-

creasingly relies on the drug effects as a participant in its functioning [Wieder and Kaplan, 1969, p. 402].

Many researchers see chronic drug use as a consequence of ego pathology, which takes on a life of its own, adding to and increasing the pathology through repetitively induced regressed ego states. Substance abuse is not employed for "kicks" or highs per se, but as a form of self-medication to reduce tension and stress; homeostasis cannot be achieved by the individual's own mental efforts.

Wieder and Kaplan (1969) using Mahler's concepts of symbiosis and separation and individuation (1969) stated that specific drugs commonly appear to offer particular regressive conflict solutions. LSD and related drugs are sought to provide the user a sense of object connection or to regain autistic unity (p. 404); opium and its deriviates provide fantasies of omnipotence, magical wish fulfillment, and self-sufficiency characterized by the symbiotic state (p. 429); amphetamines, methedrine, and cocaine, which diminish fatigue also lead to an increase in the feelings of assertiveness, self-esteem, and a decrease in accuracy of judgment reminiscent of the "practicing period." Alcohol, marijuana, or hashish lessen defenses against drive and impulse discharge and accentuate exteroperceptual and interoperceptual acuity (ibid). Thus there is ego compliance to id demands and a consequent lowering of internal oedipal-level conflict. In all, drugs are not chosen casually or randomly and are not fully interchangeable, selected because of particular conflicts and intrapsychic deficits.

Specific behavior patterns appear consistently in adolescent addicts who demonstrate opiate dependence:

> Underlying depression, often an agitated type which is frequently accompanied by anxiety symptoms, impulsiveness, expressed by a passive-aggressive orientation, fear of failure, use of heroin as an anti-anxiety agent to mask feelings of low self-esteem, hopelessness and aggression; limited coping strategies, and low frustration tolerance, accompanied by the need for immediate gratification [Kaplan and Sadock, 1981, p. 496].

These young people may also present such distinct physiological and behavioral signs as rapid withdrawal, physical fatigue, physical deterioration, abrupt shift of friends, and decline in academics, work, athletic, and social performance (DSM-III, 1980).

Once initiated, generally in a social peer situation, drug use is repeated, based upon (1) the pleasurable effects; (2) their effect in terminating the discomfort of narcotic withdrawal symptoms; and (3) non-pharmacological factors (Kaplan and Sadock, 1981, p. 503). Eventually legal difficulties, and severe intoxication with accompanying hallucinations and delusions, accompany the inability to reduce or stop drug use (DSM-III, 1980).

Diagnosis is made on the basis of a history and a physical exam, which generally reveals

> needle tracks, bluish phlebitis scars, ulcerating nodules, round punched-out atrophying lesions, brawny subcutaneous edema, and subcutaneous abscesses. Tattoos are frequently found in the drug-abusing population. . . . the presence of miatic pupils is invariable. Icteries, an enlarged liver or lymphadenopathy, may also be seen [pp. 506–7].

Zinburg (1975) differed with the above clinicians and was critical about what he labeled a misconception about a one-to-one relationship between personality maladjustment, and drug use and addiction. It was his contention that orally fixated individuals, borderlines, and schizophrenics

> make up only a fraction, and probably a small one, of even the addict population, let alone the general drug-using population. The idea that certain personality types seek out drug experience because of a specific, early, unresolved developmental conflict and that such people predominate in the addict group or in the much larger group of controlled users, is based on restrospective falsification. That is, looking at drug users and especially addicts, after they have become preoccupied with their drug experiments, authorities assume these attitudes and this personality state are similar to those the user had before the drug experience and thus led to it. Then "evidence" from the user's developmental history and previous object relationships is marshalled to show that the addicted state was the end point of a long-term personality process [p. 568].

Internal factors and history cannot be completely discarded in considering the decisions to use drugs and in understanding the extent and effect of the drugs on the individual. But, stated Zinburg (1975), there is no consistent profile or pattern of ego deficits, internal conflicts, or phase-specific patterns that can be considered the determining factors in the history of drug abuse and addiction. In contrast, many emphasize the power of the social setting which sustains drug and alcohol use. (Chafetz and Demone, 1962; Powell, 1973; Zinburg and Jacobson, 1974).

Drugs are used today by an increasingly large variety of personality types. Zinburg attributed much of this increase to the social turbulence that began during the 1960s and this country's engagement in Vietnam, when our youthful military occupation force widely used heroin. This heroin addiction of a wide variety of soldiers refutes stereotypes about who can and do become addicts. Further, the vast majority (over 90 percent) gave up heroin upon return to the United States, which, Robins (1974) believed, indicated that the determining factor in heroin use was the intolerable setting of Vietnam. Once these soldiers returned home, neither the power of the drug nor a susceptible personality proved decisive in keeping them drug dependent.

Based on this conception of etiology Zinburg (1975) strongly recommended that treatment interventions should not focus on the abuser's past family relationships, early traumata, and presumed motivations or "explanations" for drug dependence, such as loneliness and
anxiety. Rather, treatment that questions the current premises of the
abuser's behavior and stresses the adolescent's choices and the need to
accept responsibility offers containment and limits. "If it is carried out
with respect for the dignity of the patient, . . . it is neither punishing nor
gimmickry" (Zinburg, 1975, p. 585). This focus requires that the therapist be acutely aware of the crucial role of the social setting in the current ego state of the addict, because "personality conflict is no longer
seen as the direct cause of the addict's deterioration" (p. 586).

Miller (1973) concurred with the above noted emphasis on social
and cultural determinants, rather than personality conflicts as the
cause of drug dependency. "Some unsuccessful attempts have been
made to equate various types of pharmacological effects of drugs with
different levels of ego regression" (p. 71). The adolescent who does not
experiment with smoking, drugs, and alcohol does not necessarily have
strong ego controls and may, in fact, be overly repressed and unable to
reexperiment with infantile sexuality. Before significance is ascribed to
a lack of tolerance of ego regression, "cultural and social class attitudes
need to be taken into account" (p. 73). Miller noted that the drugs used
differ from country to country, within institutions, social groups, and
social class and also vary with fashion and culture.

> Early adolescents use glue and paint thinner for their intoxicant effects in
> parts of the United States and Continental Europe. In Britain their use is
> rare except in penal institutions. Marijuana was used in Sweden many
> years before it was used in its neighbor Finland. Its use is common among
> students in Britain and in the United States and among deprived and black
> adolescents in the ghettos of American cities. The British working class
> used amphetamines for years and only now recently began to use hashish
> [p. 75].

Miller (1973) observed three etiological reasons for drug abuse,
which are not necessarily indicative of any severe personal pathology or
based on early traumata, deprivation, or distorted parenting. One or all
can stimulate drug use:

1. Problems of identity, created by stress in emancipating from parents can slow down maturation and originate, not from the adolescents deficits, but from "isolation from extra-parental adults"
   (p. 85). This isolation is not created by the teenagers' impaired
   object relationships—but rather, is due to their increasing social
   instability, mores, and transient connection to schools, teachers,
   and varied institutional personnel. (Marijuana can stimulate

peer group internal imagery and hypercathexis to sensory perceptions of such stimuli as music.)

2. Sexual conflicts, including the adolescent's anxiety about heterosexual strivings, normal masturbatory activity, and normal
preconscious homosexual impulses. (Methedrine and ampheta-
mine use will inhibit potency.)

3. The relief of intrapsychic pain, especially the avoidance of experiencing anxiety. (Large doses of marijuana or hallucinogens
medicate against feelings of deprivation, inferiority, or depression over loss of a love object.)

The history of explanations of addictive behavior is rooted in many
disciplines, including history, sociology, psychology, medicine, psychoanalysis, physiology, and pharmacology. Early theories viewed addicts
as morally deficient; this was followed by formulations that emphasized
addicts' inherent weaknesses, which "gave nourishment to the psychoanalytic perspectives that were concerned with ego regression and
eventually ego adaptive mechanisms associated with pharmacologically
altered states of consciousness. These views still exist and flourish today" (Shaffer and Burglass, 1981, p. 482). Other perspectives emphasized sociological and environmental theories.

More recently various schools of thought have disagreed on what
drug dependence represents for the user. Is it a progressive effort, an attempt to correct impaired ego functioning, to cope, or to produce the
regressive states of withdrawal and isolation? Currently the steady increase of middle-class white addicted adolescents from privileged
homes suggests that the peer influence is most important in initiating
drug experimentation and use. Heroin users to be initiated at ages 16
and 17, but of late "the age of initiation has dropped steadily below the
age of 14. Some 10 and 11 year olds are now experimenting with
opioids" (Kaplan and Sadock, 1981, p. 497).

Regardless of theories of etiology, drug abuse creates specific and
serious therapeutic problems. Acute toxic states produce confusion, often unremembered by the adolescent; thus fear of a repetition is not recognized and so cannot deter continued abuse. Often there is no knowledge of what has been ingested. Rarely is a drug user available to engage
fully in the relationship and dialogue inherent in conventional psychotherapy. There is insufficient observing ego to reflect and think clearly.
Heroin addiction creates psychotherapeutic and medical problems, and
the patient may require hospitalization for the liver tests necessary
prior to prescribing any substitute chemical medication to facilitate
withdrawal. If drug abuse continues, it can stimulate underlying psychopathology; and withdrawal, even forced, is necessary before the underlying emotional problems and ego deficits can be treated.

No treatment has been accepted as providing solutions to all the complex personality, health, and legal problems. Detoxification and methadone substitution are the most prevalent treatment methods employed. Clonidine has then been used with reported success to effect later withdrawal from methadone. However, permanent methadone maintenance is the most widely used method of treating heroin addiction.

Advocates of this approach compare controlled addiction to methadone to insulin administered daily to diabetic patients. This removes the addict from danger of injecting himself with unsterile materials, often of questionable purity. The current AIDS epidemic has frightened many addicts and altered their casual attitudes about injections. The use of methadone maintenance eliminates the need for obsessive preoccupation and planning and, perhaps, illegal activities to procure the next fix. There are many professionals who feel the disadvantages of methadone maintenance outweigh the advantages—the continuation of addiction, the recent black market of methadone by patients or staff of methadone clinics, the accidental ingestion of methadone by children, and the yet unknown side effects of this drug. However because of its low cost, it will indubitably continue to be the prescribed mode of treatment for adolescent and adult addicts.

Therapeutic communities are another common approach in attempts to deal with addiction. They demand total commitment from the residents to engage in drug-free detoxification and to maintain abstinence. Many of these self-help programs are harsh and confrontive, employing mortifying group encounters, humiliating punishment procedures, reeducation, hard physical work, and stringently enforced rules and restrictions. These programs usually are staffed by former addicts and are not professionally oriented. The milieu involves peer pressure, group encounter sessions, and behavior modification. It has been noted that three-quarters of the population of these communities drops out in the first month. Additionally, the rate of recidivism among those who complete these programs is very high. It would appear that the harsh assaultive regime of these settings is counterproductive for residents who enter with long-standing low self-esteem. The "treatment," often a barrage of continuous narcissistic injuries and insults, is contraindicated for narcissistic character disordered patients and others who are perfectionistic and have exaggerated needs for achievement, unlimited success, talent, and admiration. These needs originally created their mortification and shame at earlier disappointments of "underachievement," which commonly created the drive to forget and withdraw via drug abuse.

Owing to the prevalence of information and education programs regarding drug use and the recent spread of AIDS with its fatal outcome,

ADOLESCENT PATHOLOGY

drug abuse has shifted somewhat in the 1980s, with an increase in the use of noninjected drugs, specifically cocaine. Cocaine can be taken by injection but "by far, the most commonly used route is sniffing or snorting; the average dose is 20 mg. to 50 mg" (p. 516). If used occasionally, cocaine appears to create no serious problems. Taken daily in sizable amounts, it can seriously disrupt eating and sleeping habits and interfere with psychological functioning, causing marked irritability, temper eruptions, disturbed concentration, and psychological dependence. Though there is no physical dependence, withdrawal causes overwhelming anxiety and depression. The lining of the nose can become inflamed, ulcerated, and swollen.

Marijuana is commonly used and "only the unsophisticated continue to believe that cannabis leads to violence and crime. Indeed, instead of inciting criminal behavior, cannabis may tend to suppress it. The intoxication induces lethargy that is not conducive to any physical activity, let alone the committing of crimes. The release of inhibitions results in fantasy and verbal expressions, rather than behavioral expression" (p. 513). The "high" or intoxication created by marijuana may heighten sensitivity to external stimuli, such as color, sound, and smell. A sense of time is distorted. Long-time users are "typically passive, nonproductive, slothlike and lacking in ambition. This finding suggests that chronic use—in its stronger forms—may have debilitating effects as prolonged heavy drinking does. . . . Many of those who take up cannabis seek to soften the impact of an otherwise unbearable reality" (p. 514). Pathological use results in an inability to reduce or stop use and causes impairment in social or occupational functioning, e.g., "marked loss of interest in activities previously engaged in, loss of friends, absence from work, loss of job, or legal difficulties" (DSM-III, 1980, p. 99). Although there is little evidence to suggest a cannabis psychosis, this drug can precipitate several types of mental dysfunction, e.g., clouding of consciousness, confusion, bewilderment, disorientation, fear, panic, sense of distortion in body perception, and paranoid ideation.

Amphetamines initially produce a sense of energy and a feeling of exhihilaration. Female adolescents can start dependency on this drug, beginning with its use of weight reduction. Chronic users show signs of flushing, fever, tachycardia, serious cardiac problems, elevated blood pressure, nausea, loss of sensory abilities, fights and loss of friends, and job and legal difficulties. Extreme usage can precipitate a paranoid psychosis and malnutrition or lesser psychological effects as confusion, tension, acute panic, and fear.

Treatment efforts may include antipsychotic and/or antidepressant medication; possibly a hospitalization; and a treatment relationship and therapeutic alliance, once the drug dependency has been modified. Until then psychotherapy will be difficult or impossible to institute.

Barbiturates known in the adolescent black market as "red devils," "downers," "yellows," "rainbows," and "double trouble" often are of questionable quality and purity. Dependence is usually caused by an adolescent seeking relief from tension, anxiety, and a sense of inadequacy. Patterns of use include chronic intoxication, episodic intoxication, and intravenous use, the latter by those heavily involved in the illegal drug culture, who have experienced extensive pill-popping, speed, and heroin. Barbiturates injected produce a rush effect "which is described as a pleasurable, warm and drowsy feeling. Like speed freaks, these barb freaks are disliked by the rest of the subculture because of their irresponsibility and . . . tendency to be violent and disruptive" (Kaplan and Sadock, 1981, p. 518). All patterns of barbiturate use are considered real danger, with barbiturate poisoning "becoming a significant public health problem. Barbiturates are the cause of death in 6 percent of suicides and cause more accidental deaths than any other single drug. About fifteen thousand deaths in the United States are attributed annually to barbiturates" (ibid.). Because judgment and memory are impaired, previous doses are forgotten, and overdosing without intent to suicide is common. Mild barbiturate intoxication resembles intoxication with alcohol; and symptoms such as sluggishness; difficulty in speaking, comprehending, and concentrating; faulty judgment; poor memory; and eruptive anger are common. Heavy users often experience hallucinations, psychosis, and convulsions.

Careful medical care is required in the detox period. The dosage must be reduced gradually and the proper amount is hard to determine because the patient's memory is impaired and thus his or her report is highly unreliable and often underestimates the dosage. Some recommend substituting nonbarbiturate sedatives, much as methadone is substituted for heroin. Treatment follow-up is essential to attempt to combat the usual pattern of relapse and resumption of drug abuse.

Methaqualone is a nonbarbiturate sedative increasingly used by adolescents in recent years. Some report that it has become popular among college students, who use it with alcohol or wine; results due to this combination can be fatal. Until recently it was thought not to lead to physical dependence, but currently withdrawal symptoms are noted.

Meprobamate and benzodiazepines are lethal because of their acute toxic effects, which often produce shock, loss of consciousness, respiratory depression, convulsions, and death. The overall treatment requires a gradual, monitored withdrawal from the drug. Glue and other volatile solvents, such as paint thinners, benzene, and lighter fluid, have been used by preadolescents and adolescents and are dangerous because of severe psychological dependence and a risk of tissue damage—particularly to the bone marrow, brain, liver and kidneys.

PCP or phencyclidene—commonly known as "angel dust"—first

appeared as a street drug in San Francisco in the late sixties and by the seventies was used increasingly. It is apparently regarded as something like a cross between a psychedelic drug and a tranquilizer or sedative. Although it may be taken orally, intravenously, or by sniffing, it is usually sprinkled onto joints of parsley or marijuana and smoked because this mode affords the best means of self-titration. Early use produces fantasies, bodily warmth, peaceful sensations, and not uncommonly, depersonalization, estrangement, and sometimes hallucinations. Body-image distortions are common, such as the user perceiving his or her body as shrunken or weightless; and there are similar distortions of time and space and disorganizations of thought. Anxiety can be reported. Following a high, depression, confusion, difficulties of speech, irritability, paranoia, and blank staring are common, as is assaultive and violent behavior. This drug produces many of the psychedelic qualities of LSD. Higher dosages produce stupor and comatose states; muscle rigidity followed by seizures and respiratory arrest can cause death. If recovery from a heavy dose occurs, psychosis can last for several weeks, producing echolalia, staring into space, paranoid ideation, depression, and in severe cases, public masturbation, violence, public nudity, inappropriate schizophreniclike laughter and crying. Following this there is amnesia and the adolescent has absolutely no memory of the entire period or series of events during the psychotic episode.

LSD is the most widely used psychedelic drug. "It almost always produces profound alterations in perception, mood and thinking. Perceptions become unusually brilliant and intense. Colors and textures seem richer . . . music more emotionally profound, smells and tastes heightened" (p. 524). Emotions are intense; charged and incompatible feelings may be experienced simultaneously. A heightened state of memory, reality, and religious and philosophic thoughts and insight are common. Flashbacks and a sense of time expansion are reported. Psychedelic drugs can magnify and bring into consciousness unconscious internal conflicts. Very marginal individuals with basic schizophrenic and prepsychotic personalities often have adverse reactions. There is no physical addiction, and psychological dependence is rare; but heavy users generally suffer chronic anxiety, depression, and a sense of inadequacy; and escape via a psychedelic trip continues to diminish their capacity to tolerate frustration, cope, and adapt.

All in all, adolescent drug abusers are rarely motivated for therapy, much as normal young teenagers have little capacity for self-observation, reflections, and introspection. Referrals for help constitute threats to early adolescents' self-esteem, autonomy, and sense of self-determination. Conscious desires for help and treatment occur more frequently in middle and late adolescence, when psychological consolidation normally occurs. Often, in the early stages of treatment, the drug-dependent teenager needs to be seen daily to substitute the treatment relationship for the soothing self-medicating drug habit; he or she must be faced with reality consequences of incarceration or probation as an impetus for conforming with a treatment regimen.

Therapy is impossible if the teenager identifies the therapist with his own harsh, immature, punishing conscious or superego. Thus, the nonmotivated drug-abusing adolescent will have to be involuntarily hospitalized, forcibly detoxified, and often, coerced into treatment. Later the treatment approach can be converted to a more usual neutral psychotherapy stance without the earlier interventions in, and controls on the teenagers life-style, choice of friends, and activities. Drug abuse that represents a profound rebellion against parents and/or therapist, requires a lengthy hospitalization, until the adolescent is reachable, accessible, self-observant, honest, and willing and able to assume age-appropriate responsibility for his or her behavior. While drug use can make some adolescents seemingly unreachable, it does not necessarily make the majority inaccessible, over the long term. Parental and therapeutic support and commitment can eventually reach many who, later, will accomplish, master, and cope in a drug-free age-appropriate fashion. Continued efforts and commitment are crucial, because drug dependencies are all but epidemic among our youth. Drug abuse not only compromises the developmental aspects of adolescence but also is generally implicated in cases of adolescent suicide, traffic fatalities, and other self-destructive behavior patterns. These young people must be identified as a high-risk population.

Case of Sophia

Sophia was almost 20 when she sought individual therapy, acknowledging an extensive drug-abuse history, which for the first time, concerned her sufficiently to motivate her to get some help. In college Sophia worked part time at a rock-music record company, as a secretary, girl Friday. Sophia was bright, anxious, given to depression, mood swings, and fluctuations between over-immersion in drug related "partying" with friends and protracted periods of social estrangement. She described her mood shifts as causing her to change friendships endlessly and to transfer from one college to the next. She had no clearcut professional goals and felt generally at sea about her current life and future. Her parents had become angered and exhausted by her shifts, moods, and temper eruptions. Currently she was residing in her parents' apartment while they spent the winter months in Florida. Upon their return, it was expected that she would have found her own housing—preferably a share in an apartment. Sophia was the youngest of four children; her siblings were employed college graduates and two were married. She described no real closeness with them, or with her parents. She viewed herself, the much younger last child, as unplanned and unwanted. Her family was white, Jewish, and middle class.

Sophia viewed herself as the marginal family member, less attractive and intelligent than her sisters and always anxious and insecure about her social status, school work, and goals. She described herself as the "skinny dumb bunny" in her family, who has always caused her parents displeasure and disappointment. Because her parents were older when they had her, she believed they had less time, interest, or energy, to deal with her. She recounted her habit of crying a lot, giving in to temper tantrums, and indulging in a lot of wild drinking and drug use in her teen years.

Her continued drug use had included anything and everything but heroin, and she affiliated with others similarly using drugs at whatever college she attended. She viewed her peer group as victims of the aftermath of the 1960s, and characterized them and herself as passive, nonproductive, and lacking in ambition and purpose. When not in a rage at her family, Sophia said she was overcome with apathy and self-pity. She had made extensive use of various amphetamines, barbiturates, and psychedelic drugs. LSD pleased her the most and she currently alternated between it and other peer-sanctioned drugs. In the rock world where she was employed, she reported that all this was "par for the course."

While Sophia could present her history and profess a wish for therapy, attendance at sessions often was erratic and marked by considerable lateness and absences due to her oversleeping, being "hung over," and being "out of it." This kind of erratic attendance had been her pattern for years, at college and at jobs. Her academic functioning was far below her intellectual potential; she "got by," passing with C's and D's despite missing class, being late with assignments, etc. At work she had often been fired because of lateness or for being dazed and spacey. At her current job, she worked with other drug users who were not demanding about punctuality and alert behavior.

After a month or more of therapy, characterized by Sophia's repeated lateness and coming to therapy sessions in what she acknowledged was a "wasted" state, the therapist queried the benefits of their continuing the current treatment plan. The therapist explored treatment alternatives and ultimately referred Sophia to a program that offered outpatient group and individual therapy to older adolescent substance abusers on a scaled fee basis. Sophia was appreciative of the appropriate referral and acknowledged relief at the prospect of group treatment and group pressure, which she thought she needed. Because of the rapport established with her therapist, Sophia experienced some stress at the time of transfer. She acknowledged, however, that "her symptom" interfered with therapy, following an arrival to a session forty minutes late. "I took the subway in the wrong direction. I'd used LSD the night before . . . after a 'Who' rock concert and blasted myself out of my mind. When I start group therapy I'll want acceptance by the others and know that kind of group pressure will help me. You accept me but have no leverage over me, especially when I can't make it to appointments."

Bibliography

CHAFETZ, M. E. and DEMONE, H. W. (1962). *Alcoholism and Society*. New York: Oxford University Press.

AMERICAN PSYCHIATRIC ASSOCIATION (1980). *Quick Reference to Diagnostic Criteria from the Diagnostic and Statistical Manual of Mental Disorders, Third Edition*, pp. 91–101. Washington, D.C.: APA.

HARTMAN, D. (1969). Drug-Taking Adolescents. *Psychoanalytic Study of the Child*, 24:384–98. New York: International Universities Press.

KAPLAN, H. and SADOCK, B., EDS. (1981). Drug Dependence. In *Modern Synopsis of Psychiatry III*, pp. 496–525. Baltimore/London: Williams & Wilkins.

MILLER, D. (1973). The Drug Dependent Adolescent. In *Adolescent Psychiatry, Vol. 2: Developmental and Clinical Studies*, eds. S. C. Feinstein and P. Giovacchini, pp. 79–97. New York: Basic Books.

POWELL, D. H. (1973). Occasional Heroin Users. *Arch. Gen. Psychiatry*, 28:586–94.

RADO, S. (1933). The Psychoanalysis of Pharmacothymia. *Psychoanal. Q.*, 2:1–23.

ROBINS, L. (1974). A Follow-up Study of Vietnam Veterans' Drug Use. *J. Drug Issues*, 4:62–81.

SAVITT, R. A. (1963). Psychoanalytic Studies on Addiction: Ego Structure in Narcotic Addiction. *Psychoanal. Q.*, 32:43–57.

SHAFFER, H. and BURGLASS, M. E. (1981). Epilogue; Reflections and Perspectives on the History and Future of Addiction. In *Classic Contributions in the Addictions*, eds. H. Shaffer and M. E. Burglass, pp. 481–96. New York: Brunner/Mazel.

SPITZ, R. (1965). *The First Year of Life*. New York: International Universities Press.

WIEDER, H. and KAPLAN, E. (1969). Drug Use in Adolescents—Psychodynamic Meaning and Pharmacogenic Effect. *Psychoanalytic Study of the Child*, 24:399–431. New York: International Universities Press.

ZINBURG, A. (1975). Addiction and Ego Function. *Psychoanalytic Study of the Child*, 30:567–880. New Haven: Yale University Press.

ZINBURG, N. E.; HARDING, W. M.; and WINKLER, M. A. (1977). A Study of Social Regulatory Mechanisms in Controlled Illicit Drug Users. *J. Drug Use*, 7: 117–33.

ZINBURG, N. and JACOBSON, R. C. (1974). The Social Basis of Drug Abuse (unpublished).

_____ (1974). The Natural History of Chipping (unpublished).

II. Alcohol Abuse

In considering adolescent patients' use of alcohol, distinction must be made between alcohol abuse, alcohol dependency, alcoholism, alcoholic psychosis, and alcoholic intoxication.

Alcohol abuse, as defined by *DSM-III*, is the nonpathological recreational use of a substance; there are episodes of intoxication without a pattern of pathological use. Duration of the disturbance is of at least one month, with social complications of alcohol use, including impairment in social or occupational functioning, such as arguments or difficulties with family or friends over excessive alcohol use; violence while intoxicated; work missed; being fired; and legal difficulties, such as being arrested for traffic accidents while intoxicated. Although there may be periods of temporary abstinence, there exists psychological dependence—an inability to cut down, or stop drinking despite repeated efforts to control or reduce excess drinking. The above characteristics strike this author as indeed pathological; similarly, Kaplan and Sadock (1981) noted that in their view the separation of alcoholism and alcohol abuse is "somewhat arbitrary, and has little relevance from a treatment viewpoint. Clinically, patients probably shift back and forth between these two categories" (p. 525).

Alcoholism, as described by *DSM-III*, indicates a pattern of pathological (daily) alcohol use as a prerequisite for adequate functioning; an inability to cut down or stop drinking, despite repeated efforts, or efforts to restrict drinking to certain times of the day; binges that result in intoxication throughout the day for at least two days; blackout or amnesic periods; and continued drinking despite a serious physical disorder that the individual knows is exacerbated by alcohol use. Impairment in social or occupational functioning due to alcohol is characteristic. Classic examples are violence while intoxicated, absence from work, loss of one's job, such legal difficulties as arrest for intoxicated behavior, traffic accidents, and arguments with friends and family because of excessive alcohol use. Tolerance indicates the need for markedly increased amounts of alcohol to achieve the desired effect, or there is a markedly diminished effect with regular use of the same amount.

Alcoholic withdrawal refers to morning "shakes" and malaise which are relieved by drinking; they are characterized by nausea and vomiting, anxiety, sweating and elevated blood pressure, depressed mood, or irritability.

Alcoholic psychosis, such as alcoholic hallucinosis or organic delusional syndrome, presents hallucinations or delusions as the predominate clinical feature(s), respectively. Distinction and differential diagnosis require consideration of schizophrenia. Severe dementia associated with alcoholism presents a clinical picture of extreme impairment of functioning with marked deterioration of personality (irritability and social inappropriateness) and an inability to function independently. In contrast, alcohol intoxication presents a less extreme picture following ingestion of alcohol. Physiological signs of the latter include slurred speech, poor coordination, unsteady gait, and flushed face; psychological signs are mood changes, irritability, loquacity, and impaired attention.

The majority of alcoholics begin early in life, somewhere in middle or late adolescence, though it appears that an ever-increasing younger population is engaged in alcohol experimentation, intoxication, and abuse. It is suggested that any lessening of drug abuse in the last dozen or more years has been matched by an increase in alcohol consumption.

Core developmental conflict, ego deficits, flawed character, and childhood traumata due to parental inadequacies postulated in dynamic etiological theories of drug abuse, also appear in theories regarding alcoholism. Classic psychoanalytic theorists (Freud, Abraham, Knight, Hartman, Tausk, Fenishel, etc.) conceived of alcoholism as a result of instinctual conflict and drive reduction. Oral fixation and a close relationship between alcoholism and homosexuality was posited.

There is considerable controversy over the causes of alcoholism. Earlier explanations were based in symbolic and other psychological theories. Rado (1933) stated that alcohol addiction was not related to the pharmacologic effect, but to the unconscious meaning of the substance. The pleasure was "brought about by the ego itself" and thus, addiction was conceived of as a psychological problem due to a libidinal fixation. The effects of alcohol were seen as secondary symptoms. Rado's conception created the famous psychological equation that bottle equals or signifies breast and that drinking, like drug abuse, is a symbolic infantile incorporation of the symbiotic mother.

Ego psychologists explain alcoholism in terms of ego deficits (Knight, 1937; Mack, 1981) or flaws (Balint, 1969) in the infant-mother relationship. Kernberg (1975) believed that a borderline character structure is basic to alcohol addiction. The basic ego deficits, lack of self and object constancy, and failure to separate and individuate are seen as causing continued attempts to reunite and merge symbiotically. This view suggests that alcohol is used by the borderline as a symbolic transitional object, or bridge toward reunion with the mother. Kohut, from a self-psychology perspective, saw the alcoholic as a narcissistic character, with structural deficits, perfectionistic strivings, and unstable self-esteem. Alcohol use is therefore a psychic maneuver used in an attempt at self-repair (self-soothing) of the structural self-object flaws (Pattison, 1984, p. 364).

In contrast, Chein et al. (1964) and Pattison (1984) maintained that oral-erotic breast symbolization, suggested by classic id psychology and drive theory, is not characteristic of most alcoholics. It is in fact only discernable for those diagnosed as having an underlying schizophrenic or manic-depressive diagnosis or those severely regressed from an extensive and lengthy alcoholic addiction.

Writing from a physiological perspective, Bean (1981), Vaillant (1981), and Zinburg (1982) contended that premorbid and morbid personality studies of alcoholics do not consistently demonstrate the presence of a borderline or narcissistic character disorder and that seeming borderline or narcissistic behaviors are the result of regression due to the effects of alcohol on ego operations. This group, described as the pharmacodynamic psychologists, put little focus and emphasis on premorbid character development. The dynamic consistent patterns frequently observed in alcoholics are the result of "pharmacologic effects upon ego operations which result in [reactive] degradiation or deterioration of ego functions combined with neurotic or quasi-adaptive ego responses to these deficts and the associated alcoholic life style" (Pattison, 1984, p. 365). Pattison (1984) noted that this perspective is compatible with much neuropsychological data on long and short decline of ego functions or data that examines abstaining alcoholics but appears to ignore premorbid ego deficits and character disorders in some alcoholics. This perspective is also compatible with the reality that some alcoholics function extremely well, without deterioration of ego functions, despite extensive alcohol use.

Most alcoholism treatment programs, especially the Alcoholics Anonymous and Alanon programs, prefer a medical disease model, emphasizing the physiology of alcoholism and the fact that "it has a progressive course with clear-cut symptoms and . . . is fatal if not treated" (Chernus, 1985, p. 67). This orientation is based on studies of genetics and physiology showing that the alcoholic's metabolism was different from nonalcoholic's before drinking was begun (Forest, 1975; Milam and Ketcham, 1981; Goodwin and Guze, 1974; Goodwin, 1976; Mendelson and Mello, 1979).

According to this view, behavioral patterns are effects rather than causes of alcohol usage, and personality and environmental variables are secondary to biological and genetic determinants influencing individuals' alcohol use and drinking habits. Clinicians who subscribe to this disease model often surrender the nondirective stance characteristic of the psychoanalytic psychodynamic approach.

Researchers do not agree on the precise causes of alcoholism. Some authors contend that there is no uniform alcoholic personality, common character disorder, or uniform pattern of fixation, regression, or basic psychodynamics. However, we can observe in alcoholics more depression, aggressive feelings and actions, paranoid thinking, and reduced self-esteem and self-control than in the nonalcoholic population. Questions remain as to whether these traits preceded or followed alcohol abuse.

Some researchers have suggested that alcoholism is an unusual allergic response to drinking alcohol. In the same way as people respond differently to the same medication, some people cannot drink more than small amounts of alcohol without experiencing unpleasant reactions, while others can consume large amounts with little effect. Hereditary factors, body type, and body weight may contribute to these idio-syncratic reactions.

What appears beyond dispute is the fact that "alcoholism is famil-ial; various studies of alcoholic groups reveal that 50 percent of their fa-thers, 30 percent of their brothers, 6 percent of their mothers and 3 percent of their sisters are also alcoholics" (Kaplan and Sadock 1981, p. 526). We can only query if this finding relates to psychological or ge-netic familial factors. Commonly, alcohol dependency begins in the teen years, followed by the steady, often moderate to ever-increasing in-take and ultimately, addiction. Alcohol consumption replaces other in-terests and activities with increasing social penalties: familial and work difficulties, blackouts, and temper eruptions to the point of family vio-lence. Episodes of remorse and depression (with thoughts of suicide by 40 percent) are followed by futile attempts at self-cure, and continued postponement in seeking help "until something shocking happens, or a coercive force with direct influence on the patient—such as an em-ployer [the police or courts] or spouse, intervenes" (pp. 534–35). This in-tervention can take the form of separating the drinker from his job, his family, or the issuing of an ultimatum regarding mandatory contact, e.g., with a therapist, probation officer, or Drunken Driver Education program. This reality pressure often becomes necessary because so many alcohol-addicted individuals consciously or unconsciously deny or camouflage their excessive drinking. Some quiet alcoholics superfi-cially manage their daily lives and may only binge and become inebri-ated episodically or on weekends.

Alcoholics have not generally been amenable to traditional forms of psychotherapy or psychoanalysis and hence have not been of great in-terest to clinicians. They, like drug addicts, often anger therapists, who thereupon act out their frustration and sense of impotence in the treat-ment situation or, not uncommonly, refuse to treat them altogether. Chernus (1985) suggested that the psychoanalytic psychotherapist must depart from traditional nondirective techniques and be able and willing to be emphatic and insistent with clients, strong in recommending, for example inpatient treatment "sometimes even in [direct] opposition to the client's wishes" (p. 69).

Treatment handled on an outpatient basis may include detoxifica-tion, frequent therapy sessions, and possibly such medication as Lib-rium and Antabuse if the severity of the withdrawal symptoms warrants it. This outpatient approach requires a most cooperative patient and, of-ten, supportive family member(s).

By contrast, hospitalization increasingly is necessary for older ado-lescents who have become addicted to alcohol early in their lives. Ka-plan and Sadock (1981), Chernus (1985), and others have noted that vol-untarism for drug addicted patients and alcoholics is a "specious" issue in that virtually all such patients come in response to some form of coercion and that it is the rare alcoholic who seeks treatment because he alone has admitted that he is alcoholic. In fact, these patients who are coerced into treatment by circumstances or persons who are meaningful to them are more apt to remain in treatment and have a successful outcome, than are alcoholics who are not forced into treatment.

Sobriety is required before any actual psychotherapy can occur, and this might require concurrent involvement in AA and/or family therapy or marital treatment. Intensive, uncovering psychotherapy is frequently unsuitable, particularly in the initial stages. The reality of drinking, its physical, legal, emotional, familial, academic, and employment consequences are crucial issues to face in the push toward and maintenance of sobriety.

Half-way houses and group homes for adolescents are frequently suitable placement facilities, if the familial home is seen as fostering or permitting regression and any danger of resumption of alcohol abuse. Groups for parents and Alateen for children and siblings of alcoholics can offer education and peer support for relatives afflicted and affected by alcoholic family members. In some settings behavioral approaches have been employed with varying success rates. These teach relaxation techniques, assertiveness training, coping skills, stress cues, and strategies to change social and environmental realities. Education in schools and other prevention programs are used but as yet, there is little hard evidence regarding their impact on curtailing alcohol use in the adolescent population.

Case of Michael

Michael was 16 years old when he was referred by his mother for emergency therapy. She made the referral with the help of her own therapist. Michael's school was threatening him with expulsion unless treatment was secured immediately. Michael, a white Catholic, was a tall, blonde, extremely handsome adolescent. He was enrolled in a midwestern public high school for gifted children, which rarely faced, or tolerated, discipline problems. Michael and a friend were described by teachers and the school principal as belligerent and surly of late and given to provocative antics. The final precipitant for the threat of expulsion was an incident when the two boys scared peers and teachers by spraying with water pistols that looked like real weapons. Michael's grades had sharply declined recently. Yet while he registered concern about his grade point average, he was derisive and scornful that there was much ado about nothing. "Water pistols, a little spring sport, and we're being treated like bona fide delinquents."

Michael's resistance and anger increased when his therapist did not give him a clean bill of health and accept his rejection of ongoing therapy. During the evaluation of Michael, the inordinate stress in his family was revealed and was seen as precipitating his current problems. Thus, a firm recommendation was made for ongoing sessions, which was strongly supported by Michael's mother and school. Michael's father reluctantly complied, but his resistance was manifested through repeated bouncing payment checks, despite his training and employment as an accountant. Michael valued his school and so reluctantly kept scheduled sessions over a four-month period, though his preference was that, at the conclusion of the assessment phase, his therapist write the school a letter disclaiming his need for help. As reported by Michael and his mother, his companion in the water pistol episode was seen once by a psychiatrist and was not required to have ongoing therapy. Michael considered his therapy an unnecessary punishment and struggled to avoid making any genuine therapeutic alliance. Ultimately, he did develop some rapport with his therapist.

The history shared by Michael and his parents revealed the following: The parents had been separated for over five years. After many attempts in individual and marital therapy, the mother had concluded the marriage because of the father's recurrent alcoholic patterns, which resulted in his erratic irresponsible handling of family finances and episodic explosiveness and physical abuse of her. Michael's younger brother had severe symptoms and incapacitation due to his abuse of psychedelic drugs and alcohol. At the time of Michael's school difficulties and referral, the younger brother was hospitalized in an adolescent closed unit, after what appeared to be a drug-induced series of psychotic episodes, during which he had cut up furniture at home, torn his mother's clothes to shreds, smashed through walls, and broken all of Michael's records and the china and glassware in his mother's apartment. The boys resided mainly with their mother but spent protracted intervals and weekends with their father, who had no control over his younger son. This younger teenager cut school and lay about the house using drugs, while the father morosely gave in to alcohol use and, similarly, avoided work and his office. Michael would thereupon return to his mother's and attend his classes, full of fury and scorn for father and brother. Presumably he did not drink at this point, although he later demonstrated dire effects from excessive drinking.

Michael, older, handsome, intellectually gifted, and most outstanding in his general performance, was seen as the parents' favorite and as unlike the younger brother, who historically floundered socially and academically. The hospital was having inordinate problems containing this younger brother, who had run away several times, most recently by jumping out of a third-story window that he had broken on a "secure closed unit." Michael was enraged at his brother and at the hospital for not being able to contain him, and early in therapy, he acknowledged his refusal to visit his brother or participate in family sessions conducted at the hospital. He wanted his brother simply to be locked up and hoped that "the key would be thrown away." This brother was being considered for long-term nonvoluntary placement in an adolescent residential treatment facility that the parents were hoping would accept him when their insurance coverage ran out. Otherwise, the hospital would discharge him or transfer him to a state hospital.

Believing that Michael was understandably reactive to these severe familial stresses, his therapist recommended continued therapy so that he would have a place to ventilate, abreact, and share his feelings in a way that would not create the social consequences noted above at school. He attended sessions promptly but maintained anger and resistance, manifested in abusive racist comments delivered at his therapist, who he accused of being a fleecing, money-gouging Jew. He articulated admiration and respect for Hitler, "who had the right idea." His therapist perceived these views as symptoms and, more easily than might be anticipated, contained and managed counterreactions, given her genuine curiosity and need to understand the etiology of this virulent vicious prejudice. The tone of the sessions could be lightened with some humor to which Michael responded briefly. The therapist would ask whether if the parents paid $1,000 a session, would it really suffice, under the circumstances? Michael would momentarily laugh—and then be off again on a tirade about the therapist serving as his doormat to abuse for fifty-minute intervals.

In his musings about Hitler, Michael revealed his fantasies and his immersion in books, television series, and documentaries about Hitler and pondered the irony that Hitler himself was part-Jewish. This association led him to examine his own self-hate. He crossexamined his therapist to determine whether "you've fallen for my anti-Semitic charade." For weeks following, he was choked up, finding it hard to speak and to swallow, as he admitted his actual close friendships with Jewish peers and his preference for his stereotyped idealization of them.

> Those friends live well, in attractive homes, with no money worries. But most special is the fact that the parents aren't divorced and the fathers aren't drinkers, like my soused shanty-Irish bum of a father. You know . . . the stereotype ideal Jewish family where the closeness really is there. My father's another stereotype—an Irish Catholic alcoholic, blotto most of the time. I can't blame mom for kicking him out. He hit her around a lot!

After a four-month period, characterized by angry tirades and productive sharing of pain and disillusion, Michael chose to terminate his therapy. His therapist advised against this decision, trying to sustain Michael's introspection and better understanding of himself and his feelings. However, with grades back to the superior level he had always achieved, Michael insisted that now he was better, calmer, and able to concentrate. He had joined a rock band at school, planned a summer bicycle hostel trip—and, in general, felt better and functioned well.

Several months later, Michael's therapist received an anguished call from his mother. On a train to the West Coast friends had gotten completely inebriated and a terrible accident had occurred. Michael had climbed up onto the train roof and, drunkenly cavorting about, was thrown off when the train went into a tunnel. He broke his neck and was hospitalized awaiting surgery. The mother was understandably terrified, given the medical realities that Michael could conceivably be crippled for life. The doctors had queried his unconscious suicidal behavior and wanted him evaluated by a therapist at the hospital; they also wanted information from his prior therapist. Michael refused any and all contact with his former therapist and all hospital psychiatric staff.

Michael seemed to have demonstrated a short-lived transference-cure that dissipated when he chose to conclude his therapy. Following this, insidious alcohol abuse commenced. His mother further reported that his surgical recovery was miraculous and complete with no residual physical problems. Nevertheless, he would not engage in self-observation or ponder his self-destructive behavior and reengage in therapy. The alcohol abuse Michael began in his high school senior year seemed to have been a way to medicate and anesthetize himself, as he struggled alone with his rage and despair over the ongoing problems in his family, as well as his own fears regarding the separation of departure for college.

Bibliography

ABRAHAM, K. (1927). The Psychological Relations Between Sexuality and Alcoholism. In *Selected Papers*. London: Institute of Psychoanalysis and Hogarth Press.

BALINT, M. (1969). *The Basic Fault: Therapeutic Aspects of Regression*. London: Tavistock. Reprinted 1979 by Brunner/Mazel, New York.

BEAN, M. H. (1981). Denial and the Psychological Complications of Alcoholism. In *Dynamic Approaches to the Understanding and Treatment of Alcoholism*, eds. M. H. Bean and N. E. Zinberg, pp. 55–96. New York: Free Press.

CHEIN, I.; GERARD, D. L.; LEE, R. S.; and ROSENFELD, E. (1964). *The Road to Hard Narcotics, Delinquency and Social Policy*. New York: Basic Books.

CHERNUS, L. (1985). Clinical Issues in Alcoholism Treatment. *Social Casework*, 66(2):67–75.

FENICHEL, O. (1945). *The Psychoanalytic Theory of Neurosis*. New York: Norton.

FOREST, G. G. (1978). *The Diagnosis and Treatment of Alcoholism*. Springfield, Ill.: Thomas.

FREUD, S. [1910] (1930). *Three Contributions to the Theory of Sex*. Authorized translation by A. A. Brill with Introduction by J. Putnam and A. A. Brill. 4th ed. New York and Washington: Nervous and Mental Disease Publishing Co.

GOODWIN, D. W. (1976). *Is Alcoholism Hereditary?* New York: Oxford University Press.

GOODWIN, D. W. and GUZE, S. B. (1974). Drinking Patterns in Adopted and Nonadopted Sons of Alcoholics. *Arch. Gen. Psychiatry* (August 1974):164–69.

HARTMANN, D. (1969). A Study of Drug-Taking Adolescents. *Psychoanalytic Study of the Child*, 24:384–98. New York: International Universities Press.

HARTMANN, H. (1925). Kokainismus und Homosexualität. *Zeitschrift fur die Gesamte Neurologie und Psychiatric*, 95:79–94.

KAPLAN, H. I. and SADOCK, B. J. (1981). *Modern Synopsis of Psychiatry III*. 3rd ed. Baltimore/London: Williams & Wilkins.

KERNBERG, O. (1975). *Borderline Conditions and Pathological Narcissism*. New York: Jason Aronson.

KNIGHT, R. (1937). The Psychodynamics of Chronic Alcoholism. *J. Nerv. Mental Disease*, 86:538–48.

KOHUT, H. (1971). *The Analysis of the Self*. New York: International Universities Press.

MACK, J. E. (1981). Alcoholism, A.A., and the Governance of the Self. In *Dynamic Approaches to the Understanding and Treatment of Alcoholism*. eds. M. H. Bean and N. E. Zinberg, pp. 128–62. New York: Free Press.

MENDELSON, J. H. and MELLO, N. A. (1979). Biological Concommitants of Alcoholism. *New England J. Med.*, 301 (October 1979): 912–21.

MILAM, J. and KETCHAM, K. (1981). *Under the Influence: A Guide to the Myths and Realities of Alcoholism*. Seattle: Madrona Publishers.

PATTISON, E. M. (1984). Types of Alcoholism Reflective of Character Disorders. In *Character Pathology: Theory and Treatment*, ed. R. Zales, pp. 362–78. New York: American College of Psychiatrists, Brunner/Mazel.

RADO, S. (1933). The Psychoanalysis of Pharmacothymia. *Psychoanal. Q.* 2:1–23.

TAUSK, V. (1915). Zur Psychologie des Alkoholischen Bescháftigungsdelirs. *Internationale Zeitschrift fur Psychoanalyse*, 3:204–26.

VAILLANT, G. E. (1981). Dangers of Psychotherapy in the Treatment of Alcoholism. In *Dynamic Approaches to the Understanding and Treatment of Alcoholism*, eds. M. H. Bean and N. E. Zinburg, pp. 36–54. New York: Free Press.

ZINBURG, S. (1982). Psychotherapy in the Treatment of Alcoholism. In *Encyclopedic Handbook of Alcoholism*. eds. E. M. Pattison and E. Kaufman, pp. 999–1010. New York: Gardner Press.

PART IV

Adolescent Sexual Behavior

16

Introduction

In examining the value system of our rapidly changing culture and the value system of human psychology, Esman (1977) proposed that psychoanalysis "reexamine some of its general and clinical theoretical assumptions in the light of changes in the social matrix within which it operates" (p. 31). Central to the value system of psychoanalysis, according to Esman, are the primacy of reason, the concept of delayed gratification in the service of future goals, the principal of stable monogamous heterosexual bonds, and a commitment to a lifelong career. Clearly, these values are challenged, to varying degrees by the changing values, realities, and implications of adolescents' behavior, particularly their prevailing sexual mores and patterns. Adolescents have been affected by the sexual revolution and feminism, which many believe complicate the consolidation process of late adolescence. Gagnon (1974) has said that among contemporary adolescents, sex has become "like Mac-Donald's hamburgers," by which, Esman (1977) concluded, that he meant "it is easy to get, cheap, and essentially tasteless" (p. 26).

Patterns of heterosexuality have changed; teenage pregnancy is a problem of epidemic proportions; increasing numbers of adolescents have rejected a heterosexual orientation in favor of a bisexual or homosexual lifestyle; and, for both gay and straight youth, sexually transmitted diseases are running rampant. Regardless of one's theoretical orientation, these recent phenomena must be recognized by any clinician working with the contemporary adolescent. Successful engagement and sustenance of the therapeutic relationship requires the clinician's sensitivity and, when appropriate, willingness to modify concepts or therapeutic postures that alienate vulnerable young people as they attempt to master a whole new set of demands and expectations that further threaten autonomy and self-esteem. Clinicians must beware of interpreting personal conflict solely in terms of social and cultural trends or malaise. The fact that certain behaviors are widely observed does not mean they can be dismissed as simply a manifestation of the youth culture. Indeed, pathologies and casualties of youth are on the increase.

Kaplan (1984) noted the current cult of immediacy with its emphasis on sensation saps the vitalities of the young and "incites their sexual passions to precocious consummation, stultifies their intellect, [and] trivializes their imaginations" (p. 336). In addition to today's rapid sociocultural and technology changes which have complicated career choices, familial breakdown and reduced institutional support heighten the problems of maturation. Rather than "blaming the victim," we must recognize these interfamilial and cultural realities as contributing to the accelerated modes of drive expression of today's youth. Their contributions are clear in the new forms of sexual behavior as well as aggressive expression. The following chapter examines adolescent sexual patterns and realities, namely, homosexuality, heterosexuality, teenage pregnancy, and sexually transmitted diseases.

17

Heterosexuality

Adolescence is viewed as a second chance. Every previous developmental issue, quiescent during latency, reappears in intensity. The final steps to complete separation and individuation and resolve the reawakened oedipal struggle all resonate in the adolescent's varied sexual fantasies, yearnings, and actual attachments. This time of life requires a complete and irreversible surrender of the forbidden incestuous desires connected with both parents. The irreversible and final farewell to the early passionate attachments to parents invokes anxiety, depression, and profound sadness. For some adolescents, the pain is so intense that they cast about frenetically seeking substitute incestuous objects; others preoccupy themselves with daydreams and lengthy, detailed fantasies and hopes of love. Some adolescents accompany their fantasy life with masturbation and trial attempts to reconcile the inner life and imagination with sexual urgency so characteristic of this age of life.

Genital masturbation is a phase-specific positive adolescent activity. In fact, some clinicians (Laufer, 1968; Eissler, 1958; etc.) suggest that its absence connotes psychological immaturity, arrest, or significant disturbance. The absence of masturbation is perceived as interfering with an appropriate integration of infantile and genital desires. Submitting to parental prohibitions often results in a subsequent disapproval of pleasurable sexuality and coitus.

Some sexual fantasies and dreams provoke shame and fear, because they are "of having relations with someone of the same sex, of having sex with a close relative or friend, of having sex in unusual or hurtful ways, or of watching secretly while others make love" (Greenberg, 1982, p. 54). Such fantasies use current people in a teenagers life as the day residue, or substitute characters to mask experiences, people, and events from early childhood. Laufer (1968) stated that in normal adolescents, perverse fantasies remain predominantly unconscious and in general a heterosexual fantasy predominates. He later (1977) noted that the ability to accept one's sexual body and to masturbate free of guilt is essential for a full integration of genital and pregenital fantasy and successful adolescent development. Some subsequent problems like phobias, compulsions, impotence, and frigidity when actual sexual activity begins, require therapeutic intervention. Such phenomena are normal and common at the beginning of sexual activity, or following a few unpleasant sexual experiences. They can properly be considered significant when they occur repeatedly over a protracted period of time. Sexual problems are not necessarily revealed in performance difficulty. "Instead a problem with sex may show up in the form of having sex in adolescence too early with too many unattractive, unappetizing partners and little real pleasure" (Greenberg, 1982, p. 56). Early adolescent heterosexuality is regarded as being primarily motivated by defensive counter-oedipal maneuvers and struggles against strong homosexual strivings (Deutsch, 1967; Blos, 1967).

The prevailing psychoanalytic position maintains that healthy intact adolescents will experience arousal of aggressive and sexual feelings but will refrain from immediate heterosexual activities. Instead, they will sublimate sexual impulses through intellectual, athletic, and aesthetic activities (A. Freud, 1936). Sexuality will also be handled by masturbation, fantasies, and homosexual strivings, during the period when time is required for clarification of identity (Erikson, 1968), and consolidation of the varied narcissistic selves (Kohut, 1972).

Currently, there is divergent opinion on the actual extent and desirability of heterosexual activities of adolescents but little disagreement on the passion and importance of the first crushes and love relations. The attachment can command complete attention and devotion. This first bond is a test of how important and desirable the boy or girl is, and the course of the relationship frequently "leaves an indelible impression that may fester in the psyche well into adulthood" (Giovacchini, 1981, p. 141). Some young people forestall entry into any sort of an exclusive relationship and engage in group activities. In fact, "there is more companionship than ever between adolescent boys and girls of both high-school and college age. There is a stronger alliance between them, by no means reserved to social and educational affairs" (Gardner, 1970, p. 173). In an unprecedented fashion, youth today live together in co-ed dorms and apartments at college and following graduation, and engage in social, political, and athletic activities relating as asexual Platonic friends. The ultimate romantic pairing varies according to the individual's background, maturity, and situation. Overall, sexual fondling is common during early and middle adolescence. "At the beginning of adolescence girls are usually more interested in dating than boys are [and in fact] early dating has more social than sexual significance" (Schowalter and Anyan, 1979, pp. 52–53).

The early falling-in-love experience of adolescence is accompanied by erotic arousal and physical intimacy. This experience is commonly characterized by the narcissistic quality of the attachment, with its absorption, ecstasy, and maintenance of a state of absolute perfection. Kaplan (1984) suggested that often the passionate first loves are simply narcissistic exploitations, where one or both parties get hurt. Despite the frequent devastating aftermath, "it is an honest outpouring and genuine expression of the stream that links the love-hates of the past with the future and with present living in the world" (Kaplan, 1984, pp. 219–20). Often the lover has been selected because he or she represents an early adored significant object, a parent or a sibling. Later, no matter how extensive the passage of time, no love can compete with this first consuming passion.

First-love relationships may continue for a period, or be short-lived, following by a subsequent intense exclusive attachment. These relationships were described by Josselyn (1974) as monogamous adolescent heterosexual relationships that have the characteristics of an ideal marriage. In considering the tasks of adolescence, Josselyn questioned this form of sexual expression and suggested that it was not a mature solution, but an attempted resolution of reactivated immature needs related to compromised early child-rearing practices. As noted earlier, the frequency of this pattern may be due to the lack of pathways for adequate sublimation.

The exclusive relationships of early and middle adolescence, are replaced by less, rather than more, commitment in the late adolescent phase. Nonexclusive dating patterns and, later, trial cohabitation without future plans for marriage have characterized the 1960s, 1970s and early 1980s. The consistent postponement of marriage, commitment, and parenthood seems to have begun to abate in 1985, and we are witnessing a return to the mores—somewhat characteristic of the 1950s—which emphasize marriage and parenthood. The sexual freedom that followed the widespread use of the pill and other "safe" contraceptives and altered the established rules have recently been challenged by the recognition of the epidemic proportions of sexually transmitted diseases. Herpes has risen dramatically since 1983 and become the number one fear among those engaged in heterosexual relations. This disease is not physically debilitating but can create severe psychological reactions.

Herpes, is not the only feared sexually transmitted disease. "Unlike syphilis and gonorrhea, which usually respond to antibiotics, some of the new diseases cannot be cured, and result in chronic pain, sterility, abnormal pregnancies, brain damaged children and cancer: in the case of AIDS the outcome is almost-certain death (Seligman et al., 1985, p. 72). It is now recognized that hepatitis B and shigellosis, a gastrointestinal disorder, are transmitted sexually. The fastest growing, little-known disease is chlamydia trachomatis, which strikes enormous numbers: "3 to 4 million Americans each year, causing sterility in eleven thousand women annually, often without producing any symptoms that might have sent them to a physician before the damage was done" (p. 72). These newly recognized diseases, like venereal warts and genital herpes pose special threats to women and babies. Babies can be born with neonatal herpes, and in infants venereal warts can lodge in the larynx, trachea, and lungs. AIDS, the most dread sexually transmitted disease, is no longer confined to the drug abusing or homosexual populations.

Fear of disease and the absence of protective vaccines have moved many to abandon their uncommitted, free-wheeling approaches to sex. Group sex and open relationships, popular in the sixties and seventies, seem to be on the wane, with a recent visible, statistically significant return to the safety of monogamy. The mutual masturbatory relationships, i.e., gratification of the biologically genital level of sexuality without a genuine relationship, seems to be increasingly renounced.

Some researchers contend that they did not find evidence of rampant promiscuity and the so-called sexual revolution in groups they studied in the sixties and seventies. Offer and Offer (1977) studied a very special group of normal, healthy, white adolescent males from middle- to upper-middle-class backgrounds. They reported that juniors in high school disapproved of sexual intercourse for teenagers, out of fear of impregnation, developing a bad reputation, contracting a disease, or the worry about handling sexual intimacy. "The phrase 'we are not mature enough' was heard repeatedly." This nonrepresentative sample is, nevertheless, significant and documents a discrepancy of several years between biological maturity and emotional readiness for heterosexual relationships. Follow-up study showed that half the sample group engaged in sexual intercourse by the third year out of high school. The appropriate cautions and fears of this well-educated group may herald a new era of restraint across socioeconomic, racial, and class lines.

18

Teenage Pregnancy
and Parenthood

In the 1960s, protest, rebellion, violence, homicide, suicide, drug abuse, running away, and "dropping out" were the major worries about adolescents. Collectives, communes, and large numbers of drug abusing comatose teenagers in such areas as Haight Ashbury dominated the scene. By the mid-1970s there were fewer signs of counterculture protest, but new issues had arisen.

> An important problem of adolescence has emerged . . . and has been somewhat insidious in its development. Having emerged with considerable destructive force, the problem of adolescent pregnancy is a complex issue that requires careful definition and perspective. It is part of the overall phenomenon of precocious adolescent sexuality, marriage, pregnancy, motherhood, and abortion that is currently so existent. While adolescent sexuality is not new, the incidence of premarital teenage coitus has increased greatly. This is true not only in the United States, but in a number of countries throughout the world, including, England, the U.S.S.R., West Germany and Japan. Adolescent pregnancy in the United States is now the fourth highest in the world [Copeland, 1981, p. 245].

Fisher and Scharf (1980) observed that 95 percent of lower-middle-class and working-class girls keep their babies. These researchers highlighted class differences in patterns of adolescent pregnancy outcome. Increas-

---

ingly, abortion is becoming the acceptable solution to the unwanted pregnancies of middle- and upper-class American females. Middle-class girls can be pressured to pregnancy by the same psychological conflicts as their lower-class counterparts, but can resist the push toward parenthood more easily, thanks to the availability of other options. Lessons, activities, and college plans can help fill social and psychological loneliness and emptiness and thus can offer alternatives to keeping one's baby.

Given the recent dissemination of birth control information with no apparent diminution of pregnancies, but rather a rise, we must recognize that prevention, education, and intervention have little impact on the dominating psychological factors, namely a

> peculiarly tenacious quality of the symbiosis within the maternal line. The pregnancy may reflect several overlapping psychodynamic issues: an attempt to replace a lost object, an attempt to cure the mother's depression, an attempt to avoid separation, or an attempt to overcome early deprivation through identification with the new baby. The baby may be a hostage to the mother/grandmother for the daughter's own liberation, with a subsequent arrest at a phallic level [p. 395].

Statistics are alarming: "there are just under one million American teenage pregnancies per year, resulting in approximately six hundred thousand births and four hundred thousand abortions" (United Nations, 1975). "In the last 40 or more years, illegitimate births for black teenagers have doubled, to 90 per 1,000 in 1975; for whites, 10 per 1,000 in 1975, and given the large white population, the actual number of illegitimate pregnancies and resultant babies is considerable for both groups" (Chilman, 1977). Few adolescents desired marriage, despite pregnancy; and there is a high degree of marital failure in the teenage groups who actually marry.

Biological factors associated with adolescent pregnancy are numerous; and Copeland (1981) pointed to an elevated mortality rate, toxemia, anemia, prematurity, and the repeated finding that the babies of young mothers are considered as being at risk. Social consequences are enormous for both mother and baby. "By virtue of an increased incidence of academic failure, repeat pregnancies, and a 50% divorce rate, many of these girls remain in the lowermost socioeconomic ranks of society, requiring enormous amounts of support for themselves and their children for many years" (p. 345). Precocious sexual activity and pregnancy do not serve as an avenue for emancipation and independence but are a way of consciously or unconsciously complying with the symbiotic tie with the mother, noted by Fisher and Scharf (1980), and in fact produce a reinforced heightened dependency (Copeland 1981). Copeland (1974) attributed adolescent repeat pregnancies to an incomplete sense of identity and poor self-esteem; and other authors (Bandura and Walters, 1963 and Douvan and Adelson, 1966) have observed early closure in personal development and overidentification with mothers who themselves were teenage mothers. Teenage maternity interferes with the completion of developmental tasks of adolescence, limiting educational, vocational, social and emotional growth and life choices (Copeland, 1981). Arrest in age-adequate development may take the form of nonsexualized socialization and peer relationships, or regression to experience nurturance and support. Such nurturance and support in the regressed state may enable the adolescent to progress to a more mature level, by reworking and modifying early harsh superego identifications, developing skills and hobbies that would lead to career choices, and autonomous emotional and physical self-care (Fisher and Scharf, 1980).

The inadequate development of the teenage mothers affects their babies as well. Fraiberg (1982) stated that the emotional problems of attachment and detachment experienced by the more disturbed teen mothers were mirrored in severe disorders of attachment in the babies, who were "the most severely impaired children in our case load" (p. 8). "Failure to thrive," an ominous syndrome, results in grave impairment of psychological functioning. Such babies are joyless, listless, inconsolable, and often retarded in physical and emotional development. This syndrome reflects many teenage mothers' virtual incapacity to parent. Depressed young mothers frequently become neglectful and severely abusive, particularly when they and their infants are living in poverty and miss supports from family, an extended kinship network, and/or the community.

The treatment focus that Fraiberg described is a form of undoing the past, by way of examination of the intense internalized rage of teenagers towards their own abusive and frequently neglectful parents. Unsatisfied longings, hopes for mothering, wishes for a fantasy baby, who will offer rebirth or fill the sense of emptiness, must be articulated. Helping teenaged mothers identify with their own early selves and experiences rather than with their abusive aggressor parents facilitates maturation, separation, and individuation, as the adolescent mother surrenders symbiotic ties to her mother in the safety of the therapeutic relationship. The goal is to help the overwhelmed young mothers identify with and empathize with their babies, via an empathic identification with themselves in their earlier years.

Effective programs offer far more than birth control information. Fisher and Scharf (1980) noted that perhaps only ten percent of girls who become pregnant do so because they do not understand contraception. Effective treatment programs provide a peer group and adults who nurture and set limits for the young mothers, while demonstrating infant care and gentle effective limit setting for babies. Additionally, effective programs provide educational and career facilities for the teenage mothers and outreach to, and involvement of, the teenage father whenever possible. Most necessary is the need for long-term services and "client contact beyond the separation-individuation phase of the child" (Fisher and Scharf, 1980, p. 397). This is a crucial period for these mothers, in that they have not effected separation and individuation in their own lives. "It is at this juncture that the most abuse and foster placement, as well as new pregnancies occur. . . . it is at this point that social institutions and the community at large express the greatest hostility to young mothers" (p. 398). Developmental theory (e.g., Spitz, Mahler) would predict mothers that will be most vulnerable when changes in their own lives and major developmental events in the baby's life occur simultaneously. For example, as the babies begin to talk and walk, the mothers, ideally, have begun employment and require longer home child care (see Spitz, 1965; Mahler, 1961, 1971; Mahler, Pine, and Bergman, 1970). At this point, the mothers often feel most fragile, explosive, and subject to feeling overwhelmed and depressed. They are tempted by ideas of placement for their babies; and they often regress and demonstrate poor impulse control, which leads to neglect, severe physical abuse, and/or a new pregnancy.

All in all, the effective programs create a "holding environment" in which the mother-to-be or teenage mother "is properly nurtured, perhaps for the first time in her life, and is therefore, better able to hand down this newly discovered experience to her own offspring" (Fisher and Scharf, p. 403). Some programs, with follow-up studies showing impressive results, offer various levels of therapeutic intervention, based on an assessment of the teen mothers and the infants in an effort to delineate those at minimal, moderate, and high risk.

> Mothers of infants consistently placed at high risk presented serious characterological and borderline characteristics. They appeared to feel negative and unconcerned about their babies or see them as a burden. Becoming pregnant was a form of acting out. Their babies were at very high risk for failure to thrive during the first year and for abuse and neglect during their second year. Their family backgrounds were chaotic, and there were no role models for these [young] mothers to emulate. Their own mothers were in some cases having more children of their own and had very little time or love to give these adolescent daughters [Salguero et al., 1980, p. 419].

These unwed adolescents received comprehensive medical, nursing, dental, psychiatric, nutritional, educational, psychological, and pharmacological services in a community-controlled health facility.

19

Homosexuality

Most of the clinical literature about the homosexual adolescent deals with etiology, the various pathological forms, and the appropriate treatment foci and interventions. Robinson (1980) suggested that the relative paucity of studies dealing with adolescent homosexuality "may be attributed to the acceptance of an allowable homosexuality in adolescence, which, under favorable circumstances, is gradually replaced by heterosexual development" (p. 422). Other authors have also suggested that homosexual activity is a normal phase in adolescence, in fact a step toward sexual mastery, at which time a choice is made whether to move on to heterosexuality. Offer and Offer (1971) noted that there can be frequent intense conflict during the period of choice but that most youngsters handle it very well, with a final heterosexual resolution.

For the female adolescent, the surrender of hope for the mother's exclusive love is manifest in her moving on to her intense crushes and close ties with "best" friends. Homosexually oriented activities and fantasies are common in male and female latency-age children, when object choice is narcissistic, i.e., friends are sought for being like oneself or because they possess admirable skills and qualities. Blos (1962) posited a similar later normal homosexual stage, which lasts into early and middle adolescence and is of positive value because it contributes to the evolution and maturation of the ego ideal.

Traditional psychoanalytic theory suggested that when there is not an ultimate heterosexual orientation it is due to a pathologic deficit or arrest, caused by the adolescent's having experienced early sexual trauma—often molestation, overstimulation, or unresolved problems in the parent-child relationship. This prevailing deficit theory is currently under attack, and has received increased attention from various quarters. Some clinicians assert that homosexuality is "a normal variation in both sexual orientation and sexual behavior" (Martin, 1982, p. 52). The recent *DSM-III* distinguishes between patients who present ego-dystonic or ego-syntonic affects about their homosexuality, with only those in the former group viewed as exhibiting any form of psychopathology. Some perceive this distinction as a political appeasement reflecting the desire of clinical professional groups to disengage from stigmatization. Other clinicians disavow engagement in discussion about the health or pathology of homosexuality versus heterosexuality but maintain the "unequivocal position that in the absence of developmental interference, preferential adult heterosexuality is the species, as well as the mammalian norm" (Gadpaille, 1978, p. 139).

The traditional view holds that problems in child-parent relationships, namely, an overly close relationship or a poor relationship, can predispose a child toward a permanent homosexual orientation (S. Freud, 1905; A. Freud, 1958; Looney, 1973; Swanson, et al., 1972; etc.). Originally homosexuality was explained in terms of drive theory, and emphasis was put on the unresolved oedipal conflict and the intense castration anxiety caused by the interplay of a child's and/or parent's inability to surrender the erotically charged oedipal relationship. This tenacious attachment may be due to weak parental coalition and marital difficulty, where a child is used as a spouse surrogate. When a parent has died or is inordinately weak, absent, cold, hostile, or frightening, the child may not identify with this absent or negative parental figure. Ego psychology and object relations theory—focusing on symbiosis, separation-individuation, and object and self constancy—note that some children (e.g., borderline youth) never effect genuine separation and individuation, but remain symbiotically bound to the original object, the mother. Staller (1974) noted that when boy babies remain tied to their mothers, it leads to their feeling like women. This would cause the male adolescent to seek love and intimacy with other males, rather than females.

> However, even if he does not identify with her, a boy who is overly close to mother may become homosexual if his wishes to remain faithful to her cause him to give up other women permanently. On the other hand, absence of the mother and an overly close relationship between a boy and his

father can lead to powerful love feelings for father and a male object choice for sexual activity even though the identification is masculine [Robinson, 1980, pp. 424–425].

Female homosexuality may be caused by an overly strong attachment to the father and a need to reject other males or by the fearful reaction to the mother's envy over the daughter's bond with her father. Some female children reject the feminine role out of distaste for their mother's submissive role, in which she has been dominated or abused by the father. Nagera (1975) viewed "feminine" girls' homosexual stance as emanating out of parental rejection and disapproval of the girls' oedipal strivings; this would include the girls fear of paternal rejection and/or mother's envy and disapproval.

As contemporary psychoanalytic theory focuses increasingly on pre-oedipal disorders, homosexuality, too, is explained in terms of pre-oedipal arrests and deficits. An incomplete early symbiosis with the mother can, for example, cause female offspring to seek maternal nurturance in their subsequent object choices. Incomplete mirroring, merger, and empathy in the first two or three years of life can later cause the child to seek a narcissistic object choice, a mirror image of the self, resulting in homosexual objects sought by male and female children.

Early traumatic sexual experience at the hand of family members is receiving renewed attention, as the actual incidence is increasingly documented in the 1980s. No longer are such experiences routinely attributed to fantasy wishes and childish distorted reports. Family violence, the increase in substance abuse, and the subsequent loss of drive regulation have created many child victims, particularly when children are raised in nonintact families, in which parents' lovers and series of partners are not restrained by incest taboos. Trauma can occur when a child witnesses or overhears parents engaged in intercourse. The young child misperceives sex as terrifying, particularly endangering the mother. The child raised in a home where sexuality is excessively public, and outside of the context of a loving attachment between the adults, is frightened and overstimulated by the phenomenon.

Robinson (1980) noted nonsexual determinants of homosexuality. The recent activities of gay liberation groups, and their proclamation that "homosexuality is a normal, even superior, alterative life-style" has attracted many older adolescents. Defries (1976) described what he termed "pseudohomosexuality" in female college students. In recent years, many adolescents struggling to make attachments and resolve identity conflicts, have combined ideological and political feminist issues with sexual identity issues. Thus a specific heterosexual population now appears to maintain a homosexual public position over a protracted number of years. For some, this becomes permanent, for others it is another form of adolescent experimentation.

Some researchers have distinguished between gender identification and object choice. Individuals who choose a homosexual love object may not have gender identity problems but individuals with gender identity confusion, often discernable in early childhood, are prone to a homosexual adaptation (Whitman, 1977). Gadpaille (1978) took issue with the traditional psychodynamic perspective that states that sexual identity and object choice, i.e., sexual orientation, remain fluid and modifiable through adolescence; he suggested essential developmental processes during critical earlier periods. Current child-rearing practices, in this researcher's view, are falling short in preparing adolescents to handle sexuality optimally and are causing a lack of what is labeled "heterosexual readiness." Gadpaille noted Western middle-class constraints and prohibitions of early childhood sexuality as contributing to the magnitude of sexual problems among contemporary adolescents, in contrast to the "remarkable infrequency of either sexual deviations or sexual dysfunctions in cultures permissive of childhood homoerotic sex play and curiosity" (p. 151).

Cultural permissiveness and prohibitions were also addressed by Josselyn (1974) in her discussion of changes in the sexual mores of adolescents. She observed that researchers tend to hold extreme positions and points of view. Some clinicians view open homosexual gratification as indicative of superego lacunae, while, at the opposite extreme, others consider guiltless sexual behavior as evidence of a healthy achievement of freedom from repression. Josselyn suggested an alternative to the above theoretical stances. She suggested a pseudosexuality—a pseudoheterosexual activity, whereby many teenagers use sexual behavior to express reactivated immature needs because of the failures of the culture and family to provide and encourage constructive sublimation of the adolescent sexual drive. "Such a hypothesis is based upon the assumption that in phases of growth, sublimation, rather than direct expression or repression of an inherent drive pressing for discharge, fosters the psychological maturation of that drive" (p. 116). Any attempt to reconcile advocacy of sexual freedom with sublimation will emphasize cultural changes in general child-rearing practices, namely, greater permissiveness in early childhood and increased limit setting and constraints during puberty and adolescence.

Irrespective of one's conception of the etiology of homosexuality, the question of whether to treat, or not to treat, homosexual adolescents remains germane. There is no agreement on the advisability, and focus for treatment of adolescents who are homosexual. The traditional psychodynamic position has regarded homosexuality as a problem that requires either "the beneficial passage of time to allow for maturational processes" (Winnicott, 1965); the postponement of analysis of homosexual tendencies, until the adolescent has achieved his sex-appropriate

orientation, to avoid intensification of the self-doubts and identity conflicts (Blos, 1953; Fraiberg, 1961), or immediate therapeutic intervention, even if it requires coercive actions by family members. Socardies
(1978) stated that homosexual behavior through adolescence in the absence of anxiety, guilt or conflict together with perverted fantasies is an
alarming sign. It is imperative to initiate therapy in order to create a
conflict for the patient (in Martin, 1982). The notion that self-motivation
is immaterial and that guilt and anxiety must be generated is shared by
many other prominent psychoanalysts. Fraiberg (1961) suggested that
there is a good possibility of changing the orientation while anxiety and
guilt about homosexuality is present. Marmor (1965) noted that psychotherapy is indicated for children and adolescents who demonstrate failure in making appropriate gender identification because, so long as society views homosexuality as a deviation, optimal adjustment requires
prevention of homoerotic patterns.

In contrast to the prevailing traditional view, Szasz (1965) stressed
the inadvisability of forcing treatment aimed at a heterosexual adaptation on unwilling homosexuals. Many homosexual adolescents and
adults seek treatment for depression or academic difficulty and do not
acknowledge conflict about their homosexuality. This reality is no
longer viewed by all clinicians as a form of denial, but instead, as a po-
tent preference. The therapist's values and assumptions and the way
they fit or misfit with those of their patients will influence the therapeutic process. Kohut (1966 and 1971) has raised extensive questions about
therapists' therapeutic stances and their foisting their Judeo-Christian
ethic and notions of heterosexual object love onto patients. Different
aims and therapeutic goals are articulated by self psychologists and others who accept client preferences and follow only the patient's concerns during the process of therapy. Self psychology has commanded
the attention of many traditionally trained psychotherapists and other
clinicians serving homosexual adolescents and adults.

Concerns about the repeated acts of deception, social isolation, hiding, stigma, and discrimination have stimulated the development of special programs for homosexual youth. The newer programs, clinics, and
schools have arisen out of concerted efforts "to provide gay adolescents
with the opportunity to have social [and clinical] environments in which
they can develop their personal and social skills free from fear of exposure and censure" (Martin, 1982, p. 63). Such settings provide therapeutic assistance in self-identification as a homosexual. Additionally, staff
is frequently composed of professionally trained gay personnel who
provide suitable gay adult role models. Clark (1977) pointed out that social and familial pressures have conditioned the gay person to feel different and self-conscious. There is commonly a distrust or disavowal of
the person's own feelings, which causes depression, immobility, and a

gnawing sense of emptiness. This frequently precipitates substance abuse to dull the pain and loneliness. Because of the above factors, the therapy may be sought. Help can be offered, but not forced.

A number of practice principles or ground rules are offered for professionals working with a homosexual client population, be they adolescent or adult. A therapist's primary objective is to help the person become more truly himself or herself, and that may mean becoming comfortable with his or her homosexuality. All effective clinical work requires the therapist's self-awareness and sensitivity to countertransference phenomena, in this case, one's own homophobic or antigay feelings. To work with any minority group (ethnic and racial minorities, the disabled, etc.) self-examination is required to avoid blind spots, prejudices, or counter-transferential acting out. The therapist's recognition of his or her own homosexual feelings and attraction is also critical for effective treatment.

Most heterosexuals, unfamiliar with homosexuals, tend to believe that regardless of sex, age, race, socioeconomic and educational status, all homosexuals are alike. An extensive study by Bell and Weinberg (1978) of the Institute for Sex Research demonstrated the need for specificity of race, sex, age, educational and occupational lives, individual experiences and expressions, and patterns of relationships to comprehend the full diversity of the homosexual orientation. For, they found as many "homosexualities as there are heterosexualities" (p. 219). Therapists engaged in clinical work with adolescents must be sensitive to these realities as their patients struggle with sexual orientation and personal and social identity. Straight therapists might well be surprised by one of the major findings of the Bell and Weinberg study.

> It would appear that homosexual adults who have come to terms with their homosexuality, who do not regret their orientation, and who can function effectively sexually and socially, are no more distressed psychologically than are heterosexual men and women. Clearly, the therapist who continues to believe that it is by fiat his or her job to change a homosexual client's sexual orientation is ignorant of the true issues involved [p. 216].

Confidentiality and the right to privacy is a cornerstone of all effective therapeutic work. Breach of confidentiality, divulging facts about a client's gay identity "is an absolute violation of trust as well as an ethical violation of confidentiality" (Clark, 1977, p. 150), and this includes sharing information with parents, police, an employee or a spouse.

Other decisions beyond homosexual or heterosexual choice are viewed as crucial in adolescence.

> The central dynamic issues, then, are not whether the adolescent makes a homosexual or a heterosexual adjustment, but how he/she arrives at that adjustment and the relative balance between self-love and a capacity to love

others. Is the person able to commit herself (himself) to lasting love relationships? Are the relationships dominated by the narcissistic longing to see mirrored in the other what one wishes to be oneself? Does the person have the sexual capacity to be caregiver and lawgiver to the next generation? As we have seen, heterosexuality is no guarantee of sexual or moral maturity. Social conventions make it possible for a heterosexual adult to hide his or her less-than-adequate solutions in a social role. Unless they are pressured into a role of deviant by social conventions, homosexuals also have available to themselves a variety of successful or failed solutions to the incest taboo [Kaplan, 1984, p. 164]

20

Sexually Transmitted Diseases

Infections spread by sexual contact must be understood by adolescents and all personnel engaged in professional work with teenagers and young adults. Quick diagnosis and immediate intervention reduce the risk of serious complications for most of these infections. Follow-up and watchfulness are also crucial.

> Sexually transmitted diseases are running rampant in America today, especially among the teenage population. . . . Public health statistics in 1984 estimate that there are two million new cases of gonorrhea annually in the U.S., along with 500,000 new cases of genital herpes, 2.5 million cases of nonspecific urethritis, and 80,000 new cases of syphilis. More than half of the people affected are between the ages of 15 and 24 [Kolodny et al., 1984, p. 85.]

These diseases are not always transmitted by sexual intercourse; most can be spread by oral sex and even kissing.

Gonorrhea is easily diagnosed in males. It will cause a puslike discharge from the penis and frequent, painful urination. It is not easily detected in females; and when the symptoms do occur (vaginal discharge, burning with urination, and abnormal menstrual patterns), they are often mild and overlooked, which is serious, because untreated, this disease can cause permanent sterility. Treated with large dosages of penicillin, gonorrhea is almost 100 percent curable.

Syphilis is less common today and affects males more frequently than females. An early sign is a painless sore that might appear on the genitals or near the anus, but also, on a finger, the lips, or inside the mouth. Untreated this sore heals in a matter of weeks, creating the false impression that the infection has gone away. However, the infection moves into what is know as secondary syphilis and may not be visible or apparent for as long as six months.

> Common symptoms in this stage include a pale red rash on the palms and soles, sore throat, fever, and aching joints. If the disease is still untreated, a latent stage occurs where the infection invades tissues such as the spinal cord and brain; in the most devastating stage of late syphilis, serious heart problems, eye problems and brain damage can occur. It is effectively treated (best in the earlier stages) with penicillin [pp. 85–86].

In the last three years we have heard about genital or venereal herpes continually, on radio, television, and in the newspapers and in feature magazine articles; and we are informed of a literal epidemic. Cold sores, mononucleosis, chicken pox, and shingles are all caused by herpes viruses. The real increase in the herpes virus family, however, has been in genital or venereal herpes, which undoubtedly has spread because of today's more casual sexual liaisons and varied forms of oral, anal, and genital contacts minus the conventional contraception that has been abandoned with the development of the contraceptive pill. "We now know that approximately twenty million people have type 2 genital herpes; nearly one out of every 10 people" (Langston, 1983, p. 4). The psychological impact has been enormous on those who have the disease and on those who fear contracting it. The extent of the fear relates to the incurable nature of the disease and its possible serious consequences, particularly for women and infants. A first genital infection during pregnancy poses a much greater threat to the baby than recurrent disease, in that neither mother or child have the necessary antibodies to fight the virus. Herpes in a newborn may be diagnosed on the basis of skin, eye, or mouth blisters alone, or on the taking of a brain biopsy and culture. Symptoms in a newborn often include unusual sleepiness, fever, irritation of the eyes, or convulsions and coma. While few women with genital herpes actually develop cervical cancer, evidence suggests a connection between herpes and cancer, and thus regular medical follow-up is critical for women who in fact have this virus.

Herpes is passed on by kissing or sexual intercourse, genital to genital; or lovemaking, mouth to genital, rectum to genital, and mouth to rectum. Herpes sores thus can be found in the mouths and throats of those who practice cunnilingus. "It should be remembered that venereal herpes is frequently associated with and may initially be hidden by other forms of genital infection, as fungal infection, trichomonas, bacterial vaginitis, syphillis and gonorrhea" (ibid.).

The first infection usually occurs three to seven day after sexual exposure and may appear as a few tiny blisters. Mild tingling and burning may precede the actual appearance of lesions. Watery blisters soon develop, and it is at the blistering stage that the disease is most infectious. However, it may be passed on to a sex partner during the tingling stage. There may or may not be accompanying low-grade fever, headache, aching muscles, and swollen painful lymph nodes in the groin. A florid first infection can last three to six weeks. The course of this disease is not understood: Some patients have repeated episodes of active ulceration; others never have obvious symptoms again; and for many, the disease quiets down spontaneously.

One infected with herpes can pick up new herpes virus following sexual activity with someone with active herpes, though commonly new blisters are a recurrence of one's original virus. Causes of recurrence are not certain, but it is suspected that stress, tension, menstruation, pregnancy, and trauma to the genitalia can precipitate a new attack. "Perhaps the greatest contributing factor to spread of herpitic venereal disease is the silent but contagious stage of infection in both men and women. Some may spread live infectious virus without ever having developed noticeable evidence of the disease" (Langston, 1983, p. 38). Virus culture and Pap smears are the surest diagnostic procedures. Venereal herpes can spread to various sites on the body: the buttocks, back, mouth, throat, and fingers. Dentists, physicians, nurses, and oral hygienists can pick up the disease on their fingers from patients.

Genital herpes infection is no different in incidence, severity, and management in the homosexual community. "There is, however, another lesser known herpes virus which is causing severe problems which are largely confined to the gay population. It appears to be a venereal illness. In 1981 the medical world first became alerted to an epidemic of a chronic and potentially lethal herpes virus infection associated in a number of cases with a malignant tumor known as Kaposi's sarcoma. . . . Cytomegalovirus (CMV) infection is the most common binding factor among cases reported thus far" (Langston, 1983, pp. 158 and 159). CMV appears to interfere with the body's ability to fight infection, and is related to the development of a particular form of cancer known as sarcoma. Kaposi's sarcoma tumors, if diagnosed promptly may respond well to early X-ray therapy. The CMV infection and drug abuse are suspected of inhibiting the white blood cell system and thereby destroying the body's immune system. This illness is similar to acquired immune deficiency syndrome (AIDS).

At present, genital herpes is increasingly better understood, and thereby can be adequately managed on a medical and personal basis, if prompt attention is given at the time of initial and subsequent outbreak. This disease routinely is not considered dangerous unless it is transmitted to the eyes or infects the brain.

The personal emotional reactions of herpes patients are intense. Commonly physical and emotional alienation, sexual isolation, and lowered self-esteem follow the diagnosis of herpes. "Psychological factors are important in both the resistance to genital herpes and in the adaptation to the disease. The fact that it attacks young people during vital periods of psychosexual development makes it a pervasively crippling disorder in virtually all areas of living" (Luby, 1981, p. 35). Luby enumerated a sequence of general responses:

1. Initial shock and numbing when the diagnosis is offered
2. A frantic search for cure and/or reassurance
3. Development of a sense of isolation and loneliness, with concerns about the future possibilities emotionally, sexually, and (for women) regarding pregnancy and childbirth
4. Anger can develop against the self, the person who passed on the infection, and toward doctors and therapists
5. Fears are articulated regarding contagion and the need to tell partners about the disease
6. A "leper" effect may set in, followed by
7. Deepening depression and possibly the reactivation of underlying pathology

Laskin (1982) wrote about what he called the herpes syndrome, the sense of being impaired, damaged, anguished, and in isolation. Support groups, psychotherapy, group therapy, hypnosis, and relaxation techniques are noted as successful avenues to explore to regain self-esteem and self-confidence. It has been observed that herpes is only as devastating as a patient allows it to be. In fact, this disease is profoundly dependent on mood and emotion; and, thus, once a patient is more emotionally stable, outbreaks are often more easily managed and diminished.

AIDS (acquired immune deficiency syndrome), once dismissed as the gay plague, now has become the number one public-health menace, affecting ever increasing groups of individuals. There have been 12,067 cases recorded in the United States in the last few years since the disease was given its name. "No one has been known to recover. Once infected, a person is infected and infectious for the rest of his life" (Clark et al., 1985, p. 20). This disease lies latent, in incubation for as long as three years; thus thousands of people are infecting others unknowingly.

The disease is no longer passed on solely by drug users or between men, but now has struck women, children of parents carrying or with AIDS, patients receiving blood transfusions, and hemophiliacs. In Africa, it strikes women and men in equal proportions. AIDS is common in Haiti, but Haitians in the United States have been dropped as a high-risk group. In the United States the identified lethal virus is labeled T-cell lymphotropic virus (HTLV III), and it attacks white blood cells. "The leading theory holds that AIDS spread from Africa to the Caribbean, and then was picked up by American homosexuals vacationing in Haiti. Indeed, AIDS has turned up by now in practically every European country" (p. 23).

AIDS symptoms include Kaposi's sarcoma, a type of skin cancer; swollen lymph glands; fatigue; fever; night sweats; diarrhea; and gradual loss of weight. Because the virus invades brain cells, mental and neurological problems such as impaired speech, seizures, and tremors may be noted. The disease is spread by bodily fluids during sexual activity, intravenous drug use, and blood transfusion.

The threat of this dread disease has resulted in a rapid decline in high-risk sexual activity—namely, multiple sex partners—in the gay and bisexual world. Civil libertarian considerations and pressures from various groups have stopped any kind of official legislation or regulation of those commercial sex establishments and bathhouses that continue to operate. Unmarried heterosexuals have also begun to alter their behavior in response to this disease, out of fear that possible partners may have bisexual preferences or encounters with prostitutes.

In all, the poor prognosis of AIDS results in particular emotional responses over and beyond what is observed to accompany the other sexually transmitted diseases. Acute depression, suicidal ideation, and a high incidence of actual suicide commonly follow the onset of undeniable symptomatology. The estrangement and depression are affective responses to the disease and to the social isolation frequently experienced by AIDS patients, who are often abandoned by lovers, family, and friends. In addition, many health professionals recoil from treating AIDS patients, fearful of becoming contaminated by this plaguelike disease.

Specialized medical centers and highly trained treatment teams generally provide more adequate care than general hospitals and clinics. Hospices for fatally ill AIDS patients recently have started providing medical and nursing care during the terminal stage of the illness. In most urban areas support groups, particularly within gay communities, offer psychological counseling to AIDS patients.

Bibliography

AMERICAN PSYCHIATRIC ASSOCIATION. (1980) *Quick Reference to the Diagnostic Criteria from Diagnostic and Statistical Manual of Mental Disorders, Third Edition.* Washington, D.C.: APA.

BANDURA, A. and WALTERS, R. (1963). *Social Learning and Personality Development,* New York: Holt.

BELL, A. P., PH.D. and WEINBERG, M. S., PH.D.(1978). *Homosexualities—A Study of Diversity Among Men and Women. New York:* Simon & Schuster.

BLOS, P. (1953). The Contribution of Psychoanalysis to the Treatment of Adolescents. *Psychoanalysis and Social Work,* ed. M. Heiman, pp. 210–41. New York: International Universities Press.

_____ (1962). *On Adolescence.* New York: Free Press.

_____ (1967). The Second Individuation Process of Adolescence. *Psychoanalytic Study of the Child,* 22:162–86. New York: International Universities Press.

CHILMAN, C. (1977). *Adolescent Sexuality in a Changing American Society.* Washington, D.C.: Department of Health, Education and Welfare.

CLARK, D., PH.D. (1977). *Loving Someone Gay.* Milbrae, Calif.: Celestial Arts.

CLARK, M.; GOSNELL, M.; WITHERSPOON, D.; HAGER, M.; and COPPOLA, V. (1985). AIDS. *Newsweek,* August 12, 1985.

COPELAND, A. D. (1974). *Textbook of Adolescent Psychopathology and Treatment.* Springfield, Ill.: Thomas.

―――― (1981). The Impact of Pregnancy on Adolescent Psychosocial Development. In *Adolescent Psychiatry, Vol. 9: Developmental and Clinical Studies,* eds. S. Feinstein, J. Looney, A. Schwartzberg, and A. Sorosky, pp. 244–53. Chicago: University of Chicago Press.

DEFRIES, Z. (1976). Pseudohomosexuality in Feminist Students. *Amer. J. Psychiatry,* 133:400–04.

DEUTSCH, H. (1967). *Selected Problems of Adolescence.* New York: International Universities Press.

DOUVAN, E. and ADELSON, J. (1966). *The Adolescent Experience.* New York: Wiley.

EISSLER, K. R. (1958). Notes on Problems of Technique in the Psychoanalytic Treatment of Adolescents: With Some Remarks on Perversions. *Psychoanalytic Study of the Child,* 13:223–54. New York: International Universities Press.

ERIKSON, E. H. (1968). *Identity: Youth and Crisis,* New York: International Universities Press.

ESMAN, A. H. (1977). Changing Values: Their Implications for Adolescent Development and Psychoanalytic Ideas. In *Adolescent Psychiatry, Vol. 5: Developmental and Clinical Studies,* eds. S. Feinstein and P. Giovacchini, pp. 18–34. New York: Jason Aronson.

FISHER, S. M. and SCHARF, K. R. (1980). Teenage Pregnancy: An Anthropological, Sociological and Psychological Overview. In *Adolescent Psychiatry, Vol. 8: Developmental and Clinical Studies,* eds. S. Feinstein, P. Giovacchini, J. Looney, A. Schwartzberg, and A. Sorosky, pp. 393–403. Chicago: University of Chicago Press.

FRAIBURG, S. (1961). Homosexual Conflicts in Adolescence. In *Psychoanalytic Approach to Problems and Therapy,* eds. S. Lorand and H. I. Schneva, pp. 78–112. New York: Harper.

―――― (1982). The Adolescent Mother and Her Baby. In *Adolescent Psychiatry, Vol. 10: Developmental and Clinical Studies,* eds. S. Feinstein, J. Looney, A. Schwartzberg, and A. Sorosky, pp. 7–23. Chicago: University of Chicago Press.

FREUD, A. (1936). *The Ego and the Mechanisms of Defense.* New York: International Universities Press.

―――― (1958). Adolescence. *Psychoanalytic Study of the Child,* 13:255–78. New York: International Universities Press.

FREUD, S. [1905] (1953). Three Essays on the Theory of Sexuality. *Standard Edition,* 7:3–243. London: Hogarth.

GADPAILLE, W. (1978). Psychosexual Developmental Tasks Imposed by Pathologically Delayed Childhood: A Cultural Dilemma. In *Adolescent Psychiatry, Vol. 6: Developmental and Clinical Studies,* eds. S. Feinstein and P. Giovacchini, pp. 136–55. Chicago: University of Chicago Press.

GAGNON, J. (1974). Quoted in *New York Society for Adolescent Psychiatry Newsletter*, January 1975.

GARDNER, G. (1970). *The Emerging Personality—Infancy Through Adolescence.* New York: Delacorte Press.

GIOVACCHINI, P. (1981). *The Urge to Die—Why Young People Commit Suicide.* New York: Macmillan.

GREENBERG, H. (1982). *Hanging in: What You Should Know About Psychotherapy.* New York: Four Winds Press.

JOSSELYN, A. (1974). Implications of Current Sexual Patterns: A Hypothesis. In *Adolescent Psychiatry, Vol. 3: Developmental and Clinical Studies,* eds. S. Feinstein and P. Giovacchini, pp. 103–17. New York: Basic Books.

KAPLAN, L. J. (1984). *Adolescence—The Farewell to Childhood.* New York: Simon & Schuster.

KOHUT, H. (1966). Forms and Transformations of Narcissism. *J. Amer. Psychoanal. Assn.* 14(2):243–72.

_____ (1971). *The Analysis of the Self.* New York: International Universities Press.

_____ (1972). Thoughts on Narcissism and Narcissistic Rage. *Psychoanalytic Study of the Child,* 27:360–401. New York: Quadrangle.

KOLODNY, R.; KOLODNY, N.; BRATTER, T. E.; and DEEP, C. (1984). *How to Survive Your Adolescent's Adolescence.* Boston/Toronto: Little, Brown & Co.

LANGSTON, D. P., M.D. (1983). *Living with Herpes.* Garden City, N.Y.: Doubleday & Co.

LASKIN, D. (1982). The Herpes Syndrome. *New York Times Magazine,* February 21, 1982.

LAUFER, M. (1968). The Body Image, the Function of Masturbation, and Adolescence. *Psychoanalytic Study of the Child,* 23:114–37. New York: International Universities Press.

_____ (1977). A View of Adolescent Pathology. In *Adolescent Psychiatry, Vol. 5,* pp. 243–56. *See* Esman (1977).

LOONEY, J. (1973). Family Dynamics in Homosexual Women. *Arch. Sexual Behavior,* 2:329–41.

LUBY, E., M.D. (1981). Psychological Responses to Genital Herpes. In *Herpes—A Complete Gujide to Relief and Reassurances,* ed. Freudberg, pp. 000–000. Philadelphia: Running Press.

MAHLER, M. (1961). On Sadness and Grief in Infancy and Childhood: Loss and Restoration of the Symbiotic Love Object. *Psychoanalytic Study of the Child,* 16:332–51. New York: International Universities Press.

_____ (1971). A Study of the Separation-Individuation Process and Its Possible Applicaton to Borderline Phenomena in the Psychoanalytic Situation. *Psychoanalytic Study of the Child,* 26:403–24. New York: Quadrangle.

MAHLER, M.; PINE, F.; and BERGMAN, A. (1970). The Mother's Reaction to Her Toddler's Drive of Individuation. In *Parenthood: Its Psychology and Psy-*

chopathology, eds. E. J. Anthony and T. Benedek, pp. 257–74. Boston: Little, Brown.

MARMOR, J. (1965). Sexual Inversion—The Multiple Roots of Homosexuality. New York: Basic Books.

MARTIN, A. D. (1982). Learning to Hide: The Socialization of the Gay Adolescent. In Adolescent Psychiatry, Vol. 10, pp. 52–65. See Fraiburg (1982).

NAGERA, H. (1975). Female Sexuality and the Oedipus Complex. New York: Jason Aronson.

OFFER, J. and OFFER, D. (1971). Four Issues in the Developmental Psychology of Adolescents. In Modern Perspectives in Adolescent Psychiatry, ed. J. G. Howells. New York: Brunner/Mazel.

———— (1977). Sexuality in Adolescent Males. In Adolescent Psychiatry, Vol. 5, pp. 96–107. See Esman (1977).

ROBINSON, L. (1980). Adolescent Homosexual Patterns: Psychodynamics and Therapy. In Adolescent Psychiatry, Vol. 8, pp. 422–36. See Fisher and Scharf (1980).

SALGUERO, C.; YEARWOOD, E.; PHILLIPS, E.; and SCHLESINGER, N. (1980). Studies of Infants at Risk and Their Mothers. In Adolescent Psychiatry, Vol 8, pp. 404–21. See Fisher and Scharf (1980).

SCHOWALTER, J. E., and ANYAN, W. R. (1979). The Family Handbook of Adolescence. New York: A. Knopf.

SELIGMANN, J.; RAINE, G.; COPPOLA, V.; HAGUE, M.; and GOSNELL, M. (1985). A Nasty New Epidemic. Newsweek Feb. 4, 1985, pp. 72–73.

SOCARDIES, C. (1978). Homosexuality, New York: Jason Aronson.

SPITZ, R. A. (1965). The First Year of Life: A Psychoanalytic Study of Normal and Deviant Development of Object Relations. New York: International Universities Press.

STALLER, R. J. (1974). Symbiosis Anxiety and the Development of Masculinity. Arch. Gen. Psychiatry, 30:164–72.

SWANSON, D. W.; LOOMIS, S. D.; LUKESH, R.; GRONIN, R.; and SMITH, J. A. (1972). Clinical Features of Female Homosexual Patients: Comparison with Heterosexual Patients. J. Nerv. Mental Diseases, 155:199–210.

SZASZ, T. S. (1965). Legal and Moral Aspects of Homosexuality. In Sexual Inversion—The Multiple Roots of Homosexuality, ed. J. Marmor. New York: Basic Books.

UNITED NATIONS DEPARTMENT OF ECONOMIC AND SOCIAL AFFAIRS (1975). Demographic Yearbook, 1974. New York.

WHITMAN, F. W. (1977). Childhood Indicators of Male Homosexuality. Arch. Sexual Behavior, 6(2):89–96.

WINNICOTT, D. W. [1965] (1971). Adolescence: Struggling Through the Doldrums. In Adolescent Psychiatry, Vol. 1, Developmental and Clinical Studies, eds. S. Feinstein, P. Giovacchini, and A. Miller, pp. 40–50. New York: Basic Books. Reprinted from D. W. Winnicott, The Family and Individual Development. London: Tavistock.

PART V

Selecting a Treatment Plan

21

Criteria for Family, Group, and Individual Therapy

The specific stages and phases of adolescence often play a significant role in the consideration and formulation of an appropriate treatment intervention. As noted earlier, the perspective prevailing today subdivides adolescence into three stages: early adolescence, ages 12–15; middle adolescence, ages 16–19; and late adolescence, ages 19–24. In this view, the achievement of adult personality consolidation and financial independence extends beyond the college years.*

Early adolescence is generally recognized as one of the most difficult age groups to treat. There exists considerable controversy over which therapeutic mode to use. Some clinicians and researchers do not believe that adolescents this age can actually engage in and maintain a therapeutic alliance. Others believe that only short-term periods of therapy are possible, with adolescents coming for help periodically, when stress becomes overwhelming. Gereerd (1957) emphasized the setting of only moderate goals in treatment of young teenagers, specifically, to in-

*This chapter is based on my papers "Criteria for Selecting Treatment Interventions with Adolescents;" *Child and Adolescent Social Work Journal*, 1 (4, Winter 1984): 219–34, and "Clinical Implications in the Selection of Treatment Resources for Troubled Children and Adolescents" (Paper delivered at the Twelfth Annual Vista del Mar Child Care Conference, Mareanner S. Applebaum Institute, May 16, 1985).

crease the ego's tolerance for conflicts and to improve reality testing. The young adolescent often uses the therapist as a substitute parent. These treatment parameters require acceptance of limited goals in the "working through" process and change expected. The transference is not genuinely worked through, nor does the therapist attempt to handle it as he or she would with older patients.

Blos (1962) observed that the unique character of early adolescence is caused by the decathexis from the incestuous love objects, which results in free-floating object libido and, therefore, requires new attachments and accommodations. Simultaneously with his or her push for more independence, the young teenager searches for new love objects, often predicated on a narcissistic model. The admired ego-ideal is most commonly a peer or peer group, rarely an adult, such as an available therapist. As young adolescents are attempting to disengage from their parents, they commonly resist any dependent relationship with an adult parental figure; thus, individual psychotherapy frequently is contraindicated. Many young adolescents can only be engaged in, and made accessible to, a therapeutic intervention, such as group treatment, that provides distance from the adult and the protection of peers.

Comparing and contrasting the male and female young adolescent, Blos (1962) noted that girls form crushes that extend to adult men and women an idealized and eroticized attachment, but only with women will they appear in an unadulterated form. The objects chosen out of infatuation generally possess some similarity, or striking dissimilarity to the parent. Thus, it follows that individual psychotherapy proceeds with greater ease with the young adolescent female, than with the young adolescent male.

The middle adolescent phase, i.e., adolescence proper, is characterized by more fervent and intense emotional life and a turning toward heterosexual love, as the withdrawal from the parents continues at an increased rate. This decathexis frequently results in impoverishment of the ego because of the pain and mourning over the increasing loss of the close and loving parent-child ties. This mourning process leaves little ego energy for attachment to an individual therapist. Mourning or anxiety over the separation from parents is most acute with the less intact teenager, such as the borderline adolescent. This leave-taking, in search of more autonomy, is experienced as a most painful relinquishment, and Masterson (1974) noted that borderline youth often act out to ward off what he termed "abandonment depression." Frequently, with such troubled teenagers, one must adopt an aggressive outreach stance to engage them in a treatment relationship. This very pursuit by the therapist demonstrates significant concern and care and can, on occasion, constitute the beginnings of a treatment alliance. The oft-proclaimed "leave me alone" frequently masks dependency longings and hope for a genuine attachment to a significant caring adult. Adolescents generally de-sire and deserve autonomy in the decision-making process regarding the seeking of therapy. However, many chronological adolescents have not actually achieved a developmental and psychological adolescence. Rather, they demonstrate arrests and fixations and behave, in fact, like much younger impulsive children. They cannot be awarded such decision-making powers; many in fact are seen as nonvoluntary clients, forcibly referred for treatment by parents, schools, and courts; and while they overtly protest that they need no help, in fact, unconsciously they desire limit-setting and the caring stance of a therapist. Thus, man-ifest opposition to a referral for therapy is not necessarily a contraindi-cation for treatment.

Late adolescence normally heralds what Blos (1962) described as "gains in purposeful action, social integration, predictability, constancy of emotions and stability of self-esteem" (p. 128). Personality consolida-tion is marked by control of affects and increased capacity to compro-mise and tolerate frustration and delay. Thus, at the end of adolescence, there is greater clarity and finality about identity and decisions related to choice of career, life goals, and love attachments. The age—appropriate demand for clarity and closure motivates many older ado-lescents to seek treatment, even after prior resistance and denial of the need for any help. The recognized need for stability, integration, and au-tonomous functioning become undeniable; and this often is a turning point that stimulates the seeking of therapeutic help.

Family Therapy

There is a fundamental theoretical struggle in the field of family ther-apy. Two distinct movements or schools of thought and practice exist; they might best be described as the psychoanalytic perspective and the systems analysis perspective (Offer and Vanderstoep, 1975). The psy-choanalytically oriented practitioners have debated the indications and contraindications for family therapy, while few systems analysts have explicitly examined this issue, believing "that the question of indica-tions and contraindications is a 'nonquestion'" (p. 145).

Some psychoanalytically oriented and well-published family thera-pists are Ackerman (1966), Jackson (1959), Kramer (1970), Wynne (1965), and Williams (1967). They use a nosological psychiatric classification system and view individuals and families from a psychodynamic point of view. Conducting a diagnostic family interview enables the psycho-therapist to diagnose psychopathological processes and thus arrive at both the family and individual diagnoses. According to these clinicians, certain problems and families should be offered family therapy, and oth-ers should not.

Assessments reveal stable and unstable families, situations with severe physical or emotional illness, rigidity or flexibility of defenses, honesty versus deceptions by one or both parents, varied forms of marital disorders, and, specific disturbances in the relationships of parents, children, and adolescents. Offer and Vanderstoep (1975) recommended that the field of family therapy evaluate both its achievements and failures and move to a more circumscribed offering of this mode of therapy; this is particularly pertinent with adolescents who generate and demonstrate atypical intergenerational conflicts. These authors distinguished among adolescents—regardless of their individual diagnoses—according to the preferences of the teenager. Some teenagers are adamant that they have problems and issues that they want to examine privately; and under no circumstances can they or will they tolerate a treatment plan that requires that they meet conjointly with their parents. Others refuse to consider therapy unless the entire family participates; while still others, concerned with peer group problems, want no part of a treatment program that includes the parents. Similarly, parents have their preferences. "It is important to stress that the therapist should take into account the initial biases that the patient brings with him" (p. 155). In summary, psychoanalytically oriented clinicians have delineated those families where family treatment is or is not the appropriate intervention.

By contrast, the systems analysts in the field of family therapy make none of the above distinctions. Haley (1971) strongly objected to considerations of indication and contraindication for family therapy. He believed that focusing on assessment and diagnosis was merely a device to deal with the therapist's anxiety. He advocated replacement of the assessment process with an action-oriented point of view. Psychopathology is viewed not as lodged in the individual(s) but rather in the relationships within a family. Thus, the unit for attention is not the individual but the family system.

Unterberger (1972) noted that considerations of when to offer family therapy are in fact an externalization of a clinician's question of his or her own professional competence and/or willingness to reach out, make home visits, etc. This perspective appears based on the conviction that if

> a therapist takes the time and energy to convene the family network, a considerable amount of therapeutic work is accomplished in that process. . . . In the systems analysts' view, everyone—therapists and patients alike—is limited by the developmental level of his current systems. Good therapy takes place when patients are fortunate enough to encounter a system with which they can accomplish mutual growth. Hence all concerns about disease and psychopathology become irrelevant. The only important thing is the potential for mutual evolution and change in the two intermeshing systems [Offer and Vanderstoep, 1975, p. 152].

Other systems analysts believe that the only contraindication for group therapy is the absence of a skilled family therapist or inability or refusal of the family to convene.

Adherents of both schools of thought believe that family therapy can be particularly helpful in situations that involve here-and-now struggles in regard to interpersonal conflicts, such as marital disorders, and in disturbances in the adolescent's relationship with the family. Psychodynamically oriented clinicians often recommend family therapy in conjunction with individual and/or group treatment. Systems analysts rely solely on the family modality, with the family as the single unit of attention.

Group Therapy

Ginott (1961), Heacock (1966), Josselyn (1972), and Berkovitz and Sugar (1975) noted the value of group treatment under specific circumstances and the need for caution in other cases. Josselyn (1972) stated that group therapy can in fact, be a dangerous intervention for some adolescents who become more acutely disturbed by the group experience. They feel threatened and assaulted by group pressure or succumb to acting-out conflicts, which previously had been adequately defended against and repressed. In such cases, the group experience produced ego exhaustion, which would not have occurred if the adolescent had been seen in supportive individual therapy.

While adolescence is a time of life when heightened narcissism, or overriding self-reference, is common, this must be distinguished from more pathologic forms of unstable self-esteem. Highly narcissistic adolescents exhibit a "primary defect of the self" (Kohut, 1977, p. 50). This deficit is defended against with grandiosity, exhibitionism, and a striking lack of empathy for others (Kohut, 1971). The more normal path of development entails self-involvement in the quest for narcissistic perfection in one's sense of self and an evolving capacity for intimacy and affiliation, which entails sacrifice and compromise. Those adolescents exhibiting a narcissistic personality disorder are "inhibited from such affiliations, compromises and sacrifices because they threaten to limit his pursuit of narcissistic perfection for his self-representation" (Rothstein, 1980, p. 247). Rothstein (1980) observed that such adolescents rarely seek help from mental health professionals and that, when they do, it is commonly in response to mortification, narcissistic injury, or failure in their quest for perfection. Thus, such teenagers are generally inappropriate candidates for a group therapy experience. They cannot empathize with other peers or tolerate public self-exposure because of their struggle regarding their self-esteem or self-regard. Such youths may well require individual supportive treatment prior to any successful involvement in a group. A group can be very threatening to someone who is overly sensitive to criticism and who is self-conscious with peers. Not infrequently, the shy, socially inept, friendless adolescent is referred for group therapy to be helped to gain peer acceptance before he or she is emotionally ready to relate in a socially acceptable manner. This well-intended referral will fail because such an adolescent will be unsuccessful in relating to peers and will therefore experience trauma, assault, and shame. This kind of experience may well interfere with any future efforts to venture forth and seek further treatment.

The adolescent who demonstrates deficient self-control and minimal frustration tolerance is generally most difficult to help in group therapy. Resistances manifest by clowning, lateness, provocativeness, and defiance of the leader are typical. Heacock (1966) excluded the "severely delinquent and hyperactive [young client] who 'acts in' during the sessions. [The] disruptive behavior spreads to the others who are quite responsive to this, and so therapy becomes impossible. Suggestible patients who are easily led would be stimulated to more acting out in groups" (p. 41). The macho rebellious adolescent commonly acts out to save face and may more easily relate, without bravado, in individual treatment, where defiance is not rewarded by peer support. This phenomenon is most common in the junior high school population where group contagion and acting-out behaviors are noted even in formerly cooperative students who were diligent and self-controlled in elementary school. Experimentation with drugs and alcohol occurs most frequently among this younger adolescent population which struggles to defy adults and comply with the social mores of peer groups.

Ginott (1961) listed several criteria for the exclusion of specific adolescents from group therapy. When teenagers are suffering intense sibling rivalry, they often need the undivided attention of the therapist in individual treatment. They cannot share the adult with symbolic sibs— peers in a group. Sociopathic adolescents who present shallowness, cruelty, persistent stealing, and impulsivity generally are better reached on a one-to-one basis than via the group modality. Adolescents who have been eroticized by exposure to critical perverse sexual and aggressive activities also need individual help. All in all, those who have been traumatized often need supportive help, provided without delay.

Consideration of success or failure in handling developmental tasks offers additional guidelines in assessing indications and contraindications for group therapy. Berkovitz and Sugar (1975) suggested examination of the degree of separateness from parents; the quality and durability of significant peer attachments; the stability of the sense of self esteem; and whether or not there was a sustained sense of identity demonstrated in the familial, social, sexual, and work areas. Additionally, hopes and life goals for the future are critical. Thus adolescents who are totally confused, or deficient in these areas are best helped in individual therapy.

Successful group therapy requires the availability of a suitable group. Group composition is crucial. Too uneven a group will be doomed to failure. There is a danger in mixing too widely divergent an age range of adolescents and in combining non-acting-out and severely acting-out adolescents. If one has a candidate for group therapy, but no suitable group, this may well motivate a recommendation for individual treatment.

Individual Psychotherapy and Psychoanalysis

Psychoanalysis entails four or five sessions a week, whereas intensive individual psychotherapy involves one, two, or at most, three sessions weekly. The goals of these modalities are different. Analysis aims for a reconstruction of the personality with changes in the balance and nature of ego, id, and superego. Psychotherapy strives for symptom reduction, behavioral changes, and a return to the path of normal development and mastery of age-appropriate tasks. In analysis the therapist attempts to help the adolescent examine inner conflicts, the immediate past, and the earlier childhood past, to comprehend what has gone awry. In psychotherapy, the focus is on the here-and-now and the current relationships with parents and peers.

Some analysts question the analyzability of teenage patients, given their state of vulnerability and emotional turbulence, their preoccupations with the present, and their overall lack of insight and personality consolidation. However, there is less question about offering analysis to the older adolescent, who is more introspective, self-absorbed, and psychologically minded. Psychoanalysis is the treatment of choice if there is adequate intellectual capability, a preponderance of internalized, non-acted-out conflicts, and support from the family. Severe pathology in either the parents or the adolescent is a contraindication for analysis. Those teenagers who suffer ego deficits and deviation, failures in separation-individuation and attainment of object and self constancy, cognitive deficits, or a propensity to fragment under the onslaught of aggressive feelings cannot handle a demanding uncovering treatment. They would become more disturbed by closer contact with preconscious and unconscious material. Thus, only the relatively intact teenager with more circumscribed pathology is a suitable candidate for psychoanalysis or very intensive individual psychotherapy.

Policy in agencies and clinics—in contrast to therapists in private practice—usually dictates supportive individual treatment once a week. This mode of work is very valuable in inviting bonding and attachment and provision of a role model, who serves as a developmental transitional parental figure to aid in the building of structure and development of self-soothing mechanisms. Adolescents reactive to trauma or evidencing impoverished coping with age-appropriate tasks can benefit from an intervention designed to stabilize self-esteem and ego functioning. Individual psychotherapy is appropriate for a wide range of adolescents: the severely disturbed; the teenager in a traumatic home situation; or one who presents a habit disorder, ego deficit(s), or developmental disability. Many adolescents only desire pointed, goal-directed therapy. The work must be supportive; empathic; and respectful of repression, resistances, and defenses. In supportive work, counseling, advocacy, parent guidance, and collaboration with school personnel is often required. Caution about confrontation is crucial. A well-intentioned clinician often wants to make an adolescent see reality, yet such interventions can backfire and be interpreted as an assault and a failure of empathy. Ideally in work with more disturbed adolescents, the therapist will offer empathic communications that clarify the content, affect, and function of the patient's self-object configurations, which resurface in the face of threats of regressive fragmentation and dissolution (Stolorow and Lachman, 1980).

Bibliography

ACKERMAN, N. W. (1966). *Treating the Troubled Family*, New York: Basic Books.

BERKOVITZ, I. H. and SUGAR, M. (1975). Indications and Contraindications for Adolescent Group Therapy. In *Adolescents Grow in Groups*, ed. M. Sugar, pp. 3–26. New York: Brunner/Mazel.

BLOS, P. (1962). *On Adolescence—A Psychoanalytic Interpretation*. Glencoe, Ill.: Free Press.

GEREERD, E. (1957). Some Aspects of Psychoanalytic Technique in Adolescence. *Psychoanalytic Study of the Child*, 12:263–83. New York: International Universities Press.

GINOTT, H. (1961). *Group Psychotherapy with Children*. New York: McGraw-Hill.

HALEY, J. (1971). Family Therapy. *Internat. J. Psychiatry*, 9:233–42.

HEACOCK, D. R. (1966). Modification of the Standard Techniques for Out-Patient Group Psychotherapy with Delinquent Boys. *J. A. M. A.*, 58:41–47.

JACKSON, D. (1959). Family Interaction, Family Homeostasis and Some Implications for Therapy. In *Individual and Family Dynamics*, ed. J. Masserman, New York: Grune & Stratton.

JOSSELYN, I. (1972). Prelude—Adolescent Group Therapy: Why, Where and a Caution. In *Adolescents Grow in Groups*, ed. I. H. Berkovitz, pp. 1–5. New York: Brunner/Mazel.

KOHUT, H. (1977). *Restoration of the Self*. New York: International Universities Press.

_____ (1971). *The Analysis of the Self.* New York: International Universities Press.

KRAMER, C. H. (1970). Psychoanalytically Oriented Family Therapy: Ten Year Evolution in a Private Child Psychiatry Practice. *Family Institute of Chicago Publication* 1:1–42.

MASTERSON, J. F. and WASHBURNE, A. (1966). THE SYMPTOMATIC ADOLESCENT: PSYCHIATRIC ILLNESS OR ADOLESCENT TURMOIL? *Amer. J. Psychiatry,* 122:1240–48.

OFFER, D. and VANDERSTOEP, E. (1975). Indications and Contraindications for Family Therapy. In *The Adolescent in Group and Family Therapy,* ed. by M. Sugar, pp. 145–60. New York: Brunner/Mazel.

ROTHSTEIN, A. (1980). *The Narcissistic Pursuit of Perfection.* New York: International Universities Press.

STOLOROW, R. E. and LACHMAN, F. M. (1980). *Psychoanalysis of the Developmental Arrests—Theory and Treatment.* New York: International Universities Press.

UNTERBERGER, L. (1972). Personal communication to E. Offer and E. Vanderstoep.

WILLIAMS, F. S. (1967). Family Therapy: A Critical Assessment. *Amer. J. Orthopsychiatry,* 37:912–19.

WYNNE, L. C. (1965). Some Indications and Contraindications for Exploratory Family Therapy. In *Intensive Family Therapy: Theoretical and Practical Aspects,* eds. I. Boszormenyi-Nagy and J. L. Framo, pp. 289–322. New York: Harper & Row.

22

Placement in Group Residential Care
Hospitals and Residential Treatment Centers

Despite society's attempts to strengthen family life and clinicians' preference for prevention, early intervention, and deinstitutionalization, there will always be some adolescents in need of group care "away from home." While most of the literature on group care states that the home is the best place for the child, many children have no home, or only a psychonoxious home, to return to, and are too severely damaged to be adoptable. Too many severely disturbed children and emotionally limited adoptive parents have been linked in the legalities of adoption, which then are disrupted by the need for separation and placement of children in residential treatment facilities. With the emphasis on "deinstitutionalization" and "permanancy planning," the reality of the fit between adoptive home and child is often overlooked.

Indications for Placement

Because many disturbances of adolescence are transient and reactive, and correct themselves, an important question is whether treatment is indicated and, if so, where and how the therapeutic intervention should occur. There are different perspectives regarding indications and contra-indications for individual, group, and family treatment. There are, however, clearer and less controversal indications for therapeutic group care in hospitals or residential treatment centers:

(1) Symptomatic behavior which is dangerous to the self or others, which appears as a response to perceived frustration. . . . For potentially homicidal behavior or that which is dangerous to others, complete containment is clearly necessary. A spillover of potential suicidal behavior is tolerable providing the patient can give a trustable absolute assurance that no action will be taken without first giving the opportunity to a therapist to intervene. This assurance is possible in some types of suicidal personalities; it does not seem to be observable with those who are potentially homicidal. Projection of badness onto others, as a preliminary to attempts at destruction, is harder to contain than the projection of badness onto the self. (2) Developmentally destructive behavior which cannot be contained and may include chronic drug abuse, alcoholism and sexual promiscuity. (3) Psychic pain of such intensity, or symptomatic attempts at pain resolution, which make it impossible for the adolescent to function in an age-appropriate way. This pain cannot be attenuated by out-patient therapeutic intervention with the patient or the family. (4) A psychonoxious environment which makes the patient inaccessible to therapeutic intervention. The disturbance of the patient is so needed by the family or society that no successful treatment is possible while the patient is being stimulated or provoked, consciously or unconsciously, to disturbed behavior [Miller, 1980, p. 478].

Hospitalization

Adolescent patients ages 12 through 25, began increasingly to be admitted to psychiatric hospitals during the 1950s. In the last thirty years, they have comprised "50 to 80 percent of psychiatric hospital populations" (Barish and Schonfeld, 1973, p. 340); and there has been a corresponding increase in provision of hospital facilities for them. Admission of teenagers to hospitals creates special dilemmas; and institutions have struggled with, and experimented with, the use of special adolescent units or mixed-population units. Currently, many hospitals maintain adolescent units, while others have returned to mixing adults and teenagers, with the adolescent group off the unit, in school and special programs, large portions of the day. This latter generic approach permits nursing care and attention for adult patient needs and concerns. Advocates of the generic milieu believe that it recreates a family or community setting and that it thereby approximates the normal adolescent experience. They claim that adults have a calming influence on teenagers and that, by contrast, all-adolescent units are chaotic, disruptive, and close to unmanageable. They also feel that isolating teenagers from the rest of the hospital community gives a negative rejecting message.

The generic units are thought to decrease the typical antagonism between staff and patients by providing neutral adults as well as allies, "particularly concerning patient complaints" (p. 364).

Benefits to adult patients have been documented: They are sought out for advice and comfort, and they appreciate the adolescents bringing life and zest to a hospital setting. "Adults cohabiting with adolescents have an opportunity to exercise their parenting skills and adult roles and to reexperience their own adolescence, which they may have repressed. All this can enhance their self-esteem" (pp. 264–65). While teenagers do have special needs, advocates of the generic unit believe that they can be effectively addressed in mixed units, which afford adults and teenagers an opportunity to learn and grow together.

Other researchers posit that many younger and more vulnerable adolescents are best served in inpatient units that include teenagers and younger children. Olas (1982) described adolescents who cannot be treated by conventional dynamic psychotherapy because of their lack of tolerance for the anxiety that would be aroused. Their lack of an observing ego and age-appropriate defenses makes them more reachable through games and stories commonly used in treating the younger latency-age child. Sib relationships in fact can be improved via hospitalization with younger children. The environment is structured to provide clear limits; imaginative stories and play therapy are employed without toys that would humiliate adolescents. There is an attempt to provide help in problem solving even though the adolescent is reluctant to ask for it directly. Frequently adolescents can safely and vicariously satisfy their own needs and wishes for nurturance and support by the teaching and comfort they give to younger patients with whom they reside.

Adolescents' high level of activity and energy, their

> provocative behavior, bizarre modes of dress, sexual preoccupations, profane language, and musical tastes are disruptive to standard adult worlds [thus] they have been isolated on special adolescent units. Unfortunately, separating adolescent from adult patients creates as many problems as it attempts to solve. Inevitably, the adolescent becomes a scapegoat and is seen either as too rowdy, making unreasonable requests of the staff or the institution, or, as too pampered, given special opportunities not afforded others by the staff [Bond and Auger, 1982, p. 360].

On the adolescent units, attempts were made to provide and utilize structure, therapeutic milieu; group activity, and peer pressure. However, as reported by Bond and Auger (1982), this approach in no way solved the difficulties of providing adequate services and protection. It led to less focus on the individual and more on the group as a whole, and often resulted in intense chaos and turbulance on the adolescent units.

The special adolescent units did stimulate the development of an extensive array of services appropriate for teenage interests and needs. School programs of five hours days replaced inadequate tutoring programs. Art, music, and dance therapy programs, physical education, and crafts are all needed in any facility serving adolescents.

Residential Treatment Centers

For adolescents not in need of medication and/or the special security protection of a hospital setting, residential treatment centers are the alternative group-care plan. Barish and Schonfeld (1972) stated that such programs generally have a social work or educational orientation. The oldest are the social work settings, which emphasize group living while also providing special education and recreation programs, psychological and psychiatric services, and work with parents and families of children in care. The programs that emphasize education focus on academics and social relationships and commonly utilize concurrent psychotherapy. By contrast, some less sophisticated hospital programs do not provide significant educational and/or therapeutic recreational programs. Barish and Schonfeld (1972) generalized: "the first two forms of residential care emphasize the mobilization of healthy aspects of the personality, whereas psychiatric hospitals have tended to stress the relief of psychopathology" (p. 340). Hospitals, by and large cannot provide protected group living in a complete milieu that would meet the needs of adolescent patients by offering long-term residential or inpatient treatment: social, educational, and recreational programs; psychotherapy (individual, family, and group); and transitional care and after care to support the adolescent's return to family and community, where possible, or to specific work, educational or foster care programs when return to the natural family is ill-advised.

> In short, comprehensive residential treatment is more than the management and treatment of adolescents away from home. The designation is not appropriate for facilities that limit themselves to crisis intervention, short-term hospitalization or partial hospitalization; nor does it apply to day schools, half-way houses, group residences or foster family placements, though there is admittedly, some overlap in facilities and functions and many of these services are, by definition, included [p. 341].

Therapeutic Milieu

Bettelheim and Sylvester (1972) define a therapeutic milieu by its inner cohesiveness, which permits the child or adolescent to develop and internalize a consistent frame of reference. This is based on a program that is clear and structured, where adults respond benignly, predictably, and firmly and thus facilitate meaningful child and adult interaction and relationships. The management of group living, daily activities, and education is intended to be growth promoting and noncustodial. A gratifying responsive environment requires skilled and well-supervised staff who aid children in emotional growth and drive control. Regression per se is not encouraged, except in the service of ego growth. Adolescents requiring twenty-four-hour care have failed to develop adequate ego structure and generally are fixated on primitive modes of expression and impulsivity as their mode of instinctual expression.

While the group living units and a therapeutic milieu must be tolerant of symptomotology, the adolescent and the institutional staff must feel safe and in control. Allowing wild acting-out behaviors, aggression and destructiveness further alarms the out-of-control adolescent, who indeed feels safer with limits, controls and boundaries presented in a nonpunitive fashion. Adversarial postures between staff and adolescents are common in all hospitals and residential treatment programs. The adolescent patients require endless nonthreatening reality clarifications, external limits, and interpretations and reflections from staff. Fritz Redl (1959) developed what he called the "life space interview," an on-the-spot means of responding therapeutically to children's explosive tantrums, fighting, and vandalism. It is an intervention used by house parents, nurses, or child care personnel in charge of the child's living situation.

Acting-out, violent adolescents are most difficult for all institutions to treat. Mayer, Richman, and Balcrzak (1977) enumerated problems of control created by misconceived state regulations. These regulations were geared to correcting abusive coercion; but, in reality they often render personnel helpless, so that fear of very aggressive children creates serious barriers to treatment and leads administrators to refuse to admit such needy youth to many hospitals and residential centers. Commonly, such extremely aggressive adolescents need a closed hospital setting or a locked unit where they can be segregated to avoid group contamination. Some institutions have quiet rooms, stripped of furniture, where a violent adolescent can be contained and supervised by staff. It is critical that no patient be left in isolation unattended. This is an unhuman, unethical procedure that can have grave and dangerous consequences. Usually medications must be utilized to calm such an adolescent.

Child Care Staff

The variations of organizational models and staffing patterns in child care facilities include centralized and decentralized systems, hierarchies (as in hospitals), democratic staff structures, professionalization divisions of personnel, and charismatic leadership. Whatever the formal structure of the group care facility, clear and open channels for communication allowing staff members optimal input of their personalities, ideas, and skills will enhance patient care. The counselors, nurses, or child care staff, who "live" with the children, handling all aspects of daily living, participating in treatment conferences, and, frequently working with parents, must provide the following to the children: "(1) need fullfilment at the most primitive level, (2) acceptance of primitive expression of need and feeling from the children, (3) working through some conflicts in "marginal" or [life space] interviews and (4) working through other problems in specially scheduled individual interviews" (Kessler, 1966, p. 472).

Child care work in this country is marginal, a low status occupation in terms of level of education expected, salary paid, and power permitted. Research, however, has shown that in many cases this is not the reason for the high turnover of staff that has consistently plagued residential facilities. "A lack of sufficient nurturance [of staff] was a major factor" (Fant and Ross, 1979). Barrett and McKelvey (1980) focused on organizational issues and personal stresses on the worker.

Education

Education is essential for normal adequate emotional adjustment during adolescence, and for future employment and self-sufficiency. Thus, school classes are essential in any residential program. They may be offered through tutoring or at an adjacent local school if the adolescent can be allowed off campus to attend. Most commonly, they are provided within the hospital or residential institution. An educational assessment is always needed to plan properly for the adolescent in residential care. Placed youth are commonly uneven in academic performance and need a flexible curriculum and individualized school program. Nichtern (1974) enumerated the ingredients of a meaningful educational assessment: "(1) identification of learning needs, (2) identification of blocks to learning and (3) evaluation of the current level of capacity to learn." (p. 432). Teachers in such settings occupy a significant therapeutic role and need access to records and open communications with other staff members via routine discussions and attendance at case conferences. They must be trained and supervised to work effectively with the disturbed adolescent whose emotional state has a profound effect on learning and mastery of academics. The seriously troubled adolescent will bring to the classroom a high degree of anxiety. He or she is generally subject to severe episodic or chronic disorganization, which will interfere with cognition, memory, sensory perception, and concen-

tration. Despite the occasional adequate or superior academic performance of some youth in care, we generally observe "mistrust, suspicion,
alienation and egocentrism well beyond that expected of an average adolescent classroom population" (Rinsley, 1974). Teacher and school
must contribute to case planning and determine, for example, if an adolescent should be in a coed or noncoed class, be assigned homework, be
placed in a one-to-one or group class, be expected to handle abstract
ideas and concepts or rote work, or be permitted to attend school off
campus. Resistance, defenses, and transferences all manifest themselves in the academic realm; and it is to be hoped that in the course of
care, learning and academic performance will become part of the
conflict-free sphere of ego functioning. Too frequently the teachers'
therapeutic, limit-setting, and nurturing role is overlooked in residential
programs; and the therapeutic implications of learning are ignored. The
special therapeutic educational program ideally aims to: "(1) foster secondary process thinking in disturbed patients and teach social skills; (2)
provide students with a learning experience calculated to produce feelings of success; and (3) rekindle adolescents' intellectual curiosity in the
hope of propelling them once again toward formal training." (Copeland,
1974). Thus this program is an indispensable component in any comprehensive treatment program for adolescents in residential care.

Recreation

After educational classes, recreation occupies the next major portion of
the adolescent's day and must be integrated into the therapeutic milieu.
Adolescents with severe ego defects often reflect disorientation in time
and space, feelings of omnipotence, and confused concepts of cause
and effect and rely on primitive defenses, such as denial and projection,
which impair their abilities to sublimate and contain aggression. This
interferes with the ability to be creative, focused, and sustained in play
and group activities. Successful recreational activities can help the
child develop internalized controls. In therapeutic recreation for disturbed youth, it is generally essential to minimize competition and pressures to succeed. Activities must be geared to help institutionalized adolescents handle their aggression through relationships with others.
Often this is a neglected and under-financed aspect of a residential program. Many institutionalized adolescents who are, at least initially, unreachable through traditional treatment interventions are more accessible through sports, art, music, dance, or drama, all of which aim to
provide "forms and transformation of narcissism" (Kohut, 1966).

Psychotherapy in Residential Group Care

Most adolescents placed today in residential treatment centers or in hospitals have had many bouts of attempted outpatient treatment. The failure of these efforts in the face of continued psychic pain, serious acting-out and self-destructive behaviors (drugs, alcohol, auto accidents, sexual promiscuity, delinquency, anorexia nervosa, etc.), and inaccessible or unsupportive parents commonly make placement necessary.

Most teenagers placed in group care are diagnosed as borderline, schizophrenic, or personality or character disorders. Their chronological adolescence is not matched by a genuine psychological adolescence. The customary themes and conflicts center about "impulse control, body image, dependency versus independence, peer relationships, sexual adequacy, identity, competition, authority and so on" (Barish and Schonfeld, 1973, p. 342). The adolescent's repetitive, symbolic acting-out patterns communicate inner conflicts and anxieties and at times are dangerous, socially disturbing, and slow to lessen under containment and treatment. Commonly, long-term treatment is required; but often the cost of care, inadequate hospital insurance, and diminished state and local funds for placement interfere with appropriate long-term treatment planning. Thus all psychotherapy planning must embrace the reality of the length of possible placement and consider immediate treatment interventions as well as long-term ones, while the adolescent is in a closed setting or is subsequently transferred to a group home, day treatment program, halfway house, or the like.

Most residential programs provide several modalities of therapy: usually some combination of individual, group and family therapy. (See Chapter 21, Criteria for Family, Group, and Individual Therapy.) The living unit has already been described as a major ingredient in the therapeutic milieu. In addition, many settings provide clinical treatment groups and community or management groups, which focus on ward or cottage life, child-staff relationships, stealing, scapegoating, vandalism, etc. These management groups may address developmental transitional steps, such as intake, discharge, transfer to public schools, and the like. The clinical groups can include activity group treatment, peer socialization, and insight-oriented interventions. Treatment of whatever modality must be directed to the central issues these adolescents struggle with, namely, helplessness, autonomy, and inadequate separation and individuation.

Miller (1980) observed that developmental issues and psychodynamic understandings commonly are omitted in the case planning for adolescents in care. Generally the more disturbed the adolescent, the shorter the time spent with the therapist. As a general rule the schizophrenic, who cannot pay attention for more than a few minutes or who is genuinely frightened by too much closeness, can only be seen for about fifteen or twenty minutes at a time during acute stages of the illness; once it is in remission, longer sessions are possible. The frequency of sessions is determined by

> (1) the patient's capacity to make a therapeutic relationship, (2) the level of anxiety, (3) the intensity of pain inflicted on others and felt by the patient, (4) the presence of regressive symptomatology, especially drug abuse, which needs to be attenuated or no therapeutic contact is really possible and (5) the patient's conscious motivation for treatment [p. 479].

Treatment can be behavioral, supportive or insight-oriented. Caution is necessary in using interpretation which is frequently misperceived by the adolescent as a lecture, a persecutory experience, or a distancing device. Miller (1980) noted that different interventions are geared to invite bonding, provide developmental models, or resolve conflicts. Which type of treatment is appropriate depends on diagnosis. "The failure to make an adequate assessment of which type of therapy and its frequency is appropriate can convert a seriously disturbed adolescent to one who is intractably ill" (ibid.).

Parents: The Role of the Family

Despite the recognition that the role of the family is crucial, parents receive more lip service than real service in too many residential settings. Some institutions try unconsciously to sever or diminish parent-child ties, viewing the families in perjorative terms and trying to "rescue" the child. Many institutions are not genuinely supportive or expectant of familial cooperation and involvement through regular visits, letters, and meaningful collaboration with the staff of the institution.

In residential programs, children repeat the past, replicating the early distorted relationship with parents, now with therapist, teachers, and child care staff. It is crucial that staff resist stepping into the role of the exhausted, hostile, and frequently ambivalent parent and, instead, handle the inevitable transference and counter transference phenomena that always arise in response to the adolescent's rage, aggression, wildly fluctuating ego states, bizarre symptoms, glaring hatred, distorted sense of reality, and disorganized behavior.

Commonly, the placement of an adolescent is a crisis intervention, following on the heels of a series of acting-out episodes. This generally means that there has been little or no preplacement work and the placement causes both the adolescent and the parents pain, anger, guilt, and a sense of helplessness. Grief and depression over separation are common affects, which surface and get acted out later. For successful treatment of the adolescent, the parents must establish a bond of trust and an alliance with the staff of the institution. This need is most clear in evaluating work with the child who lacks any genuine familial ties. Studying the treatment of the child without the family, Albert et al. (1965) commented that the findings were "far from optimistic." Barnes (1972) observed the all-too-common practice of placing youth with insufficient attention to the adolescent's need for genuine guardianship. Barnes believed that in those instances when adolescents are placed in residential care, the hospital or treatment institution is expected to be the "parent." Thus the community or placing agency all but abdicates all responsibility, which is an unrealistic approach, since sooner or later these adolescents will be discharged and will need support, funding, and care. Barnes (1972) emphasized guardianship over treatment, in that no genuine therapy can be affected unless "proper guardianship is established first" (p. 139). Child welfare agencies that act as guardians frequently cannot exercise their surrogate parental obligations firmly and consistently due to heavy case loads and endless staff turnover. Thus, unvisited adolescents frequently experience a series of unsuccessful revolving door placements.

Appropriate, consistent contact and work with the parents of adolescents in placement increases the parents' identification with the treatment program and, ideally, diminishes their ambivalence and unconscious resistance to their child's growth and change. Some residential programs have engaged parents as treatment collaborators—helping parents learn child management skills—and set up formal expectations for reports from parents after visits. Given the declining funds for long-term placement and the adolescent's probable return home, alliances with families are crucial.

Krona (1980) described a model of placement that involves parents in a myriad of clinical procedures including assessment, treatment, and discharge planning. They receive training to help and support their children in the program and to sustain behaviors once children are discharged. Over and beyond family therapy sessions, parents are contacted weekly and also receive weekly written reports about their teenagers. Any and all disciplinary action and granting of privileges is discussed with them. The staff of the residential facility then remain available for months after discharge to provide support, consultation, and help in crisis. The success of such extensive involvement of parents appears to be predicated on both agency philosophy and the reality of fairly intact parents and children who can benefit from behavior modification techniques. While not universally applicable, this approach is

an concouraging departure from the historic patterns of all but total severance of child and family.

Countertransference in Group Care Programs

Staff countertransference in a residential program is generally intense,
and of great significance in transactions between the adults and adolescents. It is important to recognize the adolescent's transference manifestations toward the adults, based upon what Ehrlich (1983) called the
four aspects of the parental "gestalt": (1) the *real* actual parent, (2) the
internalized or introjected image of this parent, usually couched in infantile levels of fantasy, affect, and meaning; (3) the *projected* image of
the parent, as it finds expression in the adolescent's view of the world;
and (4) the parental *function*, comprising those parental behaviors and
roles to which the adolescent still needs to relate in everyday dealings
with reality, whether these take place with the actual parent or a surrogate figure. Residential staff must be prepared to be responded to on a
split-level basis, the transferential and the realistic. In addition to the
disturbed adolescent's propensity for the primitive defense of splitting,
that is, dividing people into all good or all bad objects, these youngsters
frequently come from one-parent homes, or intact families that have
been marred by collusions, inapproriate alliances, and various family
pathologies. Given such familial training in addition to basic ego deficits, adolescents in placement often are or become masters at dividing
staff members, creating rivalries, misunderstandings, inappropriate alliances, and collusions. These phenomena, combined with the adolescent's defiances, rage, and contempt, will arouse staff member's repressed or unresolved feelings in day-to-day treatment interactions with
the adolescent population.

Countertransferential responses will vary in accord with each staff
member's personality and early life history. In addition, Bonier (1982)
contended that "most severely disordered individuals, and particularly
adolescents, because of the greater age-appropriate intensity and confusion, evoke in significant others, exactly those responses which serve to
confirm their disordered views of self and others, of causality and predictability" (p. 385). The usual intensity of the interchanges can "rekindle those never fully resolved themes in all of us" and "not infrequently
the exchanges are best measured in decibels rather than in substance"
(pp. 386–87). The adolescent's substance abuse, vandalism, and physical threats can prove most intimidating and alarming to staff—not
infrequently out of proportion to the actual danger. What appears overdetermined and countertransferential are elevated, highly personalized,
extreme responses. When there is an impulsive wish to act without re-

flection and self-examination, meetings, consultations, and supervision are always necessary to examine and review staff transactions and feelings. "Powerfully felt imperatives to act are often an indication of matters which need to be relocated in the adolescent, rather than acted out by the adult" (p. 390). In all, countertransference problems are greatest in work with impulsive, acting out and highly narcissistic patients.

Kris (1959) listed the following integrative functions of the ego, which are essential for a therapist, for the treatment process, and for the achievement of insight in both patient and therapist: (1) self-observation, in which the ego is split into the observing and experiencing parts; (2) control of the discharge affect, which is related to the therapists' tolerance of tension over need gratification in themselves and patients; and (3) control over regression, which permits therapists to empathize with patient's regressions, manifested by their transferences, without loss of their own reality testing function or identity. Thus, staff engaged in intense work with very ill adolescents must be in touch with their own adolescence, their own infantile needs, and thus effectively live "guardedly" in the world of adolescents; in a sense, they live in two worlds, the past and the present, the real and the unreal, and as themselves and the children in their care (Olden, 1953).

Voluntary and Nonvoluntary Placement and Civil Rights of Adolescents

Currently courts and legislatures are regulating access and detention of adolescents in residential facilities. Previously placement or hospitalization was effected by the parents of the adolescent or the juvenile courts. Teenagers had no voice in the decision. But now, new laws allow the hospitalized adolescent to reject the placement and seek redress through lawyers and the courts. The result is that, because of the new legal issues raised, many fine programs reject any nonvoluntary adolescent patients. The legal "reforms" have arisen out of recognition of the inadequacies of many residential facilities, particularly those under the auspices of the juvenile court; and as a result, all residential programs have come under suspicion; and placement has become near to impossible without the explicit consent of the adolescent. Miller and Burt (1977) stated that these new critiques and legal rules are based on fundamental misconceptions of adolescent psychology.

If treatment interventions and policy are to be appropriate, we must understand adolescent techniques of communication. Miller and Burt (1977) pointed out that some adolescents are concrete in their thinking, have a poor sense of the future, and see themselves as persecuted. Authorities must appreciate that an adolescent's words are less important than his actions. Specifically, acting-out asocial behavior, designed to test adults, provoke limits, care taking and control is more significant than cries for autonomy and independence. Legislatures and courts appear blind to these covert but real messages from adolescents and have chosen to intervene in parent-child relationships, virtually stripping parents of the right to hospitalize their adolescent, who frequently causes danger to himself or others. Little recognition is given to parental ambivalence about nonvoluntary placement. (Some view parents as willfully and wantonly abandoning or incarcerating their children.) Additionally, civil rights advocates mistakenly assume that psychiatrists unnecessarily contain children and adolescents in hospitals for excessive lengths of time.

Currently no one languishes, unattended and ignored, in the back wards of hospitals. Rather, we see that the pendulum has swung the opposite extreme, to "deinstitutionalization," a process once referred to as reform of the mental health systems. In the 1960s there was revulsion against huge and cruel institutions that warehoused the mentally ill. Patients of all ages were discharged in the hope that community care would be more humane. Tranquilizers became the panacea, and patients were discharged often to ill-prepared families or programs. The recipient community systems of care and support have been underfunded and understaffed, resulting in a major societal tragedy. Because they are not provided with mental health care or even such basic needs as food and shelter, millions have been cast adrift to roam the streets seeking shelter. Recently more and more disturbed adolescents have joined the ranks of the homeless street people.

Lengths of stay in inpatient programs are too often determined by hospitals' short-term care and/or the coverage prescribed by insurance companies, rather than patient need. The nonvoluntary patient, increasingly, receives short-term hospitalization and community treatment mandated by legislative reforms and administrative mental health policy, despite the frequent medical need for more protective custody. Families commonly are ill-equipped to resume care of their adolescent after a twenty-one-, thirty-, or sixty-day hospitalization. Thus, we see many "revolving door" adolescent patients, repeatedly rehospitalized and prematurely discharged.

The *Harvard Law Review* (1976) noted that most of the legal reform directed at correcting the abuse of the confinement process has been ill-conceived, and thus fails to address the real problems. Because there is little empirical evidence that psychiatrists or any other behavioral scientists can predict dangerousness, courts, parents, and doctors who wish to commit often can take no step until some harmful act has been committed. The legal reforms of the past decade have had a profound effect on the incompetent patient, with particularly dire effects on the psychotic population, which includes schizophrenic patients and those suffering from drug-induced psychosis. This is particularly relevant in contemplating involuntary hospitalization of the resistive adolescent substance abuser. These patients are commonly considered too much trouble for hospitals, who refuse to admit them or offer only a brief stay. Families who now seek to use legal interventions to control their adolescents will get little assistance. "Although it is usually ignored in the libertarian calculus, the suffering and the behavioral manifestations of the mentally ill do have a deleterious effect on those around them" (Sone, 1979, p. 566). Incompetent adolescents who may or may not pose a danger to themselves and/or others often end up in jail, rather than a treatment milieu. Or they may be placed in settings ill-suited to meet their actual needs. The "least restrictive alternative" may not be available or appropriate for the adolescent needing placement out of the home.

Group residential care in hospitals or institutions is only part of a genuinely coherent system that offers preplacement, placement, and postplacement services. The child welfare, child mental health, and juvenile justice systems are plagued with fragmentation and profound disorganization of services. Funding and benefit cutbacks by local and federal government and insurance companies have severely limited provision of care for adolescent youths of all classes, races, and ethnic backgrounds. There are growing numbers of severely ill people wandering the city streets and living in welfare hotels. Many of them are homeless adolescents, unprotected, unserved, and on the loose.

Because of the current concern over patient rights, it is now necessary for clinicians to invoke court hearings where appropriate and testify with parents regarding specific youths' need for secure closed placement programs. To assume that "all residential psychiatric facilities for adolescents are equally prisons, no matter how open, estranges the possibility of therapeutic work for adolescents who are otherwise amenable to treatment" (Miller and Burt, 1977, p. 50). The decision as to the type of residential placement required for disturbed adolescents must not be based solely on the severity of the adolescent's symptomatic behavior, but rather on the basis of how successfully that behavior can be contained within the context of human relationships, with parents, therapists, extra-parental adults, peers and general social systems.

Bibliography

ALBERT, A., ET AL. (1965). Children Without Families. J. Acad. Child Psychiatry, 4:163–278.

BARISH, J. I. and SCHONFELD, W. A. (1973). Comprehensive Residential Treatment of Adolescents. In Adolescent Psychiatry, Vol. 2: Developmental and

Clinical Studies, eds. S. C. Feinstein and P. Giovacchini, pp. 340–50. New York: Basic Books.

BARNES, M. E. (1972). The Concept of "Parental Force." In *Children Away From Home*, eds. J. K. Whittaker and A. W. Trieschman, pp. 132–39. Chicago/New York: Aldine Atherton.

BARRETT, M. and McKELVEY, J. (1980). Stresses and Strains on the Child Care Worker: Typologies for Assessment. *Child Welfare*, 59(5):277–85.

BETTELHEIM, B., and SYLVESTER, E. (1972). A Therapeutic Milieu. In *Children Away From Home*, eds. J. K. Whittaker and A. W. Trieschman, pp. 70–86. Chicago/New York: Aldine Atherton.

BOND, T., and AUGER, N. (1982). Benefits of the Generic Milieu in Adolescent Hospital Treatment. In *Adolescent Psychiatry, Vol 10: Developmental and Clinical Studies*, eds. S. Feinstein, J. Looney, A. Schwartzberg, and A. Sorosky, pp. 360–72. Chicago: University of Chicago Press.

BONIER, R. (1982). Staff Countertransference in an Adolescent Milieu Treatment Setting. In *Adolescent Psychiatry, Vol. 10*, pp. 382–90. See Bond and Auger (1982).

COPELAND, A. (1974). An Interim Educational Program for Adolescents. In *Adolescent Psychiatry, Vol. 3: Developmental and Clinical Studies*, eds. S. C. Feinstein and P. Giovacchini, pp. 422–31. Basic Books.

EHRLICH, H. S. (1983). Growth Opportunities in the Hospital: Intensive Inpatient Treatment of Adolescents. In *The Psychiatric Treatment of Adolescents*, ed. A. Esman, pp. 261–76. New York: International Universities Press.

FANT, R., and Ross, A. (1979). Supervision of Child Care Staff. *Child Welfare*, 58(10):627–41.

HARVARD LAW REVIEW. (1976). Developments in the Law: Civil Confinement of the Mentally Ill. Vol. 87:1190.

KESSLER, J. (1962). *Psychopathology of Childhood*. Englewood Cliffs, N.J.: Prentice-Hall.

KOHUT, H. (1966). Forms and Transformation of Narcissism. *J. Amer. Psychoanal. Assn.*, 14(2):243–72.

KRIS, K. (1956). On Some Vicissitudes of Insight in Psychoanalysis. *Internat. J. Psychoanaly.*, 37:445–55.

KRONA, D. (1978). Parents as Treatment Partners in Residential Care. *Child Welfare*, 59(2):91–96.

MAYER, M. F.; Richman, L. H., and BALCRZAK, E. (1977). *Group Care of Children: Crossroads and Transition*. New York: Child Welfare League of America.

MILLER, D. (1980). Treating the Seriously Disturbed Adolescent. in *Adolescent Psychiatry, Vol. 8: Developmental and Clinical Studies*, eds. S. Feinstein, P. Giovacchini, J. Looney, A. Schwartzberg, and A. Sorosky, pp. 469–81. Chicago: University of Chicago Press.

MILLER, D. and BURT, R. (1977). On Children's Rights and Therapeutic Institutions. In *Adolescent Psychiatry, Vol. 5: Developmental and Clinical Studies*, eds. S. Feinstein and P. Giovacchini, pp. 39–53. New York: Jason Aronson.

MISHNE, J. (1983). *Clinical Work with Children.* New York: Free Press.

NICHTERN, S. (1974). The Therapeutic Educational Environment. In *Adolescent Psychiatry, Vol. 3*, pp. 432–34. See Copeland (1974).

OLDEN, C. (1953). On Adult Empathy with Children. *Psychoanalytic Study of the Child*, 8:111–26. New York: International Universities Press.

OLAS, J. (1982). The Inpatient Treatment of Adolescents in a Milieu Including Younger Children. In *Adolescent Psychiatry, Vol. 10*, pp. 373–81. See Bond and Auger (1982).

PROCTOR, J. (1959). Countertransference Phenomena in the Treatment of Severe Character Disorders in Children and Adolescents. In *Dynamic Psychopathology in Childhood*, eds. L. Jossner and E. Pavenstedt, pp. 293–309. New York: Grune & Stratton.

REDL, F. (1959). Strategy and Techniques of the Life-Space Interview. *Amer. J. Orthopsychiatry*, 29:1–19.

RINSLEY, D. (1974). Special Education for Adolescents in Residential Psychiatric Treatment. In *Adolescent Psychiatry, Vol. 3*, pp. 394–418. See Copeland (1974).

STONE, A. (1979). Legal and Ethical Developments. In *Disorders of the Schizophrenic Syndrome*, ed. L. Bellak, pp. 560–84. New York: Basic Books.

23

Therapeutic Work with Parents

The process of referral sets the tone of the ongoing work with the referred adolescent's parents. Kessler (1966) believed that an effective referral should communicate genuine concern for the child's welfare, rather than portray the child as a disruptive nuisance. It should emphasize the child's and parents' inner feelings, pain, and confusion and involve the parents in preliminary work that deals with their initial resistances and objections. The latter frequently are related to fear of stigma, concern about confidentiality, and parental guilt.

In examining how and why clinicians work with parents, Hamilton (1947) stressed the need for clarity about the emotional tone and relationships within the family. She noted that the objective in work with parents is to develop their insight into the connections between their problems and those of their child, to thereby enlist their efforts and involvement to help meet the child's evolving developmental needs. Chethik (1976) suggested similar goals focusing on the phenomenon of repetition compulsion and the fact that parents relive their own earlier problems and, in particular, adolescent struggles through their children. This treatment approach would not necessarily entail referral of the parent for direct personal therapy; rather, the child's therapist might well effectively work through these temporary impasses with the parent. However, if this working through takes a protracted period concurrent with treatment of the adolescent, it might well not best be handled by the teenager's therapist. Work with parents is often most taxing, requiring great skill and sensitivity. It often determines the success or failure of the treatment of the young patient.

Considerable controversy exists in regard to the parent-child-therapist relationship. Some therapists advocate seeing the parents as rarely as possible; some are adamant that, in the course of treating an adolescent, there be no parent-therapist contact. The reasoning behind this point of view is that the therapist-parent contact obstructs the teenager's development of a therapeutic alliance and interferes with confidentiality and autonomy. Those who emphasize therapist-parent contact note the fact that parents often need advice and explanations to help them understand that the goal is greater autonomy, self control, and age-appropriate development, rather than symptom reduction alone.

Esman (1985) recommended parent-therapist contact in the treatment of adolescents. "Not only is valuable information to be obtained from such meetings, but I believe that parents have the right to see the person to whom they are entrusting the care of their child and to whom they are paying . . . a fee" (p. 130). This author concurs with Esman's perspective and also with his belief that the approach should vary according to the age of the teenager and the presenting complaints or symptoms. When a voluntary adolescent is in the middle or late teen years, initial contact with him, or her rather than the parents, emphasizes that the therapist is there for him or her, rather than as a referee or champion of the parents' complaints. The older adolescent is encouraged to make the treatment contract, schedule his or her own appointments, and have decision making power regarding parent-therapist contact and whether or not the adolescent wishes to be present at such sessions. The treatment parameters for work with fairly intact middle and late adolescents closely parallels those in work with adults, when the patient is a suitable candidate for insight-oriented psychoanalytic psychotherapy. Such a patient possesses considerable ego strengths, and symptoms that do not preclude normal school attendance and continuation of life in the family and community. Overall, with such youths, difficulties emanate from phase-related intrapsychic conflict or reactive responses to such events as divorce, illness, or remarriage in the family.

Minimal to frequent parent-therapist contact is necessary when one is working with a more disturbed younger adolescent who presents more florid behavior, such as serious substance abuse, delinquency, or criminality. The question of confidentiality raises continuous clinical dilemmas in situations where the therapist is attempting to determine the meaning and extent of symptomatic behavior. Is the teenager experimenting with drugs, or in fact addicted? Is the adolescent recounting sexual experimentation, or potentially dangerous promiscuity? Are the exploits described actual criminal acts, or minor delinquent escapades? Experience and gradually evolving practice wisdom, fortified by supervision and consultation, will instruct the beginner clinician in making appropriate distinctions.

Confidentiality is maintained when appropriate. However, failure to meet appointments, specific impulsivity, sociopathic behavior, extensive substance abuse, sexual acting out, and injurious behavior cannot be kept secret from parents or those parent surrogates responsible as guardians for the adolescent patient. Therapists cannot collude or enter into what Keith (1968) termed "unholy alliances" with patients. However, communication cannot take place behind the back of teenage patients. The clinician must inform the patient of the need to communicate with parents, given the extent of dangerous or self-destructive behavior. Fear of the teenager's anger often mistakenly inhibits beginner practitioners, until they experience the actual relief the adolescent eventually shows at realistic limits and boundaries, which constitute caring and nurturance. Often after a barrage of protests and threats, the adolescent demonstrates feeling safer when the caring adults, therapist and parents, form a protective coalition. Many adolescent patients seen in treatment have exploited the reality of a divorced home, in which there is no cooperative joint parenting. They frequently attempt to replicate this split in the treatment transference relationship, namely, between their parent(s) and their therapist. Not uncommonly, interpretations fail to curtail the acting out, often dangerous, behavior; and thus parents, foster parents, probation officers or others must be contacted and recruited by the therapist to actively join the treatment "team" to fortify intervention efforts with the teenager.

Confidentiality does require that the therapist not communicate with the parents until the adolescent has been informed that the therapist will take this action, with or without permission. Confidentiality requires protection of the teenager's communications and only informing the parents of specific concerns about, such dangerous acts and preoccupations as suicidal ideation and drug and criminal activities. The necessity of such communication may well be the first step in arranging for a stronger, more protective structure (as in a residential treatment institution or hospital) if the acting out does not abate. In general, however, under less extreme circumstances, what the teenager shares in therapy is kept private. What the parents share in an appointment or by phone is not similarly protected, but rather is shared with the teenager. This is to demonstrate that there exists no collusion between therapist and parent(s) and that the clinician "belongs," if you will, to the adolescent. Similarly, no advice or guidance is given parents behind the teen-ager's back. It should be noted that

> direct advice to parents is seldom effective, particularly early in treatment, unless the parents' attitude towards the child is empathic and their under-standing is sufficient to enable them to interact meaningfully with the child. . . . Direct prohibitions to the parent, specifically in matters of sexu-ality and seduction, is not effective and may be disruptive to therapy [Sours, 1978, p. 624].

Case Example: Patient-Therapist-Parent Contact with a Healthy Family

Jim, age 16, a white, upper-middle-class teenager, residing in an affluent sub-urb, had been complaining in therapy sessions about his parents' intrusions and nagging. He claimed they did not like his current circle of friends, clothes, study patterns, endless phone calls, and frequent social plans on school nights. He felt that he had always adequately handled his studies and should not be subjected to their supervision, monitoring of calls, or obsessive questions about his comings and goings. While his therapist acknowledged his irritation, it was pointed out that a number of things may well have pro-voked parental anxiety and renewed attempts to supervise and control him. His grades, although adequate, had declined in the last grading period. Addi-tionally, since he had been secretly engaged in some drug experimentation, he had become more irritable and moody, and in all, parental worry and sus-picions had been aroused. Jim acknowledged these realities, but neverthe-less requested that the therapist get "his parents off his back," in the upcom-ing session they had requested with his therapist.

> Jim: "Since you're seeing Mom and Dad tomorrow, calm them down somehow. They'll drive me to defy them more and more. I'll lie a lot, if they keep spying like this."
>
> Therapist: "Look, Jim. I indeed can talk to your folks about a teenager's need for privacy and wish for freedom to make choices, decisions, even mistakes. I agree with you that your grades are your grades, not theirs, and that, in fact, you and you alone bear the consequences of your grade point average and what college you'll get into. What do you think they'll say? What do you think is their reason for trying to monitor your activities?"
>
> Jim: "I've always been perfect—a grind—an achiever—and that's what they've come to expect. Sure, in their way, they want the best for me. But who says what they think is best, really is in my best interests. Ivy League colleges aren't the end-all and be-all. They'll tell you they're disappointed in me, want the best for me-and that I'm getting into deep trouble, getting worse, in-stead of better, lately. Who knows what they'll say. They may even blame you for not shaping me up."

Therapist: "All possible, Jim. And of course, our work together relates to finding out what you want for yourself, making choices and decisions independently. It appears that you need my help in getting your folks to see that."

Jim: "That's right, Doc. And now I've seen you long enough to know you're on my side—and aren't trying to make me over in accord with their expectations. Their image is hurt if their son isn't Mr. Perfect, Big Man On Campus. I don't care now. You will keep private all of that I told you about trying out reefers and coke. You know what to say to them. You don't think I'm some derelict addict. I know you don't approve of drugs—but you do know that kids my age try out lots of things. I'm not stealing or dealing. I use my own money I earned for my drug use, which is hardly a habit. You'll give me the script—word for word, tomorrow, after your appointment with them; and you'll tell me what they said and how you replied. We've been through this before. I expect it will happen again, too. I'm glad they're coming tomorrow. Give 'em another lesson on the fifth Amendment. I'm entitled to refuse to answer all their questions."

The following day, Jim's parents came in for a session with their son's therapist. Jim had accurately described his parents' anxiety about him. They were concerned about his lower grades, choice of friends, secretiveness, and moodiness. His disinclination to participate in sports worried them. His reduced attention to grooming suggested depression to them. After reviewing their areas of concern, they were able to listen to the therapist's discussion of their son's age appropriate experimentation with new interests and friends, as well as his fairly normal depression, in response to the underlying developmental issues Jim was struggling with, as he attempted to master separation and individuation. His need for intense peer relationships, i.e., substitute attachments, as he disengaged from the strong love bonds with his parents, was discussed in detail. The parents were helped to see that they could no longer protect, guide, direct, or insulate their son as they had when he was younger. As noted by Barnes (1965), the parents did not have to effect basic personality changes to modulate their modes of discipline and handling of their son. Jim's parents had demonstrated from the onset of therapy that, supported by education and a trusting alliance with their son's therapist, they could effect empathic parenting that reflected sensitivity to normal developmental issues.

Jim was informed of all that his parents shared with his therapist. He was told of their worry and concern regarding his current choice of friends, his new stance of secretiveness, and decline in academic and athletic achievement. His therapist also revealed what she attempted to impart, namely, his need to experiment, and proceed without parental concern and guidance, as he prepared himself for more disengagement and independent living. The parental love for Jim was emphasized as the underpinning of their concern, despite their frequent manifestation of anger and frustration. Significantly, Jim acknowledged his affection and regard for his parents as he demonstrated insight, and acknowledged his provocativeness.

Probably if I were more open, they'd worry less. Actually, Mark, Sally, and Tom aren't what they appear to be. I mean, they look kind of weird, hippy, or punk and messy—but actually Mark is a talented musician, composes his own music, and Sally and Tom are artists, or trying to be. Sally paints amazing stuff, and Tom makes mind-boggling things out of trash he collects, huge pieces of sculpture. We all use drugs some, to expand our senses, to free our minds, but we're serious about things we read and think about, and talk about. We all plan to go on in school. I've just gotten sick of the preppie look and my conformist life to date and can't explain it all to my folks. I love them, but feel my interests and values are very different than theirs. I can bring my grades back up, if I want; but at the moment, I'm bored with my courses, and don't want to study like I used to. I have a good record to date, and my PSATs were good. I bet my SATs will be even better. I'll get into a decent college, if I want. As for team sports, I'm sick of them and all the backbreaking practice time. I'm not All-American, so why waste time with sports? Since age ten, I was captain of Little League and every team. My priorities have changed. I want something new. Hearing and making cool music, clubs and discos are fun—for a change. I'm sure I'll continue to have new interests and ideas, and not throw my life down the sewer. My folks just have to learn that being different from them or the way I used to be is not the ruination of my life or a sign that I've stopped loving them.

Parent-Therapist Contact with Less Intact Families

In contrast to the above vignette, clinicians in mental health clinics and social agency practice generally work with more disturbed adolescents and families, which requires, not infrequently, being available almost on demand and offering "consistency, reliability, concern, and deep involvement in the welfare of the family and its everyday problems. The degree of investment necessary to maintain the contact over time varies with the adaptive and supportive capacities inherent in the family" (Anthony and McGinnis, 1978, p. 333). These authors emphasize the importance of respect and gentleness in work with borderline and psychotic individuals, who generally feel unworthy and have low self-esteem. Such families require flexibility, patience, and a gradual nonconfrontive approach. Severely disturbed parents commonly relate to the present as if it were their own chaotic past, and therefore are easily subject to regression and withdrawal. Their weak ego boundaries and primitive defenses make them subject to intense dependency longings and a propensity to make a symbiotic merger with the therapist. Frequently, these extremely disturbed parents are consumed with trivial preoccupations, recriminations, and obsessive questions, and therefore engage in prolonged and frequent phone calls to the therapist.

Parents are commonly seen in individual, family, and group therapy. Additionally, parent education groups are useful in providing ego support and clarification, as well as peer support with others engaged in similar parenting dilemmas. Factual information is provided to help parents to know what to expect, what is age appropriate, and what might well constitute effective handling. Parent groups affirm the importance of continued parent-adolescent ties and the crucial nature of the parental role.

Continued parent-adolescent bonds are crucial, even when severe pathology requires separation, via placement in residential care or hospitalization. Successful treatment of adolescents in placement requires establishment of a bond of trust, an alliance with the staff of the institution. Excluding parents makes them fearful and distrustful of staff, thereby creating severe loyalty conflicts for the teenager. Parents may become alarmed by their adolescent's complaints and requests to return home and may ignore staff recommendation and remove their teenager.

Rosenthal (1975) suggested that authoritative work on the psychology of adolescence has for too long disregarded the reality of a sense of filial obligation in adolescents, even in those who are seriously disturbed or whose parents have accepted very little responsibility for them. It is suggested that the teenager struggles against this sense of obligation with rebellion and withdrawal, while often unconsciously yearning to repay parents or make reparation for real or fantasied damage done to loved or needed objects. Such conflicting feelings, if and when worked through, help an adolescent achieve a cohesive sense of self and improve the parent-child relationship; as it feels safer to have some tie, even a negative one with a demanding parent, than none at all. Concerns regarding damage done to one's family are recurrent themes frequently expressed by even the most disturbed teenager.

Summary

The goal of establishing empathic relationships with and within the family is now more generally recognized. We have moved beyond viewing the troubled teenager as the helpless victim of bad parents and place greater emphasis on reality experiences, life stressors affecting parents and teenagers, and parents unconsciously reexperiencing their own symbiotic parent-child ties. Recognizing parent-child bonds, even in the face of parental neglect, has enabled us more effectively to comprehend filial obligations and loyalty conflicts when children "protect" even abusive parents. It is hoped that treatment will enable parents and adolescents to relinquish their defensive dismissal of each other and to experience each other more realistically, without the above noted unconscious assumptions and projected identifications. The crucial clinical issue is the avoidance of a misalliance, predicated on old stereotypes, staff's rescue fantasies, and/or common negative countertransference responses to parents, which generally mirror the distorted relationships within the family.

Newer, more effective clinical approaches in work with the parents of a severely disturbed adolescent avoid any hint of patronizing or ignoring parents. The teenager's need to see the parents treated with respect is now more clearly recognized. Disrespect and conflict is accepted within the family system but is feared and abhorred by the adolescent if it comes from outside. The deeply troubled adolescent is psychically unseparated from the parents, despite physical separation in the case of placement or hospitalization. Thus, teenagers commonly mirror or experience parental anxieties, anger, and resistance. It is often easiest to reach them as they experience some adult alliance and coalition between staff and parents, for they then feel allowed to move outside their family system to make new attachments.

Bibliography

ANTHONY, J. and McGINNIS, M. (1978). Counseling Very Disturbed Parents. In *Helping Parents Help Their Children*, ed. E. L. Arnold, pp. 328–41. New York: Brunner/Mazel.

BARNES, M. (1965). Casework with Children. Smith College Studies in Social Work, 35(3):173–188.

CHETHIK, M. (1976). Work with Parents: Treatment of the Parent-Child Relationship. *J. Amer. Acad. Child Psychiatry*, 15.

ESMAN, A. (1985). A Developmental Approach to the Psychotherapy of Adolescents. In *Adolescent Psychiatry Vol. 12: Developmental and Clinical Studies*, eds. S. Feinstein, M. Sugar, A. Esman, J. Looney, A. Schwartzberg, and A. Sorosky, pp. 119–33. Chicago: University of Chicago Press.

HAMILTON, G. (1947). *Psychotherapy in Child Guidance*. New York: Columbia University Press.

KEITH, C. R. (1968). The Therapeutic Alliance in Child Psychiatry. *J. Child Psychiatry*, 7:31:53.

KESSLER, J. (1966). *Psychoapthology of Childhood*. Englewood Cliffs, N. J.: Prentice-Hall.

ROSENTHAL, M. (1975). Filial Obligation in Adolescence: An Orientation. In *Adolescent Psychiatry, Vol. 5: Developmental and Clinical Studies*, eds. S. Feinstein and P. Giovacchini, pp. 151–74. New York: Jason Aronson.

SOURS, J. A. (1978). The Application of Child Analytic Principles to Forms of Child Psychotherapy. In *Child Analysis and Therapy*, ed. J. Glenn, pp. 615–46. New York/London: Jason Aronson.

PART VI

The Treatment Process

24

The Treatment Relationship

Alliance, Transference,
Countertransference,
and the Real Relationship

In her seminal paper, "Adolescence," Anna Freud (1958) likened this time of life to states of mourning and unhappy love affairs; mourning for the parental objects of the past is inevitable, as are the crushes and unhappy love affairs outside of the family. These emotional struggles and the pursuit of new loves are fraught with extreme urgency and immediacy, leaving little emotional energy or libido available for investment in the past or in the treatment process.

> If this supposition as to the libido distribution in the adolescent personality can be accepted as a correct statement, it can serve to explain some of our young patients' behavior in treatment, such as their reluctance to cooperate, their lack of involvement in the therapy or in the relationship to the analyst; their battle for the reduction of weekly sessions; their unpunctuality; their missing of treatment sessions for the sake of outside activities; their sudden breaking off of treatment altogether [p. 263].

The course of the psychotherapeutic work with adolescents is widely acknowledged to be difficult, ambiguous, and challenging.

Treatment can be behavioral, supportive, uncovering and reconstructive, or interpretive and reflective. Mistakes, failures to assess the adolescent patient properly, or inflexible provision of all patients with one modality or form of treatment can cause a disturbed teenager to become intractably disturbed. Some clinics only offer short term treatment for all; others provide only a family or group therapy form of intervention. Too frequently slogans, panaceas, and agency bias guide practice. Such programs do not respect individualism and deny the necessity for diagnostic and assessment planning. The assessment process has been presented fully in Part II, and ideally provides guidelines to determine the following: the appropriate model of intervention; the adolescent's level of anxiety, conscious motivation for therapy, and ability to relate and form a therapeutic relationship; the extent of pain experienced, and inflicted on others; and the nature and extent of arrest and regression, defenses and resistance.

Most, if not all, therapists would agree that the young teenage patient is not a candidate for thorough and complete psychoanalysis or intensive psychotherapy. The adolescent often comes for help unwillingly, at the behest or pressure of parents; schools; and in some cases, courts and probation departments. As the young person is attempting to separate from the family, form an identity, and make important peer attachments, he or she is commonly loath to enter into a relationship and attachment with a new adult. Fear of therapy, of a new powerful adult, and of the discovery of one's inner troubled self, is generally much stronger than the wish for assistance in self-understanding and development of one's new identity. This common lack of motivation and responsibility for initiating therapy dictates the modified goals of psychotherapy. It is generally unrealistic to expect total resolution of conflict. The goal, rather, should be to assist the young person sufficiently to facilitate better ego functioning and improved self-esteem, thereby enabling the teenager to move forward developmentally and to achieve mastery and gratification within the limits of social reality.

In treatment with adults we seek to restore or facilitate relatively normal functioning, but in work with adolescents, "we clear the way for further development, but we cannot predict where it is going to lead. Withstanding this pain of uncertainty, often disguised as a scientific dilemma, is a capacity the therapist must acquire in order to cope with adolescent patients who revive in him the uncertainty of his own adolescence" (Ekstein 1983, p. 145).

Rarely in work with adolescents is the conclusion of therapy a genuine completion or cure. Treatment frequently is interrupted abruptly. The teenager may withdraw or rebel and refuse future appointments. It is always preferable that the termination not be abrupt, but rather be effected over a period of time to permit patient and clinician to separate with mutual respect and regard, even when they are not in accord with the decision to end their work together. Ending on a reasonable note is preferable to the adolescent's desperate rebellion or angry submission and pseudo-compliance with scheduled sessions. This gentler conclusion often enables the adolescent to reenter therapy at some later point, when he or she wishes to assume initiative and responsibility for treatment.

I. The Therapeutic Alliance

The therapeutic alliance is seen as emanating out of the adolescent's "conscious or unconscious wish to cooperate and his readiness to accept the therapist's aid in overcoming intense difficulties and resistances" (Sandler, Kennedy, and Tyson, 1980, p. 45). The alliance does not arise solely out of the adolescent's wish for pleasure in the treatment situation, but "involves an acceptance of the need to deal with internal problems . . . in the face of internal resistance or external resistance, as from the family" (p. 45). Some clinicians and researchers query the validity of distinguishing between the therapeutic alliance and transference. Arlow and Brenner (1966) and Brenner (1980) made no distinction. The terms *working alliance* and *therapeutic alliance* have been borrowed from the field of adult psychoanalysis. Discussion of the therapeutic alliance dates from Zetzel's 1956 paper on transference. Greenson's later paper (1965) suggested the term *working alliance*. Curtis (1977) noted that in the last twenty-seven years, analysts have expanded their sphere of interest beyond the patient's intrapsychic life to embrace all aspects of the therapeutic relationship. The therapeutic alliance is not an end unto itself, but rather a means to the end, a way of facilitating the treatment process. It is based upon a new and correct relationship, "a fund of trust" (Basch, 1980, p. 133), whereby the patient views the therapist as an important adult with whom the adolescent is willing to work. Additional to the positive feelings for the therapist, the alliance is based upon the ego's accurate appraisal of a need for understanding and its gratification in being understood. Adolescents will only look to therapy for relief if they have the capacity for self-observation and some awareness that there is an internal problem. Not all troubled adolescents have enough inner ego structure for self-awareness and self-observation.

> Most psychotic and borderline [adolescents] are able to form a symbiotic relationship with the therapist. This merging of ego boundaries means that for a long period of therapy, the patient will use the therapist's ego as his own observing and synthesizing ego. This merging of the therapist's and [adolescent's] ego can be called a "pseudoalliance" since it does not represent a true therapeutic splitting (self-observing and self-experiencing) of the child's own ego. The therapist consistently and repetitively interjects

his own secondary process and rational behavior into the treatment situation [Keith, 1968, p. 38].

Often teenagers do not experience their symptoms as painful. When their self-injurious or maladaptive behaviors are ego-syntonic, rather than ego-dystonic, they do not experience anguish or anxiety. Rather the adults (namely, parents and teachers) suffer and commonly forcibly refer the adolescent for therapy. In such situations, the parents usually make the initial alliance, which can support their determination and commitment to bring their oppositional teenager for treatment. Hopefully, even the resistive adolescent eventually will participate in the engagement and treatment process and extend the therapist "provisional credibility, that is, a belief that he can help" (Basch, 1980, p. 67).

Basch (1980) noted that clinicians cannot prove themselves, or convince a patient of their goodwill or ability. The therapist tries to show the patient that neither anger nor doubt will deter him or her from the goal of trying to be of help. Some adolescents cannot enter therapy and sustain an alliance because of an overpowering wish to keep their private lives private. Some are fearful of sharing sexual and masturbatory fantasies. Others are mortified by shame, envy, and profound self-consciousness, oblivious to the universality of the age-appropriate anxieties that burden them.

Even without an alliance, some adolescents improve as a result of treatment, gaining symptom relief and rentering the path of normal development. Sandler et al. (1980) cautioned that such improvement may be treatment compliance rather than treatment alliance. Many family realities interfere with the teenager's freedom to use treatment. Family secrets, loyalty conflicts, parental ambivalance about therapy, all can interfere with the development of an alliance. The slow progress of therapy and lack of immediate gratification, cause some teenagers to terminate therapy quickly. Then there is the puzzling situation of the adolescent who continues in treatment without seeming to progress in sessions, but whose outer life shows marked improvements. This phenomenon may well be due to the sheer presence of a therapist with specific personal characteristics, e.g., patience and humor, that impress a given teenager, in spite of an apparent lack of a trusting dialogue and communication.

The engagement and development of a therapeutic alliance often proceeds in a tenuous fashion. The alliance commonly is precarious and fragile, in part, because of the pervasive adolescent alienation in society today. Meissner (1985) stated that alienation is basically a pathology of the self, interfacing between intrapsychic dynamics and the existent social and cultural realities. Alienation includes a basic sense of loneliness and estrangement; continued frustration; and chronic despair, hopelessness, and helplessness. Common adolescent responses are a disinclination to ask for help and, instead, seeking of escape through drugs, cults, alcohol abuse, and rebellion against prevailing adult values and standards. Gedo (1972) cautioned us about many unexplained and unpredicated failures in work with adolescents caused by "covert adherence to unreason, certainty and simplicity. At any rate, times are now out of joint, and many patients whose personality structure should permit successful [therapy] are impossible to treat because of the content of their value system" (p. 220). These extremes of alienation distort the young person's growth and interfere with adaptive later resolutions. In the more normal course of things, alienation is not so extreme or long-lasting; and eventually, it is resolved into new and adaptive adult patterns of identification and role functioning.

As the adolescent seeks bridges and transitional objects to support separation and emancipation from families, therapists often can be used as the trusted adult friend, educator (Meeks, 1971), ego ideal or role model, or transitional parent (Ekstein, 1983). Thus, in the course of the shaky alliance, the therapist, transitional-object parent substitute, must remain firm, consistent, and not engulf or tenaciously hold the adolescent patient. The teenager must be permitted intermissions, or intermittent courses of treatment. Often permission given for this trial and error disruptive course of therapy is the crucial ingredient in maintaining a continuous therapeutic alliance with an adolescent patient, serving to bring the adolescent back, time after time, in the course of recurrent stress and pain.

II. Transference and Countertransference

Transference

There is considerable difficulty in defining transference and countertransference. These terms have been mistakenly used to explain any and all behavior, reactions, and feelings experienced and expressed between patient and therapist. In his earlier considerations of transference, Freud (1912, 1915, 1916–1917) stated that all people unconsciously displace and transfer the libidinal aspects of their primary object relationships to current object relationships. The term *transference* is derived from adult psychoanalytic therapy and refers to the views and relations the patient presents about significant early childhood objects, namely parents, sibs, and significant caretakers. Transference phenomena are expressed in the patient's current perceptions, thoughts, fantasies, feelings, attitudes, and behavior in regard to the analyst (Sandler, Kennedy, and Tyson, 1980). In the course of work with children and adolescents, the relationship between the young patient and the analyst is "often a complicated mixture of elements of a real relationship, and extension into the analysis of current relationships, and a repetition or even a revival of the past" (Tyson, 1978, p. 213).

In 1966, at a panel considering problems of transference in clinical work with young patients, there was overall consensus that transference neurosis cannot take place in children until there has been sufficient structural development to allow for internalized intersystemic conflicts. Tyson (1978) did not believe that this structural development can be present until the superego is independent of parental influence, which is usually at the time of puberty, or early adolescence. Blos (1972) dated it later. In his view, the infantile neurosis only acquires delineation and structure as a central unconscious conflict in late adolescence, with the greater solidification of the personality. Tolpin (1970) restricted the definition of infantile neurosis to the repressed conflicts of the phallic-oedipal phase, for patients whose early development has been normal. Anna Freud (1971) underscored the reality that development and structure that results in an infantile neurosis, represents a positive sign of substantial personality growth. This relatively well-endowed and highly developed child is the rare patient in contemporary clinics and social agencies. More commonly treated are children assessed as "less than neurotic," connoting early traumata and developmental failures with pre-oedipal levels of arrest. Due to constitutional deficits, lack of suitable objects, and improper environmental handling, children in this latter group have inferior object relationships; weak identification; incomplete structuralization; permeable id-ego boundaries; and distorted, deformed and immature egos (A. Freud, 1971). These children, lacking precise self and other distinctions and self and object constancy do not have the capacity to form genuine transference. They more commonly merge, relate in a part object fashion, or evidence a habitual style of relating. Even the healthier children seen in psychoanalysis present only a short-lived, circumscribed transference neurosis.

Tolpin (1978) emphasized that "for patients with structural deficits, genetic reconstructions and interpretations of conflict are ineffectual because these interpretations bypass and obscure the central pathology" (p. 181). Such young patients have faulty self-esteem, lack of sense of direction, and manifest anxiety, depression, and a lack of firm values and ideals; they develop self-object transferences that must be distinguished from the classic definition and understanding of transference. Self-object transference (i.e., merger and mirror transferences) are not the displacement phenomena of classic transference, but rather a use of the therapist to provide for the patient a missing part of the self.

Subtypes of Transference

Because children and adolescents commonly still reside with the significant early objects, they generally do not displace feelings and defenses and perceptions from their past. Rather, more generally they demonstrate:

1. Habitual modes of relating [revealing in treatment various aspects of character and behavior as they would to any person]
2. Transference of current relationships [whereby in treatment the child's and adolescent's mode of relating is an extension of, or defensive displacement from, the relationship of primary objects]
3. Transference which is predominantly that of past experiences [i.e., when past experiences, conflicts, defenses, and wishes are revived in treatment, as a consequence of analytic work and are displaced onto the therapist in the manifest or latent preconscious content]
4. Transference neurosis [meaning the concentration of the conflicts, repressed infantile wishes, fantasies, etc., on the person of the therapist with the relative diminution of their manifestations elsewhere] [Sandler, Kennedy, and Tyson, 1980, pp. 78–104]

Externalization in the Transference

Furman (1980) discussed various forms of externalization (in attributing any aspect of the self to the external world) in transference. Children and adolescents commonly do battle with their environments and use the therapist to represent a part of their personality structure. During the adolescent upheaval and rebellion, externalization and projections are common defenses, whereby the teenager wards off inner conflict, and the superego function is relegated to outside authority figures whom the teenager defies, but also invites to control or punish the displayed disobedience and defiance (Furman, 1980).

> "However, the externalization not only changes an inner battle into an outer one; it also supplants a very harsh inner threat into a usually milder punishment from the outside. The visible misbehavior is seen as less of a violation than the inner forbidden activity or wish, e.g., masturbatory activity or sexual or aggressive feelings towards forbidden objects [p. 271].

The reawakened oedipal passions often create profound need for punishment and parental disapproval. If parents and educators mistakenly fulfill the assigned superego role of harsh disapproval or punishment or lower expectations and offer overgratification and permissiveness, they fail to keep the young person in the age-appropriate inner conflict and developmental struggle. Massive frustration and restrictions, overgratification, inconsistency, and the lethal combination of both create a fertile ground for pathologic outcomes. These commonly stimulate the adolescent's regressive sadomasochistic strivings for even harsher punishments and/or failure to develop self control.

Adolescent Transference Patterns

There are specific types of transference phenomena, which may be the adolescent's habitual style of relating, or extensions of the relationships with the primary objects. Commonly these patterns will disrupt the therapeutic alliance and obstruct ego growth. Thus, they require early identification and active management (Meeks, 1971). Meeks noted the following problematic adolescent transference phenomena: (1) the erotic transference; (2) the omnipotent transference; (3) the negative transference; (4) the superego transference—the therapist as superego.

The erotic or sexual transference is common in treatment of adolescent clients. It may prove to be alarming, as the young teenager especially is not comfortable with his or her burgeoning sexuality; and thus panicky feelings can erupt, causing flight or extreme withholding during sessions. Often such feelings arise out of reawakened oedipal feelings or in direct response to attraction to the therapist as a sexual and exciting person. Often adolescent patients cannot tolerate a young therapist of the opposite sex because of the alarming intensity of their fantasies and attraction. Thus seeing a clinician of the same sex serves to suppress excitement, and therapy can be maintained more comfortably. Obviously, sexual excitement can also be created in same sex patient-therapist dyads, when the young patient experiences homosexual erotic arousal. The therapeutic stance of objectivity, calm, and actual unavailability does much to quiet and defuse the teenager's excitement and alarm in the wake of heterosexual or homosexual erotic transference patterns.

The idealizing or omnipotent transference puts the therapist in the role of the all-powerful, all-knowing, perfect person. This idealization can abruptly shift to a view of the therapist as a devalued, deidealized object. These forms of relating commonly reflect the narcissistic disorders in adolescent patients. Their self-esteem regulation is faulty and highly dependent on outside accolades and approval. As the treatment process unfolds and the adolescent's narcissistic balance improves, there will be a correspondingly more realistic appraisal of the therapist. Many adolescents do idealize the therapist and require that the therapist serve as a mirror or extension of the patient's self, giving back or mirroring the same idealizations. Goldberg (1972) recommended that the therapist not confront, but "accept the narcissistic disorder of the patient as existing alongside a relative paucity of object love, and not try to change narcissistic investment into object love. Treatment consists ... of a gradual undermining of the grandiosity and exhibitionism of the patient as well as a diminution of his search for unattainable ideals" (Goldberg, 1972, p. 5). In all, the therapy focuses on recognition and acceptance of the adolescent's narcissism in a nonjudgmental fashion, utilizing the transference to demonstrate the use of the clinician as a regulator and modulator of self-esteem.

The negative transference can rarely be tolerated by the child or adolescent patient. Negative feelings may be habitual hostile attitudes toward all adults. Defensive hostility may cover painful feelings of shame, anxiety, and inadequacy. Anger in response to a confrontive interpretation or to a therapist's rage and frustration is not a transference phenomenon; rather, it is an affective response to the reality in the therapy interchange. "True negative transference reactions occur [only] when situations in therapy reactivate earlier experiences in which negative attitudes towards important loved objects predominated" (Meeks, 1971, p. 129). Meeks discussed management of the negative transference and emphasized objective acceptance of the adolescent's feelings, avoidance of counterattack, and firm refusal to accept unrealistic blame and excessive criticism. As the adolescent is helped to explore and comprehend his anger, the empathic therapist tries to reflect his or her recognition of how things appear and feel from the patient's perspective.

The therapist as superego evolves out of the rigid, often brittle and harsh, superego of latency. Because the adolescent cannot independently assume firm impulse control, he or she often assigns the therapist the role of conscience, moral prohibitor, restrictor, or educator. It is obvious that clinicians do have their own value systems and are not neutral about moral questions. Commonly these moral biases must be articulated and shared in a climate of fairness, calm, and control. The therapist cannot force his or her views on patients, but "neither does he attempt to avoid his responsibility as an adult to offer his ethical conclusions ... such openness in discussions also encourages the adolescent to think about his own assumptions and to use his own powers of logic to the best possible advantage" (Meeks, 1971, p. 135). Kohlberg and Gilligan (1971, 1980) stated that many current adolescent moral dilemmas arise because some adolescents possess formal logical capacities without having developed equally mature moral judgment.

In summary, transference as manifested by adolescents must not be understood to represent displacement from early objects. The teenager residing with his or her family most commonly evidences current thoughts, feelings and behavior patterns that relate to parents in the here and now. Thus, there may be nothing special or unique in the way the adolescent relates to the clinician. We see habitual modes of relating and transfer or spillover of current relationships in therapy (Sandler, Kennedy, and Tyson, 1975). There is a spillover—often both ways—in that the teenager may act out at home and school as a result of therapy, while simultaneously presenting the therapist with all of the behavior that originated in and is currently enacted in the parent-child relationship. The adolescent who suffers structural deficits, depends on an external object, and therefore, creates a self-object transference relationship.

Countertransference

Countertransference, like transference, is an overused term that commonly covers any and all feelings and reactions from the therapist in response to the patient. Giovacchini (1985) noted that adolescents have a propensity for creating stress and difficulty in the course of treatment because of their reticence about becoming involved in therapy or because of their inclination to express themselves through action rather than words and feelings. The therapist's reactions and responses to these stresses are currently viewed, not as obstacles, but as valuable assets in providing technical guidance to deal with taxing treatment dilemmas. Commonly a frank and nonanxious examination of feelings facilitates resolution of various therapeutic impasses. Countertransference is distinguished by its arising, not out of a patient's behavior alone, but from unconscious and preconscious forces within the therapist that cause the therapist to react to the patient in ways inappropriate to the current reality of the therapeutic relationship. Such unrealistic, unprovoked reactions are displacements from significant early relationships with the therapist's sibs and parents (Dewald 1964). Giovacchini differed with the above formulation and (1985b) offered a broader definition of countertransference (and transference):

> I believe countertransference is ubiquitous; it is found in every analytic interaction in the same way transference is. Everything a therapist or a patient thinks, feels, or does can be viewed as being on a hierarchal spectrum, one end dominated by unconscious, primary process elements, and the other end dominated by reality-oriented, secondary process factors. When a patient directs his feelings towards the therapist, the primary process elements of the spectrum represent transference, and in a similar fashion, that part of the analyst's responses that stems primarily from the more primitive levels of his psyche can be viewed as countertransference [p. 451].

Some clinicians would make distinctions along Giovacchini's spectrum, and designate reality-oriented factors as counterreactions, and those that emanate out of unconscious primary process variables as countertransference.

Racker (1968) considered two types of countertransference: one that is rooted in concordant identifications, where the therapist is empathic, and the other that is based on complimentary identifications, where the therapist is the recipient of unwanted projections. Giovacchini (1985b) also divided countertransference into categories: (1) homogeneous, the responses and reactions most commonly expected from most therapists; and (2) idiosyncratic, unique responses of a given therapist, based on his specific character, personality, and life history. Negative idiosyncratic responses are viewed as due to the therapist's untamed or unmodified personal pathology. Positive idiosyncratic responses may result in increased tolerance, talent, charisma and fit with the most difficult adolescent patients. There is wide variation in the patient-therapist fit. One cannot work with equal effectiveness with all patients. "Rather than view treatability only in terms of the patient's limitations, it is more realistic to consider the patient-therapist relationship as the axis that determines treatability. A patient may not be treatable by a particular therapist, but that does not make that patient untreatable" (Giovacchini, 1985b, p. 450).

Marcus (1980) defined countertransference as a reaction to the specific patient, to the patient's transference response, or to other components of the patient's material. When countertransference is used defensively, it can interrupt or disrupt the therapist's analyzing function, because it "activates a developmental residue and creates or revives unconscious conflict, anxiety, and defensiveness" (Marcus, 1980, p. 286). Thus, it is a negative contaminant or a positive therapeutic tool to aid in the interpretation of patients' unconscious. Interpretation of the therapist's own reactions or countertransference can be a most effective treatment technique but this communication requires skill, correct timing, and empathy.

Many researchers (Proctor 1959; Epstein and Feiner 1979; Giovacchini 1985; Wallace and Wallace, 1985) note that countertransference dilemmas are greatest with impulsive, acting-out, and highly narcissistic patients, who tax, provoke, and immobilize therapists. Counterresistance is a common response. Frequently clinicians are tempted to counterattack, or mobilize infantile aspects of their superego against the patient's id, which can result in rejection, punishment, or hostile demands for compliance. Not infrequently, the therapist falls into the patient's family's pitfalls, and thereby unwittingly replicates the negative parenting responses. When relating to professional colleagues, a therapist can unconsciously use a patient as a narcissistic extension: as a source of pride and praise, or as a source of shame and professional mortification. Patients may be misused and abused to satisfy drives of voyeurism and curiosity or to gratify unconscious aggressive or masochistic needs in the clinician. Signs of countertransference dilemmas are the therapist's chronic lateness, boredom, fear of and anger at a patient, repeated forgetting of the patient's sessions, and scheduling mistakes (Litner, 1969). Supervision, consultation, and personal treatment help the therapist to stay in touch with, and in control of, his or her own unconscious and preconscious unresolved early conflicts.

III.   The Real Relationship

In a recent extraordinary little book, Bruno Bettelheim (1983) attempted to correct what he viewed as the mistranslation of Freud and many of his most important psychoanalytic concepts. Bettelheim's thesis is that the English translations of Freud are seriously flawed, and erroneous conclusions have been reached about Freud the man and also about the process of psychoanalysis. Bettelheim's goal is to show the humane Freud, who he presents as a "humanist in the best sense of the word. His greatest concern was with man's innermost being, to which he most frequently referred through the use of a metaphor—man's soul—because the word 'soul' evokes so many emotional connotations" (p. xi). Drawing from one of Freud's letters to Jung, Bettelheim quoted, "Psychoanalysis is in essence a cure through love."

Perhaps the abounding mistranslations and misunderstanding of Freud have led analytically oriented clinicians to select a posture of a rigid blank screen, presenting themselves as unaffected by a patient's verbal and behavioral manifestations. Adherents to this mode are impassive, silent, and unresponsive to all they hear or see.

> The result is that too often perfectly decent, friendly, curious and helpful people act like robots when they begin to function as psychotherapists. They literally wonder whether they should smile or shake hands upon greeting a patient the first time, worry whether such behavior might already "contaminate" the field, as if a relationship between two living beings could be reduced to the artificial atmosphere of a physics or chemistry laboratory [Basch, 1980, p. 4].

This misunderstanding of Freud's teachings has created what Basch called the dogma and myth of the therapist's anonymity. He recommended injection of a personal note when appropriate. In work with adolescents, often one does not wish to stimulate their fantasies or encourage a regression, which is the goal and outcome of the blank screen stance. Adolescents generally cannot tolerate a passive silent, stilled approach. Meeks (1971) suggested that because of their age-appropriate narcissism, distrust of adults, and expectation of criticism, they react to silence, withholding, and formality with intense anxiety, flight, and increased defensiveness. Alexander (1963) was one of the first to challenge the neutrality of the analyst, and stated emphatically that the analyst's values are subtly learned by the patient through verbal and nonverbal communications, and the experience of genuineness, warmth, and respect is a corrective emotional experience with a real person. Seductiveness, verbosity, intrusiveness, and effusiveness are counterindicated. Marmor (1982) emphasized the value of empathic warmth, active attentive listening, and active participation in the treatment process.

In very recent years, some self-disclosure has been recommended, particularly in work with teenagers. Adolescence is a period of life that commonly reflects some transient ego impoverishment and impairment. Personal openness has been advocated "to show the therapist as a real person, apart from the patient and his parents, who can recognize the adolescent and respect him as an individual" (Weiner and King, 1977, p. 458). The interpersonal interactional rule is suggested by Blanck and Blanck (1979) in their description of the therapist as developmental reorganizer of the patient's subphase inadequacies. In essence, therapists serve their adolescent patients as new object and role models, and as trusted private adult friends who provide guidance in the fight and struggle for self-understanding. Recent writings acknowledge the nontransferential ways in which a therapist's gender, age, humor, style, and physical features affect child and adolescent patients (Tyson, 1980).

Anna Freud (in Sandler, Kennedy, and Tyson, 1980) noted the realistic difficulties in keeping separate and distinct the transference relationship and the real relationship, particularly in situations where there has been parent loss through death or abandonment. When natural parents are present, children and adolescents frequently try to compel the therapist to act as an intermediary between themselves and their parents and/or reject their parents in new allegiances and identifications with the therapist. The nonanalyst clinician generally sees a teenager once or twice a week; and this infrequency of contact creates, by design, more of a real relationship than a transference relationship. Support, reflections, enhancement of self-esteem, education, and guidance in a talkative and responsive interchange are more frequent interventions than interpretations of the transference, defenses, fantasies, and unconscious primary process material.

In contrast to the uncovering inherent in psychoanalysis, with the goal of reconstruction of the personality, psychotherapy aims for symptom reduction, behavioral and personality changes, and a return to, or resumption of, normal progressive development. In therapy, the emphasis is on the here-and-now and the adolescent's current significant relationships; in analysis, the primary focus is on the inner conflicts, reconstructions of the past, and reexperiencing through examination of feelings, displacements, and the transference observed in the treatment situation. Overall, the focus of adolescent psychotherapy is on current ego functioning, object relationships, and regulation of self-esteem. This does not rule out making use of symbolic productions presented in the treatment hour. Many creative adolescents wish to share dreams, daydreams, hopes and fantasies, poetry, prose, and paintings. They may be less interested in interpretations about their production or their wish to share them, than in receiving empathic support, acceptance, soothing, and admiration from a trusted and private real person who clearly demonstrates warmth, affection, and respect.

The Treatment Relationship: Case of Carol

Carol, a 17-year-old white middle-class Protestant girl, was referred for therapy by her mother at the recommendation of a friend of the family. The mother's concerns about her daughter were not new. She described Carol as "gifted, impossible, fragile, weak, and given to falling apart." She said that Carol's current profound depression and indecision alarmed her and that Carol was in need of help now to support her continued studies. Carol was enrolled in a highly competitive drama program. Of late she had become indecisive about her course of study and had become nonfunctioning over the summer, doing almost nothing. The mother expressed alarm and anger at Carol's lying about, monosyllabic and immobilized, erratic in her eating and sleeping patterns, and evidencing severe depression. The mother was able to provide a rich and detailed history and expressed the hope that her daughter and the therapist would connect.

The divorced parents were not willing to have regular or even occasional contact with Carol's therapist. Though the parents remained remote, a therapeutic family perspective kept in bold relief the parents' own enormous needs and pressures and their allocation of the sparse emotional and financial resources for themselves and their two children. They jointly paid a scaled-down fee for Carol's treatment until the time when she could handle her payments independently.

Carol was a beautiful young girl, ingenue in appearance, with a cameo face and long straight blond hair worn loose or in a ballet dancer's bun or braid. She was lithe and graceful, demure in manner, anxious to please, shy, and highly motivated for treatment. Very early on, she expressed profound relief at having liked the therapist, stating that she felt they clicked from the start. She was a gifted actress, accepted at several of the finest drama departments. She evidenced considerable additional talent and studied ballet and music seriously; she showed remarkably sophisticated knowledge of literature and real ability in creative writing.

Carol was quite isolated socially and felt shy and inarticulate particularly with female peers. She was more at ease with male peers and received considerable attention from them. At the onset of treatment, she was living with a male fellow student, an actor, and was conflicted and ambivalent about this affair. She experienced depression about her lack of romantic love for this young man and guilt that she used him to take care of her. She described depression, a sense of emptiness, and recurrent feelings of being out of control in regard to disciplined sustained involvement in her drama studies, management of food, and overall care of herself and her belongings. She wanted to be model thin but not a skeleton and at times starved or gorged. She wanted constant reassurance about her beauty, all the while despising herself for being vain and narcissistic, and with shame recounted haranguing her boyfriend a thousand times a day to tell her she was beautiful. She was meticulous about her grooming; but in her eyes, she was slovenly beyond belief in her lack of care of her things and her apartment. Her chaotic room had been a chronic angry battleground between her and her mother since she entered adolescence, and Carol believed the disorder reflected her psychological inner chaos.

Carol's quick establishment of trust was striking, and she experienced great relief to be in therapy with someone she could talk to with ease. She consciously wished to cooperate and recognized the need to deal with internal problems; thus she made a strong and enduring therapeutic alliance. She was always scrupulous about keeping her appointments promptly and regularly and worked hard in the sessions, using insight and responding positively to the therapist's efforts at providing a consistent empathic relationship. Confrontations were avoided as were classic interpretations. Carol's mother had often overpsychologized and been assaultive in her explanations of their conflict and Carol's behavior. Carol benefited from the therapist's deliberate disinclination to make conventional interpretations, her patience, and her waiting for Carol to demonstrate insight and self-observation. During the course of the treatment, this young patient internalized the empathic stance of the therapist, which served to allow her more self-respect and more stabilized self-esteem. This corresponded with Carol's increased understanding of her preconscious and unconscious conflicts. She became more open and spontaneous and delighted in her increased freedom and ability to laugh and enjoy humor. She often commented on feeling 100 percent better in the therapist's presence. Her insights, imagery, creativity, and dream material consistently reflected a most imaginative and intuitive young person in close touch with her unconscious.

Dream material and associations revealed transference feelings toward the idealized, omnipotent, all-good, admiring and loving "mother." Mirror and merger transference phenomena were repeated in Carol's wish to emulate her therapist, who she knew specialized in work with children and adolescents. She chose similar areas of interest. She described wanting to do similar "admirable things so I guess my respect for you and wanting your respect stimulated my donations to a Korean orphan and my volunteer work with abused children." Carol volunteered several hours per week for a year at a child welfare agency, offering art and acting lessons to children in care. "It's time I think of someone besides myself. It feels good to care about those children and not be so obsessed by how I look, how much I weigh, and what they thought of me in class and at auditions."

Carol could describe her need for the therapist to admire her, protect her, and help her modulate overwhelming feelings of depression, anger, or low self-esteem. When she faced auditions she would become frantic and anxious and would request additional sessions each week. She said she took solace in the therapist's belief in her, trust, and hopes for her future. She could articulate a need that the therapist find her exquisite and special, a gifted person of talent and potential. Only after twenty months was she able to stop acting completely perfect and careful and let the therapist see her "infantile, nasty, and complaining bitchy side." She could express grandiose notions about her potential alongside feelings of low self-esteem—that she was sinking to ignominious mediocrity. When she succeeded at auditions, she was sure it was not her acting ability but her beauty which impressed teachers and directors. She spoke of controlling and manipulating others to do her bidding—be it by temper tantrums or becoming immobilized, depressed, and suicidal and dramatic. These patterns ultimately ended as she made therapeutic gains during the lengthy course of her psychotherapy. Aggression became appropriately modulated and no longer turned onto the self or others. She no longer vascilated between idealizations and devaluations of herself and others.

Outside changes were apparent in her being able to live apart from a continuous series of caretaker boyfriends and, instead, develop relationships with female peers and romantic liaisons that involved more equality and mutuality. She became more empathic and less narcissistic in her relationships. She surrendered her perfectionist strivings, shyness and self-consciousness. She used to believe that she was nothing and that acting and drama defined her and gave her life meaning. At the conclusion of therapy, she was more able to consider herself a person of emerging worth who also had acting talent. Instead of striving for superstar fame and fortune, she valued a meaningful career and a personally satisfying life. She no longer viewed conventional experiences such as marriage and children as mediocre and beneath her. Her ever-increasing success at auditions and school, plus receipt of specific honors and recognition were handled with greater calm, less grandiosity and/or fear of imminent failure lurking around the next corner. Her relationships with her parents became more neutral and calm. She no longer depended on bonds of hostile explosive fighting or trying to please and satisfy them with professional triumphs. Carol became more compassionate in her accounts of her parents, having surrendered her unrealistic idealizations and devaluations of them.

The therapist's counter transference responses were varied; early and short-lived frustration about the unavailability of the parents and positive maternal feelings for Carol were tempered by concern about becoming a backstage Pygmalion mother, pushing Carol in her artistic career. At times, Carol's idealizations followed by devaluation of her self, her therapist, and therapy became assaultive and hard to bear with calm equanimity and empathy. Introspection, clarity about Carol's painful history, and empathic recognition of the roots of her narcissistic imbalance enabled the therapist to tolerate the shifts in the transference. Additionally, the therapist consciously contained her demands for compliance when Carol exhibited her "bitchy side" and revealed her sadistic, selfish, and manipulative impulses and actions.

The real relationship was one of warmth and respect. Carol was curious about the therapist and some self-disclosure was provided. The therapist never withheld reasons for schedule changes, when a professional meeting necessitated a shift of hour or day. The patient often brought to sessions tapes of monologues and scripts she had prepared for auditions. The therapist deliberately chose not to reject these offerings or withhold her genuine admiration and respect for the patient's productions. The therapeutic stance of a silent blank screen was scrupulously avoided.

Carol had to terminate her therapy abruptly following success at a most significant audition, which earned her an acting scholarship in Europe. She kept in touch with her therapist and when home, asked for an appointment, or a visit. She wrote on occasion and wanted to share any and all achievements. These letters were answered, and appointments were offered gratis, because of Carol's most limited financial realities. This degree of flexibility was seen as appropriate after the course of a five-year relationship, the actuality of the real relationship, and the therapist's unbroken bond of commitment, respect, and interest in Carol.

Bibliography

ALEXANDER, F. (1963). The Dynamics of Psychotherapy in the Light of Learning Theory. *Amer. J. Psychiatry.*. 120:440–48.

ARLOW, J. and BRENNER, C. (1966). The Psychoanalytic Situation. In *Psychoanalysis in America*, ed. R. E. Litman, pp. 22–43, 133–138. New York: International Universities Press.

BASCH, M. (1980). *Doing Psychotherapy.* New York: Basic Books.

BETTELHEIM, B. (1983). *Freud and Man's Soul.* New York: Knopf.

BLANCK, G. and BLANCK, R. (1979). *Ego Psychology I—Theory and Practice.* New York: Columbia University Press.

BLOS, P. (1972). The Epigenesis of the Adult Neurosis. *Psychoanalytic Study of the Child*, 27:106–35. New York/Chicago: Quadrangle Books.

BRENNER, C. (1980). Working Alliance, Therapeutic Alliance and Transference. In *Psychoanalytic Exploration of Technique—Discourse on the Theory of Therapy.* ed. H. Blum, pp. 137–57. New York: International Universities Press.

CURTIS, H. [1977] (1980). The Concept of Therapeutic Alliance: Implications for the Widening Scope. In *Psychoanalytic Exploration of Technique: Discourse on the Theory of Therapy*, ed. H. Blum pp. 159–92. New York: International Universities Press.

DEWALD, P. A. (1964). *Psychotherapy: A Dynamic Approach.* New York: Basic Books.

EKSTEIN, R. (1983). The Adolescent Self During the Process of Termination of Treatment: Termination, Interruption, or Intermission. In *Adolescent Psychiatry, Vol. 11: Developmental and Clinical Studies* eds. M. Sugar, S. Feinstein, J. Looney, A. Schwartzberg, and A. Sorosky, pp. 125–46 Chicago: University of Chicago Press.

EPSTEIN, L. and FEINER, A. H. (1979). *Countertransference.* New York: Jason Aronson.

FREUD, A. (1958). Adolescence. *Psychoanalytic Study of the Child*, 13:255–78. New York: International Universities Press.

_____ (1962). Assessment of Childhood Disturbances. *Psychoanalytic Study of the Child*, 17:149–158. New York: International Universities Press.

_____ (1971). The Infantile Neurosis—Genetic and Dynamic Considerations. *Psychoanalytic Study of the Child*, 26:79–90. New York: Quadrangle Books.

FREUD, S. (1912). The Dynamics of Transference. *Standard Edition*, 12:97–108. London: Hogarth Press.

_____ (1915). Observations on Transference-Love. *Standard Edition*, 12:157–71. London: Hogarth Press.

_____ (1916–1917). Introductory Lectures on Psychoanalysis. *Standard Edition*, 12:15–16. London: Hogarth Press.

FURMAN, E. (1980). Transference and Externalization in Latency. *Psychoanalytic Study of the Child*, 35:267–84. New Haven: Yale University Press.

GEDO, J. E. (1972). The Dream of Reason Produces Monsters. *J. Amer. Psychoanal. Assn.*, 20:199–223.

GIOVACCHINI, P. (1985a). Introduction: Countertransference Responses to Adolescents. In *Adolescent Psychiatry, Vol. 12: Developmental and Clinical Studies*, eds. S. Feinstein, M. Sugar, A. Esman, J. Looney, A. Schwartzberg, and A. Sorosky pp. 447–48. Chicago: University of Chicago Press.

_____ (1985b). Countertransference and the Severely Disturbed Adolescent. *Adolescent Psychiatry, Vol. 12*, pp. 449–67. *See* Giovacchini (1985a).

GOLDBERG, A. (1972). On the Incapacity to Love—a Psychotherapeutic Approach to the Problem in Adolescence. Arch. Gen. Psychiatry, 26 (January): 3–7.

GREENSON, R. R. (1965). The Working Alliance and the Transference Neurosis. *Psychoanal. Q.*, 34:155–81.

KEITH, C. R. (1968). The Therapeutic Alliance in Child Psychiatry. J. Child Psychiatry, 7:31–53.

KOHLBERG, L. and GILLIGAN, C. [1971] (1980). The Adolescent as a Philosopher: The Discovery of the Self in a Postconventional World. In *New Directions in Childhood Psychopathology*, eds. S. Harrison and J. McDermott, Jr., pp. 221–57. New York: International Universities Press.

LITNER, N. (1969). The Caseworker's Self-Observations and the Child's Interpersonal Defenses. *Smith College Studies in Social Work*, 39(2):95–117.

MARCUS, I. (1980). Countertransference and the Psychoanalytic Process in Children and Adolescents. *Psychoanalytic Study of the Child*: 35. New Haven: Yale University Press.

MARMOR, J. (1982). Changes in Psychoanalytic Treatment. In *Curative Factors in Dynamic Psychotherapy*, ed. S. Slipp, pp. 60–70. New York: McGraw-Hill.

MEEKS, J. (1971). *The Fragile Alliance: An Orientation to the Outpatient Psychotherapy of the Adolescent*. Baltimore: Williams & Wilkins.

MEISSNER, W. W. (1985). Adolescent Paranoia: Transference and Countertransference Issues. In *Adolescent Psychiatry, Vol. 12*, 478–508. *See* Feinstein (1985a).

PROCTOR, J. (1959). Countertransference Phenomena in the Treatment of Severe Character Disorders in Children and Adolescents. In *Dynamic Psychopathology in Childhood* eds. L. Jessner and E. Povenstaedt, pp. 293–309. New York: Grune & Stratton.

RACKER, H. (1968). *Transference and Countertransference*. New York: International Universities Press.

SANDLER, J. KENNEDY, H. and TYSON, P. L. (1980). *The Technique of Child Psychoanalysis: Discussion with Anna Freud*. Cambridge, Mass.: Harvard University Press.

TOLPIN, M. (1978). Self Objects and Oedipal Objects. *Psychoanalytic Study of the Child*, 33:167–84. New Haven: Yale University Press.

TYSON, P. (1978). Transference and Developmental Issues in the Analysis of a Prelatency Child. *Psychoanalytic Study of the Child*, 33:213–36. New Haven: Yale University Press.

―――― (1980). The Gender of the Analyst—In Relation to Transference and Countertransference in Prelatency Children. *Psychoanalytic Study of the Child*, 35:321–38. New Haven: Yale University Press.

WALLACE, N. L. and WALLACE, M. E. (1985). Transference/Countertransference Issues in the Treatment of an Acting Out Adolescent. In *Adolescent Psychiatry, Vol. 12*, pp. 468–77. *See* Feinstein (1985a).

WEINER, M. F. and KING, J. W. (1977). Self Disclosure by the Therapist to the Adolescent Patient. In *Adolescent Psychiatry, Vol. 5: Developmental and Clinical Studies*, eds. S. Feinstein and P. Giovacchini, pp. 449–59. New York: Jason Aronson.

ZETZEL, E. R. (1956). Current Concepts of Transference. *Internat. J. Psychoanaly.*, 37:369–78.

25

Resistance and Working Through
Foci in the Middle Phase of Treatment

Resistance, defenses, regression, arrest and "working through" are dealt with during the middle phase of treatment, following the assessment phase and the selection of the appropriate intervention, which includes determination of therapeutic frequency.

Fixation or Arrest

Many disturbed teenagers have experienced puberty but have never made a genuine entry into adolescence. They have become physically mature but are unable to demonstrate appropriate behavioral and psychological responses to the stage of adolescence. They lack an autonomous sense of self and are commonly unsuccessful in the initial separation-individuation resolution, which makes the "secondary separation-individuation, a sine qua non of adolescence, effectively impossible" (Mahler, 1971). In essence, those teenagers masquerade in the bodies of an adolescents, but emotionally, they are suspended in the psychological stage of toddlerhood and are tied to the mother. Their teenage attempts to master the tasks of adolescence are futile, and they cannot maintain a progressive line of development.

The fixation is due to residuals of earlier developmental stages that have acquired and retained strong "charges" of psychic energy and play an important role in later development of mental functioning. Delays in development occur in instinctual, superego, and ego organization and in the unfolding of a sense of self-regard or self-esteem. Such arrests cause various degrees of persistence of primitive ways of gaining satisfaction, of relating to people and to the self, and of reacting defensively to old, even outmoded, dangers. In addition to constitutional reasons for fixation, e.g., intellectual and ego endowment, there are inevitable life experiences and stresses that overwhelm some immature egos. Trauma produces helplessness, due to the inability of the psyche to understand, cope, and adapt to the injury or shock; and fixation can be the result. Frequently, there is also the unfortunate combination of excessive gratification and excessive frustration, which contributes to the cessation of development. A three-year-old boy would not understand his parents' separation and divorce; and the frustration at loss of the father and overgratification through complete possession of the adored oedipal object, the mother, could well constitute a trauma. The mother, in turn, might be overly indulgent and overattached to her son, especially if the separation was followed by sparse paternal visiting and parenting of the son. Such a series of life events could easily produce in the child, arrest or fixation at the initial separation-individuation and early oedipal phase and arrests in his development of self-esteem due to the narcissistic injury at the loss of the father. The impact of those identical circumstances on a seventeen-year-old boy would be considerably different because of the accumulated cognitive, ego, and superego development and more fully established self-esteem.

Regression

There are three types of regression: (1) Libidinal or drive regression is evident in a teenager's retreat to an earlier phase of instinctual organization, as for example, the adolescent's demonstration of temper tantrums when frustrated or resumed use of head banging as a retreat from the danger of masturbation and accompanying sexual fantasies. (2) Ego regression is manifested by a return to an earlier stage of mental organization, e.g., when a 13-year-old boy with unresolved oedipal conflicts faces surgery and regresses to the magical thinking of toddlerhood. The mental constructs are that of a much younger child, causing the teenager to believe he is being retaliated against because of his guilt and anxiety over aggressivity and rivalry with the father. He thinks primitively and denies the reality need for surgery. The retreat from and relapse in development occurs when a predetermined maturational step and/or a need to cope with stress confronts the young person with difficulties that he or she is unable to master. Regression is often due to unresolved repressed, unconscious earlier difficulties that the child was unable to handle. It can also occur even in the well-developed person in response to profound external stress such as exposure to terrorism or violence or severe and terrifying bodily illness. (3) A regression to infantile omnipotent gradiosity can follow a blow to one's self-esteem. A narcissistic injury, e.g., rejection by a boy or girl friend, can cause a teenager to disavow the pain and retreat from heterosexual interests, regressing to the games and tasks of latency—with childlike preoccupation with fantasies of prowess and superstar athletic achievements.

Regression serves as a defense, attempting to protect the individual against the intolerable anxiety that is aroused. The emerging genital sexuality of adolescence and accompanying incestuous wishes prove overwhelming for some youth, to such a degree that the sexual body image is rejected or denied expression (Laufer, 1978). Laufer (1980) concluded that many adolescents secretly believe they are abnormal and that their fantasies and secret sexual wishes are proof that they are seriously damaged. Teenage patients will generally not confess that they believe that something serious is amiss with their sexual bodies—but rather, commonly complain of loneliness and isolation. Anorexia, depression, delinquency, and substance abuse are common symptoms that the adolescent demonstrates in the attempt to divert or anesthetize himself in the retreat from age-appropriate roles and tasks.

> The regressive affects of such substances as marijuana and alcohol reinforce the regressive developmental pull which is always present in early and mid-adolescence and becomes an impediment to further emotional development . . . It would appear that the severity of problem presentation in adolescents does not necessarily relate to the severity of the underlying illness. . . . [Regressive] symptoms become intractable when youngsters receive so much instinctual gratification from their problems that they cannot abandon them [Miller, 1980, pp. 470–71].

Thus, the immediate clinical task is to attempt to halt the regression so that no more loss of functioning occurs. Crisis work should attempt to restore, as quickly as possible, the highest level of development once attained to enable the adolescent to cope with the urgent life tasks at hand and not to lose further ground or access to age-appropriate roles and expectations. Longer-term therapy initially aims for some degree of reconstruction of the immediate past overwhelming events and stressors to help the adolescent understand his or her present fragmentation, anxieties, depression, and shame. "Unless this is done [promptly] the power of the trauma at puberty continues to operate and prevents the adolescent from undoing the immediate past and integrating (and mastering) the experience of the breakdown" (Laufer, 1980, p. 463).

Laufer conceptualized the adolescent as having two pasts, the immediate past and the preadolescent past. One would not attempt to engage a patient in examining his or her early formative years, while ignoring current pressures and failures. Rather, the therapist strives to support a cognitive and emotional grasp of the recent past so that it can be a link rather than a barrier to immediate ongoing development.

Resistance

Anna Freud (1958, 1978) discussed adolescents' and children's inability or unwillingness to maintain a stable therapeutic alliance, tolerate frustration, and translate feelings into words rather than actions. All of these characteristics can add to conscious and unconscious resistance in the course of psychotherapy. Resistance must be distinguished from a lack of motivation for change or lack of interest in forming a relationship with a professional person. Resistance is defined as the obstruction that evolves in the process of therapy. It may be related to transference phenomena and the defenses which arise against facing or experiencing anxiety-ladened issues and feelings. With adolescents, communication and cooperation can be withheld and sessions missed. Some resistances are present from the very beginning of treatment and are characteristic of the emotional structure of the patient. "These may be called 'character resistances.' As with adults, there is a type of juvenile patient who does not allow anxiety to find expression in thought or words but constantly negates it" (Sandler, Kennedy, and Tyson, 1980, p. 58). This character resistance is distinguished from the opposition that arises in the course of therapy. This latter arises because internal conflict is defended, and there is always some degree of resistance to removing these defenses.

Dewald (1964) noted that resistances emerge during the treatment process at varying levels of consciousness. They are caused by the patient's fear of change; gratification from regressive infantile and childish drives, patterns, and relationships; and the need to maintain repression of the unconscious conflicts that produce anxiety and guilt. Resistances should not be viewed pejoratively, as they operate through the ego and demonstrate ego development. A total absence of defenses and resistance is an ominous sign, suggesting lack of psychic structure, decompensation, or a propensity to merge and comply indiscriminately. (This dangerous compliance, obedience, and merger is seen in youth who join cults.) It is important to come to understand why, what, and how the patient is avoiding. Therefore, resistances and defenses should not be assaulted with confrontive or intellectualized reflections and interpretations.

Adolescents demonstrate resistance before and during the course of therapy; and this may be stimulated by their own lack of motivation or fear of stigma and/or parental resistance to the therapy process. Many teenagers resist the parents' referral because of their wish for autonomy and their fear that the therapist—the agent of the parents—will attempt to transform them in accord with the parents' needs and not the adolescent's preferences. Silences, broken appointments, tardiness, action rather than verbalization, passive aggressive "putting in time" and wasting the session, impatience, boredom, and resentment all are standard adolescent manifestations of resistance.

Defenses

Defense is a term used to described struggles of the ego, unconsciously employed, to protect the self against perceived danger. The threat of recognition or conscious awareness of repressed wishes or impulses causes anxiety and guilt and must be avoided. Thus, defense mechanisms are developed as a means of controlling the impulses or affects and thereby shape the individual's personality and style of coping with reality (Campbell, 1981). Assessment and diagnosis determine whether the defenses are age-adequate, primitive, or precocious and whether or not they prove to be effective in binding impulses and anxiety to promote coping and adaptation. Some patients' defenses are ineffectual, allowing interference and disequilibrium. In such cases, the ego has struggled vainly to repress or deny intolerable wishes or impulses, resulting in full-blown anxiety and panic states and, commonly, regression.

Denial and *projection* are primitive defense mechanisms employed when the ego attempts to avoid painful reality. Adolescents commonly deny their substantial difficulties and lack of adaptation and often *project* or *displace* all blame outside themselves onto parents, teachers, and peers. *Identification with the aggressor* is another primitive defense, as when a teenager bullies and scapegoats a peer, possibly out of fear of his or her own helplessness and fright at social ostracism by high-status peer members or gang leaders. The primitive defense of *splitting* reflects defective object relations and a lack of self and object constancy. Thus, people (e.g., mother and self) are perceived as all good or all bad. There is a lack of tolerance of ambivalence and ambiguity; and the adolescent cannot remain permanently attached, irrespective of frustration or gratification. *Reaction formation* is a more advanced defense and entails replacement in conscious awareness of a painful idea or feeling by its opposite. For example, an adolescent's hate and resentment of a stepsib may be repressed and extreme solicitude and concern is exhibited instead. *Isolation of affect* is demonstrated through a division, or compartmentalization, of thinking—keeping things apart. An adolescent will remember a powerful emotional experience in detail but feel or show no emotion. For example, an adolescent might describe parents' fierce marital strife and sordid divorce with no sentiment or sensation. *Reversal of affect* takes place when, for example, sad feelings about the self are transformed into excitement; clowning and gaiety may reflect the young person's inability to tolerate sadness and depression. *Intellectualization and rationalization* may provide emotional distance from overwhelming affects, moods, stimuli, and feelings. *Withdrawal* into solitude or philosophical preoccupations is often an attempt to ward off painful acknowledgment of a teenager's social isolation and ineptness. *Sublimation*, a high-level defense, involves the neutralization and transformation of drives, ego energies, and sense of self into activities that promote cohesion and consolidation of the personality such as academics, athletics, artistic, musical, and political activities, which are conflict-free efforts and interests. Self-psychology describes transformations of narcissism into creativity and wit.

The defenses must be recognized, understood, and accepted as the adolescent's needed protection against anxiety. Despite the often objectionable, assaultive, and wearing quality of the defenses, a nonretaliating therapeutic stance must be sustained in a benign consistent holding environment that constitutes the milieu for the development of a corrective emotional experience. The management of counterreactions and countertransference responses is taxing, as discussed above. Through the therapist's nonpunitive, empathic response to unpleasant maladaptive defenses and negative behavior, the adolescent can gradually drop some of the reflex defensive patterns and examine the underlying perceived threats and dangers. It is always critical to note secondary interference with ego achievement, that is the price paid by the adolescent for the upkeep of the defense organization (Eissler et al., 1977).

The absence of defense is a danger sign, leaving an individual unprotected from external and internal stimuli. The defenses of latency are often insufficient to protect the teenage patient from the rearousal of oedipal incestuous feelings, increased genitality and pubescent hormonal changes. Thus, the therapeutic process must distinguish between adaptive and maladaptive defenses and aid the adolescent to maintain age-appropriate adaptive defenses which effectively protect the ego, while maintaining a good relationship with the self and the external environment. An example would be the adolescent's surrender of denial and projection of all blame for his difficulties onto the parents; assumption of responsibility for grandiose arrogance and petty delinquent angry actions; and development of sublimatory channels for anger, shame, and low self-esteem. Immersion in academics and athletics (i.e., sublimation) is an adaptive age-appropriate defense to handle continual pain and anger over the real strains in the home.

Working Through

The realities of public clinic and agency practice often dictate that a reconstruction and integration of the immediate past (Laufer, 1980), enabling the adolescent to resume progressive development, concludes the case. Depending on the policies of the agency—its practical considerations regarding service delivery, staff time, and waiting lists—and the patient's preferences, motivation, psychological mindedness, and money or insurance for ongoing treatment, there may be a continuation of therapy to effect a genuine understanding of the client's early history. This longer course of treatment is aimed at effecting a more complete "working through" process. The thoroughness of reconstruction and working through of trauma is greater in analysis than in psychotherapy and in treatment of older adolescents than with children and young teenagers. As indicated earlier, motivated adolescents may seek repeated periods of therapy. The treatment process rarely is over a protracted uninterrupted course. Life events, age-appropriate activities and demands, schooling, and the like commonly intervene in the young person's pursuit of self-understanding and movement toward stable self-definition and personality integration. In-depth conflict resolution is rare and Blos (1962) concluded that the stage of "adolescence does not aim at conflict resolution per se nor would the accomplishment of such a task be desirable." One only hopes that the adolescent has been helped to return to a progressive line of development, following the achievement of making conflictual and complex themes ego-syntonic in nature.

The term *working through* was originally used by Freud to describe the continuing application of analytic work to overcome resistances persisting after the initial interpretation of repressed instinctual impulses. "It is the goal of working through to make insight effective, i.e., to bring about significant and lasting changes in the patient. Despite initial improvements, unless these traumatic events are thoroughly worked through, therapeutic changes will not be maintained and the patient will relapse" (Moore and Fine, 1968, p. 95). In applying the concept of working through to adolescent psychotherapy, one must keep in mind Blos's above-noted caution and the practical and personal realities, in considering the modified goals achieved following successive therapeutic experiences. As each stage of adolescence concludes, it is to be hoped that the teenage patient has been helped to achieve ever-improved functioning, stable self-esteem, and greater harmony with earlier expectations, wishes, goals, and commitments.

In therapy, adolescents present material through moods, affects, symptoms, defenses, stories, daydreams, night dreams, fantasies, hopes, complaints, fears, and activities. By following the adolescent's lead in regard to choice of material and mode of presentation, the therapist can sense how much to reflect and interpret at any given point in the treatment process. Confrontation might be useful on occasion; it can also be nonproductive and in fact assaultive, causing the erection of defenses and resistances and creating a power struggle reminiscent of the adolescent's conflict with parents. Active empathic listening is essential. As noted earlier, the "blank screen" therapist has no place in work with adolescents: "Prolonged silences in therapy mobilize projective mechanisms with the result that the patient's ego boundaries become blurred and anxiety drives the adolescent into acting out, withdrawal, or negativism. It is necessary in adolescent therapy constantly to keep in mind the disorganizing influences of silences" (Blos [1962], 1980, p. 75).

One often wonders about trying to understand everything at once, and what is the correct timing for interventive interpretations and reflections. Practice wisdom has shown that significant activities, affects, fears, and relationships will reappear repeatedly and cannot be handled when initially recognized. Many adolescents will stop talking if interpretations are too quick and direct, bringing the patient too rapidly into painful material, especially sexual and aggressive material and feelings of shame and low self-esteem. Often adolescents flood therapists with material. Sandler, Kennedy, and Tyson (1980) noted that "it is very necessary to differentiate between the problem of phrasing an interpretation so that the unconscious and repressed material can be made conscious and acceptable to the patient, on the one hand, and the problem of choosing the right time to give the interpretation to the patient, on the other" (pp. 178–79). When the therapist has ascertained what has been expressed, the adolescent may be far from ready to accept the therapist's observation or reflection. The patient's readiness is based on the patient's ego state, the nature and strength of the treatment relationship, the current transference phenomena, and external factors such as stress and deprivation.

The therapist wants to avoid colluding with defenses, like for example, the adolescent's propensity to deny and blame the parents for the current state of stress. A stance of nonjudgmental acceptance, however, is necessary in order to make and sustain an alliance and empathic relationship. In general, based on sensitive assessment of the adolescent's readiness, it is advantageous to proceed slowly in offering reflections. If the patient is engaging in self-injurious behaviors, the same slow step-by-step process is obviously inappropriate; and crisis intervention efforts and protective limits must be employed. Anna Freud (recounted in Sandler, Kennedy, and Tyson, 1980) described situations of stress and deprivation where the concern of the patient is wholly engaged in the present. This demand for coping and handling stress precludes in-depth comprehension of unconscious and preconscious material. Thus, "working through" can only follow later after mastery of reality and life issues.

Introspection and insight are linked with working through. Sterba (1934) described introspection as a phenomenon in which one part of the patient's ego identifies with the analyst, shares in the analyst's increased understanding, and takes part in the therapeutic effort. Similarly, Kris (1956) defined insight as a process that makes use of the ego function of self-observation in both experiential and reflective form. Anna Freud (1965) stated that while introspection and insight are normal in the adult, they are not present in the child. Children and many adolescents are not self-observant; rather, they are preoccupied with action and the outer world. Some teenagers at the time of puberty become excessively introspective as a part of the heightened narcissism that is inherent in the adolescent process. In general, adolescence proper or the middle adolescent phase is characterized by greater introspection and efforts at self-understanding. Commonly, efforts are not directed toward the distant past to comprehend conflict and compulsions to repeat behavior. Adolescents focus on their current real difficulties and apprehensions about the future. It is rarely until late adolescence that young patients internalize the analyzing, observing, and reflecting function of their therapists, and begin to acquire and retain an understanding of their genesis of their difficulties.

It is critical to bear in mind the limitations of insight. Self-understanding does not produce immediate magical change and relief. Working through and resolution of both internalized and externalized conflict requires considerable time and repeated encounters and experience with mastery. The varied levels of insight and working through are pertinent in work with adolescent patients. What is semiunderstood and controlled in middle adolescence may well be truly mastered and comprehended in far greater depth and richness at a later point in development. Object relations, defenses, and issues of self-esteem are viewed more realistically and tolerantly in the older, and/or increasingly successful adolescent, who has been helped to move on effectively to direct his or her life responsibly. Sandler, Kennedy, and Tyson stated that "sufficient working through has taken place when the [young patient] has moved to the next level of development and established himself there" (1980, p. 184).

Working Through: Case of Vivian

Vivian, a 19-year-old, white, lower-middle-class, Jewish girl, was seen in intensive biweekly and triweekly psychotherapy over a three-year period. She had been referred to the outpatient psychiatry clinic of a large teaching hospital by her advisor, who was concerned about her erratic academic record in the physical therapy program affiliated with the same teaching hospital. Because of her limited financial resources and because she was a student at the hospital, she was not charged a treatment fee. Vivian demonstrated motivation and interest in seeking therapy and throughout the course of her treatment, was scrupulously prompt and consistent in keeping all appointments.

Vivian initially shared her depression and uncertainty about career goals and aspirations. She acknowledged not being happy in her studies because she felt that the program called for exacting order, manual dexterity, and excessive routine, whereas she was more interested in communicating with patients and providing supportive relationships to allay their fears and anxieties during their hospitalization. She felt more intellectually curious than her peers and believed her creative approaches to written papers assignments, and questions in class were discouraged by her teachers. She felt she had made a mistake in leaving college but wanted to try to continue in therapy training, as it enabled her to live separately from her family. She expressed grief and sadness at the impossibility of continued residence at home. Vivian's exceptional intelligence was immediately discernable. She demonstrated an articulate, expressive, and insightful manner. Her depression was obvious, and Vivian could acknowledge having struggled with sadness and hopelessness for some time. She recognized the connection between her depression, episodic overeating, chronic weight problem, and erratic grooming.

Vivian was assessed as suffering from a reactive depression due to her career conflicts and dependency conflicts. Her wish to be taken care of was appropriate, given her young age and academic aspirations. Familial stress and financial constraints did not afford her the parental supports needed. Vivian's ego strengths and object relationships placed her at a high point of developmental growth (A. Freud, 1971). She had reached the neurotic level of development; she demonstrated self-other distinctions, achievement of separation and individuation, a triadic mode of relating, and entry into the phallic oedipal stage. Her depression and sense of helplessness kept her continuously close to tears or engaged in efforts to ward off her sense of abandonment, sadness, and hopelessness.

She was able to provide a rich and detailed history, with appropriate affectual responses to her painful past. Vivian's parents were divorced when she was nine years old. She was the oldest of three children and had two brothers, four and five years younger than she was. The children always resided with their mother, who remarried when Vivian was 16½. The stepfather was Catholic, whereas Vivian's mother and maternal family were Jewish. The stepfather was described as several years younger than Vivian's mother, uneducated, and never married before. Vivian was most troubled by her mother's remarriage and found the adjustment very difficult. During middle adolescence she had been accused of causing some of her mother and stepfather's marital difficulty. She acknowledged that she did rebel in her own defense and, additionally, took on an interfering and protective stance in regard to her younger brothers. The stepfather was described as hitting and belittling all the children to establish his authority over them. According to

Vivian, her mother was grateful that a man would marry her and take on her children as well. Thus, she did not intervene to attempt to protect her children.

Vivian's natural father resided in Oregon and, in recent years, had also remarried. He was a realtor. For some years following the divorce his child support payments were erratic and inconsistent. His long-distance parenting had always been erratic, with lapses of years between visits with Vivian. She was the only child he maintained contact with.

Because of this position of specialness, Vivian always felt she had been a pawn between her natural parents. She realized that she had romanticized her long-distance father and, in the course of treatment, came to have a more realistic and accepting view of him. Vivian believed she had occupied various roles in the family, that of sibling to her mother during her mother's dating years, and that of pseudo-adult mother, caring for her younger brothers since she was nine, when, after the divorce, her mother had to work full time. Vivian painfully described her conflicts over these various roles and her guilt that what the natural father gave was only given to her and never to her brothers.

Following the divorce and the mother's full-time employment, the family was in serious financial straits, moving from one apartment to another routinely. There were four moves during the time Vivian was in grammar school. Vivian could recount the anxiety generated by the moves, loss of friends, endless adjustments in new schools, and the financial pressures and worries that her mother always shared with her.

Considering the mother's stressors and surrender of the parenting role to her daughter and the genuine deprivation she had known, Vivian's strengths were impressive. It appeared that despite infantile behavior patterns and impulsivity, Vivian's mother had always been there, dependent upon, but also interested in and involved with her children.

Early in treatment Vivian was able to face some of her dependency longings and wishes for more mature and protective parenting. She was also able to consider the reasons for her attraction to and mild involvement in drug parties of college students, hippie drop-out communities, and casual sexual relations. She resisted repeating potentially self-injurious behavior, supported, she said, by her therapy, which she recognized improved her judgment and ability to plan and anticipate more realistically.

Vivian was able to face the reality of having to take care of herself and provide for her own support and college education. Her father did not answer her request for some financial assistance for school. The mother did promise her her small portion of the child support check. After six or seven months of treatment, Vivian left physical therapy training, facing her feelings about this profession—the anxiety seriously ill patients evoked and the fact that a place to live away from her family was no basis for choosing a career.

Vivian's feeling more worthwhile made her more optimistic about financing college. Earlier her guilt and masochistic patterns prohibited better provision for herself. She would give more to others than to herself. Vivian was very resourceful in finding a job with flexible hours that allowed time for class attendance at college. She enrolled at a school which had the lowest tuition in the state, and began on a part-time basis. She secured adequate living arrangements in an inexpensive apartment. Her management of her finances also reflected emotional progress and growth. She became able to set limits for herself more readily and no longer was helpless, vulnerable, and unable to say "no" in her relationships with friends and family. She was able to stop loaning money to her friends and her mother and thereby was able to focus on realistically meeting her own needs. She became more appropriate, spontaneous, and free in relationships with dates and no longer conveyed the need to be accepted at any cost to herself. The combination of employment, self-support, and part-time school reflected her treatment gains and growth after more than a year of therapy.

Because of her superior academic average and ever-emerging intellectual creativity, she received increasing attention from her professors. They were all very involved and encouraged her to consider graduate study. Vivian experienced much pleasure from the success and recognition as well as from her inclusion on faculty retreats for curriculum planning. After her successful pursuit of her undergraduate degree, she was indecisive about graduate study.

At the time of termination of therapy, she had not arrived at a final career decision. She decided that she would work at least a year teaching school prior to entering any graduate program. She felt that her college years had been gratifying, but draining, due to the financial pressures and the continued need to work excessively to support herself. At the time of graduation, Vivian thought that she might enjoy having some money without scrimping and saving without respite. Additionally, she felt an obligation to start paying back government education loans. Vivian did exceptionally well in her student teaching in her senior year and was offered a job at the school where she had done her practicum.

Vivian acknowledged her enormous therapy gains and planned her termination with care. She no longer felt inadequate, and would laugh about the distance she had come. Both therapist and Vivian believed that it would be wise to terminate prior to graduation. This timing was based on Vivian's not wanting to lose the support and structure of both college and therapy at the same time.

Vivian's vastly altered physical appearance was astounding. In the course of 2½ years of treatment, Vivian emerged as a beautiful young woman. She was twenty-five pounds thinner, well poised, and well groomed. She could assess her greater emotional maturity, which enabled her to end a pattern of involvement in neurotic and unsatisfying social and romantic relationships. She attained more compassionate and neutralized relationships with her family. All the changes in her life and improved self-esteem provided Vivian pleasure and a sense of mastery. She experienced freedom from the earlier debilitating depression of the past. In all she felt very ready to conclude her therapy.

As during the entire course of treatment, dreams, rich associations, and early memories were shared. Greater focus and insight emerged in the last half year of treatment, especially once a termination date had been set. Vivian was shaken by the emotional impact of her deeper recognition of her bonds to her father. This had been intellectually recognized before, but much emotion and feeling had been warded off when Vivian contemplated the impact of early parent loss.

Vivian was able to get in touch with her repressed oedipal longings for her father, which had been displaced onto her brothers and various boy friends. This insight enabled her to conclude a longstanding compulsion to repeat her neurotic choices of romantic love objects and enabled her to make more appropriate love attachments; she was also able to put behind her her prior immobilizing guilt and low self-esteem.

By the end of treatment, Vivian's accomplishments were extraordinary. She had supported herself financially, attended college on scholarship, and graduated with honors. She was able to give up her parenting role with her own mother and restrain herself effectively in meeting periodic unrealistic demands by her father. Freed of prior extensive guilt and repressed anger, she was no longer a victim of depression. Her prior defenses and efforts to ward off sadness with compulsive eating or provocative dangerous actions were no longer necessary. Thus, symptom relief was complete.

Vivian had entered therapy during adolescence proper, and concluded treatment during late adolescence-early adulthood. She was able to make unusual use of long-term intensive psychotherapy. Vivian had been able to deal with unconscious conflicts through sharing dreams, free associations, and memories. The dramatic improvement in her relationships and in her capacity for creative, productive work and study demonstrated gains that occur when genuine "working through" takes place. Self-esteem regulation and structural change had occurred. The diminution of the primitive super-ego and the array of previously needed defenses permitted more ego energy. Patient and therapist both concurred that Vivian could and would maintain and continue the therapeutic process independently. Follow-up contact substantiated this prediction.

Bibliography

BLOS, P. [1962] (1983). Intensive Psychotherapy in Relation to the Various Phases of the Adolescent Period. [Amer. J. Orthopsychiatry, 32:901–10.] In The Psychiatric Treatment of Adolescents, ed. A. Esman, pp. 71–86. New York: International Universities Press.

_____ (1983). The Contribution of Psychoanalysis to the Psychotherapy of Adolescence. In Adolescent Psychiatry, Vol. 11: Developmental and Clinical Studies, ed. M. Sugar, pp. 104–24. Chicago: University of Chicago Press.

CAMPBELL, R. J. (1981). Psychiatric Dictionary, 5th ed. New York/Oxford: Oxford University Press.

DEWALD, P. (1964). Psychotherapy: A Dynamic Approach. New York: Basic Books.

EISSLER, R.; FREUD, A.; KRIS, M.; and SOLNIT, A. EDS. (1977). An Anthology of the Psychoanalytic Study of the Child—Psychoanalytic Assessment: A Diagnostic Profile. New Haven: Yale University Press.

FREUD A. (1965). *The Writings of Anna Freud VI—Normality and Pathology in Childhood: Assessments of Development*. New York: International Universities Press.

——— (1971). The Infantile Neurosis—Genetic and Dynamic Considerations. *Psychoanalytic Study of the Child*, 12:79–90. New York: Quadrangle Books.

KRIS, E. (1956). On Some Vicissitudes of Insight in Psychoanalysis. *Internat. J. Psychoanal.*, 37:445–55.

LAUFER, M. (1978). The Nature of Adolescent Pathology and the Psychoanalytic Process. *Psychoanalytic Study of the Child*, 33:307–22. New Haven: Yale University Press.

——— (1980). On Reconstruction in Adolescent Analysis. In *Adolescent Psychiatry, Vol. 8: Developmental and Clinical Studies*, eds. S. Feinstein, P. Giovacchini, J. Looney, A. Schwartzberg, and A. Sorosky, pp. 460–68. Chicago: University of Chicago Press.

MAHLER, M. (1971). A Study of the Separation-Individuation Process and Its Possible Application to Borderline Phenomena in a Psychoanalytic Situation. *Psychoanalytic Study of the Child*, 26:403–24. New York: Quadrangle Books.

MILLER, D. (1980). Treatment of the Seriously Disturbed Adolescent. In *Adolescent Psychiatry, Vol. 3: Developmental and Clinical Studies*, eds. S. Feinstein, P. Giovacchini, J. Looney, A. Schwartzberg, and A. Sorosky, pp. 469–81. Chicago: University of Chicago Press.

MOORE, B. and FINE, B. (1968). *A Glossary of Psychoanalytic Terms and Concepts*. New York: American Psychoanalytic Association.

SANDLER, J.; KENNEDY, H.; and TYSON, R. L. (1980). *The Technique of Child Psychoanalysis—Discussions with Anna Freud*. Cambridge, Mass.: Harvard University Press.

STERBA, R. (1934). The Fate of the Ego in Analytic Therapy. *Internat. J. Psychoanal.* 15:117–26.

26

Termination

In all of the clinical literature the topic of termination has received relatively scant attention. This is particularly true in the writings that focus on adolescent psychotherapy; the emphasis has been on engaging and sustaining the young person in treatment and managing complex and intense countertransference responses. Therapists' difficulties in separating from and relinquishing child and adolescent (Kohrman 1968) patients undoubtedly reflect their attitudes and anxieties about endings and surrendering the parental hope of safeguarding the young person.

Some believe that the concluding phase of treatment is the one that produces the greatest amount of stress and difficulty, creating problems for the patient and the clinician. At this point, the affective meaning of the therapy and the significance of the therapist-patient relationship, is experienced most keenly, not only by the patient, but also by the therapist (Schiff, 1962). Thus, how the therapeutic relationship is brought to a conclusion may in fact be the most important aspect of the entire treatment process, in that it generally influences the manner and degree to which gains are maintained. Commonly, failure to work through the attitudes and feelings related to the ending of therapy will result in a weakening or undoing of the therapeutic work.

Ferenczi (1927) was the first to focus specifically on the conlcuding phase of treatment and noted that completion is attainable "only if unlimited time is at one's disposal" (p. 82). The next significant examination was Freud's seminal paper "Analysis Terminable and Interminable" (1937), in which he offered guidelines and criteria for concluding analytic treatment. He emphasized relief of the patient's suffering, the conquering of anxieties and inhibitions, and the therapist's conviction that the treatment was successful enough to ensure against any repetition of the patient's symptoms and pathology. Freud was not unrealistic in his expectations of treatment gains and goals, in considering when appropriately to conclude analytic treatment. He emphasized sufficient intrapsychic structural change to permit optimal functioning. This would be exemplified by the modification of a patient's harsh superego and the diminution of defenses that caused secondary interference. The pioneer work of Ferenczi and Freud raised the critical questions clinicians and health care providers still wrestle with in considering the when and how to conclude therapeutic interventions. Briefly, they are: what is the age-appropriate functioning that signifies mental health and what are the criteria for termination of long-term and short-term treatment? These questions are particularly pertinent for the therapist working with adolescents. The young patient has not achieved the personality consolidation of the adult and faces innumerable life stressors and developmental milestones. Thus, it is always easy and natural to find reasons for the adolescent patient to continue in therapy well beyond the amelioration of the problems and symptoms that originally necessitated the seeking of help. Not uncommonly, ego strengths are underestimated by the protective therapist who wants to continue to support and guide the young patient through the painful maturation process.

In the 1960s and 70s, brief or short-term therapy became increasingly recognized as a valid form of treatment, one which provides specific significant help and is not an abbreviated or watered down, inferior version of open-ended long-term treatment. Mann (1973) raised questions about the "interminability" of long-term open-ended treatment and suggested that vaguely defined goals and therapist's countertransference problems caused inappropriately prolonged therapy. Some practitioners, such as Maluccio and Marlow (1974), advocated the use of the treatment contract to ensure patient-therapist interaction and collaboration in identifying concerns, goals, conditions of ongoing service, and time allotted for the therapeutic intervention.

The specified period of treatment time is particularly germane in considering clinical work with adolescents who are bound to their present concerns and anxieties and commonly uninterested in their pasts. Novick (1977) described what he called the adolescent's "unilateral treatment plan," in which termination is planned at the onset, for example, for the end of the school year. The adolescent patient may not necessarily share the plan early in treatment, but rather will simply announce his or her departure, such as for college. This may be part of developmental maturation or an artificial attempt at separation and individuation from the parents. "Instead of separating from his parents, however, he often leaves [therapy] and ends up even more attached to them" (p. 392).

The Significance of Termination

Concluding treatment entails loss and a separation. It is appropriate to compare stages in the termination process to phases of grief work described first by Freud (1917, 1937) and illustrated by Lindemann's (1965) study of loss. Grayson (1970) emphasized loss as inherent in all ego development, and Loewald (1962) noted that separation has the significance of emancipation and growth. Throughout the clinical literature the final phase of therapy has been linked to the patient's previous experience with separation. Melanie Klein (1950) linked the termination of treatment with the infant's depression and anxieties at the time of weaning; Buxbaum (1950), Dewald (1967), and Weiss (1972) compared termination to the typical normal progression from adolescence to adulthood. Payne (1950) compared the conclusion of therapy with "the anxieties of growing up, leaving school, leaving the university, rebirth, weaning, and end of mourning, all being critical times involving a reorganization of ego and libidinal interests" (p. 205). Schafer's (1973) examination of the termination phase highlights the "unspoken promises, expectations and resistances on the part of both patient and therapist" (p. 140).

   Termination reactivates earlier losses and separations that patient and therapist have endured. There are inherent limitations based on the personal strengths and weaknesses of patient and therapist as well as the individual nature of each treatment process. Mistakes and omissions are inevitable. However, ideally, the patient will leave therapy feeling strengthened and fortified by the experience of mastering the current loss of the renewed examination and reexperiencing of old separations and possible traumas. Termination can offer an integrating corrective opportunity to rework and modify earlier separation problems. Edelson (1963) has described three major affective themes in reaction to termination.

> The theme of narcissism and the response to the narcissistic wound, including panic, rage, and a pervasive sense of worthlessness. Theme of mourning with accompanying feelings of guilt and grief. Theme of struggle toward maturity and independence, including feelings of competitiveness, defiance, envy, jealousy, and the anxiety associated with these [p. 27].

Criteria

The indications for appropriate conclusion of the adolescent's treatment are many and varied and require consideration both from the ideal and practical standpoints. Neubauer (1968) stressed that the decision to end therapy should not be soley based on symptom relief. He called for a developmental assessment to ascertain whether or not the young patient demonstrates noteworthy progress and movement beyond points of fixation (notwithstanding phase-appropriate conflicts and problems) and whether the adolescent demonstrates the capability to handle ongoing and predictable future developmental and environmental realities.

Psychotherapy, in contrast to psychoanalysis, focuses primarily on the here and now and on the interaction and interpersonal relationship between adolescent and therapist. Less attention is given to early infantile conflicts. Thus the goals in the treatment are to (1) increase the capacity for reality testing; (2) strengthen object relationships; and (3) loosen fixations. In deciding whether additional treatment is needed, Anna Freud (1965) stressed the need to examine drive expression (libidinal and aggressive manifestations) and the ego and super-ego functioning "for signs of age-adequateness, precocity or retardation" (p. 55). The primary considerations are the norms, compromise formations, and solutions that have been achieved. The child's capacity to develop progressively—or, conversely, the damage to that capacity—is the most significant feature in determining a child's mental future (A. Freud, 1962). In considering the ideal criteria for termination, one must continually return to the process of assessment since neither symptomatology nor life tasks alone serve as reliable guides. The clinician attempts to ascertain strengths and weaknesses, and external familial and environmental circumstances that may enhance or impede future growth. Nagera's discussion (1964) of arrest in development, fixation, and regression is most pertinent both in the reassessment process and in considering the ideal timing of termination.

Dewald (1964) suggested that for those patients treated in insight therapy, indication for termination would be: some structural change in the personality, lessening or elimination of symptoms, or evidence of the patient's improved capacity to tolerate specific symptoms and conflicts, improvements in relationships, capacity for work, and self-awareness, whereby the patient can handle or examine conflicts and thus maintain the therapeutic process independently. For those seen in supportive therapy, indications for appropriate termination would be reduction of symptoms, greater homeostatic balance, management of self-esteem and drive expression, and cessation or reversal of the prior regressive pull.

The Decision to Terminate

Practicality requires consideration of the adolescent's and the parents' preferences and desires. After symptom reduction occurs, many adolescents wish to conclude treatment and immerse themselves in age-appropriate activities such as summer study and/or travel or after-school sports. The decision may be based on appropriate selection of priorities or a premature flight into health to avoid examining more threatening issues and conflicts. Relieved parents may wish to conclude therapy. In some cases the adolescent may demonstrate other conflicts that do not trouble the parents, or, in fact, provide them unconscious gratification. In some situations, parents feel that the needs of their other children must be met, and they resist ongoing allocation of time and money for the patient.

An adolescent's impulsive decision to conclude therapy may be due to transference responses in the treatment relationship, for example, frustration at the lack of gratification of early infantile needs. The adolescent patient will frequently use termination or the threat of terminate in an attempt to manipulate or control the therapist. Termination impulsively determined may be analogous to a phobic reaction at the perceived threat of abandonment. The adolescent patient might make a sudden and impulsive declaration of quitting therapy, or announce a refusal to return for the next appointment. Dewald (1964) noted that when such a sudden decision to discontinue treatment is accompanied by anxiety, intense affect, and reluctance to discuss it openly in advance, there are unconscious components in the termination. In such a situation, the therapist must weigh issues of confidentiality in deciding whether to inform the parents of a minor that the adolescent is seriously disturbed and capable of seriously self-destructive behavior.

The therapist may decide to terminate therapy, and or seek consultation in the event of a stalemate. If treatment is concluded suddenly or impulsively against a patient's wishes, there will be profound difficulty in establishing a new trusting and effective therapeutic relationship. The patient will be afraid to invest in a new relationship. Such improper therapeutic handling arises out of profound countertransference problems on the part of the therapist. A more optimal handling would be to explore the therapeutic impasse and the reasons for the therapist's wish for consultation and/or transfer of the case, in a careful planned fashion. Reasonable and objective discussion prior to any change permits the patient and therapist to consider the reasons for the therapeutic failure and to assess the best future course of treatment. A therapeutic fit cannot be universally achieved with all patients, particularly adolescents; but one therapist's difficulties must not be misconstrued—by either therapist or patient—to mean that the adolescent is untreatable.

Termination decisions may be treatment interruptions created by external factors, such as therapist or family moving away or change of schools. Gould (1981) examined the termination phase of therapy created by the conclusion of trainees' practicums, conclusion of social work students' field work placements, psychologists' internships, and psychiatrists' residencies. There exists considerable controversy about whether or not clinicians should inform patients from the start about a pending termination that the therapist knows must occur. Some advocate that this reality should be withheld, as it discourages engagement in treatment and in the establishment of an alliance and stimulates separation anxiety. Other clinicians, e.g., Langs (1974), Weiner (1975), and Dewald (1965) disagree. Langs (1974) stated emphatically that the failure to share a preordained termination leads to "over-intense, paranoid-like, rageful and vengeful fantasies, [which are based on the sense of betrayal,] "because the therapist has compromised himself and no longer invites trust" (p. 481). Weiner (1975) and Dewald (1965) observed that the sharing of a planned termination date helps sort out which patients can use the circumscribed period of therapy and which might benefit from referral to another therapist for a longer course of work. For some patients, the circumscribed period enables them to make optimal use of a specified time period. This is often useful for adolescent patients who are ambivalent about commitment and dependent attachments to adults, while they struggle for autonomy and the capacity for self-maintenance.

Techniques in Termination

Dewald (1964) distinguished between how to terminate with patients seen in insight-directed therapy and those treated in supportive therapy. In insight-oriented psychotherapy, he emphasized resolution of the transference relationship, particularly the intensified negative feelings that commonly surface at the loss of a significant relationship. This desired resolution can stimulate maturation on the basis of the patient's acceptance of frustration. In supportive therapy, the therapist continues attempts to reduce conflict and stress and avoids mobilization or activation of the negative transference, by emphasizing rapport and the positive sides of the transference. When possible, the therapist, can even offer a continuing relationship via future availability should the patient require it.

According to Langs (1974), in determining the length of time allocated for termination one must consider:

1. The patient's sensitivity to separation and his history of separation traumas.

2. The extent to which the patient has formed a deep and dependent attachment.
3. The extent to which other persons are actually available to the patient.
4. Borderline and narcissistic patients tend to be more involved than neurotics with their therapist and therapy in both libidinal—dependent and hostile—paranoid ways. Their ambivalence is intense and their primitive fantasies and responses to loss are quite threatening to them. The therapist considers indications of separation anxieties that emerged during the therapy as the patient's symptoms were being explored and resolved.
5. Indications of separation anxieties.
6. Other indicators of the need for some extra time to terminate are: slow movement by a patient through treatment, long years of therapy (more than three) and open reluctance to complete therapy.
7. Termination forced by external circumstances generally requires an extra period of time for working through [pp. 449–450].

As the adolescent struggles with his or her parents, similarly will he or she struggle with the therapist in the termination stage. Adolescents commonly interrupt their treatment and then seek intermittent bouts of therapy. Ekstein (1983) recommended a therapeutic stance of flexibility during the concluding phase and cautioned against overreaction and a sense of failure when the patient imposes the conclusion of treatment. The emphasis is on appropriate letting go of the adolescent patient, based on the therapist's surrender of omnipotent hopes of safeguarding the adolescent against future dangers, life vicissitudes, and regression. One must allow the adolescent the opportunity to take the chance of independent passage.

Anna Freud doubted the prophylactic effect of early treatment, as emotional illness leaves its scars. A recovered child or adolescent is no safer from the vicissitudes of life than a person who was never ill. Therefore clinicians "must avoid carrying a case beyond the point which was originally viewed as the goal, just as [they] must abstain from continuing treatment attempts when reasonable expectations no longer promise material improvement" (A. Freud, 1957, p. 291).

Reactions to Termination

If the patient or therapist has experienced traumatic separations from key figures early in life, the likelihood is increased for intense conflict during the conclusion of treatment. Commonly there is resistance to facing and reexperiencing old losses, sadness, and grief. The work of mourning is often avoided under a defensive facade of anger and denial that the therapist and therapy were of real significance. When the denial breaks down, there is often intense grief, sadness, anger, and narcissistic hurt. This is commonly followed by absorption of loss and association to feelings that are connected with early memories of loss. To the extent that the patient and therapist can work through these affects and old losses, the termination can produce detachment and genuine resolution. Glenn (1971) cautioned against being a "one-note singer." Too often therapists focus only on anger and rage, and this can be due to their own discomfort. If the clinician avoids awareness of all affects, he is not offering skill and sensitivity in the treatment process. "If the therapist in fact pulls away and detaches himself from the leave-taking experience, the patient becomes abandoned prematurely. [The patient] may now react with mourning and anger. He grieves not for the future anticipated loss of his therapist but for his actual pulling away in the present" (p. 441).

The patient or therapist may try to induce guilt in the other, if one opposes the decision for termination. Postponement, regression, and resurgence of symptoms often occur during the concluding stage. Ideally, the therapist can maintain self-awareness and a safe holding environment, staving off his or her own regressive pulls, so that he or she can help the patient examine and resolve the conflicts mobilized by the termination. In situations where there has been a strong transference, Dewald (1964) advised maintaining the constancy of the therapist's activity as well as the basic frequency and duration of sessions up to the conclusion of the treatment. In less intensive treatment, or where the patient has more limited ego capacity, he suggests a gradual reduction of sessions during the final phase of treatment. In clinics and institutions the less intact patient will be reminded of the ongoing availability of the institutional setting, following termination.

Countertransference dilemmas are frequent during this phase of treatment. A therapist's overly intense attachment, dislike of a patient, therapeutic overambition, or overidentification will interfere with an effective termination. Fear of the patient's regression or anger may contaminate the handling of the final stage of therapy. The therapist's narcissistic response to the conclusion of therapy is an important issue. If the adolescent has not improved fast enough and if there have been struggles with the parents and/or patient, some therapists wish to rid themselves of the patient quickly, thereby avoiding a genuine termination process. If the particular case causes narcissistic injury to the clinician or stirs up old, unresolved issues, the therapist is often unable to provide skilled services.

One of the most important reasons for therapist-introduced termination is the clinician's conclusion of training or seeking of employment elsewhere. Therapist-introduced termination occurs continually in settings that provide training. The patient and the therapist will both be affected during the termination phase by the subsequent disposition of the case: (1) the case cannot be transferred and continued, despite therapeutic need for ongoing treatment; (2) the case will be placed on a lengthy waiting list for eventual transfer and resumption of care; (3) the case will be transferred to someone the current therapist admires and respects; or (4) the case will be picked up by someone the current therapist fears, is competitive with, or holds in low regard professionally. In all, the advent of a new therapist can be perceived as a threat to the old therapist's feeling of omnipotence, because the new clinician might achieve superior treatment results and will scrutinize the prior efforts and work performed (Lenzer, 1955).

Responses to termination are not confined to the patient and the therapist. King (1976) focused our attention on the immense importance of staff reactions. Staff and administrative departures, upheaval, and changes in institutions serving adolescents commonly produce anxiety, anger, and, frequently, rejection of the patients or, appeasement of them. Halperin et al. (1981) described staff's sense of helplessness and fear, which can result in necessary confrontations being avoided and surrender of reality demands. "In still other instances the acting out of the adolescent may represent a repressed part of the staff members who unconsciously identify with and encourage disregard for social limits" (p. 564).

The Real Relationship in the Termination Phase

Optimally, at the conclusion of treatment the adolescent has accepted the impossibility of obtaining infantile gratifications and continued protection from therapy and has begun to perceive the therapist in a more realistic fashion. He or she experiences the therapist more and more as a contemporary real object, and the conclusion of therapy connotes a separation between two individuals whose relationship has been in the nature of collaborative work on a precious enterprise (Hurn, 1971). Ekstein (1983) emphasized that the end of treatment with adolescents "is perhaps the prologue for the future. The ending of treatment is but the beginning of a new life" (p. 145).

Commonly, some adolescent patients maintain varying degrees of contact with their former therapists. Clinicians in private practice often receive follow-up letters and visits. Periods of contact later during the adolescent's growth and maturation, as he or she seeks final resolution of educational and vocational aims and romantic object choices, are not uncommon.

Is holding on to the therapist evidence of separation difficulty, or of the clinician's difficulty in relinquishing the young patient, or rather, an appropriate use of "transitional parents" who have often proved to be more consistent role models and supportive figures than the real parents (Ekstein, 1983)? Anna Freud concluded that there are differences in how children, adolescents, and adults handle termination and that the principles of treating adults should not be superimposed on the young patient.

> It never seemed quite logical to me that terminating [the young patient] should involve the complete separation from the analyst that it usually does for adult patients. With children (and adolescents) there is the loss of a real object as well as the loss of the transference object and this complicates matters. To make an absolute break from a certain date onward merely sets up another separation, and an unnecessary one [A. Freud, 1980, quoted in Sandler, Kennedy, and Tyson, 1980, p. 243].

Continued contact, or later reconnection, with the therapist is generally not possible in public agencies and clinics, in part because of logistical factors, and in some settings because continued contact is viewed pejoratively, as due to the clinician's rescue fantasies or need to hold on to patients. Yet, if the termination went well, a real relationship will have evolved, which can support the adolescent's maintenance of gains and serve as a bridge, rather than an obstacle, to the future seeking of treatment. This "real relationship" must have professional parameters in accord with the prior treatment relationship. Continued contact via letters, phone calls, and an occasional face-to-face meeting to seek advice or referral for later treatment, e.g., at college, only reaffirms trust in the work previously accomplished.

All in all, the concluding stage of treatment contains something of a rehearsal for the future (Ekstein, 1965) whereby energy is available for investment in new relationships and new experiences. Like parents, therapists hope their adolescent patients will not falter, but rather will be fortified to master the tasks of life, love, and attachment.

Termination of Employment in an Adolescent Residential Treatment Institution: "Cottage #1"

Like many residential treatment facilities, the Y institution had originally been an orphanage. It became a nondenominational interracial residential treatment institution after World War II. It is the hub of an extensive well-integrated child welfare program that offers a continuum of child welfare services: adoption, foster care, day care, group homes, and a program for retarded youths. The Y institution is very well respected locally and nationally, generously funded in its local community and heavily endowed by private funds, trusts, and individual philanthropists. Fees are paid by private tuition and "purchase of care" contracts by public and private agencies and child serving systems such as juvenile courts and child welfare programs. There are eighty to one hundred children from all parts of the country in care, ages eight to eighteen, most of them are adolescents. Concern about patient mix, and scapegoating, led to the decision not to admit more severely disabled (e.g., retarded and schizophrenic) young people. The majority of children served are delinquent, borderline, impulse ridden, or character disordered aggressive youth, placed for long-term treatment. Personnel include administrators, social workers, psychologists, child care paraprofessionals, maintenance and dietary personnel, plus an extensive staff of certified teachers selected by the institution and paid by the local board of education. Recreational personnel direct athletics, music, art, and drama programs. Volunteer Big Brothers and Big Sisters assist in various aspects of the program and often have ongoing one-to-one contact with the adolescent residents. A sizable group of child psychiatrists and child psychoanalysts serve as consultants to each living unit and to various portions of the rich and extensive program. Social work therapists provide group, individual, and family therapy. A few children are seen in intensive psychotherpay and classical analysis. Milieu treatment in the living units is emphasized in the attempt to provide "a therapeutically designed round-the-clock living-in experience, the purpose of which is care and treatment. Its clinical components are an integration of functions, structure, physical setting, and immediate social environment. . . . Residential treatment involves the temporary replacement of family living with group living in a controlled environment" (Maier, 1972, p. 154).

Ms. J. was the supervisor of the younger girls' unit over a period of 2½ years. In this position, she served as a "power parent" (Mayer, 1972), not a transference figure. Ms. J. supervised the daily life and discipline of the children. She supervised the child care staff and coordinated treatment care plans (those involving cottage or living unit, school, recreation department, therapy department, and contact with the child's biological parents, etc.) Ms. J. found her work very gratifying, and she approached each aspect of the job with energy and enthusiasm. Staff relationships were close, congenial, and mutually supportive, reflecting the strengths of the director of the institution. He was a charismatic figure, a talented clinician and a beloved figure in the community, called upon for guest teaching at various universities and for expert testimony by national child welfare organizations, among others.

Ms. J. enjoyed a close and warm relationship with the director, other professional personnel, her own paraprofessional child care staff, and the children in her care. However, after several years, the inherent strains and the long hours stimulated Ms. J. to consider a job change, especially when she learned that the director was leaving his post at the institution for more extensive administrative responsibility. Her decision to leave was met with denial, disappointment, and considerable overt and covert anger. Staff changes always prove disruptive and troublesome, and replacement was viewed as an arduous task. Anxiety, sadness, and a sense of betrayal and loss became prevailing themes in the ensuing discussions Ms. J. initiated with the director and her own child care staff. Because of the nature of her responsibilities, Ms. J. planned six months in advance to terminate her employment. She anticipated it would take time to work through the separation with the children in care, all of whom had suffered repeated loss and abandonment in their young lives.

Because of her limited professional experience in residential institutions, Ms. J. was unprepared for the administration and staff response, including guilt inducing tactics on the part of her own immediate staff. In supervisory conferences with the senior child care worker, she was repeatedly, and roundly confronted with denial and anger.

> How can you leave us? This cottage is organized, well run, and a happy place for all of us. Staff and children have never done so well. You will disrupt and spoil everything by leaving! I've been here over fifteen years, and am sick and tired of supervisors who come and go. I'm tired of picking up the pieces. I refuse to believe that you are leaving.

The response on the part of the child care staff was similar.

> Nothing is happening for ages, and when we see it, we'll believe it. You probably won't be able to work out the move you've planned, and will stay on here, after all. You wouldn't walk away from work that you enjoy . . . and leave us, and the kids. You couldn't be so disloyal.

The director was of little help and support because of his own reactions to Ms. J.'s plans to terminate her employment.

> Look, we've enjoyed a remarkable and close personal and professional relationship, and I don't want you to leave. I need you here, given my pending new responsibilities. I don't suffer staff changes calmly. Each time it's a real wrench and personal loss. I value you and can't believe that you, *and* M, might actually leave this place within the year. You both are important needed key people here. I obviously can't withhold superior work references, but frankly, I hope this new position doesn't work out for you, and that you'll remain on, for years to come!"

The director thereupon kept his distance, cut short all normal conferences with Ms. J. and was abruptly cold and silent. Their warm camaraderie had suddenly vanished. Mrs. J. initially felt lost and abandoned because of her professional and personal reliance on her supervisor. He had been her most significant professional mentor.

Child care staff unanimously continued to deny and resent any and all discussion about Ms. J.'s departure plans. Once an actual termination date was set, they formed a rebellious united front.

> Don't tell the children. This psychoanalytic theory about loss and mourning is just a lot of jargon. We don't want to endure the supposed "working through" process. The kids will be angry and upset and, as always, will get crazy and aggressive. We don't need to struggle with that for months. It all falls on us—not you. We're the one's who live on grounds and are bombarded night and day with their tantrums and run-away escapades.

With help and support from the child analyst consultants, Ms. J. and the staff ultimately did inform the children of Cottage #1 of the pending changes—allowing a four-month period to "work through" the termination phase. The children initially responded with anger, pain, and disbelief.

> You can't be serious. You really won't leave us. Are we so awful that you're worn out? Are you tired of us sickies? Go already! Go to hell! Who liked you anyway?

White Bitch! Who will take your job? Will you please pick the new person and make them be like you!

Despite extensive articulation of feelings, some significant aggressive acting-out behavior ensued. Several teenage girls punched out several windows, and a set of drapes were cut to ribbons. Several children showed severe regressive symptomatology—in the form of sleeplessness, running off, cursing, and tantrums—in response to their reexperience of loss and separation and the temporary breakdown of their controlled, safe, and predictable environment. Boundaries of time, space, and activity had become blurred; additionally, adult expectation conveyed mixed and confusing messages. Splitting and projective identifications emerged. Adler (1973), in studying hospitalized borderline patients and exploring staff and patient interactions, observed the defenses of splitting and projective identifications and their impact on residential staff. He recognized that when staff are recipients of cruel and aggressive behavior, they will respond in kind to the patients and demonstrate sadistic punishing behavior.

Staff and Ms. J. temporarily were in conflict over their views of the children. Mr. J., soon to depart, became idealized, and the available staff persons were depreciated and abased by the children. Adler noted that such conflicts can occur frequently between two groups of staff members, who begin to act towards one another as if each one of them had the only correct view of the patient and as if the part the patient projected onto the other staff members were the only true part of those staff members" (Adler, 1973, in Halperin et al., 1981, p. 564). Children and staff displayed anger and anxiety, destructiveness and retaliatory punishment, helplessness, appeasement, permissiveness and explosiveness. These debilitating affects were finally brought under control, as administration, staff, and children absorbed the reality of Ms. J.'s pending departure and could detach from her with sadness, controlled anxiety, and genuine acceptance of the separation.

Staff, administration, and child residents could review their prior satisfying collaborative relationships and work with Ms. J. During the final months of the termination process there was greater calm, and renewed warmth and positive feelings, highlighted by the children's preparation of a farewell reception for staff, and private cottage dinner party for Ms. J. The dinner party was a loving token of affection, prepared by the children and followed by a skit and presentation of poems, pictures, and presents. They conceded to Ms. J.'s tastes in the choice of music.

We know you enjoy rock and jazz—but much prefer classical music, so that's what it will be tonight. We're not angry any more. Donna is still a little mad and made the jello mold black; but since it tastes okay, we figured you'd understand.

Tearfulness, sadness, and recognition that Ms. J. would miss everyone at Y was finally believed, comprehended, and accepted.

In summary, the staff's ultimate mastery of the stress period demonstrated their strengths, coping ability and professional skills. The period of termination was a rehearsal for what lay ahead; the senior child care worker would be in charge, until Ms. J.'s replacement arrived. Her recognition of her own and the staff's growth and ability was genuine. Child residents and staff had moved beyond their initial sense of narcissistic injury, panic, and rage. Ms. J. and the director resumed their close professional and personal rapport—in a new context. Equilibrium had been restored in a renewed and nurtured climate of mutual respect and regard.

The Termination Process: Case of Vivian (see Chapter 25)

Once Vivian had set the date for her termination six months hence, she worked harder than ever to achieve all that she could before concluding her treatment. She had made substantial gains and nevertheless kept working at the preconscious and unconscious levels. She demonstrated deeper insights about the early derivatives of her career interests and choices of romantic objects, all of which harked back to the happier time of life when her family had been intact, and when she had the gratification of a close and loving relationship with her father. Her fascination with anthropology and mythology brought her in touch with memories of her own preschool play, her subsequent interest in fairy tales, and her gratifying kindergarten and primary grade experiences, when her teachers' innovative curriculum, using Indian and Mexican customs, folklore, art, and music, had so excited her. In that period of life, Vivian had excelled in school, and in such creative activities as drawing and painting; but thereafter, following the parents' separation and divorce, she lost her enthusiasm for study and any creative expression. Both of these had now been resurrected in late adolescence as a result, she believed, of her intensive therapy experience. Similarly, she recognized a reality denied throughout her adolescence, namely, that all romantic crushes were choices predicated on her repetition compulsion to choose exotic foreign-looking men, physical replicas of her father.

In the final phase of therapy, Vivian experienced both excitement and exhiliaration and great sadness and anxiety. She openly shared her fears and her sense of mourning and loss. She went through a short-lived period that proved temporarily frightening, despite her keen intellectual and emotional understanding of the unconscious forces. For many weeks she lost vital possessions, including her purse, her wallet, her jacket, her car keys, her calendar-address book, and several sets of class notes. She did verbalize her sense of fear at the loss of her therapist and her therapy sessions, as well as anger that her therapist was "throwing her away," despite her intellectual recognition that she had initiated plans to conclude her therapy. She wept freely and expressed loneliness and alarm that she might act out sexually if she "didn't have to report" her actions in therapy. This short-lived demonstration of intense anxiety diminished, and high-level functioning was restored in the final months of treatment. This concluding period marked Vivian's surrender of the positive and idealized maternal transference, and she responded to her therapist more as a real object and a trusted and respected friend. She maintained the therapeutic alliance in an unwavering fashion and left her final session with sadness, nostalgia about the rewarding collaborative endeavor, and a sense that she could proceed successfully now, on her own.

Follow-up

More than a year later, Vivian returned to her therapist and contracted for regular sessions over a period of many months. She had been doing very well on her own to date, but now faced some major decisions in her life. She had two major life choices to make, namely, a career shift, and whether or not to move ahead in a most significant romantic relationship. Dissatisfaction with the circumscribed role of a teacher motivated Vivian to consider how to train herself to be more useful and effective in children's lives. Although she did not want to emulate and mirror her therapist, she wisely considered the same issue from the "opposite side of the coin."

> While not wanting to overidentify with you, I recognize that a refusal to pursue my interests, which I realize have always been somewhat similar to your professional specialty, says the same thing in just another way. If I can't consider any career that is at all like yours, then I'm not as separated as I thought I was.

Months of work, examination, and analysis of motives and conflicts freed Vivian to enter a graduate clinical program.

Concurrent with the crystallization of her vocational choice was her ability to make a steadfast commitment to the young man in her life—an attractive person capable of warmth, intimacy, commitment, and a deep sense of responsibility. He was markedly different from the previous young men in her life. To date they have been married nine years and have two small children. Vivian has kept her former therapist apprised of major life events, via intermittent correspondence. The "transitional parent" (Ekstein, 1983) of Vivian's adolescence remains a trusted private friend. Thus continues an unbroken bond of commitment and profound regard and respect for Vivian.

Bibliography

ADLER, G. (1973). Hospital Treatment of Borderline Patients. *Amer. J. Psychiatry.* 1:25–32.

BUXBAUM, E. (1950). Technique of Terminating Analysis. *Internat. J. Psychoanal.*, 31:184–90.

DEWALD, P. (1964). *Psychotherapy: A Dynamic Approach.* New York: Basic Books.

——— (1965). Reactions to the Forced Termination of Therapy. *Psychiatric Q.*, 39:102–26.

——— (1967). The Termination of Psychotherapy. *Psychiatry Digest*, 38:33–46.

EDELSON, M. (1963). *The Termination of Intensive Psychotherapy.* Springfield, Ill.: Charles C. Thomas.

EKSTEIN, R., (1983). The Adolescent Self During the Process of Termination of Treatment: Termination, Interruption or Intermission. In *Adolescent Psychiatry, Vol. 9: Developmental and Clinical Studies*, eds. M. Sugar, S. Feinstein, J. Looney, A. Schwartzberg, and A. Sorosky, pp. 125–46. Chicago: University of Chicago Press.

FERENCZI, S., [1927] (1955). The Problem of the Termination of the Analysis. In *Final Contributions to the Problems and Methods of Psychoanalysis*, ed. M. Balint. pp. 77–87. New York: Basic Books.

FREUD, A. [1957] (1964). The Ego's Defensive Operation as an Object of Analysis. In *Child Psychotherapy: Practice and Theory*, ed. M. R. Haworth. New York and London: Basic Books.

—— (1962). Assessment of Childhood Disturbances. *Psychoanalytic Study of the Child*, 17:149–58. New York: International Universities Press.

—— (1965). *The Writings of Anna Freud, Vol. 6: Normality and Pathology in Childhood: Assessment of Development*. New York: International Universities Press.

FREUD, S. [1920] (1937). Analysis Terminable and Interminable. In *Therapy and Technique*, ed. P. Rieff, pp. 233–71. New York: Crowell-Collier Publishing Co.

—— [1937] (1950). Analysis Terminable and Interminable. In *Collected Papers Vol. 5*, pp. 316–57. London: Hogarth Press.

—— [1917] (1957). Mourning and Melancholia. *Standard Edition*, 14:243–58. London: Hogarth Press.

GLENN, M. (1971). Separation Anxiety: When the Therapist Leaves the Patient. *Amer. J. Psychotherapy*, 25:437–46.

GOULD, R. (1981). Students' Experience with the Termination Phase of Individual Treatment. *Smith College Studies in Social Work* (Summer): 234–69.

GRAYSON, H. (1970). Grief Reaction to the Relinquishing of Unfulfilled Wishes. *Amer. J. Psychotherapy*, 24:287–95.

HALPERIN, D.; LAURO, G.; MISCIONE, F.; REBHAN, J.; SCHNABALK, J.; and SHACHTER, B. (1981). Countertransference Issues in Adolescents. In *Adolescent Psychiatry, Vol. 9, p. 56A*. See Ekstein (1983).

HURN, H. T. (1971). Toward a Paradigm of the Terminal Phase. *J. Amer. Psychoanal. Assn.*, 19:332–48.

KING, C. (1976). Countertransference and Counterexperience in the Treatment of Violence Prone Youth. *Amer. J. Orthopsychiatry*, 46:43–52.

KLEIN, M. (1950). On the Criteria for the Termination of an Analysis. *Internat. J. Psychoanal.*, 31:284.

KOHRMAN, R. [1968] (1969). Panel Report on "Problems of Termination in Child Analysis," Annual Meeting of the American Psychoanalytic Association, Boston, May 10, 1968. *J. Amer. Psychoanal. Assn.*, 28:191–205.

LANGS, R. (1974). *The Technique of Psychoanalytic Psychotherapy*, vol. 2. New York: Jason Aronson.

LENZER, A. (1955). Countertransference and the Resident on Leaving His Patient. *Journal of Hillside Hospital*, IV:148–51.

LINDEMANN, E. (1965). Symptomatology and Management of Acute Grief. In *Crisis Intervention: Selected Readings*, ed. H. J. Parad. pp. 7–21. New York: Family Service Association.

LOEWALD, H. (1962). Internalization, Separation, Mourning and the Superego. *Psychoanalytic Q.*, 31:483–504.

MAIER, H. (1972). The Child Care Worker. In *Children Away From Home*, eds. J. K. Whittaker and A. E. Trieschman, pp. 267–73. Chicago/New York: Aldine Atherton.

MALUCCIO, A. and MARLOW, W. (1974). THE CASE FOR THE CONTRACT. *Social Work*, 19:28–35.

MANN, J. (1973). *Time-Limited Psychotherapy*. Cambridge, Mass.: Harvard University Press.

MAYER, M. F. (1972). The Parental Figures in Residential Treatment In *Children Away From Home*. eds. J. K. Whittaker and A. E. Trieschman. pp. 273–872. Chicago/New York: Aldine Atherton.

NAGERA, H. (1964). On Arrest in Development, Fixation and Regression. *Psychoanalytic Study of the Child*, 19:222–39. New York: International Universities Press.

NEUBAUER, P. [1968] (1969). Participant in panel on "Problems of Termination in Child Analysis," Annual Meeting of the American Psychoanalytic Association, Boston, May 10, 1968, reported by R. Kohrman. *J. Amer. Psychoanal. Assn.*, 28:191–205.

NOVICK, J. (1977). Termination of Treatment in Adolescence. In *Adolescent Psychiatry, Vol. 5: Developmental and Clinical Studies*, eds. S. Feinstein and P. Giovacchini, pp. 390–412. New York: Jason Aronson.

SANDLER, J.; Kennedy, H.; and TYSON, R. (1980). *The Technique of Child Psychoanalysis—Conversations with Anna Freud*. Cambridge, Mass.: Harvard University Press.

SCHAFER, R. (1973). The Termination of Brief Psychoanalytic Psychotherapy. *Internat. J. Psychoanal. Psychother.*, 11:135–48.

SCHIFF, S. K. (1962) Termination of Therapy: Problems in a Community Psychiatric Out-Patient Clinic. *Arch. Gen. Psychiatry*, 6:77–82.

WEINER, I. (1974). *Principles of Psychotherapy*. New York: Wiley.

WEISS, S. (1972). Some Thoughts and Clinical Vignettes on Translocation of an Analytic Practice. *Internat. J. Psychoanal.*, 53:505–13.

Index